The Economics of Business Strategy

John Lipczynski
John Wilson

The Economics of Business Strategy

Prentice Hall
FINANCIAL TIMES

An imprint of **Pearson Education**
Harlow, England • London • New York • Boston • San Francisco • Toronto • Sydney • Singapore • Hong Kong
Tokyo • Seoul • Taipei • New Delhi • Cape Town • Madrid • Mexico City • Amsterdam • Munich • Paris • Milan

Pearson Education Limited
Edinburgh Gate
Harlow
Essex CM20 2JE
England

and Associated Companies throughout the world

Visit us on the World Wide Web at:
www.pearsoned.co.uk

First published 2004

ISBN 0273 67625 3

British Library Cataloguing-in-Publication Data
A catalogue record for this book is available from the British Library

Typeset in 9.25/12pt Stone Serif by 35
Printed by Ashford Colour Press Ltd., Gosport

The publisher's policy is to use paper manufactured from sustainable forests.

Dedication

For my daughter, Kathryn (JW)

and my children, Sonya, Mark and Anna (JL)

Contents

Part Three Analysis of Firm Strategy

Part Four Analysis of Government Policy

List of Boxes

List of Case Studies

List of Figures

List of Tables

Acknowledgements

A number of acknowledgements are in order. We would like to thank our anonymous referees for comments and suggestions on earlier drafts of this manuscript. JW would like to thank Alan McKinlay and Chris Carter for good-humoured and illuminating discussions on various aspects of economics, sociology, management and organisation studies during numerous car journeys to and from the University of St Andrews. He would also like to thank John Goddard, Donal McKillop, Phil Molyenux and Manouche Tavakoli for various useful insights, and Barbara Lessels and Jennifer Kerr for secretarial assistance. JL would like to thank colleagues and students in the Department of Business and Service Sector Management at the London Metropolitan University for their direct and, at times, unknowing help in writing this book. He would like to give special thanks to his ex-Head of Department, Bob Greenhill, and Mark Wronski, David Glenn, George Milios, Riette van Wijnen and Jeremy Stangroom for their support and helpful comments.

Thanks are due to a number of staff at Pearson Education, who have provided support and encouragement at all stages, as the project has progressed. We are particularly indebted to Justinia Seaman (Commissioning Editor), Janey Webb (Editorial Assistant) and Rachel Daily (Editorial Assistant) for their rigorous and systematic approach to this text. Thanks are also due to Helen Baxter (copy editor) and Julie Knight (desk editor). Any remaining errors are, of course, ours.

The publishers would like to express their gratitude to the following academics who provided invaluable feedback on this book at various stages of its development: David Bailey, L'Institute, Birmingham Business School, UK; Lawrence Britt, Anglia Polytechnic University, UK; Dan Coffey, Leeds University Business School, UK; Stephen Drinkwater, University of Surrey, UK; Peder Kongsted Christiansen, Denmark; Judith Mehta, Open University and University of East Anglia, UK; Corinne Mulley, University of Newcastle upon Tyne, UK and Stuart Wall, Anglia Polytechnic University, UK.

We are grateful to the Financial Times Limited for permission to reprint the following material: Case Study 7.1 Pilsbury Dough, © *Financial Times*, 9 October 2001; Case Study 8.1 Advanced Passenger Train, © *Financial Times*, 10 July 2001; Case Study 9.3 John Lewis/Dixons, © *Financial Times*, 7 April 2001; Case Study 10.2 Flight of the navigator as Boeing spreads its wings: digital cinema is the next step for the aerospace group's diversification, © *Financial Times*, 16 April 2002;

Case Study 11.2 Medicines in supermarkets, © *Financial Times*, 16 May 2001; Case Study 11.4 UK Newspaper prices, © *Financial Times*, 17 September 2002.

We are grateful to the following for permission to use copyright material: Case Study 11.1 from Government and Regulation, *The Financial Times Limited*, 28 August 2002, © Colin Mayer; Case Study 8.3 from DTI Innovation Unit Database, www.innovation.gov.uk/bcs/index.html. Reproduced with permission of JC Bomford Excavators Ltd; Case Study 9.2 from www.oft.gov.uk/News/Press+releases/1999/PN+24-99.htm. Reproduced with permission of the Press Office at the Office of Fair Trading, London; Case Study 10.3 from Breaking up can be good to do, *The Financial Times Limited*, 13 August 2002 © Najib Hashem.

Most importantly, we would like to thank our families, particularly our wives, Nicole and Alison, for their patience, encouragement and support during the course of writing this book.

Introduction and Overview

The strategy and performance of firms is one of the central areas of discussion in the business press and research in business economics and strategic management. We are all interested in why companies perform differently. Why are some companies successful, while others are not? Much theoretical, empirical and anecdotal evidence has been presented in an attempt to answer such a question. In other words, what factors drive company performance? Many theories have been developed and frameworks extended to analyse competitive conditions in industries, so as to argue that industry-level characteristics are the main factors, which determine company performance. Other theories argue that this is in fact only part of the picture; rather it is internal resources and assets or strategies specific to an individual firm that can exert a positive or negative influence on performance. Of course, at any given point in time, industry environmental influences, internal resources and business strategies are likely to exert an influence on company performance.

This book examines how industry environment and business strategies determine company performance. It provides an introduction to the economics of business strategy. It introduces key concepts drawn from microeconomics, industrial organisation, business economics, business environment, organisation studies and strategic management. The book is written for the growing number of courses at HND, undergraduate and MBA level where readers require not only an integrated theoretical framework in economics and management, but also the practical skills and knowledge, to examine how and why firms behave in certain ways in the real world.

The book comprises 11 chapters, in four parts. The structure is shown in Box I.1.

Part One, Introduction to Markets and Production, comprises Chapters 1 and 2. In Chapter 1, we introduce the reader to microeconomic principles useful in the study of market conditions. In particular, Chapter 1 examines markets and prices. In this chapter, the reader is introduced to the behaviour of consumers and firms and basic components of economic analysis. This chapter analyses the determinants of demand and supply and how these interact at the level of the market to form equilibrium conditions. Utilising the key concept of elasticity, it also introduces various definitions of revenue, which are used in Chapters 3 and 4. Chapter 2 introduces us to production and costs. The importance of time and efficiency for operational decision making and subsequent scale and strategic development of firms is introduced. Overall, Part One of the book provides the reader with the basic

Box I.1 The Economics of Business Strategy: structure

PART ONE: INTRODUCTION TO MARKETS AND PRODUCTION
Chapter 1: Markets and Prices
Chapter 2: Production and Costs

PART TWO: ANALYSIS OF INDUSTRY
Chapter 3: Market Structure 1: Perfect Competition, Monopoly and
Monopolistic Competition
Chapter 4: Market Structure 2: Oligopoly
Chapter 5: Approaches to Competitive Market Analysis
Chapter 6: Practical Analysis of Industry

PART THREE: ANALYSIS OF FIRM STRATEGY
Chapter 7: Advertising and Product Differentiation
Chapter 8: Research, Development and Innovation
Chapter 9: Vertical and Horizontal Integration
Chapter 10: Diversification

PART FOUR: ANALYSIS OF GOVERNMENT POLICY
Chapter 11: Government and Business

foundations of economic analysis and a convenient framework to assist in understanding more advanced aspects of industry structure and business strategy introduced in later parts of the text.

Much of the research in economics and strategic management assumes that company performance is driven not only by factors specific to the firm (such as its objectives or internal resources), but also by the competitive environment within which the firm operates. Consequently, Part Two of the book is devoted to the Analysis of Industry. In particular, we examine the theoretical and practical approaches to the analysis of competition and firm performance which have been popular in economics and management. It comprises Chapters 3 to 6. Chapters 3 and 4 examine economic theories of industry structure. Chapter 3 introduces perfect competition, monopoly and monopolistic competition. This chapter defines key components of industry structure and introduces various notions of profitability. Utilising a profit-maximising framework, the chapter guides readers through the pricing and output decisions of firms operating under conditions of perfect competition, monopoly and monopolistic competition. A critical analysis of monopoly is also presented and its implication for government policy toward business. This is a theme that is examined in detail in Part Four of the book. Chapter 4 deals with theories of oligopolistic behaviour. Key notions of firm interdependence and strategic interaction are introduced. The chapter examines the behaviour of firms in oligopoly under conditions of competition and collusion by utilising well-established tools of analysis such as the kinked demand curve and game theory. The chapter also examines why firms often co-operate in order to avoid competition and the various factors that determine the success or otherwise of such co-operation. Chapters 5 and 6 deal primarily with practical aspects of industry analysis. In Chapter 5, contributions from economics, sociology and strategic management are utilised to introduce readers to the various methodologies that can be used to analyse industry structure and firm behaviour. This chapter introduces various static and dynamic approaches which have been used to explain why industries, firms or even groups of firms within industries often differ with respect to business strategies and performance. Much of the discussion in this chapter forms the basis of our analysis of business strategy in Part Three of the text. Chapter 6 examines two of the most frequently researched components of industry structure, namely industry concentration and barriers to entry and exit. These components of industry structure define not only an industry, but also the extent and nature of competition which is likely to take place in these industries. This chapter examines industry concentration and its development over time. We also identify and quantify barriers to entry and the implications of such barriers for the performance of new and established firms. Overall, Part Two of the book provides the reader with the necessary theoretical knowledge and practical skills required to analyse competitive forces that impact on firm behaviour.

Utilising the theoretical and practical frameworks introduced in Part Two, Part Three of the book presents an Analysis of Business Strategy. It comprises Chapters 7 to 10. Chapter 7 and 8 examine two non-price strategies (advertising and innovation) which firms often adopt in order to attain or sustain a competitive advantage over business rivals. Both these strategies can be seen as methods of making a firm's product *different*, thus reducing product substitutability and possibly creating a new market in which the firms have a more assured status and future. We identify and explain the nature and the role as well as the opportunities and the limitations of the two strategies. In particular, Chapter 7, on advertising, discusses how and why firms differentiate their products and services. The relationship between advertising, competition and firm profitability is also examined. The extent to which advertising provides consumers with information is also assessed. Chapter 8 discusses innovation. This chapter focuses on the stages of the research and development process. Since innovation confers great benefits to firms as well as society, special attention is drawn to the factors that can slow the pace of diffusion of new technologies within firms, industries and the economy. The chapter also examines the factors that determine a firm's decision to innovate. Various factors relating to marketing, production, finance and development time are highlighted. Chapters 9 and 10 examine the scale and scope of firms. Chapter 9 discusses vertical and horizontal integration, while Chapter 10 discusses diversification. In each of these chapters we examine the motives for integration and diversification and the implications for the competitive process of firms engaging in such activities. In particular, Chapter 9 discusses the benefits that vertical and horizontal integration can confer on firms. Chapter 10 first examines the various typologies of diversification and then discusses the reasons for diversification and identifies key concepts of corporate coherence, focus and deconglomeration. Overall, Part Three of the book provides the reader with an integrated approach to the economic analysis of business strategies. The knowledge attained in these chapters provides an invaluable complement for those readers studying strategic management.

Part Four of the book comprises Chapter 11 and examines the relationship between government and business. This chapter discusses why government intervention in industry is necessary by outlining why, in the absence of such regulation, markets fail to provide an efficient allocation of scarce resources. The merits of competition are reiterated and a rationale for government policies aimed at promoting competition is provided. The evolution of such policies in the UK and Europe is also discussed. This chapter also examines the recent deregulation (often through privatisation) and re-regulation of industries that were once government-owned natural monopolies. Notions of regulatory capture, rate of return and price cap regulation are outlined and assessed. Overall, the final part of the book brings together many of the arguments outlined in Parts One to Three of the book to provide readers with a policy-related study of government involvement in industry.

Learning Support

Each chapter in this book defines a set of outcomes from which the reader can gauge their learning and understanding of key issues. Case studies written by the authors or adapted from pages of the *Financial Times* have been included to clarify, broaden and extend these issues where possible. Each chapter also has background and advanced references for readers who require an extended discussion of the key issues. Further reading references and website addresses are also provided for readers who want to extend their research of the topics beyond that presented here. Key terms or phrases introduced in each chapter are defined in summary form in a glossary at the end of the book. End of chapter questions for use in tutorial or discussion groups are also included. Indicative answers to these are included for instructors on the accompanying website www.booksites.net/lipczynski.

Part One Introduction to Markets and Production

Markets and Prices

By the end of this chapter, the reader should be able to understand:

* the determinants of market demand
* the determinants of market supply
* how demand and supply determine market price
* the concept of elasticity
* the existence of consumer surplus
* the importance of these for business decisions.

Key Concepts

* average revenue
* complements
* consumer surplus
* determinants of demand
* determinants of supply
* elasticity
* inferior goods

* law of demand
* marginal revenue
* market equilibrium
* normal goods
* substitutes
* total revenue

1.1 Introduction

Since this book presents an economic analysis of business strategy, it is important at the outset to explain briefly what the study of economics entails. Most definitions of economics focus on three issues: consumer wants, resources and choice.

Economic activity exists because of the existence of human wants or demand. These wants are made up, first, of 'biological' wants, which refer to the demand for food, clothing and shelter: in effect, the goods necessary for our survival. Second, people exhibit 'cultural' wants. These refer to our particular taste for goods and services, which is determined by our social and ethnic backgrounds. Since all of us are unique individuals our wants are all very different and thus the first characteristic of human wants is that they are *varied*. The second important characteristic is that we can reasonably assume these human wants to be *unlimited*. Evidence suggests that the vast majority of individuals do seek better (and more) goods and services.

Resources are the necessary inputs required to produce goods and services which satisfy human wants. They are often referred to as the *factors of production*. These include such things as capital (machinery, factories) labour, natural resources and enterprise. These resources possess three characteristics. They are *substitutable*, which means that producers can vary these inputs in the production of specific goods. They are also *versatile*. In other words, they can be put to different uses. For example, a unit of labour can exhibit a variety of different skills. Finally, and most important of all, resources are *scarce*. We do not possess an infinite amount of labour, capital and natural resources.

The consequence of unlimited human wants but limited resources is that individuals, firms and governments have to make *choices*, and economics is a study of how such choices are made. Whenever a choice is made an alternative is forgone. If an individual decides to buy a PC, he or she may have forgone the opportunity of buying a second-hand car. If a government decides to spend more money on defence, it may have to forgo the building of more hospitals or schools. To an economist the true cost of any action is the alternative forgone, and this concept is referred to as the *opportunity cost*. We look at this concept in Chapter 2. Let us now turn our attention to the study of consumer wants.

In a market economy the power of consumer demand plays an important role in determining market prices. Firms produce only those goods for which demand is sufficiently buoyant to maintain prices high enough to cover the firms' costs of production. In this chapter we examine the economic issues that define and shape the operation of such markets. This begins with the study of factors which determine the behaviour of buyers (market demand) and the behaviour of sellers (market supply), which leads us to examine the concept of equilibrium market prices (see Box 1.1). The final part of the chapter examines the responsiveness of demand and supply to changes in the factors which determine them (otherwise known as *elasticity*). For example, one of the main elasticity measures to be discussed in this chapter is the price elasticity of demand. This measure allows us to examine the precise reaction of consumer demand to changes in price. A brief conclusion then follows.

1.2   Demand

A convenient start to an analysis of market demand is to examine the factors that determine an individual's demand for a good or service. This can be summarised by the following demand function:

Box 1.1 Markets and the role of market prices

Markets can be defined as *opportunities* for individuals or institutions to buy and sell (or exchange) goods and services at specific prices. Without such markets and market prices, trading would pose great difficulties. If for instance you wanted to exchange one good for another and there were no marketplace and no market price, you would have to approach people at random, asking them if they wanted to make a trade. You would have to be doubly lucky, for not only would you have to find another trader who was willing to accept your goods, but you would have to find a trader who had goods *you want*. This is known as the *double coincidence of wants*. Furthermore, you might suggest a rate of exchange that your fellow trader regards as inappropriate. Extensive 'haggling costs' may result, leading to a waste of time and effort. If there were some place where buyers and sellers were conveniently located for the negotiation of exchanges, such search costs could be minimised. Furthermore, the presence of many other traders in such a marketplace would allow people to compare different valuations of the goods on offer and reduce haggling costs.

Money in our modern economy allows it to be used as a 'medium of exchange'. A buyer acquires goods with money, which in turn allows the seller to use that money to acquire whatever she wants, thus solving the problem of the double coincidence of wants. Money also means that the rate of exchange in a market can be expressed in terms of a common unit. This solves the problem of valuation. If you were interested in acquiring a pair of shoes in a market characterised by barter, you might see one seller expressing the price of shoes in terms of beer, another in terms of potatoes and yet another in terms of chickens. This plethora of prices frustrates your ability to make realistic price comparisons. With money prices, convenient comparisons can be made between the goods offered by different sellers.

$$QD_x^i = f[P_x, P_y, Y^i, T^i, E^i, r, QD^{n-1}, u]$$

This expression is not as daunting as it may first seem. QD simply refers to the 'quantity demanded'; the subscript 'x' refers to some good or service and the superscript 'i' refers to an individual consumer. Thus the variable on the left-hand side reads as, 'the quantity demanded for an imaginary good "x" by some individual "i"'. Moving to the right-hand side of the expression we have the symbol 'f', which means, 'is a function of' or 'depends on'. The bracketed term then includes all the variables that influence our individual's decision as to the quantities of 'x' she buys. Thus the bracketed term can be thought of as a *list* of variables that most affect our individual in her choice of the quantity of 'x' she wishes to purchase. Conventionally, we refer to the variable on the left-hand side as the 'dependent variable' and the variables in the bracket as the 'independent variables'. The variables on the right can also be referred to in this case as the ***determinants*** *of demand*.

The independent variables listed in the brackets in the equation are as follows;

P_x the price of 'x'
P_y the price of other goods, which may affect the quantity demanded of 'x'
Y^i the individual's income
T^i the individual's tastes
E^i the expectations of the individual
r the rate of interest charged for borrowing
QD^{n-i} the quantity demanded of 'x' by other consumers
u all other influences (not already included).

Assessing the importance of the variables of demand

Since all these variables exert an influence on our individual to some extent, we must find a way of isolating one variable at a time. We do this by assuming all other variables are constant. Thus our analysis proceeds by examining the effect a price change has on quantity demanded, *assuming* that the price of other related goods, the individual's income, tastes, expectations, the rates of interest on borrowing, etc. remain unchanged. Textbooks often refer to this process as *ceteris paribus* or 'all other things being equal'.

Price of 'x' (P_x)

Frequent statements in our everyday lives, such as 'the price is right', 'everyone has his price', 'price busters' and even 'priceless', illustrate the large influence prices exert on consumer decisions.

On the basis of casual observation no one would disagree with the proposition that, as prices fall, consumers demand more and, as prices rise, consumers demand less. If we were to list all the possible price and quantity demanded combinations we could derive a *demand schedule* for a particular good or service. As an example, let us assume an individual is interested in opera. We could develop a demand schedule which shows the number of annual visits to the opera and the price of a stalls ticket (see Table 1.1). (We assume our individual only considers stalls tickets.)

Table 1.1 Demand schedule for tickets

Ticket price (£)	Quantity of tickets demanded per year
40	18
50	15
60	12
70	10
80	8
90	6
100	5
110	4
120	3
130	2
140	1
150	1

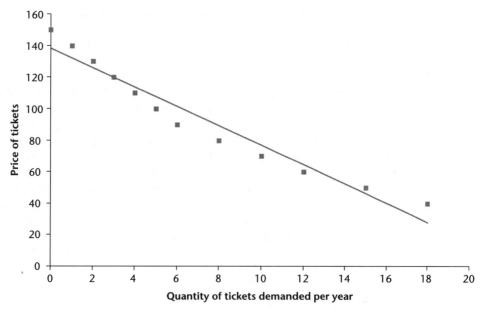

Figure 1.1 Demand curve for opera tickets

This schedule suggests an *inverse* or negative relationship between the price of the tickets and the quantity of tickets demanded. This means that, as the price of tickets increases, quantity demanded falls and, as the price decreases, quantity demanded rises. This relationship reflects the *law of demand*.

If we were to plot the data in the schedule onto a graph we could derive a negatively sloped demand function by linking the points or co-ordinates with a line of best fit. This line is traditionally referred to as a *demand curve*. This is shown in Figure 1.1.

The exact slope and mathematical relationship between price and the quantity demanded is examined later in the chapter, when we consider the issue of price elasticity of demand. For the time being all we need to remember is that most demand curves slope downwards from left to right, and this negative relationship reflects the law of demand.

Prices of other goods (P$_y$)

The prices of some other, related goods also play an important role in influencing an individual's demand for a good or service. These 'other' goods fall into two categories, namely *substitutes* and *complements*.

A substitute good is a good which competes with other goods for the attention of consumers. Thus if the price of the substitute were to fall, consumers would reduce their demand for one good (x) to buy more of the other (y). Naturally, the opposite would occur if the price of a substitute were to rise. If we refer to our opera-loving individual, then the demand for opera tickets may be influenced by the price of tickets for the ballet or orchestra recitals. Our economy is full of examples of substitute goods and services such as gas and electricity, beef and lamb, holidays to Greece and holidays to Spain, airlines and railways and, most importantly, the different brands of the same good or service. It is important for businesses to identify goods in the market which are strong substitutes for their products. This then identifies their rival producers. This also forms the basis of industry classification and for an analysis of competitive markets (an issue examined in Chapter 6).

As the name suggests, a complement is a good in joint demand with another good. The two are both necessary to satisfy a particular want. Examples of groups of complements are cars and petrol, printers and ink cartridges, strawberries and cream. If the price of one of the complements were to fall, this would encourage demand for both goods to rise. Our individual may regard an evening meal in the centre of town as a perfect complement to the opera. Thus if the price of opera tickets were to fall, our individual would visit more opera productions and consequently patronise town centre restaurants more frequently. We may tentatively conclude that the economic well-being of restaurant businesses located close to opera houses and other theatres is related to the price of opera tickets. The actual strength of this relationship, of course, depends on many other factors, such as the responsiveness of opera goers to price changes and the existence of alternative town centre attractions.

The individual's income (Y')

There are three possible relationships or responses of quantity demanded to a change in an individual's income. All these three relationships can be conveniently illustrated by curves known as *Engel curves*, named after a nineteenth-century German statistician, Christian Engel. These are shown in Figure 1.2.

The three possibilities are shown by the three curves:

(a) This is a positively sloped curve and reflects a relationship which shows that as income rises our individual increases her consumption of some good x. In our case, as our individual's income rises she attends the opera more frequently.

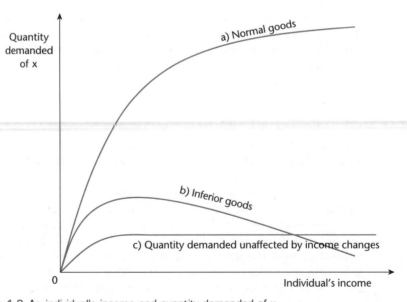

Figure 1.2 An individual's income and quantity demanded of x

These goods and services are referred to as *normal goods*. Examples of such goods might be holidays abroad, cars, eating in restaurants, clothes and DVDs.

(b) This is a negatively sloped function and shows a situation where, as an individual's income rises, quantity demanded of 'x' falls. In other words, the individual abandons or reduces the consumption of 'x' in favour of alternative goods and services. These goods are referred to as *inferior goods*. It is not too difficult to think of examples. If you were lucky enough to win the lottery there would probably be a long list of goods and services you would no longer buy or patronise, such as bus travel, eating in fast food outlets, using launderettes and chipboard furniture.

(c) This is a function which exhibits a zero slope and illustrates those goods for which demand is unaffected as incomes rise. Examples of such goods are newspapers, salt, bread and toilet paper. As our individual gets richer we might not expect her to increase or decrease her purchases of newspapers.

Again, it is important for firms to identify the effects that increasing wealth in an economy has on the demand for their goods and services. Does increasing prosperity stimulate demand or will it lead to a reduction in demand as in the case of inferior goods? It may also be possible that demand for a firm's product is recession proof: in other words, changes in consumer incomes have little effect on quantity demanded.

The individual's taste (T^i)

Taste exerts an important influence on consumer decisions. Generally, one might assume that the importance of the price of a product is only considered once a consumer has decided what he likes or dislikes. Thus our opera-loving individual may feel that opera sung in the original language is the only true opera experience. She will not consider buying tickets for operas sung in English, *at any price*. A full analysis of the effect taste has on consumer preferences would require an interdisciplinary approach, integrating economics with sociology and psychology, and this is beyond the scope of our introductory chapter. We may note, however, that much time and effort is spent by firms attempting to influence consumer tastes, and this is analysed in more detail in Chapter 7, which discusses product differentiation.

The individual's expectations (E^i)

A consumer's expectations as to the future also affect his or her pattern of demand. Such expectations may refer to prices, incomes, prices of other goods or rates of interest, as well as general political and economic events. Thus, for example, whenever the Chancellor of the Exchequer announces an increase in petrol taxes to be made effective from midnight one would normally expect to see large numbers of car owners rushing to petrol stations to fill up their tanks to beat the tax rise.

The rate of interest (r)

The rate of interest affects the demand for goods which are normally bought on credit, such as houses, cars and consumer durables. An ever-increasing variety of goods are now bought on credit and consequently the level of interest charged on borrowing has direct implications for the level of demand in the economy.

Quantity demand by other consumers (QD^{n-i})

An individual's demand is affected by observing what other consumers are buying. Leibenstein (1950) suggested three possible effects.

In the first case, a consumer may increase demand because other consumers are increasing their demand. This is referred to as the *bandwagon effect*. This reflects the desire of some people to conform with groups they wish to be associated with – a desire to be part of the 'in group' or 'one of the lads'. Examples of such goods are fashion goods, pop bands, films and children's toys. Marketing executives often create such bandwagon effects by writing copy such as 'the hit everyone is talking about' or 'four million copies sold'.

The opposite of the bandwagon effect is referred to as the *snob effect*. This occurs when consumers wish to seek exclusivity and to dissociate themselves from the 'common herd'. In this case, as other consumers increase their demand for a good or services, our individual reduces his or her demand for that good or service. If the popular destination for British holidaymakers in Spain is Torremolinos, there are some British consumers who wish to holiday *anywhere*, but Torremolinos. Note that the snob effect is not necessarily based on a desire to seek exclusive *higher priced* alternatives.

The final effect is the *taboo effect*, which refers to goods which enjoy an intrinsic utility but are only purchased if *sufficient* numbers of other consumers are seen to be buying the goods. Examples might refer to outrageous fashion, music albums by new bands and, historically, the first telephones. In the last case, telephone companies were faced with a problem of selling the first telephones to consumers who were then unable to make any telephone calls as an insufficient number of other consumers had bought the product. When faced with such a taboo effect, firms are faced with the problem of trying to break the taboo. This can be achieved either by fooling consumers into thinking that consumption is higher than is in fact the case or by charging a low or zero price for the good in question. Thus the first telephones were generally given away free of charge as a strategy of stimulating the market. A more recent example is UK TV satellite dishes, first launched in 1982, which for a limited period were also given away free of charge.

All other influences (u)

The last independent variable included in our demand function refers to all other known or unknown influences on the quantity demanded by an individual. The fact that all individuals are unique means that the variables we have identified in our equation apply only in a general sense. There are factors and patterns of consumer behaviour which differentiate one individual from another. Thus our last variable recognises the fact that other specific factors may play a part in shaping the demand function for an individual, for example age, wealth and the weather.

Changes in the determinants of demand

Changes in any of the determinants of demand can be illustrated with a reference to demand curves. In Figure 1.3 we examine the effect a price change has on the quantity demanded.

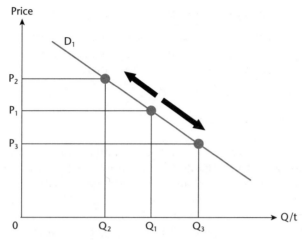

Figure 1.3 Changes in price and changes in quantity demand

If we assume price to be at a level of $0P_1$, then quantity demanded is $0Q_1$. If price were now to increase to $0P_2$, quantity demanded would fall to $0Q_2$ and if price were to decrease to $0P_3$, quantity demanded would increase to $0Q_3$. As prices change we simply read off the new quantities demanded, and we see movements *along the existing demand curve* as shown by the two arrows.

However, if one of the variables *other than price* were to change then we would see a *shift* in the demand curve.

In Figure 1.4 we assume that the initial demand curve for x is at D_1 and that price and quantity demanded of x are $0P_1$ and $0Q_1$ respectively. Let us further assume that the price of a substitute good decreases, but all other variables including the price of x remain unchanged. As the price of a substitute decreases the consumer buys less of good x at the price $0P_1$. Quantity demanded is now at $0Q_2$. This was made possible by a leftward shift of the demand curve to D_2. Had the consumer's income risen, and if x were a normal good, then at the price of $0P_1$ the consumer would have increased demand for x to say $0Q_3$. The demand curve has shifted rightwards.

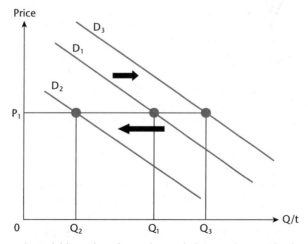

Figure 1.4 Changes in variables other than price and changes in quantity demand

Remember two things:

- For a change in a variable other than price, the demand curve shifts.
- A decrease in demand causes a demand curve to shift to the left whereas an increase in demand causes the demand curve to shift to the right.

Market demand

So far we have focused on the demand of one individual. The market demand curve can be simply regarded as the horizontal summation of all individual demand curves. The only change to our demand curve is the much larger quantities demanded at every given price. The demand function remains the same and we can drop the 'i' superscript from the independent variables and possibly add other variables such as income distribution and population change.

Exceptions to the law of demand

Before we turn our attention to supply let us consider the law of demand once again. You may remember that the law simply reflected the inverse or negative relationship between price and quantity demanded. It has been claimed, however, that there are some exceptions to this law. In other words, as prices increase quantity demanded *increases* as well. This implies a positively sloped demand curve. Let us examine three such examples and examine to what extent they do in fact undermine the law of demand: these are the Veblen effect, speculative demand and Giffen goods.

The Veblen effect

This is named after Thorstein Veblen, a 'colourful' assistant professor of Norwegian descent who, while at Chicago University, developed these ideas in *The Theory of the Leisure Classes* (1908). This argument suggests that some consumers are attracted to expensive goods as a means of demonstrating their wealth, their style and their 'good' taste. This 'conspicuous consumption' can explain the popularity of expensive branded clothes, restaurants, holidays and cars. As an extension of this argument we suggest that when consumers are uncertain about the attributes of a product they may use price as an indicator of quality. Thus in the minds of many, a cheap perfume or a cheap red wine suggests a product of low quality and certainly not one to give as a present. Quantity demanded may actually fall if prices are seen as 'too low'. But does this then suggest that the demand curve has a positive slope? In fact, what is happening is that as prices rise, consumers alter their perceptions about the good and this then causes a *rightward shift* of the demand curve. Figure 1.5 illustrates this explanation.

In Figure 1.5 we see that as price rises from $0P_1$ to $0P_2$, consumers alter their perception of the good. To some consumers this higher price now suggests a product of a higher quality or a more exclusive product. At the higher price the demand curve shifts rightwards and the quantity demanded increases from $0Q_1$ to $0Q_3$. The distance Q_2Q_1 is the pure price effect: as price rose, so quantity demanded decreased.

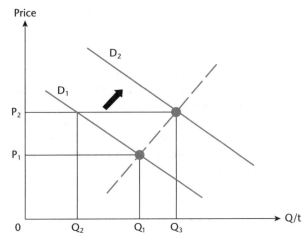

Figure 1.5 The Veblen effect

However, the distance Q_2Q_3 is the Veblen effect, the increase in quantity demanded due to the higher price alone. The positively sloped dotted line might be viewed as a quasi demand curve as it maps the combinations of prices and quantities demanded. In reality, it may be more accurate to view the dotted line as a path of equilibrium points on separate negatively sloped demand curves.

Speculative demand

It may be argued that as prices of certain goods such as stocks, shares, antiques and houses increase then quantity demanded also increases. For example, the price of houses in the UK in 2002 rose dramatically and yet demand did not fall. Does this also then give rise to a positively sloped demand curve? If people speculate that prices in the future will be higher, they view current prices as 'low' in relation to future prices. If prices are low this stimulates an increase in demand. Far from negating the law of demand, speculation can be accommodated comfortably within it.

Giffen goods

These were named after Sir Robert Giffen, a Victorian statistician who observed that nineteenth-century Irish peasants bought more potatoes as the price of potatoes increased. The reason for this behaviour was that potatoes were an inferior good and took up a large proportion of peasant income. As the price of potatoes increased, the peasants suffered a drop in their real incomes, in other words their purchasing power fell. As a consequence they could no longer afford to buy some of the better foods such as meat and fish and, to maintain their calorie intake, were forced to buy more of the relatively expensive potatoes. Although this undoubtedly does generate a positively sloped demand curve, there are few examples of such goods in the world today. Those that exist are found in the poor, underdeveloped countries.

What we have seen in the discussion thus far is that there are few, if any, real examples of exceptions to the law of demand. The inverse relationship between price and quantity demanded is firmly anchored by empirical analysis.

1.3	Supply

Let us now turn to the issues that concern producers. What factors influence a producer when deciding how much of 'x' should be produced? In the same way as we identified a demand function which listed the important independent variables that affected a consumer's demand for a good, we can also determine a supply function which lists the *determinants of supply*. Thus the variables shown in the brackets are those we consider most important when firms decide how much of 'x' to supply (QS_x):

$$QS_x = f[P_x, P_y, F, K, T^p, u]$$

The independent variables listed in brackets are as follows:

P_x price of 'x'
P_y price of other goods which may affect the quantity supplied of 'x'
F   factors of production
K   state of technology
T^p producers' tastes
u   all other influences.

Assessing the importance of the variables of supply

We shall proceed to examine each of these independent variables in turn, once again assuming all other variables are constant.

Price of 'x' (P_x)

Quantity supplied of 'x' is determined by the price a particular good commands in the market. For most goods, as prices rise, more is supplied. Higher prices mean higher revenues and consequently higher profits. Encouraged by these higher prices, existing producers expand their capacity and new producers enter the market, so as to exploit these profitable opportunities. If prices are falling, profits also fall. Some producers reduce their productive capacity and others may be forced to leave the market as market prices no longer cover their costs. Thus as prices fall, less is supplied. This positive relationship between price and quantity supplied can be illustrated with a supply curve as shown in Figure 1.6. If again we turn to opera as our example, then opera producers are keen to stage more productions if market prices are high. In addition, it is no surprise that many eastern European opera companies tour the UK, attracted by the relatively high ticket revenues.

Prices of other goods (P_y)

Producers should be aware of the prices of other goods and services which they are able to produce as well as their existing lines. If the price of good 'y' were to rise, making it more profitable than good 'x', then producers would reduce their supply of 'x' and increase the supply of 'y'. Clearly, all producers wish to use their resources

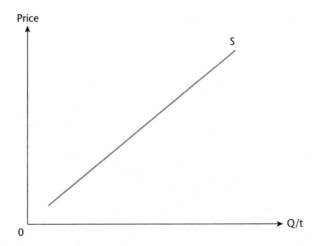

Figure 1.6 The supply curve

in the most profitable way. Thus if opera producers found that ticket prices for rock concerts were higher than ticket prices for opera, all other things being equal, they might switch their resources to the production of rock concerts. This is an example of opportunity cost introduced in the introduction to this chapter.

Factors of production (F)

As mentioned earlier, factors of production refer to the resources or inputs required to produce any goods and services. In economics we identify four main factors, namely land, labour, capital and enterprise. Land refers not only to the surface area on which a factory can be built or crop harvested, but also the natural resources found underground. Labour refers to all aspects of human effort; capital refers to property such as machines, production facilities and offices; enterprise is the talent required to organise the other resources so as to produce what consumers want. It is a moot point as to whether enterprise is just a subset of labour. All these resources have a price in the market and to a producer these prices are the *costs of production*. Changes in the price of these factors affect supply by making some goods more or less profitable. To stage an opera, producers require a number of factors of production, and each has its own market price or cost. These costs are, for example, the rental of a theatre, the wages of the singers, orchestra and stagehands, and the cost of costumes and props. Should any of these rise, while ticket prices remain constant, opera production become less attractive to producers.

State of technology (K)

Technology changes over time, and this increases the efficiency of resources in the production of goods and services. As costs of production fall (and assuming all other variables are constant), we would expect the increased profitability to encourage producers to supply more. The impact technology has on firms' strategic decisions is explored in Chapter 8.

Producers' tastes (T^P)

The actual amount supplied to the market by firms or individual producers may not necessarily be as a result of the economic variables discussed earlier. Some producers may maintain their levels of supply, even though market prices have fallen. They may do this for a variety of reasons. They may expect that the fall in prices is temporary and the costs and disruption of reducing output may outweigh any short-term losses in revenue. A producer may also speculate that market prices may rise in the future and may then withhold goods from the market. If a builder thought that house prices were to rise sharply in the following year, he might well hold on to his stock of finished houses until the next year. Finally, it is possible that producers may involve themselves in the production of goods and services for non-economic reasons. Prior to 1981, the *The Times* of London was owned by a Canadian, Lord Thomson of Fleet. In the 15 years during which he, and later his son, owned the paper it rarely made a profit and was subsidised by money earned elsewhere in his publishing empire. It was claimed that Lord Thomson derived great pleasure from simply being known as the owner of that prestigious title.

All other influences (u)

This again is simply a variable which refers to all other known or unknown influences on the quantity supplied by a producer. This might include factors such as severe weather conditions, political crises and government policies.

Changes in the determinants of supply

The analysis follows a similar path to the one developed when discussing changes in the determinants of demand. Thus changes in price cause movements along the existing supply curve, and changes in variables other than price cause shifts in the supply curves. An increase in supply shifts the supply curve to the right, whereas a decrease in supply shifts the curve to the left. Figure 1.7 illustrates these changes.

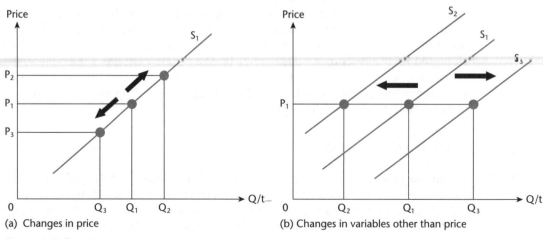

(a) Changes in price   (b) Changes in variables other than price

Figure 1.7 Supply curve

1.4   Market Equilibrium

Having presented and analysed the variables which affect market demand and market supply, we are now in a position to see how market prices are determined. By combining a negatively sloped demand curve with a positively sloped supply curve we can identify a price which balances the demands of consumers and the supply of producers. Figure 1.8 shows this equilibrium price.

At the equilibrium or market clearing price OP_e, the amount demanded is exactly equal to the amount supplied, OQ_e. We have a market equilibrium and the market is 'cleared'. There are neither shortages nor surpluses. But we may ask ourselves: how did this equilibrium come about? How do producers know what price to set? Assume price was set below OP_e at for example OP_1. Figure 1.9(a) shows that at price OP_1 the quantity demanded is at OQD_1 and the quantity supplied is at OQS_1, and there is an

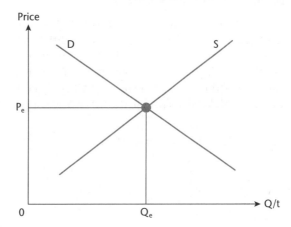

Figure 1.8 Market equilibrium

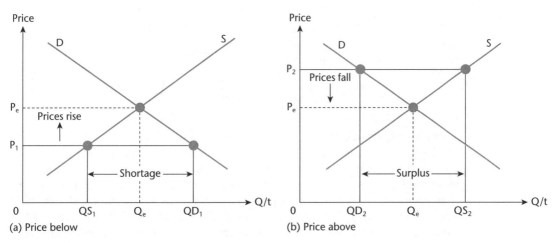

(a) Price below

(b) Price above

Figure 1.9 Equilibrium price

excess of quantity demanded over quantity supplied – in other words, a shortage. In a free market, whenever shortages occur market prices rise. Price in this context acts as a *rationing agent*, rationing out the good in short supply to those who are willing to pay higher prices. As prices rise some consumers leave the market and, at the same time, the higher prices attract additional producers into the market. Prices keep rising until the excess demand or shortage has disappeared. If price were set too high at OP_2, then it is clear from Figure 1.9(b) that quantity supplied is greater than the quantity demanded. The market experiences a glut or surplus – in other words, an excess supply of goods. With unsold stock, producers discount prices to attract consumers into the market. As prices fall, quantity demanded increases and quantity supplied by producers decreases. When price OP_e is reached, the surplus has disappeared and we have a balance or a market equilibrium (see Case Study 1.1).

Case Study 1.1

Allocation of Cup Final tickets

Every year in May, the English Football Association stages the Cup Final. In recent years this has been played in Cardiff, one of a few stadia large enough to accommodate the huge demand for this football match. Every year there is a shortage of tickets. Why does this shortage happen and what are the consequences? Could the English Football Association ensure that there was no shortage of tickets? Consider the following supply and demand diagram.

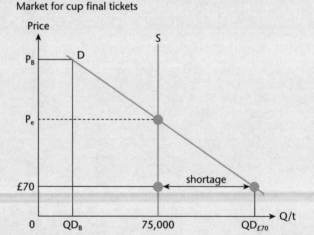

Market for cup final tickets

The supply of tickets is fixed at 75,000, the number of seats at the stadium. The supply curve will thus appear as a vertical line. A shortage of tickets occurs because the price of £70 is set *below* the equilibrium price of P_e. Thus, there are more football fans who want to attend the final than there are tickets on sale *at this price of £70*. The FA charges a price below the equilibrium price so as not to disadvantage the poorer supporters. Historically, the clubs were faced with the problem of allocating a relatively small number of tickets among a relatively large number of supporters. One solution was to allocate tickets on a 'first come first served' basis, which implied a system of queuing. This may not be fair as it treats all fans, both the casual and the passionately committed, as equal. Furthermore, queuing involves a waste of time. Thus, people who place a low value on their time such as old age pensioners could be hired as professional 'queuers' by the richer supporters who place a higher value on their time. This was common in eastern Europe in the 1970s and 1980s whenever shortages of goods appeared. An alternative approach in the 1970s was to sell tickets only to the 'committed' supporters who could produce tokens from all home match programmes and, in the case of Manchester United, away match programmes as well. Unfortunately, these schemes very quickly led to the development of a secondary market for programmes and many a programme seller was robbed by gangs not for his money but for his stock of programmes. More recently tickets are being allocated to supporters who are season ticket holders or who belong to various membership schemes. Finally, whenever shortages occur, a black market is not far behind. Since it is difficult to police all market transactions, a number of tickets will find their way onto the black market. Thus if OQ_B were the amount of tickets in the possession of touts the black market price would be around price $0P_B$. The reader will note that the steeper the demand curve, the higher the black market price and that the slope is determined by the *price elasticity of demand*.

This market equilibrium may, however, be short lived. As any of the variables other than price change, shifts in the demand and supply curves occur. This then leads to new market equilibria. Figure 1.10 shows such changes.

If we begin with a market equilibrium at e_1 with price and quantity at P_1Q_1 we can assume, for example, that interest rates fall and this causes the demand curve to shift to the right. The new equilibrium point is at e_2 at price and quantity at P_2Q_2. Should the price of resources fall, this would then cause a shift of the supply curve to the

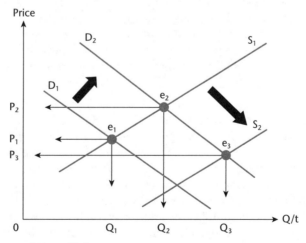

Figure 1.10 New market equilibrium

Case Study 1.2

Government housing support

Consider a deprived area of a town or some other self-contained geographical area in which most of the families are on very low incomes and pay a large proportion of their incomes as rent to landlords. Assume that the government now wishes to support these families by either a rent subsidy or a building subsidy to builders to provide affordable homes. What are the consequences of these two different policies?

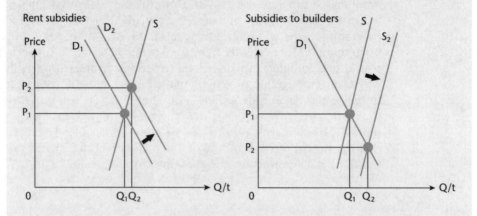

Under the rent subsidy scheme the poor family will be required to pay a proportion of their income in rent and the remainder of the rent will be paid by the government. This subsidy will be seen by the family as an increase in income. This will shift the demand curve for housing to the right, creating an initial shortage, which will pull prices up. The higher rents will lead to more housing being supplied in this area. The actual amount of additional housing will depend on the price elasticity of supply. Although poor families will gain, the biggest winners are the landlords. The losers are the taxpayers.

Under the building subsidy scheme, builders will see their costs of production fall and the supply curve will shift to the right. The initial surplus of property will lead to a fall in rents. The more inelastic the demand for housing, the bigger the fall in rents. In this case, the poor families will gain the most.

right, which would establish a new equilibrium at e_3 at price and quantity P_3Q_3. This is a very useful tool for predicting likely events in any market. (Read Case Studies 1.1 and 1.2 for real-life applications of this simple demand and supply model.)

It is important to understand that these adjustments do not happen instantaneously. For example, producers in the market are unable to respond immediately to any changes in demand and thus prices may temporarily rise to levels higher than the eventual equilibrium price. This high price will in time increase the quantity supplied. As an exercise, the reader might like to draw the relevant supply and demand diagram.

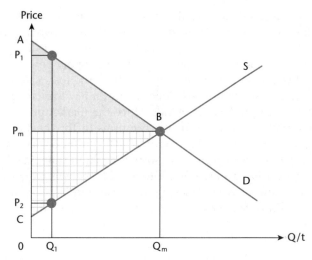

Figure 1.11 Consumer and producer surplus

Consumer and producer surplus

Consider Figure 1.11. The supply and demand curves show that the market equilibrium price is OP_m. All consumers are asked to pay this price. Consider if a price of
OP_1 were charged. What would happen to market demand? Would all consumers
abandon the market, preferring to spend their incomes elsewhere? No, the downward sloping demand curve tells us that there are still a few consumers willing to
pay this high price. They place such a high value on the good that they are willing
to pay even this very high price. We are often prepared to pay more for a good than
its actual market price. The price we are willing to pay for any good is known as our
reserve price. Whenever our reserve price is above the market price we receive a
benefit. If our reserve price is below the market price we simply exclude ourselves
from the market. The amount consumers are willing to pay is equal to area $OABQ_m$,
while they actually pay only OP_mBQ_m. The difference, triangle P_mAB, is the consumer surplus.

Why is consumer surplus important for business firms?

Producers are aware that many of their customers are paying a market price which
is below their reserve price. If producers could somehow discover customers' reserve
prices and charge them different prices, they could increase their revenues. This
is known as *price discrimination*. The objective of most market bargaining is to
discover consumers' reserve prices. But for price discrimination to work, consumers
must have different reserve prices and the producer must prevent resales or see-
pages between the consumers. Assume an aluminium manufacturer decided to sell
aluminium ingots to the cookware industry at a lower price than to the aircraft
industry. Would this strategy result in higher revenues? It would only work if the
manufacturer were able to *prevent* the aircraft industry from buying cheaper aluminium from the cookware industry. One last important condition for successful

price discrimination is that the producer must be able to control market supply. If there were competition in the market, buyers would not pay higher prices to one seller practising price discrimination. Thus successful price discrimination is often seen as proof of monopoly or quasi monopoly power by a firm.

By similar analysis we can see that producers can also enjoy a surplus. If prices were as low as OP_2 there might be just a few low-cost producers who would still be willing to produce the goods. Since the market price is OP_m these firms receive an additional benefit. Formally, the firms in this market would be willing to supply amount $0Q_m$ for a revenue of $0CBQ_m$. In fact, they receive a revenue of $0P_mBQ_m$, which results in a producer surplus equal to triangle CP_mB.

Governments are often interested in knowing the extent of consumer and producer surplus when assessing the costs and benefits of monopolies and mergers of large firms. Some of these aspects are examined in Chapters 3 and 11.

1.5   Elasticity

So far in our analysis of demand and supply we have been vague about the exact relationship of quantity demanded and quantity supplied to all the independent variables such as price, income, price of other goods and so on. Business firms wish to know precisely how quantity demanded would change, if, for example, they were to increase price; if incomes in the economy increased; or if the price of substitute goods decreased. They also want to know how quantity supplied might adjust to a new technology, to higher interest rates or lower wages. Businessmen and women with no knowledge of economics normally rely on their business experience to estimate these relationships. Such 'rule of thumb' decision making may work well in small and well-defined markets, but may prove to be too imprecise as size and complexity of markets increase. Elasticity is a measure which allows us to gauge these relationships with a greater degree of precision. We examine just four such measures: the price elasticity of demand (ED_P); the income elasticity of demand (ED_Y); the elasticity of demand with respect to the price of other goods, which is referred to as *cross-elasticity of demand* (ED_{XY}); and price elasticity of supply (ES_P).

Price elasticity of demand

Price elasticity of demand (ED_P) can be defined as the degree of responsiveness of the quantity demanded of a good or service to changes in its price.

It can be calculated in the following way:

$$ED_P = \frac{\text{Percentage change in quantity demanded}}{\text{Percentage change in price}}$$

$$\text{or } ED_P = \frac{\text{Proportionate change in quantity demanded}}{\text{Proportionate change in price}}$$

This ratio can be easily calculated in the following way:

$$ED_p = \frac{\Delta Q/Q}{\Delta P/P}$$

ΔQ refers to the change in quantity demanded, Q to the original quantity demanded, ΔP to the change in price and P to the original price. The ratio always provides a negative answer, since an *increase* in price leads to a *decrease* in quantity demanded and vice versa. Since price elasticity of demand is always negative, the minus sign can be ignored. In other words, it is only the absolute value we are interested in. But how do we interpret the value of this ratio?

A price elasticity measure of 2 would indicate that a 10% increase in price led to a 20% decrease in quantity demanded. Thus the change in quantity demanded is *more than proportionate* to the change in price. We refer to this demand as being *price elastic*. By the same token, a price elasticity measure of 0.2 suggests that a 10% increase in price led to only a 2% decrease in quantity demanded. In this case the change in quantity demanded is *less than proportionate* to the change in price and thus demand is *price inelastic*. (For a full interpretation of all measures and the relevant demand curves, see Table 1.2 and Box 1.2.)

A calculation of price elasticity

Let us consider an example for computing elasticity. Assume a firm reduces the price of a good from 60p to 59p and as a consequence finds that quantity demanded increased from 40,000 to 41,000. Using the standard formula just presented price elasticity of demand is:

$$ED_p = \frac{1000/40,000}{1/60} = \frac{0.025}{0.0167} = 1.49$$

We conclude, therefore, that demand is price elastic.

Price elasticity and directional bias

In the last example we examined a very small change in price, a change almost at a 'point'. Had we considered a price *rise* from 59p to 60p and a decrease in quantity demanded from 41,000 to 40,000, our calculation for price elasticity would have been:

$$ED_p = \frac{1000/41,000}{1/59} = \frac{0.024}{0.017} = 1.41$$

This result is not too dissimilar from the earlier measure of price elasticity. But what if we considered much larger changes in the same market? Assume we were faced with the following changes. As price fell from 60p to 50p quantity demanded increased from 40,000 to 55,000. Price elasticity of demand is:

$$ED_p = \frac{15,000/40,000}{10/60} = \frac{0.374}{0.167} = 2.24$$

Table 1.2 Interpretation of price elasticity of demand

Numerical measure	Description	Terminology	
zero	Quantity demanded does not change as price changes	Perfectly inelastic	
<1	Quantity demanded changes by a smaller percentage than price	Inelastic	
1	Quantity demanded changes by the same percentage as price	Unit elasticity	
>1	Quantity demanded changes by a greater percentage than price	Elastic	
Infinity	Consumers are willing to buy all they can obtain at this price – however, for a small increase in price they will buy nothing	Perfectly elastic	

Box 1.2 Elasticity and the slope of the demand curve

When considering Table 1.2 it is important not to equate elasticity with the slope of the demand curve. Elasticity is, in fact, the product of the slope of the demand curve and the ratio of the original price to the original quantity demanded. In fact, a linear demand curve with a constant slope exhibits a range of different elasticity values. A shallow demand curve used to illustrate elastic demand and a steep demand curve used to illustrate an inelastic demand is simply a graphical convenience. True elasticity values are computed arithmetically. The demand curve of unit elasticity means that no matter what change in price takes place, the total amount spent on the good is constant.

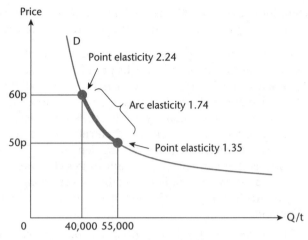

Figure 1.12 Price elasticity of demand and directional bias

Let us now consider a price *increase* from 50p to 60p and quantity demanded decreasing from 55,000 to 40,000:

$$ED_p = \frac{15{,}000/55{,}000}{10/50} = \frac{0.27}{0.2} = 1.35$$

In this case the measure is significantly different. Although the changes are the same in both cases, the measure is influenced by whether we were considering a price fall or a price rise. This is known as *directional bias*. To reduce this problem, for large changes in price we measure elasticity *over an arc* of the demand curve, rather than at a specific point. This is normally done by computing an average of the two prices and the two quantities demanded. The formula is rewritten as:

$$ED_p = \frac{\Delta Q \Big/ \dfrac{\text{New quantity + Original quantity}}{2}}{\Delta P \Big/ \dfrac{\text{New price + Original price}}{2}}$$

Referring to our example, price elasticity is now:

$$ED_p = \frac{15{,}000 \Big/ \dfrac{55{,}000 + 40{,}000}{2}}{10 \Big/ \dfrac{50 + 60}{2}} = \frac{0.316}{0.18} = 1.75$$

This answer is now *independent* of the direction of the change. If we consider a price increase or a price decrease, the price elasticity of demand is the same. Figure 1.12 illustrates these various measures.

Factors influencing price elasticity of demand

Whether demand is elastic or inelastic is of great importance to firms, industries and governments. Much research in managerial economics has been undertaken to determine the price elasticities of demand for various goods and services. Let us now turn to some of the factors that influence the size of the measure:

- One of the most important is the *availability of substitutes*. If there are many close substitutes for a good, then, as its price rises, consumers can easily switch to these alternative goods. Demand is therefore *elastic*. If there are no close substitutes then demand is *inelastic*. Consumers have little choice but to buy the higher priced good. The demand for tobacco is inelastic since there are few close sub-stitutes, a fact not lost on the Chancellor of the Exchequer should he wish to increase tax revenues. However, the demand for a particular brand of cigarette is elastic as there are many close substitutes. The demand for luxury goods is also elastic as there are many competing luxury goods, whereas necessities such as food and heating by definition have no substitutes and thus have an inelastic demand.

- If the *proportion of income spent* on a good or service is small demand is *inelastic*. A 20% increase in the price of a box of matches does not see demand fall very much, if at all. This also implies that in general as people get richer they respond less and less to price changes.

- *Habit* or an *addiction* to goods also make consumers less responsive to changes in price. Demand is therefore *inelastic*.

- If a good is a *complement* to another more expensive good then demand for it tends to be *inelastic*. For example, an expensive sound system may require specialised music discs as essential complements to the system. In this case the demand for these discs is price inelastic. (See Case Study 1.3 for a further example.)

- *Durable* goods tend to have an *elastic* demand. Since these goods are often replaced before they have worn out they can always be kept a little longer should prices rise.

- Demand is generally considered to be inelastic in the short run. If prices rise it takes *time* for consumers to discover and adjust to alternative cheaper goods. In the meantime, they may be forced to stay with the higher priced goods.

Why is price elasticity important to business firms?

Elasticity gives us a useful indicator as to the degree of control firms have over the prices they charge. This point is elaborated further in Chapter 3. The fundamental importance of price elasticity of demand to business firms is the ability to predict the likely outcome of a change in price on their sales. Firms wish to know the exact responses to a change in price. If a firm is contemplating a price reduction, it wants to know how sales are affected.

Another name for sales is *total revenue* (TR), which is the product of price and quantity demanded and can be shown as a rectangle under a demand curve. Consider Figure 1.13, which illustrates two different markets: the first is elastic, shown by a shallow demand curve, and the second is inelastic, shown by a steep curve. Bear in mind, however, that a relatively shallow or steep demand curve does not per se imply elastic or inelastic demand, since the axes may be calibrated in different ways. As was mentioned earlier, an arithmetic computation is the correct method of iden-tifying the degree of price elasticity of demand.

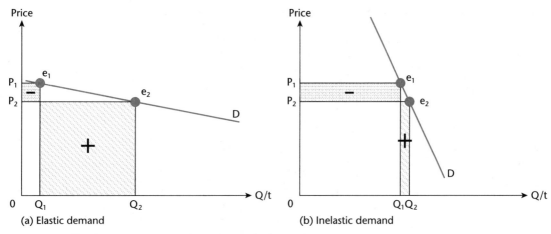

Figure 1.13 Total revenue and elastic and inelastic demand

Let us consider a price fall from $0P_1$ to $0P_2$. In both cases, the total revenue before the price fall is $0P_1e_1Q_1$, which is relatively small in the first diagram and relatively large in the second diagram. The total revenue after the price fall in both cases is $0P_2e_2Q_2$. From Figure 1.13 we can deduce that when demand was elastic, the increase in total revenue (shown by the diagonal shading) outweighed the loss of total revenue (shown by the cross-shading). In the second diagram, when demand was inelastic, the increase in total revenue was much less than the loss in total revenue. When demand is elastic, quantity demanded increases by a greater proportion than the fall in price and the firm enjoys an increase in total revenue. On the other hand, when demand is inelastic, quantity demanded rises by a smaller proportion than the fall in price and the firm suffers a decrease in total revenue.

The three revenue functions

We are now in a position to discuss three revenue functions or curves: *average revenue* (AR), *marginal revenue* (MR) and *total revenue* (TR). These functions are important for a theoretical understanding of the theory of the firm, which is discussed formally in Chapters 3 and 4 and referred to in subsequent chapters as well. Let us begin by defining the three functions:

- *Total revenue* (TR) is the product of price and quantity sold. TR thus refers to a firm's sales.
- *Average revenue* (AR) is total revenue divided by quantity sold. In other words AR is *price*.
- *Marginal revenue* (MR) is the addition to total revenue by selling one extra unit of output.

The relationship between these three functions can be shown in Table 1.3, which is then graphed in Figure 1.14.

The average revenue function plotted on Figure 1.14 is the demand curve, showing the different combinations of price and quantities sold. Economists often label demand curves as AR functions when discussing theories of the firm. Initially, as

Table 1.3 Average revenue, total revenue and marginal revenue

Average revenue (price) AR	Quantity demanded and sold	Total revenue TR	Marginal revenue MR
11	0	0	–
10	1	10	10
9	2	18	8
8	3	24	6
7	4	28	4
6	5	30	2
5	6	30	0
4	7	28	-2
3	8	24	-4
2	9	18	-6
1	10	10	-8

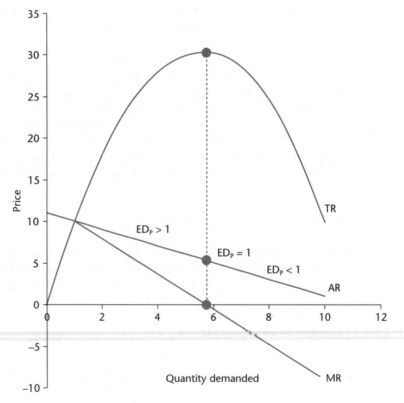

Figure 1.14 Average revenue, total revenue and marginal revenue

price falls, we see that total revenue increases and, referring to our previous discussion, this means that price elasticity of demand is elastic. After the point when total revenue reaches a maximum, further falls in price result in a fall in total revenue. The demand curve is therefore inelastic. It follows, therefore, that where total revenue is at a maximum, price elasticity of demand is unity.

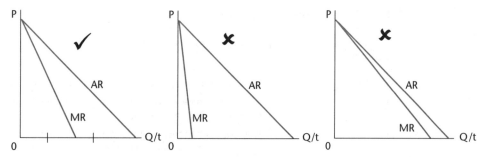

Figure 1.15 Correct relationship of AR to MR

The marginal revenue curve falls as additions to total revenue by selling one additional unit of output become less and less. When total revenue reaches its maximum, marginal revenue is zero. In other words, there are no further increases in total revenue. As total revenue begins to decrease, marginal revenue takes on negative values. One further point to note is that it can be shown mathematically that the marginal revenue curve slopes twice as fast as a linear average revenue curve. Therefore it meets the quantity axis at exactly the mid-point. Figure 1.15 illustrates the correct and incorrect relationships.

1.6 Other Elasticities

Income elasticity of demand

Let us now turn to a discussion of our second elasticity measure, income elasticity of demand (ED_Y), which can be defined as the degree of responsiveness of the quantity demanded of a good or service to changes in income.

It can be calculated in the same way as our measure for price elasticity of demand, substituting income for price, hence:

$$ED_Y = \frac{\text{Percentage change in quantity demanded}}{\text{Percentage change in income}}$$

Unlike our measure for price elasticity of demand, income elasticity of demand can be positive or negative. For 'normal' goods, for which quantity demanded increases as income increases, the relationship is *positive*. Inferior goods, for which quantity demanded decreases as income increases, are thus characterised by a *negative* relationship. If the quantity demanded is unaffected by changes in income, the measure is close to zero. These relationships are summarised in Table 1.4.

Cross-elasticity of demand

Our third elasticity measure is cross-elasticity of demand (ED_{XY}), which measures the relationship between the price of one good and the quantity demanded of another. It can be defined as the degree of responsiveness of the quantity demanded of some good X to changes in price of another good Y.

Table 1.4 Income elasticity of demand

Income elasticity of demand	Interpretation
$ED_Y = 0$	Quantity demanded does not change as income changes
$ED_Y > 0$	As income changes, quantity demanded changes in the same direction. A NORMAL good
$ED_Y < 0$	As income changes, quantity demanded changes in the opposite direction. An INFERIOR good
$ED_Y > 0$ but < 1	Changes in income and quantity demanded are in the same direction, but quantity demanded changes less proportionately than the change in income. A normal good in inelastic demand
$ED_Y > 0$ and > 1	Changes in income and quantity demanded are in the same direction, but quantity demanded changes more proportionately than the change in income. A normal good in elastic demand

Table 1.5 Cross-elasticity of demand

Measure	Relationship	Increase in price Y	Decrease in price Y
$ED_{XY} > 0$	Substitutes	Quantity of X rises	Quantity of X falls
$ED_{XY} < 0$	Complements	Quantity of X falls	Quantity of X rises
$ED_{XY} = 0$	Unrelated	No effect on X	No effect on X

Once again it can be calculated in the same way:

$$ED_{XY} = \frac{\text{Percentage change in quantity demanded of good X}}{\text{Percentage change in the price of good Y}}$$

Goods which follow a positive relationship are substitutes, since an increase in price leads to an increase in the demand of the other good. Both changes are in the same direction. Pairs of goods which have a negative relationship are complements, since an increase in the price of one leads to a decrease in the demand for the other. The closer the degree of substitutability the greater is the positive value of cross-elasticity. Equally, the closer the degree of complementarity, the greater the negative value. Goods that have no relationship record a cross-elasticity close to zero. Table 1.5 provides a summary of these relationships (see also Case Study 1.3)

Price elasticity of supply

For our fourth measure of elasticity we turn to the supply function to consider price elasticity of supply (ES_P), which can be defined as the degree of responsiveness of the quantity supplied of a good or service to changes in its price.

The reader should by now be able to anticipate the calculation of this measure, which is:

$$ES_p = \frac{\text{Percentage change in quantity supplied of good X}}{\text{Percentage change in the price of good X}}$$

Case Study 1.3

Milk consumption in the UK

As part of an analysis into the consumption of school milk in Europe, the European Commission analysed the nature of milk consumption in the United Kingdom.[1] The following table shows that, for the period 1991 to 1998, the Commission found that the total purchases of milk had fallen by 3.8% and household purchases by 6.9%, *even though the real price of milk fell* over this period. The report tried to identify the other variables that were responsible for the decline in milk consumption.

Liquid milk market (million litres), England and Wales

Year	Total liquid milk purchases	Total household purchases
1991	5752	4926
1992	5739	4873
1993	5719	4812
1994	5680	4740
1995	5568	4633
1996	5532	4588

The report suggested that the three important variables affecting the demand for milk were the child population, the extent of doorstep deliveries and the level of advertising. Of these, the first two were considered the most important. The following elasticities were calculated:

price elasticity of demand –0.2
growth of child population elasticity of demand +0.5
growth of doorstep deliveries elasticity of demand +0.25
advertising elasticity of demand +0.02

What was clear from these figures was that demand for milk is price inelastic. Thus a 10% decrease in price would increase quantity demanded by only 2%. However, although real prices fell by some 16% over this period, quantity demanded did not rise; it fell by 3.8% overall. This was caused by the fall in the UK child population and the decrease in home (doorstep) deliveries of milk.

The report also noted that 12% of milk consumed in the UK is drunk on its own, with 25% being consumed with cereals and 24% with tea. Since a large proportion of milk consumption is *a complement* to other products, it is no surprise that price elasticity of demand for milk is low (inelastic). An increase in the price of milk will not deter consumers from buying milk as they see it as a necessary complement for these other goods.

[1] Report submitted to DGVI European Commission 1999:
http://europa.eu.int/comm/agriculture/eval/reports/schoolmilk/sum_en.pdf

An elastic supply implies that the output of producers or firms responds more than proportionately to the change in price, whereas an inelastic supply implies that output responds less than proportionately to the change in price. Since the supply curve exhibits a positive slope the value of price elasticity of supply is positive and consequently total revenue always rises for an increase in price (or falls for a price decrease), regardless of whether the measure is inelastic or elastic.

The factors that determine whether supply is elastic or inelastic are as follows:

- The time or speed with which a producer can react to price changes in a given industry. In agriculture, individual producers cannot react very quickly to changes in prices as it takes a considerable length of time to plant new crops or rear new herds. Supply is thus *inelastic*. However, distributors and wholesalers of farm produce may have a less inelastic supply as they can rely on many different producers from around the world to meet increases in prices.

- In other industries the speed with which producers can react to price changes depends on how easily or how cheaply they can acquire additional factors of production such as labour, land and machinery to produce higher levels of output.

- A related issue might be the ease with which firms can switch some of their own factors of production to alternative uses. Some of their machines and labour may be so specialised as to be inappropriate for the production of other goods.

- If the level of stocks or spare capacity held by firms are high, then the response to a price rise is greater. Supply is *elastic*.

Figure 1.16 illustrates the various supply curve elasticities, which are not too dissimilar to those for price elasticity of demand. The only exception is unit price elasticity of supply. Any linear supply curve drawn from the origin, e.g. S_1, S_2 or S_3, has an elasticity of unity.

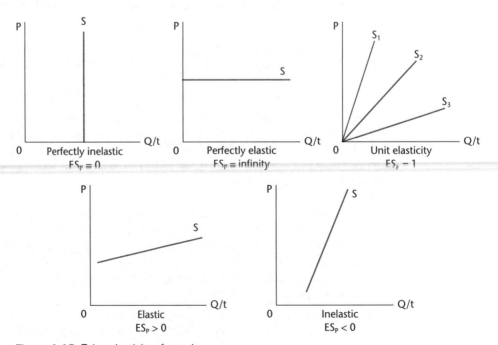

Figure 1.16 Price elasticity of supply

1.7   Conclusion

In this chapter we have shown that prices are determined by the interaction of the wants of consumers and the supply of producers. We have discussed the variables that determine the quantities demanded and the quantities supplied and have shown how these demand and supply functions determine market equilibria. The concept of elasticity, which allows us to measure the change in quantities demanded and supplied as a result of changes in variables such as prices, incomes and prices of other goods, was introduced. Even though the issues and tools of analysis presented in this chapter were intended to develop an understanding of firms' strategic decision making to be discussed in subsequent chapters, much of what we covered is also of immediate relevance to business firms which wish to have a better understanding of their consumers and markets. We also examined various revenue functions, such as average revenue, marginal revenue and total revenue. In the next chapter we consider the costs faced by producers. By bringing the two concepts together we are in a position to develop models of the firm and to discuss profitability. This is covered in Chapters 3 and 4.

Discussion Questions

1 Discuss the factors which influence demand for university degree courses in the UK.

2 Consider the market for illegal goods. What effects would you expect if the government decided to punish only the consumer or only the supplier? Draw the relevant demand and supply curves. Which of the two options would organised crime favour?

3 With reference to supply and demand curves show the cause of the shortage of sun loungers in many Mediterranean coast hotels in the summer. How are these loungers allocated? Could you suggest alternative methods?

4 Explain why some elegant restaurants require reservations while a McDonald's does not.

5 Explain why many English football clubs increase the price of tickets for European cup matches.

6 Suggest how tobacco smuggling into southeast England affects the price elasticity of demand for cigarettes in the southeast.

7 Explain the concept of *consumer surplus*. Did you receive any consumer surplus when buying this textbook? Assume a local butcher, having been party to much gossip over the years, feels that he has a good idea as to his customers' reserve prices for meat. To increase his revenue he decides to charge his customers their reserve prices (perfect price discrimination). If we assume that the butcher enjoys a local monopoly and that the townspeople are avid carnivores, will his ploy succeed? Could a doctor with similar talents succeed with such a strategy?

Further Reading

General background

Beardshaw, J., Brewster, D., Cormack, P. and Ross, A. (2001) *Economics: A Student's Guide* (5th edn). Harlow: Prentice Hall, Chapters 4, 5 and 6.

Sloman, S. (2000) *Economics* (4th edn). Harlow: Prentice Hall, Chapter 2.

Smith, P. (1999) Demanding doughnuts: getting started, *Economic Review*, 17(2). (http://www.soton.ac.uk/~peters/er/matwk.htm. Click doughnuts.pdf to read this. Article discusses consumer surplus.)

Advanced

Leibenstein, H. (1950) Bandwagon, snob, and Veblen effects in the theory of consumer demand, *The Quarterly Journal of Economics*, May, 183–207.

Veblen, T. (1908) *The Theory of the Leisure Classes*. New York: Macmillan.
(Book available on the Gutenberg site: http://promo.net/cgi-promo/pg/cat.cgi?&label=ID&ftpsite=ftp://ftp.mirror.ac.uk/sites/metalab.unc.edu/pub/docs/books/gutenberg/&alpha=853)

2 Production and Costs

Objectives

By the end of this chapter, the reader should be able to understand:

- how firms can make use of production functions
- the difference between the short run and the long run in production
- how production conditions determine the costs facing the firm
- the behaviour of average costs in the short run
- the behaviour of average costs in the long run
- the different methods used to estimate efficient methods of production which minimise costs facing the firm.

Key Concepts

- average cost
- diseconomies of scale
- economic efficiency
- economies of scale
- factors of production
- law of diminishing marginal productivity

- long run
- marginal cost
- production function
- short run
- technical efficiency
- total cost

2.1   Introduction

In the previous chapter we discussed in very general terms the issues that determine the quantity of goods and services supplied by all producers in the market. This chapter analyses these issues in more detail.

The chapter begins by examining what production actually entails and how firms attempt to achieve efficiency in their outputs:

- first, in the short run, when some factor inputs are fixed
- second, in the long run, when they are free to vary all their inputs and alter the *scale* of production.

Efficiency in the short run is subject to the law of diminishing marginal productivity, also popularly known as the law of diminishing returns. In the long run we will see that efficiency depends on the existence of economies and diseconomies of scale.

In sections 2.3 and 2.4 we focus on the money value of the inputs used by the firm, in other words the firm's production costs. We develop cost functions (curves) and examine why costs fall, rise or remain constant in both the short run and the long run. In section 2.5 we discuss how firms can estimate or calculate the cost functions they face in practice.

2.2   Production

Production in economics can be thought of as any activity which alters the form of materials, their quality and their availability over space and time. It can be thought of as a process of *transformation* of goods and services into different goods and services. This definition covers a much wider area of activity than most people imagine. Thus activities such as manufacturing, transportation, storage, retailing, marketing, etc. can all be regarded as production activities.

This wider approach is in contrast to the approach of the eighteenth-century French economists, known as the physiocrats, who believed that all true production emanated only from the land and that all other activities were non-productive. The wealth of an economy would ultimately depend on the *surplus* of agricultural production, and this surplus allowed other forms of economic activity, such as manufacturing, to exist in the economy.

Fundamentally, production is any activity which *creates* a present or future utility or use. This includes a vast range of activities. A vet immunising an animal, a composer writing a song or a student studying for a degree are all production activities in the sense that a utility is being created. The animal will avoid a future illness, the public will enjoy hearing a song and a student will improve his or her employment prospects in the future. What has happened is that something useful has been created or *produced*.

From the point of view of a firm, production takes place in response to consumer wants. Consumers wish to increase their utility by acquiring goods and services, and the firms, motivated by a desire to earn revenue, secure the necessary resources to produce goods and services which satisfy these consumers' wants.

Production functions

Production uses inputs such as labour, machinery, buildings, land, raw materials, energy, ideas and organisation. These are commonly referred to as the *factors of production*. A firm combines these inputs through a *technique* or *method of production* to produce an output. The firm also attempts to combine these inputs as *efficiently* as possible.

As discussed at the beginning of Chapter 1, factors of production possess the following three important characteristics:

- Factors are *versatile*, which means they can be put to many different uses. Thus labour can exhibit a range of abilities, machines may have different uses, and land can be used in many different ways.
- Factors can be *substituted* for one another. A given level of output can be achieved with differing combinations of factor inputs. One can, for example, erect a building with a great amount of capital equipment such as cranes, excavators, and prefabricated walls and roofs, thus relying on low levels of labour input. Alternatively, it might be possible to erect a similar building by economising on capital equipment and the use of prefabricated materials and, instead, employing more labour. The latter method would be more appropriate where labour is relatively abundant and thus cheap.
- Factors are also relatively *scarce* and thus command a price in the market. If factors were not scarce, and thus free, no price would exist. The prices paid by firms to the owners of the factors of production are viewed by firms as their *costs of production*.

A production function can therefore be defined as a technical specification of the relationship between inputs and outputs in a particular production process.

In its general form the production function simply identifies the possible outputs for given inputs and can be written as:

$$Q = f(F_1, F_2, F_3, F_4 \ldots\ldots\ldots F_n)$$

This production function shows the maximum quantity of an output 'Q' which can be obtained from a combination of factor inputs F_1, F_2, F_3, F_4, through to the last factor input used in the production process, F_n. By altering the combinations of factor inputs the firm can achieve different levels of output. With the use of statistics the production function can be worked out, *or estimated* mathematically, to give it a specific form. A very simple example of a hypothetical production function, using just two inputs, might appear in its specific form as:

$$Q = \sqrt{K \cdot L}$$

where Q is the maximum output from K units of machinery or capital, and L is the units of labour used in the production process. If we assume inputs are perfectly divisible and can be substituted for one another with no restrictions, then a given output can be produced by an infinite number of combinations. For example, with

Table 2.1 Different combination of capital and labour producing the same level of output

K	L	Q
0.5	2 000 000	= 1 000
1 000	1 000	= 1 000
8 000	125	= 1 000

reference to our earlier equation, Table 2.1 shows that an output (Q) of 1000 units can be produced by a variety of combinations of capital (K) and labour (L).

The first row refers to a labour-intensive method of production, while the last row refers to a capital-intensive method of production.

A popular production function used in economics is the Cobb–Douglas production function, which is commonly written as:

$$Q = A \cdot L^{\alpha} \cdot K^{\beta}$$

Q refers to the level of output, A is a constant which takes different values for different firms, using different technologies and located in different parts of the world. α and β are also constant and signify the contribution both labour (L) and capital (K) make to different levels of output. These are referred to as *elasticity coefficients*. On the basis of past production data, economists work out the values for A, α and β and the firm can then calculate its output for combinations of inputs. Thus if A had a value of 50, α of 0.6 and β of 0.4, and if the firm combined 30 units of labour with 100 units of capital (machinery), output per unit of time would be 2428:

$$50 \cdot 30^{0.6} \cdot 100^{0.4} = 2428$$

The reader should check this result for him or herself.

Why is the production function useful for firms?

The production function allows a firm a degree of precision in calculating its need for factor inputs. If, for example, the marketing department in a firm launches an advertising campaign and expects the firm to sell an additional 25% of its current output, the production department must calculate the additional labour and capital resources it requires. Using the previous example, a required 25% increase in output can be achieved by:

- *either* hiring an additional 14 units of labour, keeping capital fixed at 100 machines
- *or* by combining an additional 75 machines with the original workforce of 30
- *or* by any other combination of increases in *both* labour *and* capital as determined by the production function.

The actual combination depends on the *prices* the firm has to pay for its additional inputs. These are the firm's additional costs of production.

This example is, of course, a gross oversimplification of true production functions. A typical firm faces many different labour inputs, many different types of capital equipment, raw materials, energy sources and so on. Each of these inputs has its own elasticity coefficient.

Efficient production

What do we understand by the term 'efficiency'? There are two fundamental concepts of efficiency: technical and economic efficiency.

Technical efficiency relates to the actual physical ratios of material inputs to outputs. The rational firm attempts to use the minimum amount of inputs to secure a desired level of output. With knowledge gained through the study of various technologies, production managers can calculate the best technically efficient methods of production. However, the cost-minimising firm must also consider the costs of production.

Economic efficiency is the relationship between input prices or costs and output values. From a range of technically efficient input combinations, a firm selects that combination that costs the least. It attempts to economise on the use of relatively scarce resources. An oil-fired electricity-generating station may be more technically efficient than a coal-fired one, but from the point of view of economic efficiency the coal-fired station may be preferred if the price of oil, relative to the price of coal, is high.

Other concepts of efficiency can also exist, e.g. energy efficiency, social efficiency, and environmental efficiency, where we may wish to limit the production of 'bads' such as pollution. One could argue that, in time, all these ideas of efficiency could be assessed by the market and a value placed on them so as to be subsumed within the concept of economic efficiency. Nevertheless, in the short run there may well be market imperfections, such as lack of knowledge, which may create differences between these different concepts of efficiency.

Time in production

In production theory (as well as in cost theory) economists make an important distinction between the short run and the long run. The *short run* refers to a situation where some of the factors can be varied and at least one factor is fixed. Labour is traditionally regarded as the variable factor in the short run. It can be hired and fired relatively quickly. Capital and land are regarded as fixed factors in the short run. Under normal conditions it takes longer for a firm to build a new plant and acquire new machines. In the *long run*, all factors are regarded as variable. Thus, when analysing the theory of supply, economists do not measure time in the conventional sense. A large firm may regard its short run as a two-year period, whereas a market trader may regard his or her short run as a matter of days.

Law of diminishing marginal productivity

The law of diminishing marginal productivity is often referred to as the law of diminishing returns. It is concerned with *returns* to (or efficiency of) a variable factor *in the short run*. If we assume all other factors to be fixed and then examine the effect changes in the variable factor have on total output, we observe the following outcome, often stated as a 'law':

> *If increasing quantities of a variable factor of production are combined with fixed amounts of other factors of production, then after a time successive units of the variable factor make a smaller and smaller addition to total output.*

Table 2.2 Output (items processed) at a warehouse in the short run (plant and equipment kept constant)

Units of labour (variable factor)	Total product TP	Average product AP	Marginal product MP	
1	6	6	6	Increasing
2	18	9	12	returns to the
3	33	11	15	variable factor
4	40	10	7	Diminishing
5	45	9	5	returns to the
6	48	8	3	variable factor
7	49	7	1	
8	40	5	−9	

Let us now turn to an example which helps to illustrate the law of diminishing marginal productivity.

Assume a firm owns a warehouse for the delivery, storage and onward dispatch of finished goods. The chief inputs are the building, the warehouse staff and the capital equipment in the form of forklift trucks. In the short run the firm views its labour as the variable factor and the building and forklift trucks as the fixed factors. We also assume that all units of labour exhibit identical skills and supply the same effort. The output or *total product* can be measured as the number of batches of finished goods moved in and out of the warehouse per day. Table 2.2 shows the input and output figures for this warehouse.

We can use Table 2.2 to determine the following relationships:

- *Average product* (AP), which is defined as the total product divided by the number of units of the variable factor.

- *Marginal product* (MP), which is defined as the increase in total product as a result of employing *one* extra unit of the variable factor.

Figure 2.1 shows the relationships between the three measures. To ensure greater clarity the graphs are not drawn to scale and the average product and the marginal product curves are drawn on a separate graph, below the total product curve.

In the short run, as we add units of the variable factor, we first experience *increasing returns to the variable factor*, i.e. the TP curve is convex from below. This means that, as the firm hires more labour, total output rises *proportionately more*. When diminishing returns set in, the TP curve becomes concave from below, which means that total output rises *proportionately less* than the increase in the labour input. The point of inflection denotes the changeover. Diminishing returns to the variable factor set in because the expansion of these factors is not matched by an increase in the other factors. In our warehouse example, as the firm hires more staff, there are only a limited number of forklift trucks that can be used. Consequently, some of the additional staff are idle for some of the time, waiting for other staff to finish using the forklift trucks. More staff may process more goods, but the constraints of the size of the warehouse building may mean there is less and less space in which goods can be stored.

The MP curve reflects the slope of the TP curve. Thus, with increasing returns, the MP curve rises and with diminishing returns the MP curve falls. When TP falls, MP

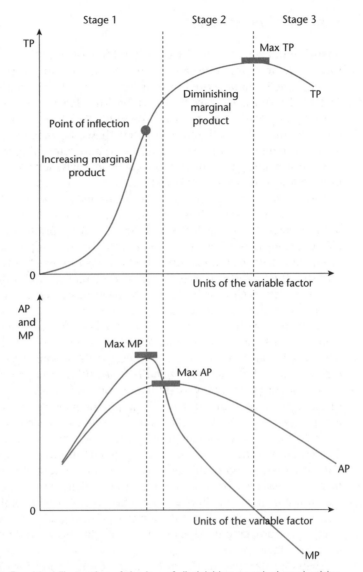

Figure 2.1 Graphical illustration of the law of diminishing marginal productivity

is negative. MP is at a maximum at the point of inflection of the TP curve and MP is zero where TP is at a maximum.

We also note that the AP curve rises and then falls. Note also that the MP curve intersects the AP curve at its maximum. This is because, whenever we add more to the total than the average, the average must rise. For example, if one worker is more productive than the one before, this has the effect of increasing average productivity. Equally, an addition to the total which is less than the average has the effect of pulling the average down.

Thus, when MP is greater than AP, AP must rise, and when MP is less than AP, AP must fall. It then follows that MP must equal AP when AP is neither falling nor rising: it is at its maximum.

Stages of production

As shown in Figure 2.1, the TP curve (and the AP and MP curves) can be divided into three stages and only one can be identified as an efficient stage of production.

Stage one is characterised by a rising AP, stage two by a diminishing but positive AP and MP, and stage three by a negative MP. Stages one and three are clearly inefficient; by implication, stage two is the only efficient zone of production. The key to understanding the distinction between these stages is to recognise that a firm is using a variable factor (in this case labour) and combining it with fixed amounts of other inputs; and that production is inefficient whenever these inputs are combined in proportions that *hinder* production.

Stage three is inefficient because it entails a negative MP. If production temporarily falls into stage three, the firm can increase output by reducing the size of the workforce. When the MP is no longer negative, production moves into the more efficient stage two. MP is negative because the fixed inputs are *overloaded* and total production falls. In our example the firm has hired so many additional warehouse staff that the forklift trucks are breaking down more often through overuse. In addition, storage space in the building may be lost by having to provide more amenities for the expanding workforce.

Whereas stage three features *too much* labour for the available capital, stage one is inefficient because *too little* labour is being employed. In stage one, the AP rises when the labour force expands. But because the labour force is small relative to the firm's fixed capital, *the fixed capital is underutilised*. In our warehouse example, one unit of labour may find it very difficult to operate a large warehouse single handedly. In addition some units of capital equipment may require more than one person to operate them. Furthermore, more labour means that individual workers can begin to specialise and concentrate on specific activities where their productivity is greater. Thus, as the labour force is expanded, output rises not just proportionately, but more than proportionately. As a result, the productivity gains (by specialisation) of the increasing workforce increase the workers' average productivity. However, remaining in stage one implies that a firm is not fully exploiting all possible gains. A firm would be inefficient if it were to stop hiring labour in the midst of these productivity improvements. The profit-maximising firm should hire enough workers to be out of stage one.

Therefore stage two is the only range of production for which labour and other inputs are combined in *efficient* proportions. We cannot determine the exact quantity of inputs a firm wishes to acquire or output produced in stage two, since these decisions depend on the *prices* of inputs and output. This decision is discussed in Chapter 3. Note that the only efficient stage of production, stage two, exhibits diminishing marginal (and average) returns throughout its entire range. We can conclude that *rather than avoiding diminishing returns, profit-maximising firms seek them out*.

Returns to scale

Our warehouse firm, faced with diminishing marginal productivity in the short run, may wish to expand its output by expanding *all* inputs. We can characterise this as the long-run period of production. Thus, in addition to hiring more staff, it acquires

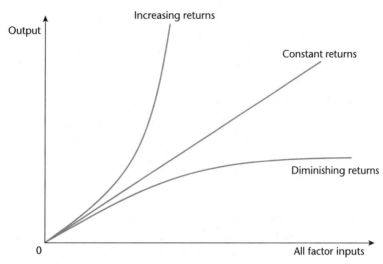

Figure 2.2 Increasing, constant and diminishing returns to scale

more forklift trucks and moves into a larger building. When firms increase the inputs of all factors of production, they alter the *scale* of production.

Returns to scale refer to the proportionate increase in output relative to the proportionate increase in all inputs. We can identify three types of returns to scale in Figure 2.2. Although the three are shown separately, firms can pass through all three phases as they expand the scale of their operations.

Increasing returns to scale occur when output increases more than proportionately to the increase in inputs. The reason for this is the advantage of specialisation, mass production and other 'economies'. These are discussed further in this chapter when we analyse long-run costs.

Constant returns to scale occur when output increases proportionately to an increase in inputs. Thus, a doubling of inputs leads to a doubling of output. Empirically, it has been shown that many firms operate under these conditions.

Decreasing returns to scale occurs when output increases less than proportionately to increases in inputs. As inputs increase, the increasing organisational complexity of the firm prevents any further proportionate increases in output. Diseconomies of scale are discussed in our analysis of long-run costs.

Cobb–Douglas production function and returns to scale

Earlier in the chapter we introduced the Cobb–Douglas production function, which was expressed as:

$$Q = A \cdot L^{\alpha} \cdot K^{\beta}$$

Q referred to the output, and L and K were the labour and capital inputs. A was a constant determined by a given technology and α and β were the coefficients which measured the relative importance of each of the inputs. The sum of these coefficients is used to determine the returns to scale. If $\alpha + \beta$ sum to unity then the firm is operating under conditions of constant returns to scale. If $\alpha + \beta$ have a value greater than 1, then we have increasing returns to scale. If, finally, $\alpha + \beta$ is less than 1 the firm is operating under conditions of decreasing returns to scale.

The reader can verify this by referring to the previous example, where A had a value of 50, α was 0.6, β was 0.4, and the firm combined 30 units of labour with 100 units of capital. The output was 2428. The reader can calculate the new output if both labour and capital are doubled, to 60 and 200 respectively, under three conditions:

- $\alpha = 0.6$ and $\beta = 0.4$ (constant returns to scale)
- $\alpha = 0.7$ and $\beta = 0.5$ (increasing returns to scale)
- $\alpha = 0.4$ and $\beta = 0.4$ (decreasing returns to scale).

In a seminal article Cookenboo (1955) estimated the production function for an oil pipeline to be:

$$T = AH^aD^b$$

where T referred to the flow of oil, measured as the number of barrels of oil per day; H was the horsepower of the machinery pumping the oil; and D was the diameter of the pipe. The constants A, a and b were dependent on the location of the pipes, the length of the pipelines and the viscosity of the oil. He estimated the production function as:

$$T = 5.4H^{0.37}D^{1.73}$$

which meant the production function exhibited increasing returns to scale. In addition, the high coefficient on the pipe diameter tells us that a 1% increase in the pipe's diameter leads to a 1.73% increase in barrels of oil per day, assuming the horsepower of the pump is kept constant. Equally, the contribution of a 1% increase in the horsepower of the pump leads to only a 0.37% increase in output.

2.3   Costs

Nature of costs

Costs refer to the payments or rewards made by firms to the suppliers of factors of production. Most of us supply our labour, in return for which we are paid a wage. This wage is a cost to a firm. A number of important points must be borne in mind.

- The word 'reward' is used as well as payment, since in many cases no formal money payment is made for the supply of an input. Thus, for example, owners of a business may not pay themselves for ploughing their own money into that business. Nevertheless, if the rewards or profits from such a personal investment were *less* than what they would have received had they invested the money elsewhere (the opportunity cost), they would soon contemplate the closure of the business. Thus, the profits made by a firm to 'reward' the owners, who have invested in a firm, can be seen as a *cost* the firm has to meet.
- The exact payment for continuing to supply factor inputs is naturally determined by market forces. Thus, the wage a worker expects to receive is determined by market opportunities, i.e. the wages paid by other firms.
- As we saw earlier, a period of time sufficiently long to generate changes in all factor inputs was termed the long run. All costs would be regarded as variable in the

long run, i.e. all costs change with the level of output. In the short run, however, some factors are regarded as fixed and, consequently, the firm would incur fixed costs. Fixed costs refer to expenditures relating to depreciation on capital equipment and buildings, rates, rentals, interest payments, insurance premiums, etc. Variable costs, by way of contrast, refer to wages, purchases of raw materials, power and fuel – in other words, all those inputs which vary with the level of production.

- It is important to note that costs simply reflect what is happening in production. If, in the short run, the firm initially enjoys increasing returns to its variable factor, usually labour, we saw that the average product of labour will rise. To maintain a constant increase in output the firm requires proportionately less labour and thus average variable costs fall. If, after a given level of output, the firm were faced with diminishing returns to the variable factor, it would require proportionately more and more labour to maintain a constant increase in output and average variable costs would rise. We can derive these average variable cost curves by examining total cost curves.

Costs in the short run

With reference to our previous example of the warehouse, our firm is faced with fixed factors of machinery and the building. It is able to increase output only by increasing its labour input. To construct a total cost curve we must calculate the required labour inputs at each level of output and multiply them by the wage rate. We add this figure to the quantity of the fixed factors multiplied by their prices. Figure 2.3 shows three possible total cost functions.

Curve 1 shows total costs rising less than proportionately to the increase in output. To increase output while keeping its capital equipment and building unchanged, the firm requires proportionately *less* labour.

Curve 2 shows that each additional unit of output uses the same proportionate inputs of labour. In this case, the firm is faced with constant returns to the variable

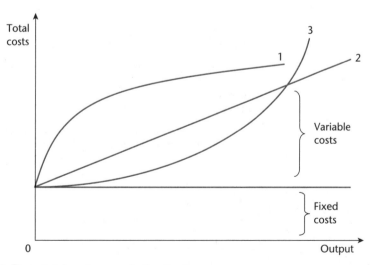

Figure 2.3 Three total cost curves in the short run

factor. This should not be confused with constant returns to scale, which refers only to the long run when all factors are variable.

Curve 3 shows that to increase output, keeping the other factors constant, requires proportionately *more* labour. The effect is then to see the total cost curve rise steeply.

The traditional total cost curve

Figure 2.4 illustrates the traditional total cost curve, which passes through all these three stages discussed above.

Figure 2.4 shows a total cost curve with increasing returns to the variable factor input followed by constant returns and eventually diminishing returns to factor input. This function reflects the total product curve illustrated in Figure 2.1. *From this total cost curve we can derive an average variable cost curve.* Average variable costs are calculated by dividing total costs by the units of the variable factor. Increasing returns to the variable factor mean that total costs are rising at a slow rate and thus average variable costs are falling. The firm is enjoying increasing efficiency by adding more of the variable factor. However, once diminishing returns to the variable factor set in, the total cost curve begins to rise at a faster rate, which leads the average variable cost curve to rise. The firm begins to suffer from an inefficient combination of its variable factors with its fixed factors. If *average cost* becomes very high, the firm may have to consider increasing the other factors, such as plant and machinery.

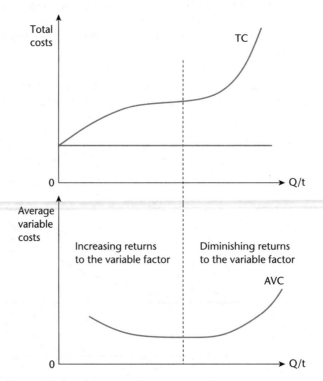

Figure 2.4 Traditional total cost curve and average variable cost curve

Table 2.3 Cost schedule

Q	TFC	TVC	TC	AFC	AVC	ATC	MC
0	50		50				
1	50	30	80	50	30	80	30
2	50	55	105	25	27.5	52.5	25
3	50	75	125	16.6	25	41.6	20
4	50	100	150	12.5	25	37.5	25
5	50	130	180	10	26	36	30
6	50	175	225	8.3	29.2	37.5	45

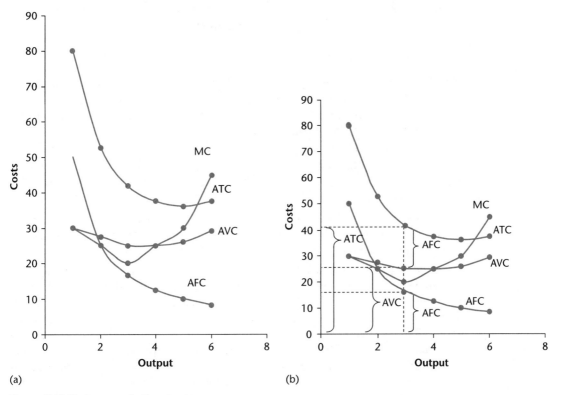

(a)   (b)

Figure 2.5 Cost curves in the short run

Let us now turn to an examination of other cost functions which face a typical firm. With the help of the simple cost schedule shown in Table 2.3 we can illustrate the functions in Figure 2.5. We begin by first defining the various cost functions, shown in Box 2.1.

We can plot the AFC, AVC, ATC and MC curves in Figure 2.5(a).

From this graph we can derive the following conclusions:

- *Average fixed costs* (AFC) decrease continually, although at a decreasing rate. This is because total fixed costs are spread over an ever-increasing output. Thus, if fixed costs are high in an industry or a firm, the firm must produce a relatively large output to reduce the high average costs.

Box 2.1 Definitions of cost

Total costs (TC)	=	Total fixed costs (TFC) + Total variable costs (TVC)
Average fixed costs (AFC)	=	Total fixed costs (TFC) / Output (Q)
Average variable costs (AVC)	=	Total variable costs (TVC) / Output (Q)
Average total costs (ATC)	=	Total cost (TC) / Output (Q) [or AFC + AVC]
Marginal cost (MC)	=	The addition to total cost as a result of producing one extra unit of output

- The *AVC curve* is U-shaped. As we saw in Figure 2.4, as production becomes more efficient (increasing returns to the variable factor) average variable costs decline. After a point, diminishing returns set in (decreasing returns to the variable factor) and the AVC curve begins to rise.

- The *ATC curve* is also U-shaped since it is the sum of AFC and AVC. ATC falls so long as the AFC and the AVC fall, and even when AVC starts to rise, since the fall in AFC outweighs the rise in AVC. When AVC rises faster than the fall in AFC, the net effect is a rise in ATC.

- The distance between AVC and ATC declines steadily with increases in output. This is so because the distance between (or difference between) ATC and AVC is AFC. This relationship is identified in Figure 2.5(b).

- *Marginal cost* is also U-shaped. When MC lies below AC, AC is falling. When MC lies above AC, AC is rising. It then follows that MC must intersect the AC curve at its minimum point. The MC curve intersects the AC curve at its minimum point for the same reason that marginal product intersects the average product curve at its maximum point. If one adds a (marginal) value to the total which is less than the average, the average falls. Equally, when the addition to the total is greater than the average, the average rises. This means that when the addition to the total is equal to the average, the average is neither falling nor rising and is at its minimum point.

Why have we introduced the concept of marginal cost?

In traditional economic analysis, it is assumed that the objective of the firm is to maximise profits. As we will see in the next chapter, this is achieved by equating marginal cost with marginal revenue.

Long-run costs

In the long run, all factor inputs can be varied. To expand the *scale* of the business our warehouse firm can acquire more capital in the form of more forklift trucks, as

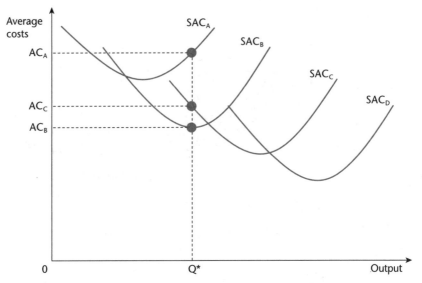

Figure 2.6 Four short-run average cost curves

well as expanding the size of the warehouse itself or moving to a bigger building. It also hires more labour.

Let us assume that the firm is faced with four possible sizes of warehouse. This implies four separate short-run average cost curves (SAC), one for each warehouse, A, B, C, and D. For each SAC, the building and the forklift trucks are the fixed factor and the firm can then vary only its labour input. The opportunities facing the firm are illustrated in Figure 2.6.

Reading from left to right, every subsequent SAC curve refers to a larger warehouse. We can see that larger warehouses generate lower average costs. This is due to *economies of scale*, which are discussed later. The decision as to which of the warehouses the firm should occupy depends on the firm's anticipated future output. If the firm expects to produce at Q* then, with warehouse A, costs are relatively high at AC$_A$, since the firm is faced with diminishing returns to the variable factor. In other words, the building is too small to house all the machinery and labour. If the firm were to acquire warehouse C, a very much larger building, costs would be at AC$_C$. These average costs are still relatively high as the firm is faced with a large warehouse but insufficient machinery and labour to make full use of the space. Warehouse B, however, would generate the lowest possible average cost at AC$_B$. Thus, for an expected output of Q*, warehouse size B would be chosen. In time, as planned output increases the firm selects larger and larger warehouses and consequently moves onto lower and lower SAC curves.

If we assume that in the long run a firm can select an infinite number of plant sizes or scales of output, we can draw an infinite number of SAC curves. This is illustrated in Figure 2.7.

At first these curves lie a little below the preceding curves due to economies of scale. After a time the curves begin to rise due to *diseconomies of scale*. If we then draw a curve to 'envelope' these curves we have the long-run average cost curve (LAC) which traces all the combinations of outputs and average costs as the scale of operations is increased. The curve is sometimes referred to as the firm's planning

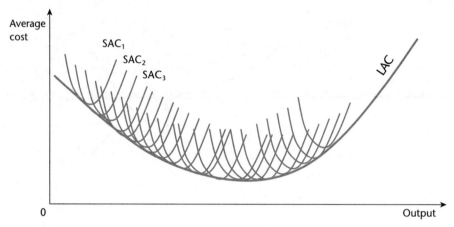

Figure 2.7 Derivation of the long-run average cost curve

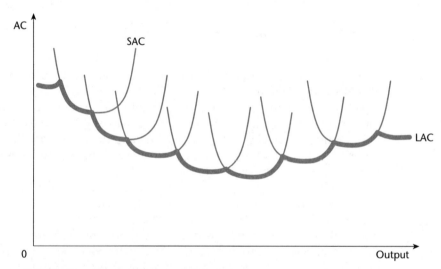

Figure 2.8 'Scalloped' long-run average cost curve

curve, since it represents all the average costs attainable at the various scales in the firm's future plans.

Two important points have to be borne in mind.

First, the smooth LAC curve implies the availability of an infinite number of different plant sizes. Each point on the LAC curve is thus a point of tangency with a SAC curve. In reality, a firm is faced with a limited choice of different plant sizes. If so, a more realistic LAC curve would exhibit a 'scalloped' shape, as illustrated in Figure 2.8.

Second, the LAC curve is not tangential to all the minimum points of the SAC curves. A point of tangency implies that the slopes of SAC and LAC are equal. Minimum points of the SAC have a zero slope and cannot therefore be tangential to a negatively sloped LAC (economies of scale) or positively sloped LAC (diseconomies of scale). This could only occur under conditions of constant returns to scale (a horizontal LAC) (see Figure 2.9 and Case Study 2.1).

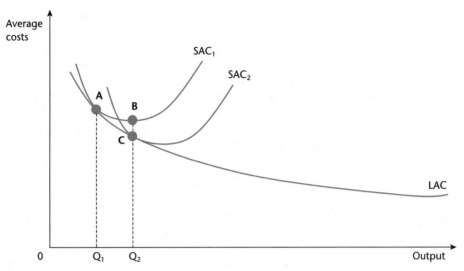

Figure 2.9 Choice of scale and short-run average cost curves

Case Study 2.1

Even top economists get it wrong!

In the 1930s Jacob Viner (the economist responsible for the LRAC curve) had asked his draughtsman to draw an 'envelope' LRAC curve so that it was tangential to the *minimum points of every SRAC curve*. The draughtsman claimed that this was impossible.

A point of tangency implies that the slopes of SRAC and LRAC are equal. Minimum points of the SRAC have a zero slope and cannot therefore be tangential to a negatively sloped LRAC (economies of scale) or positively sloped LRAC (diseconomies of scale). This could only occur under conditions of constant returns to scale (a horizontal LRAC).

When John Maynard Keynes published his General Theory in 1936, one of the critics of his revolutionary theories was Jacob Viner, who was less than impressed with Keynes's critique of classical macroeconomic theories. When Keynes arrived in the United States, he was asked to name the greatest living economist. He replied that modesty prevented him from naming the greatest, but that perhaps the second greatest was Jacob Viner's draughtsman!

If we consider Figure 2.9 it would appear that firms may wish to be inefficient in the short run, i.e. point A is preferred to point B on the SAC_1 curve. If the firm wishes to expand from Q_1 to Q_2 it can employ more of the variable factor (labour) to achieve minimum average costs at point B. However, the same output Q_2 could be achieved *at a lower average cost* had the firm acquired more fixed inputs (capital) to develop a plant associated with the SAC_2 curve. The firm has reduced average costs for output Q_2, although at point C it is still to the left of the minimum point of the SAC_2 curve.

When we consider *all costs*, the firm is not necessarily operating inefficiently. The increased plant size uses labour at an amount *less* than that required to minimise average cost; but greater economies of scale more than offset this loss.

Only one SAC curve has its minimum point tangential to the LAC curve, and that is where the minimum point of the LAC is met. The particular plant or firm size associated with this level of average cost is sometimes referred to as the *optimum firm*, i.e. of maximum efficiency, where average costs are at their lowest in the long run.

2.4   Economies and Diseconomies of Scale

Let us now turn to an examination of the LAC curve. The question is: why does the long-run average cost curve show a systematic tendency to decrease or increase with the scale of operations? We shall examine various explanations put forward to show why the LAC curve falls as the scale of output rises, i.e. economies of scale, and why the curve may eventually begin to rise, i.e. diseconomies of scale. Economies and diseconomies of scale are the cost equivalent of increasing and decreasing returns to scale respectively.

Economies of scale

Most classifications of economies of scale fall broadly into two categories: real economies and pecuniary economies. The former is associated with changes in physical input quantities, whereas the latter refers to changes in the prices paid by the firm for its inputs. These broad classifications can be further subdivided, e.g. production or technical economies, marketing economies, transport economies, stochastic economies, multiplant economies, etc. An exhaustive examination of all potential economies open to a firm would perhaps become tedious. Instead, we shall briefly cover the important economies associated with operations at the simple individual firm level.

Specialisation

As a firm grows larger it can benefit from a greater division of labour. As individual units of labour become more specialised they acquire greater skills and know-how. Their increased efficiency leads to reduced costs. Additionally, specialisation saves on wasted time when labour has to move from one job to another. This advantage also applies to management. In a small firm, a manager may have to perform several tasks, and in some may lack sufficient expertise. The large firm can benefit from acquiring specialist managers. The benefits of specialisation also reward firms in the short run as they expand their labour force, and largely explain increasing returns to the variable factor. This advantage of specialisation was noted famously by Adam Smith (see Case Study 2.2).

Case Study 2.2

Adam Smith's pin factory and economies of scale

Adam Smith (1723–90), Scottish economist and philosopher, studied the forces that determined competition, trade and markets. He was professor of logic and later professor of moral philosophy at Glasgow University and had friends in business and the government. He is considered as the founder of modern economic thought and wrote one of the first and best known books in economics, *The Wealth of Nations* (1776). The first chapter of the book deals with the division of labour and specialisation, which leads to increasing returns to scale. Although written in eighteenth-century English, it is still fresh and relevant to modern-day economics. The slightly edited extract that follows discusses Smith's observations of production in a Nottingham pin factory:

> THE greatest improvement in the productive powers of labour, and the greater part of the skill, dexterity, and judgement with which it is anywhere directed, or applied, seem to have been the effects of the division of labour. The effects of the division of labour, in the general business of society, will be more easily understood by considering in what manner it operates in some particular manufactures.
>
> To take an example, therefore, from a very trifling manufacture; but one in which the division of labour has been very often taken notice of, the trade of the pin-maker; a workman not educated to this business (which the division of labour has rendered a distinct trade), nor acquainted with the use of the machinery employed in it (to the invention of which the same division of labour has probably given occasion), could scarce, perhaps, with his utmost industry, make one pin in a day, and certainly could not make twenty. But in the way in which this business is now carried on, not only the whole work is a peculiar trade, but it is divided into a number of branches, of which the greater part are likewise peculiar trades. One man draws out the wire, another straights it, a third cuts it, a fourth points it, a fifth grinds it at the top for receiving the head; to make the head requires two or three distinct operations; to put it on is a peculiar business, to whiten the pins is another; it is even a trade by itself to put them into the paper; and the important business of making a pin is, in this manner, divided into about eighteen distinct operations, which, in some manufactories, are all performed by distinct hands, though in others the same man will sometimes perform two or three of them.
>
> I have seen a small manufactory of this kind where ten men only were employed, and where some of them consequently performed two or three distinct operations. But though they were very poor, and therefore but indifferently accommodated with the necessary machinery, they could, when they exerted themselves, make among them about twelve pounds of pins in a day. There are in a pound upwards of four thousand pins of a middling size. Those ten persons, therefore, could make among them upwards of forty-eight thousand pins in a day. Each person, therefore, making a tenth part of forty-eight thousand pins, might be considered as making four thousand eight hundred pins in a day. But if they had all wrought separately and independently, and without any of them having been educated to this peculiar business, they certainly could not each of them have made twenty, perhaps not one pin in a day; that is, certainly, not the two hundred and fortieth, perhaps not the four thousand eight hundredth part of what they are at present capable of performing, in consequence of a proper division and combination of their different operations. In every other art and manufacture, the effects of the division of labour are similar to what they are in this

> *very trifling one; though, in many of them, the labour can neither be so much subdivided, nor reduced to so great a simplicity of operation. The division of labour, however, so far as it can be introduced, occasions, in every art, a proportionable increase of the productive powers of labour.*
>
> Source: Smith, Adam (1776) *An Inquiry into the Nature and Causes of the Wealth of Nations*. Chapter 1, Of the Division of Labour; http://socserv2.socsci.mcmaster.ca/~econ/ugcm/3ll3/smith/wealth/wealbk01

Technical economies

These economies can encompass many aspects of production. We offer three examples.

Geometric relationships

These refer to relationships between inputs required to produce a piece of equipment and its output capacity. An example is the capacity of an oil tanker, which increases more than proportionally with increases in its surface area. Another example is the construction and use of pipelines. A doubling of a pipe's circumference more than doubles its capacity. It is this type of relationship that was responsible for the so-called '0.6' rule of thumb, where it was assumed by engineers in the oil industry that an average increase in capacity of 100% would lead to only a 60% increase in total costs.

Indivisibilities

Indivisibilities of capital and labour inputs are also an important source of potential economies for the large firm. If equipment, necessary to perform important operations in the firm's production process, is large, complex, highly specialised and expensive, the firm is faced with high fixed costs. Faced with an indivisible input, the firm cannot then acquire just 10% or 50% of the input. It must buy the whole machine or process. A large output thus greatly reduces the firm's average fixed costs. For example, a combine harvester is an efficient unit of capital equipment used in agricultural production. However, a farmer must have a potentially large output to justify the ownership of such a large indivisible input.

Indivisibilities may also be involved due to a *balancing process*. Assume that a firm is faced with a production process which requires only two types of machine: one which produces and the other which packages the final product. If the first machine can produce 30,000 units per day and the second can package at the rate of 45,000 per day, output has to be at least 90,000 per day (or multiples of) fully to utilise the capacity of both machines. With an output of 90,000 units per day, a firm acquires three production machines and two packaging machines. Had output been less than 90,000, the firm would have been faced with machines not fully utilised.

Length of production run

The length of the production run is also an important source for potential economies. It is argued that over time units of labour become more skilled as they repeat the same task. Thus the length of the production run becomes an important

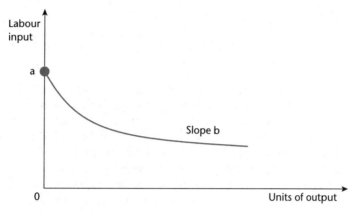

Figure 2.10 The learning curve

variable to indicate the increased rate of worker efficiency. Alchian (1963) calculated a 'learning curve' when he examined costs in the aircraft industry. He found that the level of labour productivity in the manufacture of airframes was a function of the cumulative number of frames already assembled. The estimated equation was:

$$\log m = a + b \log N$$

where 'm' referred to the labour input and 'N' the cumulative number of frames assembled. 'a' was the intercept of the curve and 'b' its slope. 'b' had a negative value, which meant that as more airframes were constructed so the firm required less labour and thus saved costs. The curve is shown in Figure 2.10.

Further studies have shown that such learning processes can be applied to cognitive skills of engineers and managers. One would eventually expect these learning effects to diminish and disappear. One would also expect different 'b' values in different activities.

Financial economies

Large firms find it easier to raise funds for future expansion. Larger firms are able to offer better security for their loans and may enjoy access to sources of finance such as the stock market and issuing their own bonds. The cost of finance may also be less as the market may consider large firms as posing a lower risk. Large firms can spread their risks by an involvement in multi-plant operations and diversification.

Marketing economies

Larger firms can buy and sell in bulk, thus reducing their purchasing and marketing costs. They can for example benefit from large-scale advertising, such as TV advertising, which is the cheapest method of advertising when considering the numbers of potential consumers reached.

Research

Large firms can afford to finance R&D, often the single most important route for growth, as well as leading to a reduction of future costs. Large firms also have the ability to exploit unexpected spin-offs from their R&D programmes.

Welfare

Large firms can offer better conditions of service, thus generating greater loyalty and improved productivity of staff.

All the economies noted above, both real and pecuniary, could be seen as *internal* economies of scale, i.e. those advantages created directly by the firm due to its own expansion of capacity and scale of operations. *External* economies of scale refer to advantages of scale created not by the firm, but by the industry. Thus a large-scale industry may enjoy the benefits of greater specialisation, a more efficient infrastructure, industry specific education and training, government and university research inputs. This reduces costs for *all firms* in the industry, large and small firms alike.

(See Case Study 2.3 for an examination of economies of scale in Scottish hospitals.)

Case Study 2.3

Economies of scale and hospitals in Scotland

The Scottish Office was asked by the Secretary of State for Scotland to recommend how resources in the National Health Service could best be allocated in Scotland. In 1999 the Executive reported its findings. One of its chief concerns was to assess the costs of delivering health services to very different geographical areas so as to ensure an equitable distribution of resources.

One aspect of this analysis was to analyse the implications of remoteness and rurality for the costs of providing hospital services and other medical services. The costs of running hospitals in rural areas were considered to be higher than those in urban areas because rural hospitals were usually of a small scale.

The report noted that large-scale hospitals had the following advantages:

- They could spread their fixed assets, such as operating theatres and diagnostic equipment, over a greater volume of patients and thus reduce average costs.

- Specialist staff in larger hospitals could be used more efficiently.

- Large hospitals required a smaller margin for reserve capacity to cope with variability of demand. Small hospitals would require proportionately more reserve capacity to deal with unexpected variations in demand such as a sudden increase in births.

- The report also noted that large hospitals provided more staff development, which led to efficiency gains.

The evidence showed that average costs of providing health services in small hospitals were greater. In the case of the large mental illness hospitals the average cost of patient care was around £700 a week, whereas the average cost in the smaller hospitals was £900 a week. Similar cost differences were found in acute hospitals, maternity units and institutions caring for the elderly.

Source: Scottish Executive Fair Shares for All Technical Report.
National Review of Resource Allocation for the NHS in Scotland, July 1999;
http://www.scotland.gov.uk/library2/doc02/fsat-00.htm

Diseconomies of scale

Let us now turn to diseconomies of scale. The popular explanation of this phenomenon is the concept of managerial diseconomies of scale. This means that, at some large scale, managers are no longer capable of running a firm efficiently. This can be due to:

- strained communications between tiers of management
- poor quality of the information flows within the organisation
- long chains of command and complex organisational structures
- poor morale among large groups of workers.

An example of one such explanation for diseconomies of scale, which covers some of the points just raised, was that provided by Williamson (1967).

Williamson's theory of control loss

A firm can be regarded as a coalition of various teams or groups which are responsible for activities such as production, marketing and finance. Since much of the firm's activity can be regarded as a 'team effort', there exist, as in all teams, incentives for 'free riders' or 'shirkers'. Some members of a team may misrepresent their abilities so as to achieve rewards higher than their real effort would merit. They could 'cover up' their poor performances by blaming exogenous factors, such as the nature of the work, the poor quality of their machines, lack of support from other staff, the weather and so on. Williamson refers to this type of situation as *information impactedness*: the desire of 'poor' staff deliberately to mislead fellow team members and supervisors. It would be irrational for shirkers to own up to the poor quality of their work. The losses sustained from such shirking fall on all the team members.

This analysis suggests that there is a need for someone to control and monitor performances of team members. Traditionally, this has been the role of the entrepreneur. In the modern organisation, the entrepreneur has been replaced by salaried managers whose main role is to monitor the performances of teams. These managers are monitored by a higher echelon of managers, who in turn are monitored by a yet still higher tier of managers and so on. We thus see the evolution of a hierarchical structure, where every level of management is monitored by the next level up. The apex of the structure is the final control exercised by the owners of the firm.

Williamson claims that these hierarchical patterns of control lead to higher costs through the concept of *control loss*. The function of the hierarchy is to handle, transmit and process or interpret information as it flows from the lowest level of the organisation to the highest. This information is subject to two distortions:

- *Deliberate distortion* (information impactedness). This occurs when managers, supervisors and team members at the lowest level misrepresent their abilities and distort the real information so as to appear in the best possible light.
- *Accidental distortion* (serial reproduction). This occurs whenever information has to flow through many channels. The children's party game of 'Chinese Whispers' is an illustration of such serial reproduction.

Williamson (1967: 127) added:

Bartlett (1932) illustrates this [serial reproduction] graphically with a line drawing of an owl which – when redrawn successively by eighteen individuals, each sketch based on its immediate predecessor – ended up as a recognisable cat; and the further from the initial drawing one moved, the greater the distortion experienced. The reliance of hierarchical organisations on serial repro-duction for their functioning thus exposes them to what may become serious distortions in transmission.

If the information is distorted, decision makers in the firm no longer have access to correct information and wrong decisions are made. Thus higher costs are incurred.

2.5   Minimum Efficient Size

The minimum efficient size (MES) is defined as the size at which long-run average costs become constant. At this point all economies of scale are exhausted and the firm cannot undertake production at a lower average cost. Figure 2.7 suggested a U-shaped LAC curve, where, once the minimum point was reached, the firm would immediately experience diseconomies of large-scale production. In reality, firms enjoy minimum average costs for a wide range of outputs where the firm is experi-encing *constant returns to scale*. Thus, a more realistic LAC curve would appear as an elongated U as shown in Figure 2.11.

Why should firms be interested in their minimum efficient size?

Entrepreneurs and managers want to have some idea of the minimum efficient size of a firm or plant if they are considering entering a particular industry. They wish to know at what scale of operations they are able to reap the benefits of all the

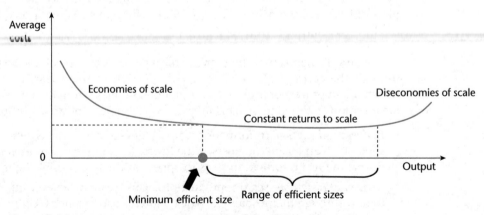

Figure 2.11 Long-run average costs and minimum efficient size

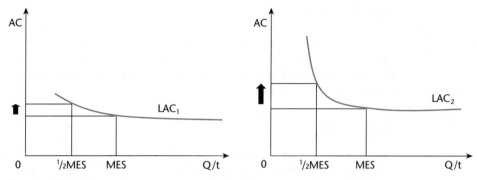

Figure 2.12 Increase in average costs of producing at less than the MES

potential economies of scale. They also like to know how many plants or firms at the MES can be borne by total market demand. If the industry is large, it may be able to bear a large number of plants and firms. In addition, calculating *half the MES* can also be used to estimate the height of the entry barrier. In certain cases, firms may be reluctant to invest large amounts in set-up costs to enter an industry at the full MES. Firms may therefore be interested in the *relative cost disadvantage* of entering at a less than full MES. In Figure 2.12 we can compare two different LACs with similar MES but very different cost disadvantages of entering the industry at less than the MES.

In Figure 2.12 the upward facing arrows illustrate these differences. If a firm were faced with LAC_1 it would experience smaller cost disadvantage if it were to enter at just half the MES, compared to the cost disadvantage of LAC_2. The shape of the LAC curve is thus an important consideration for firms.

But how can firms estimate the shape of the LAC curve and, specifically, the minimum efficient size?

We shall consider four possible methods of estimating the minimum efficient size of a plant, a firm or a group of firms. These are:

- engineering cost estimates
- statistical cost
- survivor technique
- rate of return

Engineering cost estimates

This method relies on technical experts (engineers) to estimate the cost of producing various levels of output subject to a particular level of technology. With reference to a production function which details the relationships between inputs and outputs, it is then possible to 'cost' these physical relationships. An average cost curve can then be determined. The curve is based on hypothetical data rather than actual data; however, the approach is the closest to cost theory as outlined in this chapter. Unfortunately, there are some problems in its practical application.

Time dimension

All such estimates must specify a time dimension. The quality and durability of the inputs are of great importance if the output is planned over 20 years, rather than five. Any 'learning by doing' experiences gained over time which reduce future costs also have to be included.

Human error

This approach allows for some subjectivity as engineers may disagree over the precise nature of technological relationships However, these errors may only *shift* the LAC function upwards or downwards without affecting the actual slope. Thus engineering estimates may be incorrect about the absolute level of costs, but successful at estimating the minimum efficient size.

Labour skills

While engineers may find it relatively easy to estimate the productivity of capital equipment, they may find it more difficult to anticipate the actual level of labour skill in a given plant or firm.

Non-productive activities

An engineer may also find it difficult to estimate non-productive activities of a firm, such as the administrative and marketing functions. Thus these estimates are normally applied to plants rather than firms.

No prior information

If an engineer lacks prior information it may be very difficult to make an estimate. If the largest plant to date produces 30,000 units and an engineer is asked to estimate the costs of producing 3,000,000 units, the engineer has to make many guesses.

Statistical cost

This approach does not use hypothetical data but actual data. A sample of firms in an industry is selected and an average cost for each firm as well as its size is calculated and plotted on a graph. One then draws a curve of best fit by regression analysis. In LAC estimates, cross-section data is preferred to time series data, since historical cost data may reflect changes in technology. It is most often used to estimate the cost of plants as one can rely on a *larger* sample of plants in an industry compared to a sample of firms. However, again there are a number of problems with this particular method.

Measurement

Analysis of multi-product firms leads to the problem of relating the specific costs associated with a specific product. This would then require an *adjustment* of the data, which makes the approach less attractive. Second, we may encounter the problem of lack of comparability of accounting measures in different plants. Stocks, assets, rates of depreciation, etc., can be valued differently. This, again, would mean we would have to adjust the data, which may produce errors that bias our measures. Further adjustments may have to be made if plants use different production techniques or different labour inputs, or have experienced different set-up costs.

Knowledge and experience of established firms

The output that an established firm does not sell is its knowledge and experience. However, this affects its future costs. Cost estimates based on data from well-established firms or plants may not be applicable to new entrants.

Confusion over the short run and long run

Firms or plants in one's sample may be using methods or capital that do not minimise the average costs at those levels of output, since the firms may be in *short-run equilibrium*. They may be waiting for their existing capital equipment to wear out before they install new equipment or introduce new methods of production. This has the effect of reducing average costs at the existing level of output. If this is the case, the statistical cost method confuses short-run average costs with long-run average costs. Cross-section data inevitably reflects short-run average costs unless every firm is in a position of long-run equilibrium, which is unlikely. Unfortunately, to know if a firm is in long-run equilibrium we need to know the shape of the LAC curve; but this is what we are trying to estimate in the first place!

Survivor technique

This is a technique pioneered by Stigler (1958). He explained the technique (Stigler, 1958: 56) in the following way:

> The survivor technique proceeds to solve the problem of determining the optimum size of firm as follows: Classify the firms in an industry by size, and calculate the share of the industry output coming from each class over time. If the share of a given class falls, it is relatively inefficient, and in general is more inefficient the more rapidly the share falls. An efficient size of firm, on this argument, is one that meets any and all problems the entrepreneur actually faces: strained labour relations, rapid innovation, government regulation, unstable foreign markets, etc. This is of course, the decisive meaning of efficiency from the point of view of the enterprise.

Stigler was by no means the first economist to describe this method. John Stuart Mill and Alfred Marshall (in their respective centuries) also noted the relationship between survival and efficiency, the latter undoubtedly influenced by Charles Darwin's ideas. To explain the technique let us examine a hypothetical example. We assume four sizes of plant in an industry and that size is measured by the labour force employed. We then note the market share of each plant size in one time period T_1 and then the market share in the next time period T_2. This is shown in Table 2.4.

From Table 2.4 we can infer that size 2 is the optimum size of plant. Thus plants that employ between 101 and 300 employees are the ones that are prospering and could be regarded as best suited or most efficient in this given industry. As always, there is a need for a large sample to eliminate the possibility of random errors, and consequently the technique relies more on plant data than on firm data.

Table 2.4 Market shares by plant size

Size	Labour force	Market share % T_1	Market share % T_2
1	1–100	20	15
2	101–300	35	55
3	301–600	30	20
4	601–1000	15	10

The technique does not calculate costs and no LAC curve can be directly constructed. The technique measures a much broader concept of efficiency: the ability of a plant or firm to be flexible, to adapt and to survive. Not surprisingly there are some problems in its practical application:

1 If plant 2 is the most efficient now, can we assume that it continues to increase its market share in period T_3? If we detect no further changes in period T_3, have all the plants become equally efficient?

2 Curious survival patterns have emerged from empirical studies. Assume that in period T_2 we obtain the following results:

    1   35+
    2   55+
    3   5–
    4   5–

We see that size groups 1 and 2 have increased while sizes 3 and 4 have declined. We could conclude that the upper and lower bounds of the efficient size have widened. The efficient size is thus 0–300 employees.

How can we interpret the following results in period T_2?

    1   30+
    2   25–
    3   35+
    4   10–

There are a number of possible interpretations:

• A pure random movement.

• We are faced with a badly defined industry. We have, in fact, two different products. For example, one cannot group estimates for performance cars with traditional family saloon cars. They have different production functions and scale curves, and are non-competing.

• We may be experiencing a process of convergence on size group 2 as the optimum size and the process is not yet complete.

• The industry may accommodate two different optimum sizes of firm. One may be labour intensive, while the other is more capital intensive.

3 Stigler's approach assumes competitive forces which eliminate sub-optimal firms. Consequently, this technique cannot be used where the eliminating force of competition is absent, as in the case of some oligopolies. However, the method is still appropriate for the analysis of plant sizes, as even a monopolist may view plants as in competition with one another.

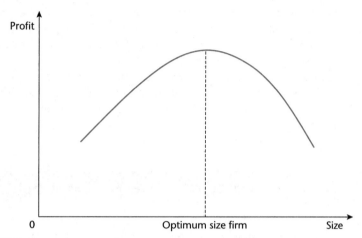

Figure 2.13 Size of firm and profits

Sub-optimal firms could survive if they were subsidiaries of larger firms or where competition law did not permit mergers or takeovers of such firms.

4 Some industries may have a constant number of firms or plants at the lower end of the size range, the 0–100 employees class. This number may be buoyed up by a relatively constant stream of new and hopeful entrants, who in due course are eliminated.

Rate of return

It might be argued that the size of firm could be correlated with accounting profits. This would then give managers the statistic they really seek: the firm size in a particular industry which is making the highest profits. Figure 2.13 illustrates such a profit curve.

We would expect profits to rise as firms experience economies of scale with an increase in their size. This would then be followed by a decrease in profits as firms face higher average costs due to diseconomies of scale. Although this may appear an attractive method it too suffers from a number of drawbacks:

1 In practice, accounting rates of return are difficult to measure with any degree of consistency between various firms.

2 Accounting profits are not only related to scale economies but can also be a function of many other variables, such as market power, diversification, vertical integration, chance and different entrepreneurial activity. We would first have to isolate all these other variables so as truly to estimate the relationship between size and accounting rates of return.

2.6   Conclusion

This chapter has discussed the theoretical concepts applied to a firm's production decision, such as the law of diminishing marginal productivity, the stages of production and returns to scale. These concepts provide the foundations for the examination of the various cost functions facing firms. The various ways in which firms estimate the size and shape of their cost curves were also examined.

Although not all firms have the knowledge or the resources to calculate such curves, most should be aware of the theoretical relationships between inputs and outputs in the short and in the long run. Without such knowledge, whether acquired directly or grasped intuitively, no firm is able to allocate its resources optimally.

Discussion Questions

1 With reference to production explain what is meant by technical and economic efficiency. Give examples of both. Are there other concepts of efficiency in production?

2 Distinguish between returns to the variable factor and returns to scale.

3 Draw *only* the traditional total product curve. Explain all the stages along this curve. At what point on the total product curve is marginal product at a maximum? At what point on the total product curve is average product at a maximum? (Hint: the slope of a line drawn from the origin is total product divided by output, i.e. average product. Thus where these lines intersect the total product curves, we have different values for average products.)

4 With reference to Alchian's learning curve, suggest occupations which may have a steep slope and those occupations where the slope is less steep.

5 Explain what might be regarded as welfare economies of scale. With reference to organisations you have worked for, assess the success of such economies.

6 Relying on your own research, identify the important inputs in the production function of a specific industry. (Use textbooks, journal articles, or the Internet.)

Further Reading

General background

Parkin, M., Powell, M. and Matthews, K. (2003) *Economics* (5th edn). Harlow: Addison Wesley, Chapter 5.
Sloman, S. (2000) *Economics* (4th edn). Harlow: Prentice Hall, Chapter 5.

Advanced

Alchian, A. (1963) Reliability and progress curves in airframe production, *Econometrica*, 31, 679–93.

Arrow, K. J. (1962) The economic implications of learning by doing, *Review of Economic Studies*, 29, 155–73.

Cookenboo, L. (1955) *Crude Oil Pipelines and Competition in the Oil Industry*. Cambridge, MA: Harvard University Press.

Haldi, J. and Whitcombe, D. (1967) Economies of scale in industrial plants, *Journal of Political Economy*, 75, 373–85.

Stigler, G. J. (1958) The economies of scale, *The Journal of Law and Economics*, 1, 54–71.

Williamson, O. E. (1967) Hierarchical control and optimum firm size, *Journal of Political Economy*, 75, 123–38.

Part Two Analysis of Industry

3

Market Structure 1: Perfect Competition, Monopoly and Monopolistic Competition

Objectives

By the end of this chapter, the reader should be able to understand:

- the key components of market structure
- the definition of and distinction between normal and supernormal profits
- the characteristics and equilibrium conditions prevalent under perfect competition, monopoly and monopolistic competition
- the advantages and disadvantages of monopoly.

Key Concepts

- accounting profit
- barriers to entry
- economic profit
- excess capacity
- market structure
- monopoly

- monopolistic competition
- perfect competition
- price discrimination
- product differentiation
- welfare loss

3.1   Introduction

This chapter examines how the output produced and prices charged by firms vary across market environments (structures). When discussing market structures we are normally interested in several indicators. Taken together these indicators give us a clear picture of competitive conditions within a given industry. As we will see later in the book, market structure has direct and important implications for firm strategy and performance. Indicators of market structure relate to:

- the number of firms and their relative sizes
- the types of products produced (i.e. whether these are different or similar)
- the ease with which new firms can enter markets and compete with established firms
- the ease with which established firms can leave markets and compete else-where
- the availability of information to firms and their customers, and how efficiently this flows between them.

These indicators determine how much freedom firms have over the prices they charge and the types of non-price strategies they employ. Overall then, by defining market structure we can assess the extent to which firms face competitive pressures. In this chapter we focus on three stylised market structures, namely perfect competition, monopoly and monopolistic competition. A discussion of oligopoly is left until Chapter 4. The rest of this chapter takes the reader through each of these market structures and shows how firms behave under each market structure and, in turn, how they perform. We assume that firms will seek to maximise profitability within any given competitive environment, although we examine other measures of firm performance in Chapter 5. Specifically, the rest of the chapter is structured as follows. Section 3.2 discusses various types of firm and examines the concepts of profit and profit maximisation. Section 3.3 introduces the notion of perfect competition, and examines pricing and output decisions of firms operating within an environment where competitive pressures facing firms are very intense. Section 3.4 examines equilibrium conditions under monopoly, and assesses whether monopolies are good or bad for consumers and society in general. Section 3.5 introduces product differentiation and examines the theory of monopolistic competition. Section 3.6 concludes.

3.2   Introduction to Firms, Profits and Market Structure

There are a number of ways in which we can define and classify organisations. A sociologist might view the organisation as a coalition of various stakeholders such as owners, managers, workers, suppliers, trade unions and customers. An economist might argue that an organisation is a planning unit which engages in the allocation of scarce resources, while an accountant might discuss the organisation in terms of what it owns (assets) and what it owes (liabilities). Finally, organisations might be defined in terms of their legal ownership or status. There are a wide variety of organisational types. These include sole traders, partnerships, limited liability firms, government owned firms, co-operatives and charities. The number and size of the first three types of organisation are shown in Table 3.1 and are now discussed briefly.

Table 3.1 Numbers of firm by ownership type and turnover

Turnover (£ thousands)	Sole trader		Partnerships		Companies and public corporations	
	Number	%	Number	%	Number	%
1–49	180 210	32	62 120	18	93 030	14
50–99	189 385	33	82 510	24	133 185	20
100–249	140 165	25	114 280	33	147 435	22
250–499	40 490	7	52 210	15	91 940	14
500–999	14 440	3	24 280	7	77 295	12
1 000+	6 205	1	14 985	4	—	—
1 000–1 999	—	—	—	—	52 670	8
2 000–4 999	—	—	—	—	39 890	6
5 000–9 999	—	—	—	—	15 865	2
10 000+	—	—	—	—	14 615	2
10 000–49 999	—	—	—	—	4 535	1
50 000+	570 890	100	350 390	100	670 455	100

Source: Adapted from Office for National Statistics (2002), Table 2.

Sole trader

This type of business can be generally defined as an organisation which is owned and controlled by a single individual. Such individuals invest their own capital in the business and consequently receive all profits or bear all losses associated with the operation of that business. In other words, sole traders put at risk their entire wealth and consequently have unlimited liability. Sole traders are the most popular form of organisation. As we can see from Table 3.1, in the UK in 2002 there were over 570,000 of these organisations (figure excludes those not registered for value added tax). However, such businesses, although popular, do have some inherent problems, which constrain their growth prospects and indeed their chances of survival. In particular, most of the funds available for expansion come from money invested by owners and retained profits earned in one period, which are then reinvested in the business for growth in successive periods. Sole traders tend to fail more frequently than other forms of organisation. Consequently, banks and other types of financial institutions are often reluctant to lend funds to sole traders, which leaves them quite small in size. As Table 3.1 shows, most sole traders have an annual turnover of less than £100,000. Although not shown in Table 3.1, sole traders tend to be located in industries such as retailing and construction where the initial costs of investment are often small.

Partnership

Partnerships generally comprise two or more people who run a business in a common interest. These individuals own, finance and control the business. In the UK, there is a legal limit of 20 partners, although some organisations (such as accounting and legal services) are exempt from such requirements. Partnerships are a very common form of business. Table 3.1 shows that there were over 350,000 of these in the UK in 2002. These partnerships are diverse in nature and range from family-run businesses to large professional organisations (e.g. solicitors and accountants), comprising various layers of partners (junior and senior). All partners share any profits made by the business, but are held jointly responsible for any losses incurred. The larger number of owners means that the risks associated with failure are more evenly spread than is the case for the sole trader. In addition, more internal finance is available to fund future growth and generate future profits. However, the average size of partnerships is still quite small. Table 3.1 shows that most partnerships have turnover of less than £250,000 per year.

Limited companies

In many industries, technical conditions require that organisations are large to take advantage of all available economies of scale. These organisations can be classed as limited liability companies. These organisations are often owned by large numbers of individuals (shareholders) and run by professional managers. Under the terms of the Companies Acts (1985 and 1989), a limited company is a legal entity. In other words, all assets or liabilities accrued by the firm belong to that firm. Limited companies are owned by shareholders, who own varying portions of the organisation. The greater the shareholding, the greater the ownership stake. This means that individual shareholders are liable only for their investment in the organisation (limited liability). Of course, the greater the investment, the greater the potential liability. This means that the liability for the firm's debts or any share of profits is limited and directly related to the extent of shareholdings. In the UK, we can distinguish between two main types of limited liability company: public and private. Public limited companies have ownership capital which exceeds £50,000. These companies are owned by shareholders and governed by a board of directors and senior managers, and are registered with the registrar of companies at Companies House. Their shares are available for sale to the general public and their accounts are available for public scrutiny. Private limited companies are similar except that their shares are not available for sale to the public and consequently they tend to be smaller than public limited companies. Overall, limited companies are, on average, much larger than sole traders and partnerships. Table 3.1 shows that approximately 20% of all companies have an annual turnover exceeding £1 million, while 1% have a turnover exceeding £50 million.

Large firms often have different organisational structures. Two of the most common types of organisational structure are the unitary (U) and multidivisional form (M), which are shown in Figures 3.1 and 3.2 and are now discussed briefly.

Unitary (U) organisational form

Under this type of organisational structure, the key activities of the firm are divided by functional area (marketing, finance, production, personnel and so on). Each department is run by a middle manager who reports to a chief executive. One of the key advantages of this organisational form is that managers must have functional expertise, which allows the clustering of particular skills or talents within

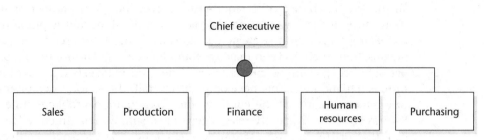

Figure 3.1 Unitary (U) organisational form

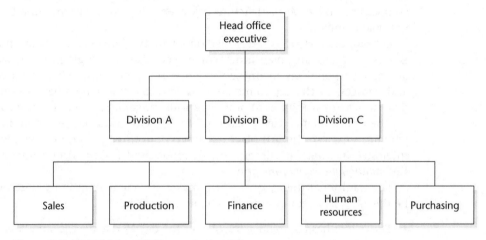

Figure 3.2 Multidivisional (M) organisational form

departments. This is particularly useful when a firm produces a single product. Consequently, this organisational structure is more common across smaller and medium-sized firms. Conversely, the U-form structure is less suited to large organisations which offer a diversified range of goods and services. This is because each function (production, finance, marketing etc.) has to deal with a wider variety of tasks and functions. Co-ordination of resources and the transmission of information between departments becomes difficult and the workload facing managers can become too heavy. This can even lead to conflict between departments.

Multidivisional (M) organisational form

Given the problems associated with the U-form structure, many larger organisations opt for a multidivisional (M) form structure. This type of structure emanated from the USA in the 1930s as the scale and scope of large organisations grew (e.g. General Motors – see Chandler, 1977). Within this type of organisational structure, the firm is split into a number of quasi-independent operating divisions. These operating divisions can be organised by geographical location (along regional, national or international boundaries) or by product type. Each division is a quasi-firm with all the key functional areas required to deliver the given product or service. The head office of the organisation oversees these divisions and is primarily involved in making longer term strategic decisions as to the future scale and scope of the organisation. Such decision making would include regular monitoring of divisional performance, governing the activities of division managers and allocating finance to research and personnel development. Overall, the M-form organisational structure removes many of the conflicts and co-ordination problems inherent in the U-form structure. A closely related type of organisational structure is the holding company or H-form organisation, whereby a holding (or parent company) has an ownership stake (which is normally a controlling interest) in other companies (subsidiaries). The holding company tends to have ultimate control over the subsidiary companies, but for the most part leaves this to the senior management of these companies. This type of structure has been adopted by a large number of multinational companies.

Overall, organisations today take on a variety of ownership forms and size characteristics. Many are small firms which specialise in a single product, while others are large corporations spanning the globe and producing a diverse range of goods and services. In the economic analysis of firms, researchers have examined what determines firms' abilities to produce a wide range of products and the consequence for their performance (see Chapters 7 to 10). Others have been more interested in why firms exist in the first place (Chapter 5). In this chapter, however, we are more interested in what we will term the textbook model of the firm, sometimes termed the *traditional theory of the firm*.

The traditional theory of the firm makes several assumptions, which will underlie the analysis in the rest of this chapter. These are:

- The owner has complete control over the day-to-day decision making within the firm.
- The firm has a single goal of profit maximisation, which is defined as the point where the difference between revenues and costs is at its greatest.
- The firm operates in an environment of complete certainty and has complete knowledge of its cost and demand conditions.
- Firm behaviour is affected (determined) by the competitive environment (characterised by market structure), and the competitive threats of rival firms.

The rest of this section introduces us to the concept of profit maximisation and the various types of theoretical market structures devised by economists to examine firm and industry behaviour.

What is profit?

Having introduced various concepts of revenue (in Chapter 1) and costs (in Chapter 2), we can now examine the profitability of firms. As we will see, the definition of profits used in economics often deviates from its everyday usage. In general terms, profit signifies the difference between an organisation's revenues and its costs or, more specifically, total revenues minus total costs. In Chapter 1 (section 1.5), we defined total revenue as simply the price of products or services sold multiplied by their respective quantities. Costs are defined as the actual expenses incurred by the firm in order to produce its finished goods and services. In Chapter 2 (section 2.3), we saw that these costs would include wages, rent, rates on building and factories and expenditures on raw material inputs. The firm's costs comprise those that are fixed and those that are variable and total costs will rise with output. The difference between revenues and costs is the profit reported by the business. This definition of profit is often referred to in many economics and finance textbooks as the *accountant's view of profitability*. In other words:

Accounting profit = Total revenue – total costs (where total costs refer to explicit costs of production)

However, the concept of profits in economics is somewhat different. This is known as *economic profit*. This measure of profit includes not only explicit accounting costs, but also implicit opportunity costs. Implicit opportunity costs reflect alternative or lost investment opportunities to which a firm could devote its scarce resources (land, labour, capital and enterprise). In other words, the owners of the firm could go and earn a salary working for another firm, while the capital invested in the firm could be invested elsewhere (e.g. equity markets or the production of other goods and services). Consequently, economic profit also includes the return on investments that has been forgone by owners in order to run the firm. Therefore, we can define economic profits as:

Economic profit = Total revenue – Total costs (both explicit and implicit costs)

In other words, Economic profit = Accounting profit – Implicit costs. To illustrate the difference, let us suppose we have a firm producing cakes, which reports an annual accounting profit of £5 million. However, the owner could have earned a profit of £11 million producing chocolates Although, the accounting profit is £5 million, the firm makes an economic loss of £1 million. This is because the implicit opportunity costs incurred are equal to £6 million. Therefore these must also be deducted from the accounting profit figure of £5 million. On the other hand, if the owner could have made £10 million elsewhere then the firm would be said to be making zero economic profit (i.e. the opportunity costs in this case would be £5 million). Therefore, firms are said to be making positive economic profits when total revenues exceed all costs (implicit and explicit).

Economic profits (often referred to as supernormal, excess or abnormal profits) serve as a signal as to how resources should be efficiently allocated. Firms that make positive economic profits are covering all their explicit accounting costs, but also earning a return for their owners that exceeds what they could earn investing funds elsewhere. Consequently, these firms (and indeed the industries in which they are located) will attract even more investment searching for economic profits. The firm makes zero economic profit when total revenues equal all costs. Zero economic profit is often termed normal profit. Firms making normal profits cover all costs, and provide owners with a return equal to what they would have earned elsewhere. Finally, when the firm makes negative economic profits (losses), its total revenues fall short of all costs. If the firm makes negative economic profits, resources will leave the firm in search of better investment opportunities elsewhere.

Firms in some industries make higher profits than those in others. This, in part, depends on the level of competition. Even within industries some firms outperform others. There are a number of explanations for why firms might earn economic profits.

Some economists have argued that profits are:

- *A reward for risk taking*. Here it is assumed that potential profits are related to risks undertaken by firms. The higher the risk, the greater the potential profits made.

- *Related to market structure*. In industries where a few large firms dominate, average profitability tends to be high. In terms of the analysis presented in this chapter, firms can make economic profits under monopoly conditions (even in the long run).

- *Related to competitive and anticompetitive practices adopted by firms*. In this case it is assumed that firms can pursue myriad competitive and anticompetitive strategies, which ultimately lead to high profits. For example, superior production and management techniques, product and process innovations may allow some firms to keep costs lower than their closest rivals, thus boosting profitability. We examine many of these assertions in some detail in Chapter 5.

- *Related to innovation*. High profits are the reward in cases where firms invest in research and development to produce product and process innovations. The extent to which these profits persist depends crucially on the extent to which the innovating firm can establish and maintain control of the property rights associated with the innovation. These issues are examined in detail in Chapter 8.

So what is profit maximisation?

Economic theory assumes that firms maximise profits where the difference between total revenue and total cost is at its greatest. Figure 3.3(a) shows (a simplified exposition of) the total cost and revenue curves of an organisation in the short run. The total cost curve is positive even at zero output due to the existence of fixed costs. Total costs are, of course, made up of fixed and variable costs, and are shown to increase as output increases (refer back to Chapter 2, pages 46–48 for a full discussion of the total cost curve). Total revenue is zero when the firm sells nothing. However, as output increases, so does total revenue. As we argued in Chapter 1, if total revenue increases, price elasticity of demand is elastic. After the point when total revenue reaches a maximum, further falls in price will result in a fall in total revenue. The distance between the TR and TC function is shown by the firm's profit function. When TR = TC, profits are zero. This is shown at points A and B in Figure 3.3(a). To the left of A, TC exceeds total revenues and the firm consequently makes losses (shown by the negative portion of the profit curve). This is also the case to the right of point B. Between points A and B, TR > TC, and the firm makes a profit. Where the distance between point TR and TC is at its greatest the firm makes maximum profits and so will produce at output level Q*.

The slopes of the total revenue and total cost curves show how the firm's costs and revenues change as output changes. More specifically, the slopes of the total cost and total revenue curves are the firm's marginal cost and revenue curves respectively (which were introduced in Chapters 1 and 2 respectively). In Figure 3.3(a) you will note that the slopes of the TR and TC curves are equal at the point of profit maximisation. In other words, profits are maximised when MC = MR. This relationship

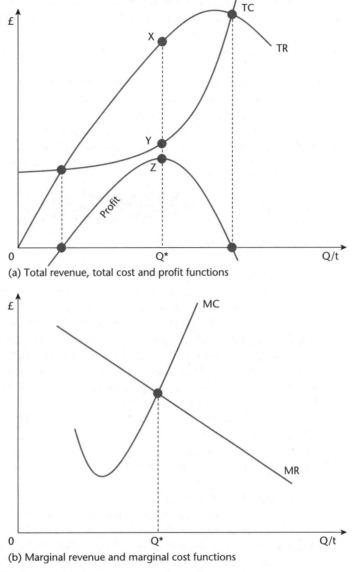

Figure 3.3 Profit maximisation

is shown in Figure 3.3(b), and examined in more detail in question 1 at the end of the chapter.

Marginal revenue has a negative slope to show that, as the firm sells more, so price falls and each successive unit of output adds less to profit. Marginal costs are initially negative to reflect that the firm uses resources more efficiently as it increases size (increasing returns to the variable factor – see Chapter 2), but also has a positive component to show that the firm's costs increase at an increasing rate as its output increases. To the left of point Q*, MR > MC, so each successive unit of output is adding more to revenue than it does to costs. In other words, the firm's *marginal profit* (= MR – MC) is positive. To the right of point Q*, MR < MC, so each successive unit of output the firm produces is adding less to revenue than it does to costs. In other words the firm's *marginal* profit (= MR – MC) is negative. Overall then, the firm produces at output Q*, which corresponds to the point where profits are maximised (i.e. where the difference between total revenues and total costs is at its greatest).

In most of our analysis in this chapter, we assume that firms' overriding objective is to maximise profits. To do this, firms adopt a strategy of marginal cost pricing (i.e. setting prices equal to marginal costs). However, many economic theorists and management practitioners have argued that firms often pursue other objectives consequently, adopting pricing strategies different from that of marginal cost pricing. Case Studies 3.1 and 3.2 provide a useful review of these views.

Case Study 3.1

Do firms maximise profits?

Can firms maximise profits?
As we have seen, the concept of profit maximisation is very complex. Firms are unlikely to have enough information to fulfil this objective. The competitive environment within which firms operate is likely to be in a constant state of flux, making it difficult to monitor costs and anticipate revenues with any certainty. Such changes may be a consequence of the entry of new competitors or uncertainties of success (and thus revenues) associated with price and non-price strategies. Technology may also cause costs to change. For example, costs may be reduced if technology improves, but increased if further discretionary investment is required. Changes in government policy with regard to taxes, subsidies, competition, employment, advertising and interest rates may also cause costs and revenues to change. Therefore, it is by no means clear that firms would have enough information to maximise profits.

Do firms have other objectives?
Firms may have other objectives that they place above profit maximisation. This can be explained by the ownership structure of the modern firm. In the modern firm shareholders own the firm, but treat ownership as an investment. It is doubtful that shareholders have enough knowledge to demand maximum profits. They can exercise some controls over senior managers through annual general meetings. However, these are often badly attended. Shareholders will tend to want a reasonable level of return on their investment. As long as managers meet this, they will not be replaced. However, managers who do not necessarily have an ownership stake within the firm may be interested in pursuing other objectives. This can often lead to conflict between managers and shareholders (see Fama and Jensen, 1983).

A number of *managerial* and *behavioural* theories have attempted to reassess the main objectives of firms.

Managerial theories argue that the managers (in control of the day-to-day running of the firm) might maximise objectives other than profits. For example, the size of the firm (through sales revenue) maximisation, growth or their own satisfaction:

- *Sales revenue maximisation.* Baumol (1959) argued that managers pursue sales revenue maximisation because their salaries are often linked to sales performance not profits. He argued that, under sales maximisation, the firm is likely to capture a greater share of the market by producing more than the profit-maximising firm produces. However, it does so by charging lower prices and consequently earns lower profits than it would under profit maximisation. However, as long as managers make enough profit to satisfy shareholders, there will be no problem

- *Managerial satisfaction.* Williamson (1963) argued that managers prefer to adopt expense preference behaviour by 'large' amounts of discretionary spending. This yields them satisfaction. In this model managerial satisfaction is a function of (S, M, D). In this model S denotes staff expenditures. Here the manager gains power and prestige from empire building; M denotes expenditures on themselves such as large offices and expense accounts, trips to the golf course etc.; and D denotes discretionary investment expenditure, where managers have discretion to spend on fixed assets or pet projects. The outcome of this process is that the manager diverts part of the firm's resources (which could be used to generate profits for shareholders) to their own use. Consequently, the firm earns lower profits than under profit maximisation.

- *Growth maximisation.* Marris (1964) assumed that firms aim to maximise growth. The model is built around the trade-off between growth and profits. The model assumes that the more finance a firm has, the more it can grow. This finance comes from the profits the firm makes. These profits, of course, come from the revenue the firm makes by selling its product and so ultimately depend on demand. This demand relies on attracting new customers, through decreasing prices, increased spending on advertising or through diversification. Therefore, the firm must strike a balance between retaining enough profits to fund growth, while simultaneously satisfying shareholders with dividends. The extent to which the firm can do this depends on how quickly the firm can attract and train new managers, and on the cost and amount of finance available to the firm.

Overall, in all of the models discussed managers sacrifice some profits to pursue other objectives.

Behavioural theories argue that the social organisation of the firm will determine its behaviour. Firms instead seek to make satisfactory profits. Firms are therefore satisficers, not maximisers. Rather than seek to maximise a single objective, satisficers aim to achieve satisfactory levels for a number of different objectives simultaneously. Firms take decisions on a rule-of-thumb basis based on past performances and expectations of future performance.

The firm is not seen as a single entity, but instead as a coalition of various *interest groups* – for example, shareholders, managers, suppliers of finance, workers, suppliers of raw materials. As a consequence of these various interest groups, the firm seeks to satisfy all groups, i.e. pay shareholders good dividends, pay workers and managers high wages, and give customers reasonably priced products. If this is the case, organisational slack is said to exist. Of course over time some groups may receive some slack while others suffer. If the firm is doing well it is easier to give slack to most groups. This may not be the case in recession.

Cyert and March (1963) argue that a firm will have a number of goals such as production, inventory, sales, market share and profits. However, it will follow satisficing behaviour. The problem is that over time the firm's objectives will change and tend to be dominated by the strongest *interest group* (see earlier).

What does the real world say?

Shipley (1981) surveyed a sample of 728 manufacturing firms, with regard to their pricing and wider corporate objectives. The sample was split into five employee size bands (<51, 51–200, 201–1000, 1001–3000, >3000), and by intensity of competition, measured by the number of competitors (0, 1–4, 5–9, 10–25, >25). Shipley asked the firms sampled to assess which objectives were important when formulating pricing decisions and of these which firms considered to be the most important. The objectives were defined as:

- target profit or return on capital employed (i.e. profits)
- target sales revenue
- target market share
- stable prices
- stable volume of sales
- price similarity with competitors
- prices fair to firm and customers.

Findings

Many firms in the sample appeared to follow multiple objectives. In other words, while profits were deemed important, they were by no means the only objective followed by firms. To assess the extent to which firms maximised profits, Shipley asked firms whether they maximised profits or whether, in fact, they made enough profits to satisfy their shareholders. Over 50% of firms surveyed stated that they maximised profits. Profit maximisation was more prevalent in industries where competition (measured by the number of firms) was more intense. Furthermore, profit maximisation (rather surprisingly, given the separation of ownership from control discussed earlier) was more important for large firms than for small firms. Firms were then asked whether profit maximisation was their overriding objective. Only 15.9% of firms answered yes to this question. Shipley argued that it is these firms that could be described as being true profit maximisers. A later study by Hornby (1995) argued that around 25% of firms (from a small sample of 77 Scottish companies) could be regarded as profit maximisers.

Overall, it is likely that profits are an important component of a wider set of firm objectives.

Case Study 3.2

How do firms set prices?

The price a firm charges for a product depends on the competitive environment or, more specifically, market structure. The elasticity of demand for the firm's product (discussed in Chapter 2), the firm's objectives (discussed in Case Study 3.1), its organisational form (further discussed in Chapters 9 and 10) and the type of product sold (in Chapter 7) can all affect the price charged.

The emphasis in much of this text is on marginal cost pricing, where the firm sets a price at the profit-maximising level of output (i.e. where marginal costs are equal to marginal revenues). Empirical research suggests that firms often follow other types of pricing strategy. Most early evidence suggested that firms calculate average costs and then add a mark-up which is calculated as a percentage of costs. This can be shown via the following formula:

$$\text{Average cost pricing: Price} = AC + X\%$$

X% is an amount to cover the fixed costs of production and allow a profit to be made.

The advantage of this is that it avoids the costs a firm may incur when collecting information in order to set prices where MC = MR. However, the disadvantage of this approach is that it often focuses on the firm's supply conditions (i.e. costs) to the exclusion of demand conditions. It may be the case that firms may act in ways consistent with marginal cost pricing by charging higher mark-ups for products which are price inelastic (normally found under conditions of monopoly and oligopoly) and low mark-ups for products for price elastic goods (normally found under conditions of perfect competition and monopolistic competition). This means then that higher prices are charged under monopoly and low prices under perfect competition.

What does the real world say?

In 1997, Hall et al. surveyed a sample of 654 UK firms from four broadly defined industry groups. These firms were asked to assess the most important factors in determining the prices they charged for their products. The results are shown in the table on the next page.

Market (industry) conditions appear to be the most important determinant of firms' pricing strategies with almost 40% of the sample indicating this as an important factor. Pricing in construction appeared to be particularly affected by market conditions. The price charged by rivals was also found to be important, particularly in retailing where over 30% of firms in this industry indicated this was important. The use of cost-plus pricing appeared to be prevalent, especially across smaller firms (not shown in table), which, it is argued, are less likely to engage in the extensive market research required to equate marginal revenues with marginal costs.

How firms set prices

Strategy	As a percentage of entire sample				
	All	Manufacturing	Construction	Retail	Other services
Market level	39	41	51	18	48
Competitor prices	25	26	11	30	23
Direct cost + Variable mark-up	20	20	22	21	17
Direct cost + Fixed mark-up	17	16	19	24	14
Customer set	5	6	3	0	6
Regulatory agency	2	1	0	0	3

Note: % values may exceed 100% as firms were allowed to indicate more than one choice.
Source: Adapted from Hall, S., Walsh, M. and Yates, A. (1997) *How do UK companies set prices?*, Bank of England Working Paper, Table A, P. 13.

Overall, it is likely that there are a number of factors likely to affect the pricing strategies followed by individual firms, given that various forms of non-price competition exist in many industries (see Chapters 7–10), that firms often indulge in illegal pricing practices (see Chapter 4), and that published prices often differ from prices actually charged.

The actual amount of profit made by firms will vary, depending on the intensity of competition facing firms. This is generally determined by the competitive structure of the market the firm is located in. Market structure generally refers to the demand and supply conditions facing firms within any given industry.

What is market structure?

Market structure refers to the various components that determine the make-up of a particular industry. No one factor determines market structure, but the number of firms and their relative sizes, the type of product produced, availability of economies of scale and the extent to which new (existing) firms can enter (exit) and (no longer) compete with (other) existing firms are all important in describing the competitive environment facing firms.

Table 3.2 shows four types of market structure (*perfect competition, monopoly, monopolistic competition* and *oligopoly*). Each market structure is cross-referenced with a number of characteristics including the number of firms, the type of product, entry barriers, the demand curve facing an individual firm and so on. Table 3.2 shows that each of the four market structures differs in at least one of the characteristics identified. As we will see (in detail in section 3.3 onwards) competition is at its most intense under perfect competition because there are a large number of firms each producing an identical product. The consequence of this is that they have very little control over the prices they charge and consequently only make normal levels

Table 3.2 Four types of market structure

	Perfect competition	Monopoly	Monopolistic competition	Oligopoly
Number of firms	Many	One	Many	Few
Product type	Identical	Unique	Differentiated	Differentiated or undifferentiated
Entry barriers	None	Difficult (especially if enforced by government)	Easy	Difficult
Demand curve	Horizontal	Downward sloping	Downward sloping	Downward sloping
Price behaviour	Price = Marginal costs	Price > Marginal costs	Price > Marginal costs	Price > Marginal costs
Objective	Profit maximisation	Profit maximisation	Profit maximisation	Profit maximisation
Economic profit	Zero	Positive	Zero	Depends on entry conditions and the strategic behaviour of firms
Examples	Selected agricultural products	Rail network	Professional services, hairdressers, restaurants etc.	Differentiated: cars, pharmaceuticals Undifferentiated: building materials, oil

of profit. Real-world examples of perfect competition are often difficult to find, but some agricultural products or stock markets may fall within this definition of market structure.

At the other extreme, we have monopoly, a market structure consisting of one firm producing a unique product and exercising complete control over the prices it charges consumers for their goods and services. Consequently, monopolists tend to make supernormal levels of profit. Monopoly power is enjoyed by firms in many industries. The extent of this power is dependent on how the market is defined (see Chapter 5). However, if we take the definition as applying to a sole producer of a good or service, monopoly power is likely to prevail and persist only when backed by government legislation. Our intermediate market structures (which are often referred to as imperfect competition in many economics textbooks) have elements of monopoly and competition. For example, under monopolistic competition firms sell products that have a small degree of uniqueness, but still face competition from a large number of rivals producing similar products. Under oligopoly, a few large firms dominate the market, but may not necessarily produce differentiated products. We examine perfect competition, monopoly and monopolistic competition in sections 3.3 to 3.5. A discussion of oligopoly is left until Chapter 4.

3.3   Perfect Competition

The model of perfect competition is the most competitive market of the four we identified earlier. To some extent, we can think of it as an ideal state of competitive conditions, where there is complete freedom of movement for resources. It is an idealised state with which we can compare competitive conditions in other markets. An analysis of perfectly competitive markets provides us with an understanding of how firms set prices and produce output under very intense competitive conditions. However, before we turn to this, we should first of all outline and examine the assumptions that underlie the model of perfect competition.

Assumptions

There are four main assumptions that underlie perfect competition:

- large numbers of buyers (consumers) and sellers (firms)
- homogeneous (identical) products are traded
- there is freedom of movement of resources (land, labour, capital) to and from the industry, and firms tend to enter or exit in response to profit signals
- all participants in the industry (buyers, sellers, workers etc.) have perfect knowledge of cost and demand conditions.

We now examine each of these assumptions briefly.

Large numbers of buyers (consumers) and sellers (firms)

One of the crucial assumptions of perfect competition is that there are a large number of buyers and sellers. The implication of this is that neither buyers nor sellers can individually exert control over transactions within the industry. In the case of sellers, because there are a large number of small firms, no one firm can dramatically alter industry supply through a change in its production. This means that no individual firm's activities can affect the output produced or the prices charged. In the case of buyers, because there are large numbers of buyers, no individual can exact preferential treatment from suppliers in terms of the prices they pay for products. Overall, then, buyers and sellers have little power to affect market conditions.

Homogeneous products

Under this assumption, firms sell identical products. This has important implications for consumer attitudes toward the products being produced, but also the prices firms can charge for these products. The implication of identical products for consumers is that they will be indifferent between one firm's products over another. This means that individual firms cannot justify, or indeed charge, a higher price than their competitors. Of course, if a firm were to find a way of making its products somehow different in the minds of consumers (even if these differences are more imagined than real), they could then exert some control over the prices they charge, as consumers would no longer be indifferent between all products. We introduce the notion of product differentiation in section 3.4 and further in Chapter 7. Suffice to say that when products are different, firms have some control over the prices they charge.

Freedom of entry and exit

This assumption stipulates that under perfect competition, resources (land, labour and capital) are responsive to changes in demand and supply. In other words, resources flow into an industry if required (in response to signals via the price mechanism) or leave again when no longer required.

If resources (land, labour and capital) are to move to and from industries, it is tantamount to assuming that firms will enter and exit the industry without any impediments. In general, firms will normally enter an industry in search of profitable opportunities. If these are no longer available then firms will exit again. In most industries, there are normally various legal (government regulation), structural (technical conditions) or behavioural reasons (what established firms do) as to why it is often difficult for new firms to enter and existing firms to leave an industry. The greater these barriers, the lesser the competitive pressure facing firms already in the industry. In the extreme, entry barriers might mean that one firm (which is effectively insulated from competition) comes to dominate the industry, as in the case of monopoly (discussed in section 3.4).

Perfect knowledge

Finally, the model of perfect competition assumes that all market participants (buyers and sellers, workers etc.) have perfect knowledge. In the case of consumers, they will know the prices being charged by all firms. If imperfect information existed, then the potential would exist for consumers to demand products from firms at higher prices than would otherwise be the case. In contrast, producers must be aware of cost and demand conditions so that they can employ the least cost factors of production, so as to operate at the maximum level of output and minimum cost given their size (technical efficiency).

So what are the consequences for competition?

We have stated already that while the assumptions of perfect competition appear somewhat extreme they provide a useful starting point (or benchmark) in an analysis of competition. The outcome of the four assumptions discussed earlier is that no individual firm has any control over the prices charged. In other words, market power is absent. Additionally, no individual consumer can unduly influence demand conditions. This has direct and important implications for the demand conditions facing an individual firm via the demand curve (and its elasticity), which was introduced in Chapter 1. Consequently, under conditions of perfect competition each firm faces a perfectly elastic (horizontal) demand curve. Figure 3.4 shows the derivation of a firm's demand curve. The figure is in two parts, (a) for the industry and (b) for an individual firm.

Given that each firm has no control over the price charged, the prices charged by all firms are determined where industry supply equals industry demand. For our purposes, each firm charges price P and faces a horizontal (perfectly elastic) demand curve D. This demand curve is perfectly elastic to reflect the fact that perfect substitutes exist for the individual firm's product. In other words, the other firms in the

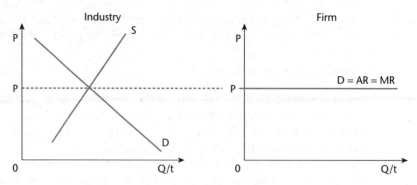

Figure 3.4 Demand curve of a firm under perfect competition

industry produce the same product. This means that an individual firm can sell an infinite amount at price P. An individual firm cannot charge a higher price than P, as it would lose all its customers to rival firms selling identical products at P. This means that an individual firm sells all it wants at P, but nothing if prices are raised above P. An individual firm, of course, would not charge a price below P, as this would lead to an unnecessary reduction in profits (given that the firm can sell an infinite amount at P).

Given that the demand curve facing an individual firm is horizontal, this has implications for the relationships between its average revenue (AR) and marginal revenues (MR) described in Chapter 1. We now briefly discuss this.

Remember from Chapter 1 that we introduced the notion of total revenue, which was calculated by multiplying the output sold by the prices charged for each unit of output. Average revenue is merely the total revenue divided by how much we sell. In other words, average revenue is the same as price (i.e. if $TR = P \times Q$ and $AR = TR/Q$, then $AR = P$). Under normal circumstances we would expect that, as more of a product is produced, its price will fall. This would mean that the additional revenue from selling each successive unit (marginal revenue) would decline. We showed in the previous chapter that the MR function falls twice as steeply as the AR function. However, because under perfect competition the price charged remains the same no matter how much is sold, the marginal revenue remains unchanged. In other words $AR = MR$. We can show this numerically in Table 3.3.

Having derived the firm's demand from the industry demand and supply curve, we can proceed to examine pricing and output decisions of firms under perfect competition. We examine these production decisions in the short run (where at least one factor of production is fixed) and in the long run (where all factors of production are variable). These are now discussed in turn.

Table 3.3 Output and revenue under perfect competition

Output (Q)	AR (Price)	TR = (P x Q)	MR = $\dfrac{\Delta TR}{\Delta Q}$
1	5	5	5
2	5	10	5
3	5	15	5
4	5	20	5
5	5	25	5

Short-run decision making under perfect competition

We will examine two possible short-run equilibrium conditions (referred to as case 1 and case 2) under which a firm might operate in the short run. In each case, we must remember that firms are price takers and set prices where industry supply is equal to industry demand.

Short-run equilibrium

Figure 3.5 shows the short-run equilibrium of a firm under conditions of perfect competition. Figure 3.5(a) shows a situation where the firm is making profits while Figure 3.5(b) shows the same but when the firm is making losses.

In Figure 3.5(a) and (b) we begin by drawing the firm's (horizontal) demand curve. Firms make output decisions based not only on expected revenues, but also on costs of production. Therefore, we superimpose the average and marginal cost curves (AC and MC hereafter) derived in Chapter 2.

Case 1: In Figure 3.5(a), the firm maximises profits where marginal costs equal marginal revenues at point X. At this point the firm produces at an output level Q_0, charging price P_0. The firm would not produce more than Q_0, as any additional output would add more to costs than to revenues (i.e. MC > MR). Conversely, the firm would not produce less than Q_0, as it would be possible to increase revenue and thus profitability by expanding output up to Q_0. The firm's average cost of production is identified where the output hits the AC curve shown as point Y. In the short run firms can earn supernormal profits, defined as returns in excess of normal profits (in other words, where average revenues exceed average costs). Normal profits are in turn defined as the minimum amount of profit necessary to induce the firm to remain within the market it occupies. The shaded area (P_0C_0YX) shows these supernormal profits. Figure 3.5(a) shows that the firm operating under conditions of perfect competition produces at output level Q_0 and makes supernormal (economic, excess, abnormal) profits.

Case 2: Of course, the firm does not necessarily make profits in the short run. In fact, it is perfectly possible that the firm could make losses. This situation will occur if the firm's average costs of production (function) lie above its average revenue (function). Again, the firm produces output where marginal costs are equal to marginal revenues (at point Y). The firm's average cost of production is identified where the output hits the AC curve, shown as point X. In the short run, firms can earn losses, defined as returns less than normal profits (in other words, where average costs exceed average revenues). The shaded area (P_0C_1YX) shows these losses. Overall then, Figure 3.5(b) shows that the firm, operating under conditions of perfect competition, produces at output level Q_0 and makes losses.

The extent to which the firm is willing or able to sustain such losses will partly depend on its supply curve or, more specifically, the relationship between its accrued costs and revenues earned from that production. As we know from Chapter 1, the supply curve of the firm traces combinations of prices and quantities. In general, we said that as prices increase, firms tend to supply more. Consequently, the supply curve is upward sloping. Under perfect competition, prices are equal to marginal costs: thus successive combinations of prices are equal to marginal costs, which allows us to derive a supply curve for the typical firm under perfect competition.

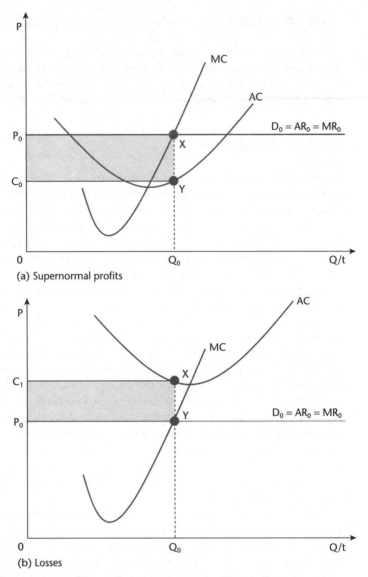

Figure 3.5 Short-run equilibrium under perfect competition

Let us take a typical firm and a series of prices, denoted by P_1 to P_4. The marginal cost curve can be used to trace out the quantity a firm wishes to supply at any given price. The extent to which the firm's marginal cost curve equates to its supply curve depends on the relationship of its average variable costs to average revenue. Figure 3.6 shows prices P_1 to P_4 and the expected output levels at those prices. Given the corresponding MC, AC and AVC curves we can identify the firm's output decisions at each of these prices. The firm will maximise profits where MC = MR. At prices P_1 and P_2, the firm would produce at Q_1 and Q_2 respectively. At both of these prices the firm would make supernormal profits (as AR > AC). However, if prices were at P_3, the situation would be less clear. At P_3, the price and thus the revenue

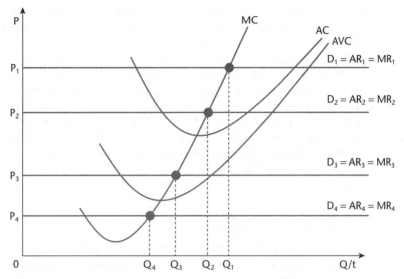

Figure 3.6 Firm's short-run supply curve under perfect competition

the firm attains are less than its costs of production. The firm could produce at Q_3, but is it in its interest to do so? To answer this question, we must refer back to our discussion of firm costs in Chapter 2. Remember that in the short run the firm incurs fixed and variable costs of production. This means that even if the firm produces nothing it must pay for these fixed costs. In the case of price P_3, the firm is earning less than average costs, but more than its average variable costs. In other words, the firm can cover its variable costs of production such as wages etc. and still have some revenue left over to pay some of its fixed costs.

Consequently, it would pay the firm to remain operating and produce output Q_3, price P_3. However, at price P_4 (to produce at Q_4), the firm will not earn enough revenue to even cover average variable costs of production. Consequently, it would be cheaper for the firm to cease trading than to continue. We can therefore conclude that the marginal cost curve (for prices P_3 and above) represents the firm's supply curve.

Do short-run equilibria persist?

As we have discussed previously, in the short run at least one factor of production is fixed, while others are variable. We have examined two possible short-run equilibria. First, case 1, where the firm maximises profits (where MC = MR) and where the price it charges (or average revenue it collects) is greater than its average costs of production. Consequently, this type of firm would make supernormal profits in the short run. We have also examined case 2, where the price it charges (or average revenue it collects) is less than its average costs of production. Consequently, this type of firm would make a loss in the short run. Neither of these two situations can persist indefinitely and thus they both have implications for the mobility of resources. In the former case, if firms are making supernormal profits, this will attract new firms into the industry in search of a share of these profits. The increase in competition will have direct consequences for the profitability of existing firms. This is because the entry of new firms increases industry supply, which depresses prices. To attain long-run equilibrium, entry will continue until all firms are making normal profits (AR = AC). Conversely, in the latter case, if firms are making losses, this will cause established firms in this position to exit the industry (either in search of new more profitable opportunities or through bankruptcy). The effect of this exit is to reduce industry supply, consequently pushing prices up. The exit of firms will continue until a long-run equilibrium is established, where all firms left in the industry are making normal profits (AR = AC). Overall, if firms are making supernormal profits, entry will take place until AR = AC. If the firm is unable to earn normal profits, in the long run, exit takes place until all the firms left operating in the industry are making normal profits.

Long-run equilibrium

In Chapter 2, we defined the long run as a period over which all factors of production are variable. In other words, firms can build new factories, buy new machines and office equipment, move location and so on. Figure 3.7 shows long-run equilibrium for a firm operating under perfect competition.

In Figures 3.5(a) and (b) initial price was at P_0 (determined by the equilibrium of the industry demand at supply curves). In case 1, firms made supernormal profits. However, these profits attract new entry, which increases supply, placing a downward pressure on the prices charged. Firms maximise profits where MC = MR, producing at Q_1 units of output. The long-run equilibrium is established at this point where the firm makes normal profits. You will note that in long-run equilibrium MC = MR and AR = AC. In case 2, the opposite happens, in the sense that at price P_0 the firm is making losses. This causes other firms to exit the industry, leading to a decline in industry supply. The reduction in supply leads to an increase in price until the firms left operating in the industry are earning normal profits.

Overall, the theory of perfect competition assumes that all firms are free to enter and exit markets, which ensures that large numbers of small firms make normal

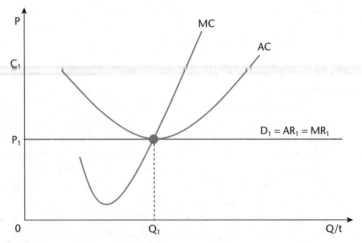

Figure 3.7 Long-run equilibrium under perfect competition: normal profits

profits. However, in reality, competitive conditions often give rise to many industries consisting of a few large firms which may have considerable influence over the prices charged, enabling these firms to earn supernormal profits. We examine this assertion later. However, before we do we must note that in the theory of perfect competition, a contradiction arises between the assumption of price-taking behaviour and the prediction that when entry takes place, prices adjust, since the theory leaves unanswered the question of who sets the prices in a world in which all firms are price takers. Furthermore, if under a perfectly competitive equilibrium, firms cannot advertise or differentiate products, it is questionable whether or not competition is taking place, at least in the sense that most real-world businesses understand the term. The theory of perfect competition as we have described earlier begins the study of competition by assuming that all market participants know all the relevant facts. This is perhaps unrealistic as it excludes discussion of many real-world features of rivalry, which are central to the notion of competition in practice. Paradoxically, competition under perfect competition is at its most intense where there is actually no rivalry. Nonetheless, perfect competition remains very useful as a benchmark from which to compare other types of industry behaviour.

3.4   Monopoly: A Critical Appraisal

In contrast to perfect competition, monopoly is a structure where competition is very limited or absent. In literal terms monopoly describes an industry comprising a single firm. In other words, the firm and the industry are one and the same. This is in fact the opposite of perfect competition discussed in section 3.3. In the absence of regulation, monopolists can exercise control over the prices they charge for products and services. Of course, in reality, it is often difficult to define industries (whether in terms of product produced or area covered), which often causes problems in defining monopolies. A discussion of these issues is outside the scope of this chapter, but they are discussed in Chapter 11. Of course, monopolies, whether privately or publicly owned, are normally subject to government regulation.

Before we proceed to examine pricing and output decisions of a monopolist, we must first outline the three main assumptions of monopoly:

- The industry comprises a single firm.
- A unique product or service is produced.
- Competition is restricted via the existence of barriers to entry and exit.

We now discuss each of these assumptions briefly.

Single firm

In a monopoly, there is a single firm which produces all the output of the industry. In other words, the firm and the industry are synonymous. Consequently, the demand curve the monopolist faces (discussed later) is in fact the same as the industry demand curve.

Unique product

Unlike perfect competition (where all firms produce identical products), the monopolist produces the only product. In other words, there are no close substitutes being produced by other firms. This means that consumers can only buy output from one firm. For example, traditionally in the UK before the deregulation of the 1980s and 1990s, customers could only buy gas (British Gas), telephony (British Telecommunications) and postal services (Post Office) from a single supplier. In Chapter 1 we argued that, when no close substitutes exist, demand is inelastic. This is why the monopolist's demand curve is downward sloping and inelastic.

Barriers to entry

One of the main reasons why monopolies arise and are sustained, is that barriers to competition exist – more specifically, barriers to entry and exit. *Barriers to entry* can be defined generally as anything that places a potential entrant at a competitive disadvantage relative to firms already established in the industry. Entry barriers can arise in three ways, namely government regulations (legal barriers), the technical conditions prevailing in the industry (structural barriers) and by the actions of established firms (strategic barriers). Legal barriers come in the form of various acts and regulations. They can arise because of various forms of regulation, which affect either industry structure (the number of firms in an industry) or how firms behave. Examples of legal barriers include registration, certification and licensing of businesses, patents, taxes, tariffs and quotas. Structural barriers arise from the inherent structural and technical characteristics of an industry. In other words, the extent of product differentiation, the size distribution of firms, the availability to firms of economies of scale and scope all determine the extent and nature of barriers to entry in any given industry. Finally, strategic barriers are erected by established firms to deter the entry of new firms. Such barriers include various forms of pricing and non-pricing strategies. These types of barrier are explored in detail in Chapter 6. Overall, in the case of a pure monopoly, the monopolist is effectively insulated from competition, by barriers to entry. Given that the monopolist faces a downward sloping demand curve and produces a unique product or service, it consequently has complete control over the prices it charges (assuming no government regulation).

Monopolist's demand curve

Given that the monopolist is the only producer of a unique product, it will face a downward sloping demand curve. This (as we have seen in Chapter 1) means that the marginal revenue curve is also downward sloping. As the monopolist lowers the price of its product to sell more, the additional units it sells results in a smaller net addition to revenue (marginal revenue). Consequently, in contrast to a perfectly competitive firm, the marginal revenue of a monopolist changes as price changes. Table 3.4 reminds us of this relationship. In this table, output (column 1) multiplied by price (= AR, column 2) gives us the monopolist's total revenue (TR, column 3). Marginal revenue is simply the additional increase in revenue as the monopolist increases its output by one successive unit.

Table 3.4 Output and revenue under monopoly

Output (Q)	Price (P)	Total revenue (TR)	Marginal revenue (MR)
1	10	10	10
2	9	18	8
3	8	24	6
4	7	28	4
5	6	30	2
6	5	30	0
7	4	28	−2

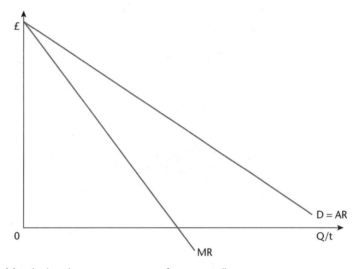

Figure 3.8 Marginal and average revenue of a monopolist

As we can see from Table 3.4, marginal revenue is less than price after the first unit of output is sold. If we assume the demand curve is linear we can show this graphically as in Figure 3.8.

In the analysis of monopoly, we adopt the behavioural assumption that all firms maximise profits where marginal costs equal marginal revenues (MC = MR). Although many monopolies face various forms of government intervention in relation to competition policies and other forms of regulations, we assume in our analysis that there is no government regulation. This means the monopolist is free to set its prices. It can do this as it is the only producer, selling a unique product and sheltered from outside competition.

Short-run equilibrium

We can now examine the monopolist's short-run equilibrium. In short-run equilibrium, the monopolist produces where MC = MR. In other words, it produces at an output level consistent with profit maximisation or loss minimisation. These two outcomes are shown in Figure 3.9.

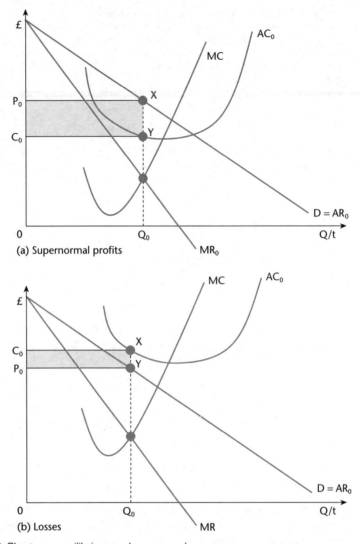

Figure 3.9 Short-run equilibrium under monopoly

In Figure 3.9(a), the monopolist produces at Q_0 (where MC = MR) and charges price P_0. Total revenue is shown by the area $0P_0$ multiplied by $0Q_0$. The total costs are shown by $0C_0$ multiplied by $0Q_0$. Supernormal profits are thus the difference between total revenues and total costs. This is shown by the area P_0XYC_0.

Monopolists do not always necessarily make supernormal profits, as is the case in Figure 3.9(b). Here the monopolist produces at Q_0. Price is P_0. Average cost is C_0. In this case, however, total costs ($0C_0$ multiplied by $0Q_0$) are greater than total revenue ($0P_0$ multiplied by $0Q_0$). Consequently, the monopolist makes a loss. This is shown in Figure 3.9(b) as the area C_0XYP_0.

Long-run equilibrium

Given that barriers to entry protect the monopolist, this means that either of the two short-run equilbria (although the former is much more likely) which we have shown in Figure 3.9 will persist in the long run. Therefore, the equilibrium of the monopolist will be the same in the long run. Of course, if the monopolist makes short-run losses greater than its average variable costs, it will have to adjust its size to become more efficient or cease trading in the long run. The existence of barriers to entry means that the normal profits are unlikely to prevail under monopoly. An exception to this is if the industry is said to be 'contestable', whereby even industries dominated by a single firm are exposed to the threat of increased competition from rivals (entry). In such an industry, even a monopolist would be forced to price products at competitive prices, thus making normal profits. (We examine contestable markets in Chapter 5.)

Are monopolies good or bad?

Although there are many reasons to criticise monopoly, many economists have argued that monopolies are not necessarily a bad thing. We now briefly examine some of the disadvantages and advantages of monopoly.

Disadvantages of monopoly

Higher prices and lower output

Monopolies often mean that prices will be higher and output lower than is the case for an industry where competition prevails. Consider Figure 3.10, in which two firms face similar costs. Firms in one industry are producing under conditions of perfect competition, while the other firm is operating under conditions of monopoly. The costs of production are the same for each industry. In the diagram firms in the perfectly competitive industry will produce where price (P_c) is equal to marginal costs (MC) and produce a competitive output equal to Q_c. The monopolist produces where marginal revenue is equal to marginal cost and produces output Q_m and charges a price equal to P_m. As we can see from Figure 3.10, prices are higher

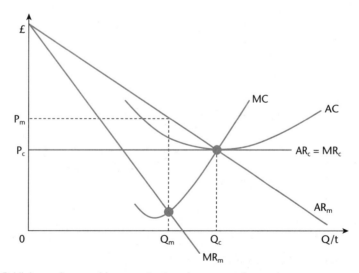

Figure 3.10 Higher prices and lower output under monopoly

and output lower under monopoly than is the case for perfect competition (i.e. $P_m > P_c$ and $Q_m < Q_c$). Following from Figure 3.10, the monopolist is restricting output in order to keep prices high. This implies that resources are not being utlised efficiently and that *excess capacity* exists within the industry. There is a consequent waste of resources equal to $Q_m - Q_c$.

Excess profits

High profits made by the monopolist are not necessarily an indication of efficient methods of production. The monopolist may, in fact, be using its market power to raise prices above marginal costs in order to increase its revenues.

Higher costs and x-inefficiencies

Under competition, firms strive to minimise their inputs to produce a given level of output. Firms do not necessarily have to produce at the minimum efficient scale to be technically efficient, as long as they produce at the lowest costs for their given scale of output. Firms which produce on the average cost curve (derived in Chapter 2) are technically efficient or x-efficient. In other words, they produce at the lowest cost possible given their respective sizes. Competition normally implies that firms will be x-efficient. However, if firms are insulated from competition, as is the case for monopoly, then there is less incentive to minimise costs. Firms may instead adopt 'expense preference' behaviour by investing in activities to maximise the satisfaction of senior managers, at the subsequent sacrifice of profitability (see Case Study 3.1). Following Leibenstein (1966) we can define x-efficiency as the difference between actual costs incurred and the best practice (technically or x-efficient) level of costs at any given level of output. Figure 3.11 shows three firms A, B and C. In this case, firms A and C are x-efficient, as they produce at the lowest possible cost, given their size (i.e. on the average cost curve). Firm B, however, is x-inefficient, as its costs lie above the average cost curve. In this case the distance between B and C measures the level of x-inefficiency, for a firm of size Q_0.

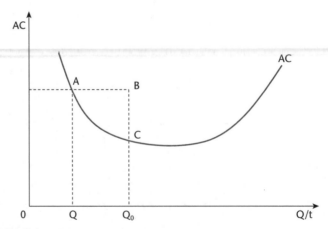

Figure 3.11 X-inefficiency

Price discrimination

Monopolists as sole suppliers can discriminate between different groups of customers (based on their respective elasticities of demand) separated into different geographic or product segments. A monopolist can practise price discrimination in several ways:

- *First-degree price discrimination.* Often referred to as perfect price discrimination, this involves the monopolist charging each customer what he or she is willing to pay for a given product. By doing this the monopolist can increase revenue and erode any consumer surplus (defined and discussed in Chapter 1) which consumers might enjoy.

- *Second-degree price discrimination.* The monopolist charges customers different prices based on their usage. In other words, consumers might be charged a high price for initial usage, but lower prices for subsequent units consumed. This type of pricing has been used in industries such as electricity, gas, water and telephony.

- *Third-degree price discrimination.* In this case, the monopolist separates customers into markets based on different demand elasticities. Customers with inelastic demand are charged higher prices than those with elastic demand. For example, train fares in the southeast of England are typically higher before 9.30 am than after.

Restrictive practices

Monopolists often use unfair practices to keep potential rivals out of the market. Even if rivals are successful in entering the market, the monopolist may choose to eliminate these firms by various restrictive price and non-price strategies such as predatory pricing and vertical restraints. (We examine some of these issues in Chapters 5 and 9, and Case Study 3.3 provides a useful example of a recent case involving a well-known car manufacturer.)

Case Study 3.3

Restrictive practices in the European car market

As we have already seen, it is possible for firms which enjoy market power advantages to discriminate against various customer groups by partitioning markets on a geographic or product basis. For example, in the mid-1990s, Audi and Volkswagen cars were found to be much more expensive in many European countries relative to Italy. However, consumers from outwith Italy could not take advantage of these lower prices.

Why was this?

By successfully partitioning European markets, Audi and Volkswagen had managed to charge consumers in different countries different prices. The European Commission found evidence that Volkswagen and Audi threatened dealers found selling cars to foreign customers with loss of bonuses and dealership. The Commission found Volkswagen guilty of infringing EU competition rules (see Chapter 11) and imposed fines of €102 million.

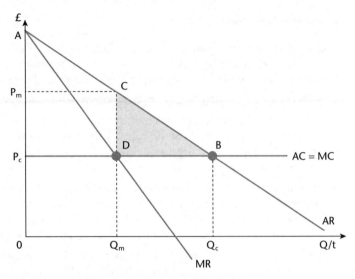

Figure 3.12 Welfare loss under monopoly

Limited technical progress

Some evidence suggests that technical progress is often slow when a single firm or group of firms dominates an industry. As they face no real competitive pressures, monopolists are under no real pressure to spend any abnormal profits earned on research and development of new product and processes, which is often seen as a risky investment. Consequently, technical progress in these industries is likely to be slow.

Welfare losses

As we saw earlier, monopolistic market structures can often lead to higher prices and lower output than is the case under perfect competition. These high prices and low outputs can lead to a loss in an economy's welfare. For example, if an industry is monopolised, prices tend to increase leading to a loss in welfare for the economy as a whole. We can examine this process in Figure 3.12.

In Figure 3.12, we assume a constant average cost curve, which is also equal to the marginal cost curve. Under conditions of perfect competition (AR = AC), output is Q_c and price is at P_c. The consumer surplus is equal to the area AP_cB. If this industry were now monopolised, output would fall to Q_m. This is because the monopolist will maximise profits where marginal revenues equal marginal costs and price would increase to P_m. Consequently, consumer surplus is now AP_mC and monopoly profit is equal to rectangle P_mCDP_c. The monopolist has eaten its way into the consumer surplus that previously existed under conditions of perfect competition. However, the criticism is not that consumer surplus is reduced from AP_cB to AP_mC, as this is merely a simple redistribution of welfare from the consumer to the producer, but the triangle BCD is lost to both consumers and producers. This area is referred to as *deadweight loss*, the true welfare loss of monopolisation. Researchers have made some attempts to assess the relative importance of such welfare losses to the wealth of various economies. For example, Harberger (1954) found that, in the USA, welfare losses accounted for 0.1% of national income. In a later study, Cowling and Mueller (1978) adopted several measures of welfare loss for the USA (1963–1966) and the UK (1968–1969). They found that, in the former case, welfare losses arising from monopoly range between 4% and 13.1% of national income, and in the latter between 3.9% and 7.2%. Such estimates of welfare loss have encouraged successive governments to direct policies at controlling monopoly behaviour in many industries.

Overall, the extent to which monopolies can be considered to be good or bad for consumers and the economy in general should be examined on a case-by-case basis. (Government policy toward monopoly is examined in Chapter 11.)

Advantages of monopoly

Monopolies do not always lead to increased prices, lower outputs and welfare losses. In fact, monopolies can often lead to increases in society's welfare as large monopolists benefit from economies of scale in production and distribution. These falls in costs can often be passed on to consumers in the form of lower priced products. We will now discuss briefly some of the potential advantages of monopolistic market structures.

Lower production costs and increased welfare

Under monopoly, greater output and standardisation can lead to lower costs. This can lead to economies of scale and scope, which can be passed on to consumers in the form of lower priced products.

Natural monopolies

It could be argued that some industries are more efficiently organised as monopolies. Industries such as water, gas, electricity and communications are often referred to as 'natural monopolies'. A natural monopoly arises when the ratio of the minimum efficient scale to industry size is so large that industries can only support one efficient firm. In natural monopolies, fixed costs form a large part of total costs. We can consider natural monopoly via Figure 3.13. In Figure 3.13, if the monopoly is in private hands, the monopolist maximises profits where marginal costs equal marginal revenues, and produces at output level Q_m and charges price P_m. The monopolist makes excess profits equal to the shaded area. If the firm were forced to charge a price that would prevail under competition, it would set price equal to marginal costs and produce at output level Q_c. At this output, the firm would make losses given that AR < AC. This could be solved in two ways. First, the government could pay the firm a subsidy equal to the losses incurred at output level Q_c. This is shown in Figure 3.13 as the distance between points A (AC) and B (AR). Alternatively governments could allow the firm to charge a price where normal profits are made. Thus the firm would produce at output level Q_r and charge a price of P_r. P_r is the price that maximises consumer welfare subject to the constraint that the firm must make normal profits. In this case, production is efficient in the hands of a single firm. The entry of new firms could lead to inefficiencies. For example, suppose we

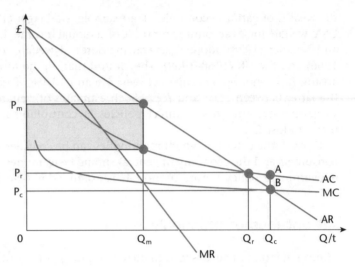

Figure 3.13 Price and output under natural monopoly

have a water company that supplies a certain part of the country through a net-work of pipes. It would be inefficient for a new firm to enter the market, set up its own system of pipes and then start supplying a segment of the market. This is because the level of output the firm produces would yield insufficient revenue to cover total costs. This competition would therefore lead to wasteful duplication (and competition) of systems. Historically, many natural monopolies were nation-alised and placed in public ownership. However, from the 1980s onwards new ways were found of managing such industries. (We discuss many of these issues in Chapter 11.)

Technical progress

Large monopoly profits may be used to finance research and development pro-grammes. As we will see in Chapter 8, monopoly profits are the reward for success-ful innovations. These innovations bring welfare gains to society in the form of new products and processes. Furthermore, these monopoly profits will not persist as there will eventually be entry by imitators or patents will lapse, which will eventu-ally dissipate these profits. These assertions have been tested empirically for manu-facturing and service industries in a number of countries. Case Study 3.4 provides a summary of the main findings.

Avoids wasteful forms of competition

Monopolies may avoid wasteful forms of competition such as advertising, which are prevalent features of many oligopolistic market structures. Given that mono-polists to some extent have a captive market, there is little incentive for mono-polies to advertise. In addition, monopolists may also generate a degree of price stability. They may be expert in accurately gauging the level of demand and supply. A monopolist may also be better placed to endure any downturn in the business cycle.

Case Study 3.4

Supernormal profitability in UK industries?

As we have already seen, the pursuit of profit has been the most widely assumed objective of firms. Although alternative theories of the firm (Case Study 3.1) suggest that firms may pursue objectives other than profit maximisation, e.g. sales, growth or managerial utility, profits are undoubtedly important in driving the competitive process. Indeed profits are seen as acting as an important signal in determining the allocation of scarce resources. In other words, entry of new firms takes place in industries when established firms are earning abnormal levels of profits. In contrast, firms will exit industries where the average level of profitability is low. Overall then, entry and exit into any industry should ensure that profits are brought quickly into line with competitive rates of return. In other words the competitive environment is efficient enough to ensure that no firm can earn supernormal profits in the long run.

What does the real world say?

At certain times some firms hold intangible assets. For example, patents, managerial skills and trademarks can often yield firms supernormal profits, which allow them to outperform rivals for many years. This is why we often observe market leaders in many industries for long periods at a time: for example, Dell in personal computers, Microsoft in operating systems, McDonald's in fast food etc. However, eventually these supernormal profits will be eroded as rivals 'catch up'.

Some attempts have been made to assess whether the competition erodes supernormal profits, by examining the extent to which firms can earn persistently high levels of profits. For example, Cubbin and Geroski (1990) examined a sample of 243 companies over the period 1951 to 1977 and found that, on average, 49% of profits persist from one year to the next. Goddard and Wilson (1996) presented evidence for the period 1972 to 1991, which showed similar results. Therefore, while UK firms' profit rates show some tendency to converge towards normal levels, this is by no means instantaneous. This is perhaps indicative of barriers to entry and specific advantages held by established firms, which prevent supernormal profits adjusting to long-run 'normal' values.

3.5   Monopolistic Competition

Monopolistic competition can be defined as a market structure comprising a large number of firms, each producing a slightly different product. Therefore, as the name suggests, this market structure has a competitive and monopolistic element. This theory was formulated by Edward Chamberlin. Chamberlin (1962) combined the previously separate theories of monopoly and perfect competition. The aim was to fill the gap between the two extremes of perfect competition and monopoly. In other words, monopolistic competition is an industry structure where competitive conditions are neither purely competitive nor completely monopolistic.

This theory was developed by observing that in the real world very few industries can be truly regarded as monopolies because close substitutes exist for most goods and services. Similarly, there are very few types of goods and services which can be regarded as homogeneous, and so perfect competition can rarely exist. In reality, many industries comprise large numbers of firms (as is the case for perfect competition), but selling products which are slightly different. These differences may be real or imaginary, but what is crucially important is that these differences exist in the minds of consumers. Forms of *product differentiation* include brands and trademarks, exploitation of national differences, catering for consumer tastes or exploiting consumer ignorance, additional technological features, offering additional services, varying the factors of production (and their quality used to produce the product) and advertising. We examine this and other forms of product differentiation in detail in Chapter 7.

The result of product differentiation is that each firm enjoys a small degree of monopoly power. However, competition exists, as the products produced are only slightly different. This means that each firm faces a downward sloping demand curve. We can outline three main assumptions of monopolistic competition:

- There are a large number of small firms.
- Each firm sells a slightly different product and there is free entry and exit to and from any individual product group.
- The price charged is determined by both competitive and monopolistic features.

Under conditions of monopolistic competition, a firm can earn abnormal profits in the short run. However, these are dissipated over the longer term by the entry of new firms. The short- and long-run equilibrium conditions under monopolistic competition are illustrated in Figures 3.14 and 3.15, which we will now discuss briefly.

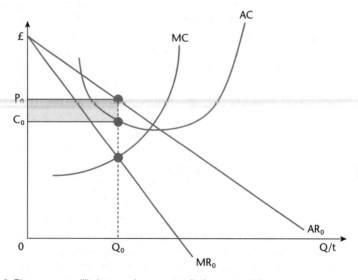

Figure 3.14 Short-run equilibrium under monopolistic competition

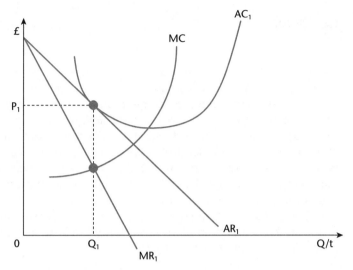

Figure 3.15 Long-run equilibrium under monopolistic competition

Short run

In the short run, the firm maximises profits where marginal revenues equal marginal costs, producing at output level Q_0 and charging a price equal to P_0. The average cost of production at this output level is at C_0. At this output level, the firm earns abnormal profits, where average revenues (AR) exceed average costs (AC). This is shown in Figure 3.14 as the shaded area.

Long run

When potential rivals see the profits which can be realised in this industry, they begin to enter. As more and more firms enter, the market share of each firm declines. In other words, at a given price each firm will expect to sell less than before the entry of new firms. The effect of entry is to shift an individual demand curve to the left. The demand curve will continue to shift to the left so long as there are abnormal profits being earned by established firms. Long-run equilibrium (the tangency solution) is achieved when average revenue (AR_1) equals average cost (AC_1). This is shown in Figure 3.15. The firm produces at Q_1 and charges price equal to P_1. At this point all firms earn normal profits.

Under monopolistic competition, if the firm increases prices, it will lose some but not all of its business to rival firms. Some customers will remain loyal to the firm in the belief that its product is sufficiently different even at higher prices. This contrasts with perfect competition, where the firm would have been left with no customers following a price rise, or monopoly, where an increase in price has little effect on demand.

3.6   Conclusion

This chapter discussed a number of theoretical market structures within which firms might operate. Adopting a profit-maximising framework, we examined the theory of perfect competition, where a large number of small firms compete based on the prices determined by industry demand and supply conditions. While firms can make supernormal profits or losses in the short run, long-run conditions mean that all firms will make normal profit. We also examined departures from perfect competition which have been influential in the development of our analysis of firm and industry behaviour. Theories of monopoly and monopolistic competition were examined, where competition is less intense leading to firms having more control over prices charged. Consequently, in some market structures (such as monopoly) firms can make supernormal profits even in the long run. Such supernormal profits may impose welfare losses on society.

Discussion Questions

1 Consider the following MR and MC schedules. What market structure does our schedule suggest? At what level of output will profits be maximised? At what level of output will total profits be zero?

Output	1	2	3	4	5	6	7	8	9	10	11	12	13	14
MR	10	10	10	10	10	10	10	10	10	10	10	10	10	10
MC	6	4	2	5	7	9	10	11	14	17	25	35	50	70

2 With reference to the following diagram explain why profits are maximised at point 'b' and not at point 'a'.

3 With reference to empirical evidence discussed in Case Studies 3.1 and 3.2, do firms maximise profits in the real world?

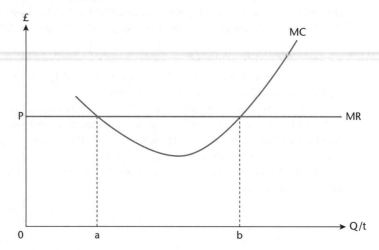

4 Draw the monopoly equilibrium.

5 Draw the short-run and long-run equilibrium conditions under monopolistic and perfect competition.

6 Are monopolies good or bad?

Further Reading

General background

Ison, S. (2000) *Economics* (3rd edn). Harlow: FT Prentice Hall, Chapters 6 and 7.

Nellis, J. G. and Parker, D. (1992) *The Essence of Business Economics*. Harlow: Prentice Hall, Chapters 4 and 5.

Sloman, J. (2000) *Economics* (4th edn). Harlow: FT Prentice Hall, Chapters 5, 6, and 7.

Stewart, G. (1998) Do firms maximise profits?, *Economic Review*, 16, 2, 31–3.

Stewart, G. (2001) Entry and entry barriers, *Economic Review*, 19, 2, 12–14.

Stewart, G. (2001) Monopoly in UK banking, *Economic Review*, 19, 2, 24–7.

Advanced

Davies, H. and Lam, P. (2001) *Managerial Economics* (2nd edn). London: Financial Times Prentice Hall, Chapter 10.

Hall, S., Walsh, M. and Yates, A. (1997) How do UK companies set prices?, *Bank of England Working Paper*.

Shipley, D. (1981) Pricing objectives in British manufacturing industry, *Journal of Industrial Economics*, 29, 429–43.

4 Market Structure 2: Oligopoly

Objectives

By the end of this chapter, the reader should be able to understand:

- that oligopolistic behaviour is essentially a reaction to the problem of interdependence
- that oligopolistic interdependence can lead to non-price competition
- the difference between tacit collusion and explicit collusion
- the economic factors which propel oligopoly firms towards collusive agreements
- why collusive agreements are often regarded as inherently unstable
- the contribution of game theory to the analysis of oligopolistic markets.

Key Concepts

- cartels
- explicit collusion
- game theory
- interdependence

- price leadership
- prisoners' dilemma game
- sequential games
- tacit collusion

4.1   Introduction

In Chapter 3, we discussed the models of perfect competition and pure monopoly as the two extremes of behaviour of producers in a typical market economy. We also discussed monopolistic competition, a model which has tried to fill in just some of the ground between perfect competition and monopoly. It is clear that these two models are unable to explain satisfactorily such business conduct as product differentiation, innovation, price wars, parallel pricing, tacit and explicit collusion, which characterise modern firms and industries. What is needed is an approach that can deal with the vast area of industry structure covering the ground between perfect competition and monopoly. This middle ground which can be referred to as imperfect competition or 'oligopoly'. The word is derived from the Greek 'oligoi' (ολιγοι) meaning 'a few' and 'poleo' (πολεω), 'to sell'.

The fundamental defining characteristic of oligopolistic markets is the recognition that a 'few' sellers account for a substantial proportion of total sales. The consequence of the fewness of firms within a clearly defined industry, where output is fairly homogeneous and entry barriers are substantial, is that firms in an oligopoly realise that they are *mutually interdependent*. Thus, an oligopolist is unable to decide its best strategy unless it knows what its rivals intend to do and, likewise, the firm's rivals are unable to determine their best strategy until they know what the firm is planning to do. Thus 'optimal' or best behaviour depends on assumptions of rivals' likely reactions and even assumptions about rivals' assumptions. *Interdependence* means that a firm is aware that its actions affect the actions of its rivals and vice versa. Oligopolists are 'outward turning'. Unlike the models we considered in Chapter 3 oligopolists cannot know the precise shape of the demand curves they face since they cannot always predict the likely reactions of rivals. Profit maximisation and survival in an oligopoly essentially depend on how a firm reacts to the strategies of its rivals.

How do oligopolists react to interdependence?

Initially, we may suggest that there are two basic reactions. Firms may either act independently or co-operate with their rivals. In fact, both independent action and co-operative (or collusive) behaviour are a matter of degree, and while examples may be found that conform to the polar cases, the great majority of outcomes fall somewhere within these extremes. Thus an oligopoly may contain elements of both independence and collusion. Figure 4.1 can help in understanding some of the likely outcomes or solutions to the oligopoly problem.

As mentioned, a firm can solve the problem of uncertainty by either deciding to act independently, which means attempting to compete with rivals for greater market share, or it may choose to collude. The desire to increase market share is in effect a desire to destroy the competition. Once rivals have been disposed of, or marginalised, the firm enjoys greater market power and less uncertainty. In its extreme form, this is known as *predation*, where firms deliberately seek to drive firms out of the market by setting very low prices or instigating a variety of restrictive practices. However, this is not a commonly observed strategy, as is shown by Case Study 4.1. Almost all oligopolists seem to shy away from rigorous price competition and if they do wish to compete, they opt for 'non-price competition' strategies instead. If price wars do break out, they could be viewed as a temporary aberration and not something which characterises traditional industry behaviour. Essentially, non-price competition focuses on product change, through strategies such as advertising, innovation, the provision of additional services and design changes.

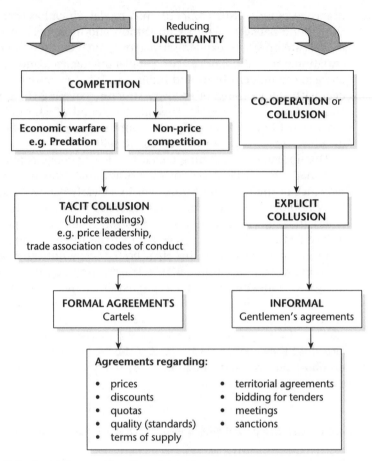

Figure 4.1 Basic solutions to the oligopoly problem

Case Study 4.1

Predation

As we see in this chapter, one consequence of the uncertainty in oligopolistic markets might be that firms will be tempted into price wars. The ultimate objective of a price war, or 'predation', is to destroy a rival by setting market prices below the costs of production so that the rival will incur losses and be forced to leave the market. The remaining firm will then supply the market as a monopoly or near monopoly at a much higher price and thus recoup any lost short-term profits.

Whenever market prices are considered to be 'too low' firms will claim this as evidence of 'predation' or 'ruinous competition'. How does the UK Office of Fair Trading investigate such claims? To answer this question we can refer to the 1998 OFT report into petrol prices.[1]

The relevant market was the retailing of petrol to the general public. The market was essentially made up of roadside sites owned by the big oil companies and the supermarkets. The OFT attempted to test whether predation did exist by considering three tests:

- Did the strategy of lower prices lead to *avoidable* (or deliberate) losses?
- Did it drive otherwise profitable rivals out of the market (the 'intent' test)?
- Once rivals had been forced out, did prices then rise to recoup the losses of such predatory behaviour (the 'feasibility' test)?

Avoidable losses

The OFT felt that the price cuts did not lead to 'avoidable' losses for the following reasons:

- First, the OFT found that petrol was not being retailed at below cost.
- Second, in the opinion of the OFT, supermarket margins were profitable and sustainable. The low prices tended to reflect their low costs as well as a competitive strategy as regards other supermarket rivals *rather than* the oil companies.
- Third, since the oil companies' sites had been losing trade to the supermarkets their response had to be to reduce price so as to increase the volume of sales to cover their own costs. Thus the price reductions were seen as helping the profitability of the roadside sites rather than strategies incurring temporary loses to force out the supermarkets.
- Finally, the OFT noted that the profitability of the roadside sites was also dependent on the sales of non-petrol items. Thus lower petrol prices might attract customers to shop for these other items, which would typically enjoy higher margins.

Intent

The OFT found that in almost all cases price reductions were made to *match* competitors' price reductions, rather than as a strategy to force competitors out of the market.

Feasibility

For the strategy to be feasible, losses made in the short term should be recouped in the long term through higher market prices. This, in the opinion of the OFT, was more likely if specific firms could be *targeted* as major rivals whose exit would reduce competitive pressures in the market. The OFT felt that it was unrealistic for the oil companies to target supermarkets, for the following reasons:

- The oil companies tended to match rather than undercut supermarket petrol prices.
- Supermarkets were the low-cost producers (due to their greater sales volumes) in comparison to the roadside sites of the oil companies.

- Supermarkets tended to focus their competitive attention on other super-markets rather than the oil companies.
- Some large supermarkets had made firm commitments to staying in the market.

The OFT also concluded that predation was equally unlikely where the targets were the roadside sites, for the following reasons:

- If one roadside site were to be forced out of business, the likelihood was that prices would not be raised since there was significant competition from other local roadside sites as well as other supermarkets.
- The disappearance of one site may only be temporary as another competitor may step in and invest in the site.
- The oil companies, as refiners of petrol, are *committed* to a minimum retail network to guarantee a market for their petrol. They will thus support their retail outlets should they face predatory practices.

On the basis of these arguments the OFT concluded that predation did not exist in the petrol retail market.

[1] *Competition in the Supply of Petrol in the UK: A report by the Office of Fair Trading*, May 1998 OFT230.

Why should firms in oligopolistic markets prefer non-price competition to price competition?

We can suggest two reasons. Firms may either regard price reductions as inappropriate in certain markets or view product changes as a more appealing strategy. Price competition may be inappropriate for the following reasons:

- Price reductions can be matched immediately by rivals and any gains are immediately diluted.
- Price reductions may be achieved by reducing the quality of the product. Even if this were not the case, consumers might equate lower price with lower quality in certain markets.
- Consumers in markets may have got used to certain 'price ranges' which accompany product subsets. To charge a different price may suggest a different product market.

Factors that might *encourage* oligopolists to change products rather than consider a price reduction include some of the following:

- Product change can be used to absorb increases in costs without the consumers being aware.
- Firms realise their ability to create and sustain consumer loyalty through strategies such as advertising and new product development. This accumulated loyalty can reward firms with increased market power.
- Much of the increase in product diversity offered by firms has been stimulated by factors such as the pace of technological change and greater disposable incomes, as well as the need to match the range of products offered by rivals.

In section 4.2 we consider one of the most famous of oligopoly models, the kinked demand curve hypothesis, which seeks to explain why oligopolists may be averse to price competition.

As suggested by Figure 4.1, an alternative route for oligopolists is to consider some degree of co-operation or collusion with their rivals to reduce the inherent uncertainties in their market. Collusion may be divided into two types, tacit and explicit. *Tacit collusion* implies that firms do not enter into direct communication with one another regarding market strategies. In time an industry tradition may evolve whereby firms learn that 'not rocking the boat' and a 'live and let live' attitude is preferable to outright competitive and potentially *ruinous* behaviour. Tacit collusion depends much on factors such as personal contacts, a group ethos and a tolerant attitude to other firms. These factors create the necessary social lubrication for successful informal tacit collusion. Personal and social contacts among competitors lessen rivalrous *attitudes*. One does not undercut or steal customers from people with whom one socialises. It will be argued later that social groupings, whether by ethnic origin, social class or even religion, have provided a powerful cement to otherwise potentially unstable collusive activities. This feeling of belonging, or an 'esprit de corps', can be further strengthened by the existence of trade associations, trade journals, conferences and social activities. In section 4.3 we examine *price leadership*, a common form of tacit collusion.

However, in some cases tacit co-operation may be insufficient to damp down the desire of some firms to act independently from time to time. Clearly, tacit collusion under these circumstances may be insufficient to reduce the degree of risk and uncertainty faced by firms. Firms may then seek more explicit forms of co-operation to ensure greater stability in their markets. *Explicit collusion* implies direct communication and agreement over various market strategies.

Figure 4.1 identifies two types of explicit collusion, the informal *gentlemen's agreement* and the more formal *cartel* agreement. Gentlemen's agreements refer to agreements that are purely oral or where written notes are at a minimum. This form of collusion has many examples. A frequently quoted example is that of the Gary Dinners, where the top firms in the US steel industry met between the years 1907 and 1911. Although the dinners were social occasions, they were, more importantly, a vehicle for fixing prices and outputs through verbal communication. The colluders also believed that they were within the law if no formal (written) agreement existed. Records of agreements at the Office of Fair Trading which pre-date the 1956 Trade Restrictions Act show that some 25% of all agreements were of this type.

Written agreements, accompanied by the development of central agencies, could be regarded as formal agreements and might be seen as distinguishing cartel organisations. Formal contracts, stipulating rights and obligations, sanctions, fines, deposition of collateral and so on would characterise these forms.

Why should firms consider formalising their informal gentlemen's agreements by setting up a cartel?

The short answer is that parties to an informal, oral agreement simply do not trust one another sufficiently to feel that the arrangement can work. If firms mistrust one another, they need to monitor each others' actions. If each firm has to monitor the market behaviour of every other firm, then the monitoring costs to the industry or market as a whole are considerable. The existence of cartels, which perform such functions, saves industry costs. The exact degree of the 'explicitness' of the agreement would depend on the number of issues covered by the agreement. The most common issues covered in the agreements are shown in Figure 4.1.

In section 4.4 we examine the economic factors which favour the development of explicit collusion as well as the factors that can lead to the instability of such agreements.

In our last section, we provide an introduction to game theory. Game theory is the study of decision making in conflict situations and is thus potentially well suited to determine oligopolistic outcomes. Theoretically, it is one of the strongest of all the models when we consider the issues of interdependence.

4.2   The Kinked Demand Curve

It had long been observed that prices in oligopolistic markets often remained unchanged for long periods, and a model was simultaneously developed by Sweezy (1939) and Hall and Hitch (1939) to explain this *price rigidity* in oligopolistic market structures. We consider the variant of the model suggested by Sweezy (see Figure 4.2).

Sweezy's solution was based on the assumption that firms do not initiate a price rise. They believe that if they did so rivals will *not follow* and consequently they will lose a sizable share of the market. However, firms *always follow* a price fall, so as to protect their market share. Prices can still be affected by large changes in demand and supply conditions in the long run.

dD is the firm's demand curve. The kink is at price P, the price at which the firm is selling $0Q_0$. Above P the demand curve, as perceived by the firm, is dP, which is

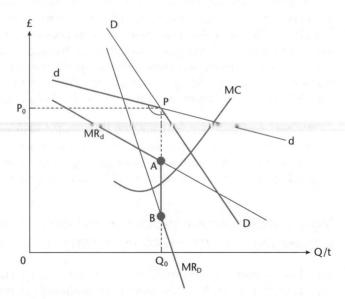

Figure 4.2 Sweezy's kinked demand curve hypothesis

relatively elastic and MR is positive. dP is elastic because the firm believes that rivals will not follow a higher price and consequently at a higher price the fall in sales would be high. PD is less elastic (inelastic) because the firm believes that a reduction in price will be matched. Although it may temporarily enjoy an increase in sales, eventually all the other firms will follow the price fall and the firm will suffer lower sales and lower profits.

The gap between A and B, which the MC curve intersects, can be regarded as the vertical section of the MR function. Profits are maximised where MC equal MR. To the left of Q_0 MR > MC, and to the right of Q_0 MR < MC: thus profit is maximised where the MC curve intersects the vertical discontinuity, which can be seen analytically as an extension of the marginal revenue function. We can now see that if MC rises or falls within the discontinuity, as shown by points A and B, *price and output remain constant*. Thus Sweezy was able to demonstrate price rigidity or 'sticky' prices.

What factors affect the degree of price rigidity?

The degree of price rigidity depends on the length of the discontinuity AB, which in turn depends on the angle of the kink, which in turn depends on the slope of the demand curves. Several factors which may affect the slope and elasticity of the curves are as follows:

- Where there are few rivals, price increases are more likely to be followed since any gains from lower prices may be quickly eroded. It could also be argued that, if there are many rivals, they are more likely not to follow a price rise but equally they may not follow a price reduction either. It might be argued that an intermediate number of firms would generate the longest discontinuity.

- The size of the rivals may also affect the size of the kink. If there is one large firm or clique of firms it may act as a price leader and all rivals will follow price increases and decreases. In this extreme case there is no kink. This equally applies to a situation where collusion takes place.

- Where goods are homogeneous with a high positive cross-elasticity of demand the discontinuity is longer and price rigidity greater, as consumers are more likely to shift to the low-price firms.

- Where entrants are unsure about the market structure or existing firms are unsure about the intentions of entrants, firms may adopt a 'wait and see' attitude and be reluctant to initiate price rises.

- A similar analysis can be applied to a 'new' industry in which firms are in the process of 'sizing' each other up.

- Finally, one might argue that, where there is substantial shareholder control, managers may be risk averse and decide to 'play it safe'.

All these features (except the last point) simply reinforce the feeling of mutual interdependence and the desire for stability. In contrast, the absence of a kink implies a normal demand curve. This could occur as suggested where we have a price leader or collusion.

How realistic is the kinked demand curve hypothesis?

- Theoretically, the model can be attacked for not explaining how prices are formed at the kink. The model begins with price as a given variable. It does not tell us how prices are determined in an oligopoly context. It explains the existence of kinks, but not their location. It is an *ex post rationalisation* rather than an *ex ante explanation* of market equilibrium.

- Second, one could argue that price rigidity can be explained in other ways. Firms may be reluctant to increase price for fear of alienating their consumers. Firms may wait for a convenient time to introduce one large price increase rather than revise prices continuously, a strategy which may negatively affect buyer psychology. Changing prices itself is a costly and complex process. In businesses where such 'menu costs' are high, changes in price are less frequent.

- Sweezy's argument that price increases are not followed but that all decreases are, can also be challenged. A price reduction need not signal to rivals that a firm has introduced an aggressive strategy to capture a larger share of the market. Rivals may reason that the products being sold are of lower quality or that the firm has financial problems. Rivals react according to *how they interpret* the price reduction. Likewise, price increases may be followed if firms believe that market conditions warrant such an increase or if they face temporary shortages in capacity and are unable to meet increases in demand.

4.3   Price Leadership

Let us now turn to another analysis of oligopoly models where interdependence is recognised, namely price leadership or 'parallel pricing'. It is a frequently observed phenomenon that firms in oligopolistic markets change prices in tandem. One firm announces a price change and soon all the other firms follow suit. There are three types of price leadership.

Dominant price leadership

As the term suggests, the industry is dominated by one firm, due to its greater efficiency (lower costs) or possibly its aggressive behaviour. The firm sets the price and other firms follow through convenience, ignorance or fear. In fact, there is no oligopoly problem as such, since interdependence is absent. The dominant firm could act as a monopolist and eliminate rivals through a price war, but this would clearly attract the attention of the government anti-monopoly agencies. A better name for this type of behaviour could be 'partial monopoly' price leadership.

Barometric price leadership

Barometric price leadership exists where a firm announces a price change that would, in time, be set by the forces of competition. It is simply the first to announce a price change. The leader is not necessarily the dominant firm in the market. Indeed, one would expect the identity of the leader to change over time. The leader acts as a 'barometer' for the market, and if it fails to interpret market conditions correctly, leadership passes on to other firms.

Effective price leadership

Barometric leadership is essentially of two types – the 'competitive' type and the more dangerous 'monopolistic' type, which is often referred to as 'effective' price leadership or 'collusive price leadership'. The benign, competitive type is characterised by:

- frequent changes in the identity of the leader
- no immediate, uniform response to price changes, i.e. a lagged response as followers consider the suitability of a price change
- variations in market share.

Effective price leadership is then characterised by the *absence* of these conditions and tends to exist where there are:

- a small number of firms, all fairly large
- substantial entry barriers
- an absence of marked product differentiation, to reinforce the feeling of interdependence
- low elasticities of demand, to prevent price cutting
- similar cost functions.

As the agreed leader changes price, all the other firms follow suit. There is no overt or explicit collusion. All firms act *independently*. They realise that it is best to co-operate tacitly in an orderly market rather than slide into the anarchy of price wars. The effect can nonetheless be similar to overt price agreements.

4.4 Collusion

As we saw earlier, oligopolistic firms, finding themselves in industrial structures characterised by interdependence and uncertainty, may attempt to avoid independent action and arrange some form of collusion in their industry.

Collusion can be viewed as a way of *easing* the pressures of competition by unified action rather than just a strategy purely intended to maximise joint profits. Three reasons can be suggested why oligopolists follow such a strategy:

- It is plausible. Collusion reduces the uncertainties of independent action and in some weak forms it need not be illegal or at least not easily detected, e.g. price leadership.
- It is realistic. Evidence shows that throughout the world anti-trust authorities are never short of work in investigating the sharper end of collusive practices.

- Lastly, collusion is simple. Co-operation reduces the complexities of interdependence. Firms no longer need to speculate about the likely reactions of rivals.

What factors may tempt firms into collusive activity?

Increased profitability

The most often quoted reason for collusion is that, by decreasing the amount of competition, firms can determine monopoly solutions and thus increase their profits. The higher profits resulting from 'near monopoly' power can be adequately illustrated by traditional microeconomic models, discussed later in this chapter.

Risk

Risk is the major influence in the setting up of co-operative structures. The risk facing firms is the variability of demand and competition from within the industry. A possible escape from these risks would be for the firm to develop market power independently on the basis of product differentiation, product innovation or vertical integration. But such a strategy would be costly and highly uncertain. Collusion is thus an obvious alternative solution to these risks.

Position and security

Both position and security matter to oligopolists, and any move towards a guarantee of status and security, via collusive action, is attractive. Perfect competition and monopoly, as theoretical ideals, are not concerned with market position. A perfectly competitive firm regards itself as sufficiently insignificant to be concerned with status. In theory a monopolist, as a sole supplier, does not consider its position as a goal or objective. It cannot better its position. On the other hand, an oligopolist is aware of market share, for it defines its status in the industry. It may well wish to improve market share or at least ensure that it is not eroded. In either event, the firm cannot ignore its position and it forms a central issue in strategic decision making.

Access to market information

The desire for information may itself be the powerful drive towards an agreement. All firms require information on which to base their decisions. The importance of such information depends on the degree of interdependence in an industry or the extent to which firms are 'vulnerable to damage' by the actions of other firms. Firms are most vulnerable when undertaking investment decisions. A firm does not wish to suffer the consequences of over- or underinvestment. The effect of such information exchange is to reduce firms' vulnerability and to increase group cohesiveness.

Cartels

The term 'cartel' refers to a form of organisation or association adopted by independent firms in an oligopolistic industry, in a clear attempt to achieve collusive rather than competitive strategies. It can cover a very wide range of organisational forms, from the very informal to highly formal, semi-legal structures. Although most people would view such associations as primarily attempting to increase joint profits by restricting competition, in reality most firms enter cartel-type agreements to protect themselves rather than from a desire to exploit the market. Agreements tend, on the whole, to keep out or keep under control potential entrants and new products that could threaten the stability of existing firms. Price fixing seems only to be of secondary importance and usually as a means to support the less efficient members. Profits are not spectacularly higher than one would suppose, thus supporting the view that firms may aim at reasonable profits rather than maximising joint profits.

Economic model of a cartel

The general model has many variants. We shall consider the simplest case, where a centralised cartel has complete control over price and output decisions and allocation of profit. We assume that entry into the industry is successfully deterred and that every firm's output is homogeneous. The maximisation of the cartel's profits is thus seen as a monopoly problem and resolved by determining output and price where the industry marginal revenue equals the industry's marginal cost. The latter is the horizontal summation of all the short-run marginal cost curves of individual members.

Figure 4.3 represents a simplified two-firm case. Total industry costs are minimised by allocating quotas in such a way that the short-run marginal costs (SMC) of each firm, when producing its quota, are equal to the SMC of all other firms. Thus the inefficient firms, those with a steeper SMC, are assigned a lower output quota than if they were independent. The reduction in output of the inefficient firms is made up by an increase in the output of the efficient firms. This rationalisation ensures that the rate of increase in total cost due to increased output of the efficient firm is less than the rate of decrease in total cost due to the decrease in output of the inefficient firms. The profit-maximising price set by the cartel is P_c and total industry output is $0X$, of which $0X_a$ is supplied by firm A and $0X_b$ by firm B. As mentioned earlier, this type of static model is simplistic and many of the real-life problems of risk, conflict and the nature of costs have been ignored.

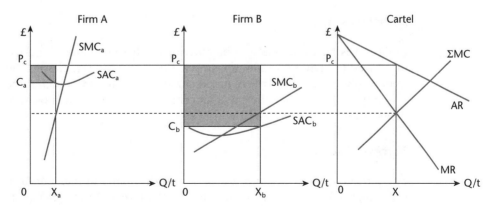

Figure 4.3 Cartel equilibrium

What factors encourage the development of and help sustain a successful cartel?

Industrial concentration and the number of firms

Firms find it easier to establish collusive strategies in industries characterised by high levels of concentration (discussed in detail in Chapter 6). Essentially, this is based on the view that, as numbers increase, the unanimity of goals diminish. With a dilution of this unanimity, the group incurs greater enforcement (or transactions) costs. As the number of firms grows so the costs of monitoring and adjusting to other firms' behaviour grow at a faster rate than the number of firms joining the collusion.

Asymmetry of market shares

The asymmetry of market shares, i.e. the size distribution of firms, is another variable that can affect the ability of firms to collude. It is commonly argued that, where firms in an industry are of roughly equal size, the chance of collusion, *ceteris paribus*, is enhanced. Substantial *asymmetry* implies a divergence of views between the large and the small firms. The smaller firms may, for example, be reluctant to adopt quotas based on existing market shares, while the larger firms may use the collusive agreement as a springboard for increased dominance.

Product differentiation

Homogeneity of output or lack of product differentiation is also seen as an important factor in facilitating efficient collusion. One would expect, *ceteris paribus*, that price fixing would be more difficult where there is marked product differentiation. Firms selling homogeneous goods need only focus on a narrow range of pricing decisions. The greater the number of variables affecting any real or perceived differences in the output, the greater the complexity for price fixing. A further complication is the degree of homogeneity over time. If a product is subject to change, due to frequent technological improvements or changes in consumer tastes, a price agreement would be all the more difficult to negotiate and sustain. Thus one would expect collusion to be more difficult to arrange in an industry characterised by high rates of product development.

Inelastic demand

Collusion is far more likely to be attempted where demand is inelastic. If higher prices lead to higher revenues it is implicit that demand is inelastic. The cost of not fixing a high price when the demand curve is inelastic is the higher profit forgone. The implication is that the price agreement must cover all substitute goods, i.e. include most of the firms in the industry.

Vertical integration

The success of cartel operations depends on the ability of member firms to be reassured that fellow members are abiding by the terms of the agreement. They must therefore be in a position to monitor deviations from such agreements. If one of the members is vertically integrated downstream, e.g. owns retail outlets, it may be able to undercut the cartel price by effectively reducing its transfer price to its retail outlets. Unless the members are fully aware of the true costs involved in retail operations, they may be unable to detect such cheating. This state of affairs would then compromise the efficiency of the cartel.

Strong trade association

The existence of a strong and efficient trade association provides the necessary operational mechanism for the setting up of the cartel. A trade association can gather, process and disseminate information, and this function can form the basis of an agreement.

Allied to a strong trade association one could briefly add the role of a strong individual leadership in the development of cartels (see Case Studies 4.2 and 4.3). This factor is discussed in more detail later in this chapter.

Pressures on cartel stability

The lack of long-run cartel stability has characterised most if not all agreements in oligopolistic markets. Writers have frequently given examples of the inevitable short-run nature of cartels. Where agreements appear to have lasted for some time their effectiveness in promoting joint profit maximisation may, in fact, have been negligible.

The reason why so many cartels fail to live up to expectations is that the 'obvious' solution to oligopolistic interdependence is far more complicated than it may at first appear. The complication is that what appears optimal for the group may not be optimal for each of the individual members. This divergence of interests necessitates some method of bargaining to reconcile these differences. One reason for the instability of co-ordinated action is that the bargaining strength of members can

Case Study 4.2

A large international cartel

European Commission press release: 'Commission imposes fines on vitamin cartels'

On 21 November 2001 the European Commission fined eight companies a total of €855.22 million for participating in eight distinct secret market-sharing and price-fixing cartels affecting vitamin products. Each cartel had a specific number of participants and duration, although all operated between September 1989 and February 1999. Because Swiss-based company Hoffman-La Roche was an instigator and participated in all the cartels it was given the highest cumulative fine of €462 million. 'This is the most damaging series of cartels the Commission has ever investigated due to the sheer range of vitamins covered which are found in a multitude of products from cereals, biscuits and drinks to animal feed, pharmaceuticals and cosmetics,' said Competition Commissioner Mario Monti. 'The companies' collusive behaviour enabled them to charge higher prices than if the full forces of competition had been at play, damaging consumers and allowing the companies to pocket illicit profits. It is particularly unacceptable that this illegal behaviour concerned substances which are vital elements for nutrition and essential for normal growth and maintenance of life.'

Following the opening of an investigation in May 1999, the European Commission has found that 13 European and non-European companies participated in cartels aimed at eliminating competition in the vitamin A, E, B1, B2, B5, B6, C, D3, Biotin (H), Folic acid (M), Beta carotene and carotinoids markets. A striking feature of this complex of infringements was the central role played by Hoffmann-La Roche and BASF, the two main vitamin producers, in virtually each and every cartel, while other players were involved in only a limited number of vitamin products. *[The heaviest fines were imposed on F. Hoffmann-La Roche AG (Switzerland), €462m and BASF AG (Germany), €296.16m. The next highest was Takeda Chemical Industries Ltd (Japan) €37.05m.]*

The cartels

The participants in each of the cartels fixed prices for the different vitamin products, allocated sales quotas, agreed on and implemented price increases and issued price announcements in accordance with their agreements. They also set up a machinery to monitor and enforce their agreements and participated in regular meetings to implement their plans.

The modus operandi of the different cartels was essentially the same if not identical ('target' and 'minimum' prices; maintenance of the status quo in market shares and compensation arrangements). In particular it included:

- the establishment of formal structure and hierarchy of different levels of management, often with overlapping membership at the most senior levels to ensure the functioning of the cartels

- the exchange of sales values, volumes of sales and pricing information on a quarterly or monthly basis at regular meetings

- in the case of the largest cartels, the preparation, agreement and implementation and monitoring of an annual 'budget' followed by the adjustment of actual sales achieved so as to comply with the quotas allocated.

The cartel arrangements generally followed this scheme, pioneered in vitamins A and E, with certain variants in other products. Hoffmann-La Roche acted as the agent and representative of the European producers in the meetings and negotiations held in Japan and the Far East.

The simultaneous existence of the collusive arrangements in the various vitamins was not a spontaneous or haphazard development, but was conceived and directed by the same persons at the most senior levels of the undertakings concerned.

Source: http://europa.eu.int/rapid/start/cgi/guesten.ksh?p_action.gettxt=gt&doc=IP/01/1625|0|RAPID&lg=EN

Case Study 4.3

A small local cartel

The Yorkshire bus cartel

Two UK national bus companies, Arriva and FirstGroup, owned Yorkshire subsidiaries. In March 2000 directors of the two subsidiaries met in a Wakefield hotel to discuss potential co-operation with regards to bus routes in the Leeds area. Arriva directors had offered to give up two routes, 1B and 96A, which involved five buses, and leave FirstGroup free of any competition. In return FirstGroup agreed that if the five Arriva buses were switched to two other routes (223 and 224) then it would 'deregister' its services on these two routes.

On the basis of witness statements and evidence of registrations and deregistrations of bus routes in question, the Office of Fair Trading concluded that the two companies had entered into a market-sharing agreement.

FirstGroup was fined around £500,000 and Arriva around £300,000. However, under the OFT's 'leniency programme', FirstGroup's fine was reduced to zero, since they were the first to admit their guilt and then fully co-operated with the OFT investigation.

Source: Based on the OFT Report *Market Sharing by Arriva plc and FirstGroup plc*, 30 January 2002 (Case CP/1163-00).

change in unpredictable ways. The consequence of these changes is that the group must fashion 'outlets' for these changes, which in turn can be regarded as mutually acceptable forms of competition within the group. These 'outlets' could, for example, allow firms some individual control over cost-saving innovations, to pursue product differentiation, to invest in innovatory activity etc. There would thus be a recognition that superior skills must somehow be rewarded. These 'outlets' would diminish the ability of the group to maximise joint profits. But, more importantly, these 'outlets' might not be sufficient to control the latent competition. As a result, skirmishes and wars often break out.

We shall examine some of the specific factors which can lead to the frustration of collusive agreements. These factors can be classified into three groups: those that arise from the internal pressures or constraints facing the firm, those that arise from the external environment, and those that might be considered as non-economic issues.

Internal pressures

Seller concentration and smallness of number

Communication among colluders is cheaper and detection of cheating is easier the more concentrated the industry. Consequently, the degree of seller concentration affects the stability of collusion. If the number of firms is small, retaliation (the deterrent to cheating) is that much faster. If the retaliation lag is lengthy, the payoff from cheating becomes more attractive since the short-run gains from cheating outweigh the long-run losses of lower future profits.

Different goals of members

When faced with a heterogeneous collection of firms, existing in an uncertain coalition, it is more than probable that the individual firms have substantially different goals. Thus, there may be an inherent internal goal conflict which may remain lightly buried in the interests of group solidarity and then rise to the surface at any time. Members may disagree over short- and long-run policies; the due regard that should be paid to potential competition; how best to treat the risks of any government reaction to anticompetitive behaviour, etc.

Extent of non-price competition

A cartel is more unstable if there are possibilities for non-price competition. If the elimination of price competition leads to the development of alternative forms of competition, such as product innovation and advertising, any advantage of co-operative action could be dissipated by these competitive 'outlets'. An effective cartel must thus ensure that firms do not gain an 'edge' over their rivals by non-price strategies.

Sanctions

The ability of a cartel to employ effective sanctions against cheats ensures cartel discipline and stability. It is a fact of cartel life that, if additional profits can be realised by cheating, then cheating occurs, unless some policy of deterrence is adopted. One should nonetheless bear in mind that if it appears to be in the economic interests of a firm to break an agreement, no sanction is likely to be very effective. At best, sanctions should be viewed as an additional constraint on potential independent action and not the prime force for stability.

External pressures

Entry

In the long run, the stability and profitability of collusion depend on the ease or difficulty of entry into the industry. If a cartel can shelter behind effective entry barriers, it may enjoy the necessary time and space to prosper and solve the often conflicting demands of its members. If, on the other hand, entry barriers are low, the cartel faces competitive pressure from potential entrants.

It follows that, in most cases, some policy of entry prevention must be instituted. The term 'entry barrier' is used loosely in this context. An entry barrier implies the entrant faces costs of gaining a foothold in the market, costs which existing firms have managed to avoid. Barriers of this type are rare. Small entrants incur disadvantages due to their scale of operations. But their scale may eventually increase and efficient organisation may result. Thus, a more valid approach in this context would be to consider the factors that lead not to increasing the height of an entry barrier but to lengthening the time necessary to achieve successful entry. (Entry barriers are discussed in Chapter 6.)

Existence of non-cartel firms

The prior discussion assumed that cartels are always threatened by the existence of firms competing outside the cartel organisation. This rests on the belief that non-cartel firms, enjoying profits higher than the loyal cartel members, will tempt the latter to desert the cartel and undermine its existence.

Changes in demand

One can argue that a reduction in market demand places strains on an agreement. As demand falls, sales drop and firms are tempted to undercut the cartel price in a bid to keep their remaining customers. The temptation need not affect all firms equally; some, which may enjoy relatively high profits, may regard the reduction in sales as temporary and may urge all firms to keep their nerve and ride out the squall; others, who are earning lower profits, may view the decline as a real threat to their future and attempt any strategy to survive. The climate of falling demand may thus create mutual suspicion and fear, which eventually leads to the breakdown of the price agreement.

An alternative view is that collusion is in fact more difficult to enforce in times of increasing demand. A firm facing an expanding market and, at the same time, being undercut by rivals may not be in a position to detect such cheating, since its own sales are rising. It would have to determine whether its sales were growing in the same proportions as those of its rivals. Suspicion that other firms may be stealing a more than proportionate share of the expanding market may force a firm to abandon the agreement.

Buyer concentration

Generally, one would expect that cartel stability is enhanced by the lack of market power of buyers. If the buyers are powerful, they may well threaten agreed prices by moving to alternative sources of supply; or by suggesting reciprocal transactions with individual firms. Equally, an atomistic group of buyers would help to maintain stability among the colluders by virtue of the difficulty of sellers to cheat on the established price. The more buyers there are, the greater is the chance of a firm being found out to be cheating.

Non-economic factors

Leadership

Most economists would naturally shy away from considering a variable such as leadership. Theory, with its emphasis on structural characteristics, tends to sit uncomfortably with such sociological aspects of organisational behaviour. The development of an agreement, nevertheless, requires that someone takes the lead and organises the initial meetings. People need to be persuaded, coaxed or even threatened to join the cartel. Thus someone must possess the leadership qualities necessary to form and control such a group. Likewise, a strong personality set against the idea of co-operation may frustrate any attempt at such a strategy.

Trust

One of the central questions surrounding successful collusion is whether the colluders can trust one another. If this trust is lacking, no amount of sophisticated price and output agreements can prevent the group from being under continual pressure. The lesson is obvious: if trust is absent, it must be built up.

Social homogeneity

If the participants to an agreement share the same social background, their group adhesion goes some way to ensure stability and trust. To cheat on one's social group is to run the risk not only of suffering the economic loss of forgone future profits but also the disutility of social stigmatisation. The cheat is branded as the outsider and denied the support and comfort of the social group.

Let us sum up the chief characteristics of a successful cartel. In the absence of legal sanctions what factors would we most likely observe in an industry to ensure cartel success? Certainly, smallness of number helps in the handling and evaluation of information flows. Similar cost functions tend to remove some of the potential conflict between firms of differing efficiencies. Attempts at an equitable and fair division of the profits should be seen to be attempted. Demand should be relatively inelastic at the pre-cartel price, to ensure increased revenues at lower levels of output. Potential members must be shown the benefits of co-operative action. The cartel must also ensure that entry is made difficult so as not to dilute too much of its gain. The cartel must guard against other external threats to its stability, notably any significant changes in demand and technology. In effect, the fewer decisions the members of a cartel are called on to make, in dealing with any structural imperfection, or changes in internal or external conditions, the greater the chance of success.

4.5   Game Theory

Game theory is an attempt to determine solutions to various outcomes based on the actions of independent players. A game is a situation where two players or firms compete, e.g. for market share. Courses open to the players are known as *strategies*, and we assume all strategies for all players are known. Strategies open to oligopolistic firms can refer to changes in price, product design, advertising, output, public relations, and so on. Each firm then faces a *payoff* for every given set of strategies. This can be illustrated by the use of a simple table or *payoff matrix* (see Figure 4.4).

Figure 4.4 illustrates the payoff matrix for two firms A and B. Firm A's strategies are 'w' and 'x', while firm B's are 'y' and 'z'. The elements in the matrix represent the payoffs (for example profits) to the two firms. The first figure refers to A's payoff and the second to B's payoff. Thus for example if firm A selects strategy 'x', while firm B selects strategy 'y', A's payoff (profit) is 6 and B's payoff is 0, i.e. no profit. Each firm then selects that strategy that gives it the best outcome, *given the likely strategies of the other firm*. If both firms can achieve this we have what is referred to as a 'Nash equilibrium', which means that no firm can *improve* its payoff, given the

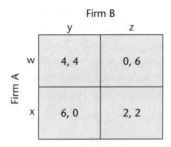

Figure 4.4 A simple payoff matrix

actions of the other firm. In Figure 4.4 we have four possible strategy pairs (wy, wx, xy and xz) and thus four possible outcomes to the game:

- *Strategy pair* 'wy' cannot be a Nash equilibrium, since firm A can *improve* its pay-off from 4 to 6 by selecting strategy 'x'.
- If we consider *strategy pair* 'wz', again, firm A can *improve* its payoff from 0 to 2 by selecting strategy 'x'. Thus this cannot be a Nash equilibrium.
- *Strategy pair* 'xy' is also not a Nash equilibrium since firm B can *improve* its payoff from 0 to 2 by selecting strategy 'z'.
- The fourth option, *strategy pair* 'xz', is an outcome that *no firm can better*, if it were to choose a different strategy. Thus, *given* the fact that firm B has selected 'z', firm A cannot do better than strategy 'x'. Likewise, given the fact that firm A has selected strategy 'x', firm B cannot do better than strategy 'z'.

It is interesting to note that, in this game, both firms would have been better off had they chosen strategy pair 'wy'. This is known as a *prisoners' dilemma* game and is discussed in the following sections.

Types of game

Broadly speaking, games fall into two categories, *co-operative* and *non-co-operative games*. In the case of a co-operative game, it is assumed that firms can negotiate a agreement. Thus, when a seller and a buyer haggle over the price of a good, we are faced with a 'game' which can be resolved by an agreement (whether verbal or written) over a mutually beneficial price. Equally, when two producers decide to collude over prices or output, we also have an agreement. However, where agreements are not possible, e.g. when two firms fight for market share, we are faced with non-co-operative games.

Games can also be classified according to their outcomes. A *constant-sum game* occurs when the sum of the payoffs to both players is always equal. Thus, if a game concerns strategies to divide up a market worth £200 million in sales, then all strategy pairs for the firms sum to that figure. Thus, if one firm were to account for sales of £120 million, the other firm would enjoy sales of £80 million. A game may be *non-constant* when the outcomes vary with different strategies.

A *zero-sum game* occurs where one firm's gain is exactly equal to another's loss. A game of poker is a zero-sum game in that one player's winnings are exactly matched by the losses of the rival player.

Finally, we can distinguish games that are *positive-sum games*, where both players are better off after the game, e.g. an exchange between a producer and a consumer; and *negative-sum games*, where both players are worse off after the game. This may occur in situations of price wars where firms force losses on each other by setting lower and lower prices. Although both lose profits in the short run, both hope that they emerge victorious and recover these losses in the long run.

Dominant strategies

The solution to a game was briefly outlined in Figure 4.4. Let us turn to a more formal analysis of how an equilibrium can be determined. An equilibrium is defined when both firms achieve a *dominant strategy*, which is a strategy that is optimal for a player or firm, regardless of what the rival does. Let us consider the game illustrated in Figure 4.5.

Assume firm A can choose one of three strategies, a, b and c, while firm B can choose from four, w, x, y and z. These strategies are shown in the payoff matrix as Figure 4.5. The elements in the matrix refer to firm A's payoff, e.g. market share, for each possible combination of strategies. We further assume that the constant value of the game (i.e. size of the market) is 20. If firm A chooses strategy 'c' and firm B chooses strategy 'w', firm A wins 6 and firm B wins 14 (the constant value of the game less A's winnings).

Firm B chose strategy 'w' because it yielded the greatest payoff, given firm A's choice. Alternatively, if we assume that firm B chose strategy 'y', firm A would have chosen strategy 'c' to maximise its gain. Firm A realises that for any strategy (row) it selects, firm B selects that strategy (column) which *minimises* firm A's winnings (and *maximises* firm B's winnings). Thus firm A has to be aware of the row minima, *the worst possible outcomes of each strategy*. Faced with row minima of 9, 4 or 6, firm A selects strategy (row) 'a' since it *guarantees* the largest return. Had it selected any other strategy (row), firm B could have forced a lower payoff on firm A. In all cases, firm A selects that strategy that corresponds to the maximum of the row minima, a procedure referred to as *maximining*. This represents firm A's dominant strategy. In a similar way firm B is interested in column maxima, which represents its worst outcomes. To ensure the best payoff, firm B selects the strategy which corresponds to

A's strategies	B's strategies				ROW MINIMA
	w	x	y	z	
a	10	9	14	13	_9_
b	11	8	4	15	4
c	6	7	15	17	6
COLUMN MAXIMA	11	_9_	15	17	9 = 9

Figure 4.5 Payoff matrix

the minimum of the column maxima. Firm B *minimaxes*. The two dominant strategies are identified by the two shaded rectangles in Figure 4.5. Since strategy pair 'ax' is determined, firm A wins 9 and firm B wins 11.

This game is known as a *two-person, strictly determined, constant-sum game*. It is 'strictly determined' since it has a unique solution or equilibrium, 'two person' since only two players are involved, and 'constant sum' since the sum of the shares of the two players is always constant (in this case 20). In reality, most games are not strictly determined, i.e. there is no convenient equilibrium. This then requires alternative approaches to attempt a possible solution to the game. These approaches can be found in more advanced textbooks in strategic management.

Prisoners' dilemma

A prisoners' dilemma game is said to exist when there are gains to be made by players colluding. However, the collusive solution is unstable since greater gains can be made if one player moves independently (cheats), on the assumption that its rival sticks with the agreement. Let us consider a situation where two prisoners are separated physically and no communication between them is possible. Each is told the following:

1 If you both confess you will receive the normal punishment (5 years in prison).

2 If neither of you confesses you will both go free (0 years in prison).

3 If you confess and your fellow prisoner does not, you will go free and receive an extra benefit of £500,000. (This is shown as 0+ in the matrix.)

4 If you do not confess and your fellow prisoner confesses you will receive a sentence of 20 years.

The strategies open to both prisoners can be illustrated by the payoff matrix shown as Figure 4.6. The matrix shows the payoffs to both prisoners in terms of years in prison. In each case A's payoff is first, followed by B's.

A considers his position and determines strategy. If he confesses and B confesses he spends 5 years in prison. If he confesses and B does not confess he gains his freedom and an additional reward. This is preferable to his other strategy which is not to confess, in which event he receives a 20-year sentence if B confesses or freedom

Prisoner A's strategy	Prisoner B's strategy		Worst outcome for A
	Confess	Don't confess	
Confess	(5, 5)	(0+, 20)	5
Don't confess	(20, 0+)	(0, 0)	20
Worst outcome for B	5	20	

Figure 4.6 Prisoners' dilemma game

Firm A's strategy	Firm B's strategy		Worst outcome for A
	Collude	Cheat	
Collude	(160, 160)	(0, 200)	0
Cheat	(200, 0)	(100, 100)	100
Worst outcome for B	0	100	

Figure 4.7 Prisoners' dilemma game – unstable collusion

if B does not confess. Thus, faced with the worst possible outcomes of prison for five years or 20 years he selects the 'best of the worst' and confesses. Similar reasoning applies to B. Thus both prisoners confess (the shaded strategy) even though it *was mutually desirable for neither to do so!*

This type of game can be applied to oligopolies where firms decide to collude. In this case the firms' mutual interest might be to abide by the terms of the oligopoly agreement, yet the temptation to cheat may be too great to achieve such a solution.

The matrix in Figure 4.7 shows the payoffs to both firms. As before, A's payoff is shown first and B's is second. It is clear that it is mutually beneficial for the firms to collude, which would result in each gaining 160. However, each realises that to stick to the collusive agreement 'invites' the rival to cheat and result in a zero return. Both decide to cheat and both lose by determining a sub-optimal solution. For a prisoner's dilemma game to be resolved in the oligopoly context, the agreement may have to be accompanied by an *enforceable contract* (whether legal or otherwise) to keep members to the 'collude, collude' strategy pair. Equally, prisoners are more likely not to confess to crimes if they know that to confess might impose greater costs in the long term in the form of a 'contract' on their life!

Do all potential prisoners' dilemma games generate sub-optimal solutions?

We may observe optimal outcomes if we relax some of the assumptions. The reasons for more stable, more beneficial outcomes may depend on the following factors:

- An optimal solution can be achieved if there is a high degree of information and communication between the rivals. If firms meet frequently they are able to exchange information and monitor each other's actions. If our two prisoners were not segregated they could determine their best strategies by a continual examination of their options. The nuclear war game 'played' by the United States and the Soviet Union in the 1960s and 1970s was likened to a prisoners' dilemma game. The choices were whether to attack the rival with a pre-emptive strike or whether to stick to the 'non-first use' agreement. One reason why the optimal solution (sticking to the agreement) was followed, was the installation of the 'hot line' between Washington and Moscow to allow the two countries to exchange regular information at the highest level of government.

- Another important feature regarding the solution to the game is the length of the reaction lags. The longer the reaction lag the greater the temptation for a player to act as an aggressor. This is especially true in cartels, where the greatest deterrence to cheating is immediate discovery and punishment. In the nuclear war game reaction lags were also crucial to ensuring that both sides kept to the agreement. Each side boasted that it could retaliate within minutes if attacked by the other, thus ensuring that there was no 'first mover advantage'. This policy became known as 'mutually assured deterrence' or MAD.

- Finally, we must also take into account the dynamics of rivalry. Is the rivalry continuous or a 'one-off' affair? If rivalry is continuous players *learn over time* that co-operation is preferable to outright rivalrous behaviour. Professional criminals have no problem with the prisoners' dilemma! Experience has taught them that silence is the best option. In the context of an oligopoly, firms change prices, alter product lines, determine advertising strategies, continuously. Thus many firms learn over time that aggressive behaviour leads to *'tit for tat' reactions* from rivals that cancel out any short-term gains. Thus a price reduction does not benefit a firm for very long as the rival responds with its price cut, with the result that both firms are worse off. Firms soon learn to 'accommodate' rivals and attempt to seek optimal solutions. These sorts of game are referred to as *repeated games*.

Sequential games

Most of the games examined so far have focused on rivals acting simultaneously. But, as in the case of a tit for tat game, there are games that follow a sequence. One firm may decide to increase its advertising budget and the rival has to decide how best to react. Choices facing a firm can then be mapped in the form of decision trees. Consider the following example.

Assume two toothpaste manufacturers are considering a new product launch. They have a choice of launching one of two products. One product's focus is on its decay prevention properties, while the other is on its taste. We also assume that the decay prevention paste is more popular with the consumers. Figure 4.8 illustrates the outcome if both firms move *simultaneously*, ignorant of what their rival is planning. Once again A's payoff is first and B's is second.

Firm A's strategy	Firm B's strategy	
	Tasty	Decay prevention
Tasty	(–5, –5)	(+10, +20)
Decay prevention	(+20, +10)	(–5, –5)

Figure 4.8 The toothpaste game

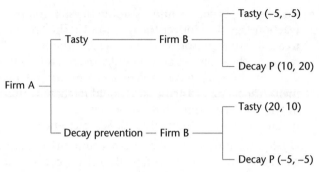

Figure 4.9 The toothpaste game as a sequential game

In this case, if both were to launch the toothpaste simultaneously, both would probably opt for the decay prevention variety. This would result in a loss for both firms. If, however, we consider a sequential game, where firm A is the first to launch the new product, a different outcome results. A realises that whatever product it launches the rational response of B is to launch the alternative. It therefore decides to launch the decay prevention paste knowing that B will react by selecting the 'tasty' paste. A will gain 20 and B will gain 10. This outcome can be illustrated with the use of a decision tree in Figure 4.9.

In Figure 4.9 the outcomes of the strategies are shown at the end of each branch. For firm A the best outcome would be to win 20. To achieve this outcome firm A launches the decay prevention paste, knowing that firm B will produce the 'tasty' paste. Clearly firm A has the benefit of 'first mover advantage'.

Game theory has undoubtedly added to the analytical toolkit of the micro-economist and the industrial economist. Nonetheless, there are two general criticisms. First, the games suggest that firms should always assume the most pessimistic of reactions from their rivals and thus follow a *minimax* (or *maximin*) strategy. There may be instances where such behaviour is not seen in oligopolistic markets, and to pursue a minimax strategy while a rival does not would imply lost profits. Second, the games do not generate unique solutions, since strategic decisions and outcomes are dependent on sociological and psychological as well as economic variables. The analyses develop a better understanding of oligopolistic behaviour but are weak at predicting that behaviour.

4.6   Conclusion

It is clear from the discussion in this chapter that oligopoly theory is inconclusive. We have no clear and unambiguous solutions to the central issue of interdependence. Firms and individuals react in many different ways and this is reflected by the great number of models that occupy the analysis of oligopolistic markets. Each one of the models we have covered, and indeed many others, reveals but a small part of wide-ranging oligopoly behaviour and we are as yet far from developing a general theory of oligopoly. It is important to remember that a proper analysis of such structures must recognise the role of rivals and that firms are *dependent* on these rivals.

Discussion Questions

1 Discuss the factors that affect the level of interdependency felt by firms in oligopolistic markets.

2 Identify the major characteristics of industries prone to collusion. Give examples of industries which might therefore be candidates for collusive behaviour.

3 Why is it necessary to police cartel agreements?

4 Discuss the difference between collusion which is covert and collusion which takes place openly, as in the case of OPEC.

5 Repeated games suggest that rivals are more likely to co-operate than to compete. Can you think of situations where firms are likely to compete in repeated games?

Further Reading

General background

Parkin, M., Powell, M. and Matthews, K. (2003) *Economics* (5th edn). Harlow: Addison Wesley, Chapter 13.

Sloman, S. (2000) *Economics* (4th edn). Harlow: Prentice Hall, Chapter 7.

Advanced

Asch, P. and Seneca, J. (1975) Characteristics of collusive firms, *Journal of Industrial Economics*, 23, 223–37.

Asch, P. and Seneca, J. (1976) Is collusion profitable?, *The Review of Economics and Statistics*, 58, 1–10.

Carlton, D. W. and Perloff, J. M. (1999) *Modern Industrial Organisation*. Harlow: Addison Wesley, Chapter 5.

Lipczynski, J. and Wilson, J. (2001) *Industrial Organisation*. Harlow: FT/Prentice Hall, Chapters 2 and 3.

Machlup, F. (1952) *The Economics of Sellers' Competition*. Baltimore: Johns Hopkins University Press.

Shepherd, W. G. (1997) *The Economics of Industrial Organization* (4th edn). London: Prentice Hall, Chapter 11.

Stigler, G. J. (1978) The literature of economics: the case of the kinked oligopoly demand curve, *Economic Inquiry*, 16, 185–204. Reprinted in Wagner, L. (ed.) (1981) *Readings in Applied Microeconomics*. Oxford: Oxford University Press.

5   Approaches to Competitive Market Analysis

Objectives

By the end of this chapter, the reader should be able to understand:

- and analyse the structure conduct performance paradigm
- the difference between static and dynamic views of competition
- the contribution of the managerial approach to competitive analysis
- and discuss strategic groups in various industries.

Key Concepts

- Austrian School
- Chicago School
- contestable market
- distinctive capabilities
- five forces model

- organisational ecology
- strategic groups
- structure conduct performance paradigm
- transaction costs

5.1   Introduction

Competitive market analysis normally involves some reference to the number and size distributions of firms, the types of product produced, the extent to which established firms control prices, the ease with which firms can enter or exit markets, and the ease with which information flows between firms and consumers and the resulting conditions facing both of these groups. This chapter provides an overview of the empirical approaches to competition analysis, drawing primarily on the microeconomic theories outlined in Chapters 3 and 4. We introduce contributions from industrial organisation, sociology and strategic management. We adopt a selective approach to examine some of the approaches that have helped illuminate our understanding of the ways in which firms and industries behave and perform. An analysis of these issues gives managers, researchers and policymakers useful information as to how buyers and sellers behave in a particular market and the implications of this for profitability and efficiency of firms and the quality and availability of products and services to consumers. The rest of this chapter is structured as follows. In section 5.2, we examine the structure conduct performance paradigm. This approach has formed the basis of an empirical understanding of the relationship between market structure, firm behaviour and firm performance. Section 5.3 discusses alternative approaches to competition analysis. Section 5.4 examines empirical evidence to assess whether any observed abnormal profits in certain industries are the result of established firms colluding to raise industry prices or merely reflect efficiency differences across firms. This section also introduces the intermediate concept of *strategic groups*, which is an approach that argues that variables specific to groupings of firms within industries can explain variations in performance. Finally, section 5.5 draws together the various approaches to competition analysis.

5.2   The Structure Conduct Performance Paradigm

The seminal writers in the field of industrial organisation were Edward Mason (1949) and Joe Bain (1959), who developed a framework for analysing the competitive conditions in industries. This framework became known as the *structure conduct performance (SCP) paradigm*. As the name suggests, the SCP approach examines how the structure of industry relates to the behaviour and performance of firms.

The structure conduct performance approach has the following uses:

- It allows industry data to be subdivided into meaningful components.
- It is grounded in the microeconomic theories of market structure (discussed in Chapters 3 and 4), which imply that there should be a relationship between industry structure, conduct and performance.
- It suggests a role for government intervention in industry. For example, regulation can be used, if necessary, to increase competition.

An overview of the SCP approach is reproduced schematically in Figure 5.1,which we now discuss.

Demand and supply conditions

The conditions of supply and demand (analysed in Chapter 1) in any industry will define the structure of that industry. Supply conditions include the availability and cost of raw materials and the state of technology. Demand conditions include the market size and methods of procurement.

We will now examine the factors that constitute the division of industry data into structural, conduct and performance variables. The basic supply and demand

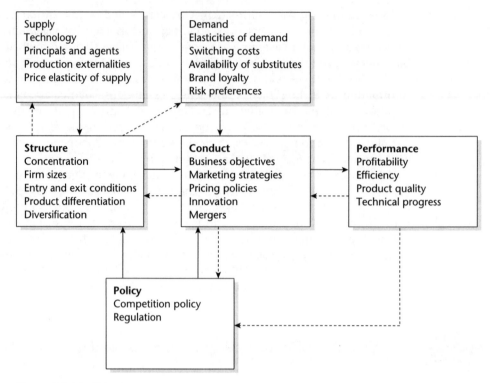

Figure 5.1 The SCP framework

conditions (outlined in Chapter 1 and earlier in this chapter) determine the industry structure, which in turn has fundamental effects on the conduct and performance of firms within any given industry.

Industry structure

Structural characteristics often change slowly and can be regarded as fixed over
time. Government policies can alter industry structure (for example, by introducing
or removing barriers to entry). We can identify the following as some of the more
important structural variables.

Concentration

This refers to the amount of market power held in the hands of a few firms and is
normally measured by the share of total industry sales, assets or employment controlled by the largest firms in the industry. (We discuss how to measure and interpret concentration in Chapter 6.)

Product differentiation

This refers to the nature of the product. To what extent is the product identical to
those produced by other firms; to what extent is it unique? If there is no product
differentiation, firms produce identical products and a market structure such as

perfect competition prevails. Any change in the nature of the product whether real or imagined will alter the elasticity of demand for an individual firm's product. This, in turn, will have implications for revenue and profitability of the established firms. (We examine the causes and consequences of product differentiation in Chapter 7.)

Size of firms

In Chapter 2, we discussed the importance of a firm's size, for efficiency. Essentially, the larger the firm, the more likely it will be able to benefit from economies of scale and scope, which ultimately feed through to lower costs and higher profits. However, firm size may also grant an individual firm market power, which can be used to charge customers high prices, ultimately leading to higher profits. Overall, we would normally expect a positive relationship between firm size and profitability. However, it is by no means clear whether the relationship is a consequence of lower costs or of large firms exercising market power by charging consumers higher prices. As we see in Chapter 11, this poses policymakers with a formidable challenge when formulating measures to ensure competition in any given industry.

Entry and exit conditions

In Chapter 3, we saw that the extent to which barriers to entry and exit exist determines both the short-run and long-run equilibrium conditions in any given industry. Entry and exit conditions determine the ease with which new firms can enter or existing firms can leave the industry. If entry is difficult, established firms are sheltered from outside competition and are likely to be able to raise prices to make abnormal profits, even in the long run. (We examine the causes and consequences of barriers to entry and exit in Chapter 6.)

Vertical integration and diversification

Vertical integration describes the extent to which firms are involved in one or more stages of the production process. For example, a firm may not only manufacture a product, but also be involved in the retailing and distribution of that product. Alternatively, a firm may source its own raw material inputs to supply its manufacturing division. Consequently, vertically integrated firms have greater certainty in obtaining supplies of raw materials and are more likely to have guaranteed distribution outlets for their manufactured products. (An in-depth discussion of vertical integration as a business strategy is provided in Chapter 9.)

Diversification describes the extent to which the firm produces a range of products across geographic or product space. In other words, a firm may produce and sell a similar product across different regions or countries or numerous products across the same geographic market. Diversified firms are less exposed to risk than their non-diversified counterparts. This is because any losses incurred in one market can be recouped by profits made in another.

Firm conduct

Conduct refers to the behaviour (or strategy) of firms under a given set of circumstances, normally determined by the structural characteristics of industry. The structural characteristics outlined earlier determine firm objectives, which in turn feed through to firms' price and non-price decisions. We examine firm conduct with respect to business objectives, price and non-price strategies next.

Business objectives

The objectives which firms follow often flow from the inherent structural characteristics of their industry. Objectives may include the pursuit of profit, growth, sales maximisation or the utilisation of managerial discretion to pursue non-financial objectives. The overall business objective of a given firm is likely to determine how the firm behaves when formulating price and non-price strategies. For example, although included under the structural heading (given earlier), firms may also wish actively to pursue strategies of vertical integration and diversification. (We examine vertical integration and diversification in more detail in Chapters 9 and 10.)

Price strategies

The extent to which firms follow a given price strategy may also flow from industry structure. As we saw in Chapter 3, under perfect competition firms price products at competitive levels (i.e. where prices equal marginal costs), while under monopoly, prices exceed marginal costs. Firms can pursue many types of pricing strategies such as entry-deterring price, collusive pricing, price leadership and price discrimination. (Case Study 3.2 provides a brief discussion of these issues.)

Non-price strategies

Such strategies may include product differentiation or expenditures on research and development.

Product differentiation

This can occur by changing the physical attributes of a product or service. Alternatively, differentiation can take place in a psychological sense, whereby consumers *believe* that similar products are somehow different.

Research and development

Expenditures on research and development activities can lead to technical advances as new products and processes are introduced. Firms may undertake basic, applied research and development work in order to produce innovative commercial products and processes, which will give them advantages over rivals. The diffusion of these new products and processes will ultimately determine the performance and growth of industries and countries.

(We discuss product differentiation and research and development in Chapters 7 and 8.)

Performance

When assessing the implications of performance for competition, one can focus on a number of variables such as profits, cost efficiency, quality of products and technical progress relating to production and distribution processes. The most popular measure of performance has been profitability.

Economists have opted for various profitability measures, many of which utilise accounting data to proxy for economic profitability (see Chapter 3). These measures have proved popular as data is readily available from the annual reports of firms. Profits are normally expressed as a return on assets, shareholder equity or sales. By comparing any observed profits with that of the relevant (industry) peer group, researchers and government policymakers can assess whether firms are making normal or supernormal levels of profitability.

As we will see later, however, it is often not clear why firms earn high levels of profits. The traditional SCP approach argues that superior profitability may result from established firms pursuing anticompetitive practices aimed at distorting or eliminating competition. However, later work contends that high profits are just as likely to arise from efficiency advantages held by established firms or returns (appropriated) from innovatory behaviour.

Overall, the SCP approach attempts to explain and predict the performance of an industry as a consequence of market structure. The emphasis is therefore on the structure of industry and how it influences conduct and performance. The solid arrows in Figure 5.1 show this. The approach assumes that the smaller the number of firms in an industry, the greater the likelihood of the abuse of market power (through collusive activities or the exercise of monopoly power) and the greater the profitability of these established firms. However, conduct and performance itself can influence the future structure of an industry. For example, a firm can reinvest profits in research and development activity to produce new products and processes, thus affecting cost and demand conditions of the industry. The dashed arrows show feedback effects of performance and firm behaviour on industry structure.

As we stated earlier, the SCP approach acknowledges the role of government intervention in industries where competition does not prevail. If competition is limited or absent, there may be a fall in product quality, lack of choice for consumers and an increase in prices charged. Consequently, policymakers have been interested in pursuing policies aimed at promoting competition. In the UK, along with most developed countries, governments have introduced successive pieces of legislation aimed at promoting competition by pursuing policies aimed at altering the structure of industries and the behaviour of firms in these industries (shown by solid arrows). Strict regulation of prices and rates of return often accompany this type of policy for firms operating in industries that can be regarded as natural monopolies. It is possible, however, that large firms can use their influence to alter government policy toward industry (shown by dashed arrows). (We examine competition policy and regulation in Chapter 11.)

Although it is a useful approach to understanding how competition can be analysed, the SCP approach is not without difficulties. We now briefly examine some of these difficulties before assessing subsequent contributions to competition analysis.

A critique of the structure conduct performance paradigm

- The SCP approach draws on theories of market structure (discussed in Chapters 3 and 4). These theories can be adapted to examine the behaviour of firms and industries. However, these theories do not always give us exact relationships between structure, conduct and performance.

- Structure can be measured by a multitude of indicators. Unfortunately, many economists tend to measure structure by concentration. This is primarily because data is easy to find in government statistics. As a consequence, there is a danger of overemphasising the importance of concentration. (We revisit this problem briefly in Chapter 6.)

- The SCP approach has been criticised for providing a 'snapshot' of competitive conditions. The approach does little to explain how the industry has evolved into its current state and what, if any, the future changes of industry structure and firm behaviour are likely to be.

- It is often difficult to decide which variables belong to structure, which to conduct and which to performance. For example, the extent of advertising, vertical integration and diversification gives useful information as to the structure of an industry.

  However, these are also strategies which firms can choose to follow to gain a competitive advantage over rivals.

- There are difficulties in measuring many of the variables. For example, how would one measure profitability? How does one measure entry barriers and the rate of entry? How do we measure the extent of vertical integration?

- What exactly do we mean by performance? Performance is some measure of the degree of success in achieving desired goals. Is it possible to have a set of uniform performance indicators? Differences in firm objectives may make the links between firm behaviour and performance difficult to assess. For example, if firms are sacrificing potential profits in order to reduce risk by investing in more certain activities, then researchers should be more interested in variability in profit rates and not profits levels per se. Alternatively (as we saw in Case Study 3.1), if managers are maximising their own satisfaction through excess expenditures, then it is no longer clear that large firms will necessarily make abnormal returns. In other words, firms insulated from competitive pressure may choose a 'quiet life' and no longer strive for greater efficiency and higher profits.

Despite its critics, the SCP approach is one of the most popular and enduring approaches to analysing competitive markets. Case Study 5.1 provides an application of the approach to the European banking industry.

Case Study 5.1

Structure, conduct and performance in the European banking industry

European banking has experienced competitive change over the last decade. Government deregulation has increased competition and allowed banks to compete not only in domestic but also in other European markets. The extent of diversification has increased, which has caused the distinction between banks, building societies and insurance companies to become blurred. There has been entry of foreign banks into many European countries, leading to intensified competition.

Structure
The number of banks has declined in many European markets in recent years. The trend is apparent across different types of banks, including the mutual

Number of banks by country, 1989–1997

Country	1989	1992	1994	1996	1997
Austria	1240	1104	1053	1019	995
Belgium	157	157	147	141	134
Denmark	233	210	202	197	197
Finland	552	365	356	350	350
France	418	617	607	570	519
Germany	4089	4200	3872	3674	3578
Italy	1127	1073	1002	937	935
Netherlands	1058	921	744	658	628
Norway	179	158	153	153	154
Portugal	29	35	44	51	62
Spain	333	319	316	313	307
Sweden	144	119	125	124	120
Switzerland	631	569	494	403	398
UK	551	518	486	478	466

Source: Central Bank reports (various).

savings and co-operative banks as well as the domestic commercial banks. However, there is still a large number of banks operating in Europe as illustrated in the table above. All countries (apart from Portugal) experienced a decline in the number of banks since 1989. What the table does not reveal, however, is that the number of foreign banks has increased in every banking market over the same period. Foreign banks constitute a significant proportion of banking activity in the UK (254 foreign banks with a 57% assets share in 1998); Belgium (eight banks with 48% of banking sector assets); France (280 banks with around 15% of banking sector assets); and Portugal (16 banks with 35% of banking sector assets). In all other European countries (except Luxembourg, of course), foreign banks generally account for less than 10% of total banking sector assets.

The widespread decline during the 1990s in the number of banks operating in Europe was matched by a similar trend in branch numbers. For example, in many of the larger banking sectors (Germany, Italy and Spain) branch numbers proliferated during the 1990s. This, in part, reflects an increase in non-price competition, but is also a consequence of deregulatory measures taken by the respective governments. Taken together, the declining number of banks and the increasing numbers of branches suggest that concentration is increasing. In many countries the combined market share of the top five banks now exceeds 60%. However, these banks do face intense competition from domestic and foreign counterparts.

Conduct

In response to these pressures, banks have attempted to adopt strategies aimed at improving efficiency, in order to expand output and increase the range of services offered. The trend towards consolidation through merger and acquisition activity can be interpreted as a response of this kind. Recent domestic activity includes the merger of Bank of Scotland and the Halifax Bank and the

Royal Bank of Scotland's acquisition of NatWest Bank. Cross-border activity includes the Dutch bank ING's acquisition of the Belgium Banque Bruxelles Lambert and the merger between Finland's Merita and Nordbanken from Sweden. Many banks have also pursued strategies of diversification and financial innovation. The outcome is that banks now offer a wider range of products and services to their customers.

Performance

The performance of European banks can been examined with reference to efficiency (i.e. the extent to which banks can minimise costs relative to their overall income). The only banking sectors which have systematically improved their efficiency levels between 1992 and 1997 are Finland, Sweden, Switzerland and the UK. Most of these improvements have come from aggressive cost-cutting strategies, including branch closures and manpower reductions.

In terms of profitability (measured by return on equity), returns improved between 1994 and 1997. Given that there is no obvious downward trend in bank performance across all countries, some would argue that this is clear evidence that competition has not increased. However, others would argue that increased profits are a direct consequence of increased efficiency and earnings from a wider variety of sources (such as insurance, consultancy and pensions). Improvements in technology (including greater use of consumer databases and call centres) mean that banks can now offer a wide variety of products at lower cost than was previously the case.

Overall, the level of competition, both between banks and between banks and other financial sector institutions, continues to intensify relentlessly. Deregulation and technological change have lowered entry barriers and made banking more competitive. The structure, conduct and performance of European banks are likely to experience marked change.

Return on equity, 1989–1997 (%)

Country	1989	1992	1994	1996	1997
Austria	10.0	6.9	7.9	9.4	5.1
Belgium	6.0	6.4	8.8	20.3	14.8
Denmark	3.0	−18.3	−0.9	16.4	11.8
Finland	1.0	19.5	25.7	11.9	19.8
France	9.4	4.3	−1.4	5.8	8.5
Germany	12.4	13.2	11.9	11.9	15.8
Italy	14.0	9.8	4.4	6.8	5.7
Netherlands	13.6	12.8	14.1	13.7	4.2
Norway	5.5	−5.8	19.3	18.0	10.1
Portugal	9.2	8.5	6.1	9.3	11.3
Spain	14.6	10.6	8.2	14.6	14.5
Sweden	5.9	18.5	19.1	23.9	8.7
Switzerland	—	8.2	7.8	9.6	9.8
UK	3.4	10.7	19.6	21.0	25.9

Source: Central Bank reports (various).

Alternative Approaches to Competitive Analysis

There are a number of alternative approaches to competitive analysis. The main ones are the Austrian, Schumpeterian and Chicago schools of thought. There have also more recently been useful contributions from the fields of strategic management and organisational ecology.

Dynamic perspectives

Austrian and Schumpeterian views

In contrast to the static SCP approach, and other models of market structure outlined in Chapters 3 and 4, the Austrian and Schumpeterian approaches view competition as a *dynamic process*.[1] They believe that competition could not be analysed using the static approaches outlined in Chapters 3 and 4. Their concern is with the roles of the entrepreneur and knowledge in a dynamic system.

Schumpeter (1950) saw the competitive process as being driven by non-price competition (i.e. innovation) and strategic decisions emanating from entrepreneurs. This innovative activity leads to a revolution in existing economic conditions by destroying old production techniques and creating new ones. Entrepreneurs introducing new innovations, which create monopoly profits, drive this process of 'creative destruction'. These monopoly profits encourage entrepreneurs in other related industries to innovate as well. Recent examples of such a competitive process can be found in the computing industry with developments in operating systems and communications with the advent of mobile telephones and digital television. The clusters of innovations have the effect of propelling the economy toward a higher state. However, following a brief 'catching up' period, imitators start to flood the market with similar innovations. This has the effect of undermining any monopoly profits, eventually bringing the economy to a new period of relative tranquillity. Abnormal profits are both the reward for past innovation and the incentive for future innovative activity. The source of any monopoly profits is the superior productivity achieved by the entrepreneurial innovation. These profits do not persist due to imitation, but eventually dissipate before a new cluster of innovations appears and the process begins again. Therefore, there is no role for government intervention to ensure a competitive (outcome) environment.

The Austrian School also views competition as a dynamic process. Entrepreneurs play a crucial role by noticing missed opportunities. They discover new pieces of information, which they spread to other decision makers who can adjust their plans in order to improve on past performance.

The Austrian and Schumpeterian views of competition are closer to everyday usage in society (i.e. it conjures up a picture of individuals battling against each other using entrepreneurial skills in an attempt to obtain larger profits). As we have already seen, in standard economic theory, any firm which has market power and can obtain supernormal profits is regarded as monopolistic in nature.

---

[1] The term Austrian School is derived from a group of economists emanating from Austria, including von Mises and von Hayek.

Chicago School

The Chicago School approach in common with the Austrian School is generally against government intervention in the market place to promote competitive outcomes. Any firms earning high profits do so as a consequence of superior efficiency over rivals. Their approach is that the best thing government can do is allow market forces to bring about desirable performance outcomes. For example, there is no point in having laws against collusive agreements, as these agreements are inherently unstable, as discussed in Chapter 4. This means that industries tend toward *competition* and not *collusion*.

Contestable markets

The theory of *contestable markets* emphasises potential rather than actual competition and so to some extent moves away from the notion that structure is directly related to performance. Contestable markets are those in which competitive pressures from potential entrants act as strong constraints on the behaviour of established firms. For a market to be truly contestable there must be no significant entry barriers. This is the case whether the market consists of a single supplier or of large numbers of firms, because it is the *potential* rather than *actual* competition that constrains the behaviour of the established firms. If potential entrants (competitors) have access to the same technology as established firms and investment costs are not irreversible (sunk), the market is said to be perfectly contestable. The theory introduces the idea of 'hit and run' (competition) entry based on three assumptions:

- A potential entrant can identify a market which will purchase its output at or below the current market price.
- The entrant has enough time to sell to this market before the established firm has time to react.
- At the prices quoted, the entrant earns enough revenue to cover all costs (fixed and variable) and then exits again before established firms can react. The theory of contestable markets does not take into account all possible reactions of the established firms. To deter hit and run entry, the incumbent firm may threaten any potential entrant with a price war.

Overall, in contestable markets it is the *perceived threat* of competition (which is independent of industry structure) and not actual competition which determines the strategies that firms follow.

Managerial approach

The separation of ownership from control in the modern organisation (i.e. where shareholders own, but managers control) enables managers to pursue objectives other than profit maximisation. Such objectives include growth, size and, through sales revenue, maximisation and managerial utility.[2] This is not to say that profit is

---

[2] A discussion of myriad alternative theories of firm behaviour is outwith the scope of this text. An excellent discussion can be found in Davies and Lam (2001), Chapter 2. Case Study 3.1 provides an overview of the main arguments.

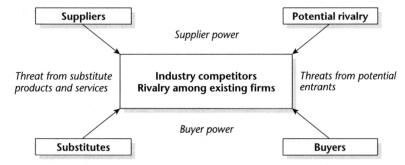

Figure 5.2 Drivers of competition
Source: Adapted from Porter (1980), page 4.

unimportant, but suggests that managers perhaps only pursue a level of profits satisfactory enough to meet owners' expectations rather than attempt to maximise profits per se.

A number of these concepts developed in economics have been used recently in the discipline of strategic management. An example is Porter (1980, 1985), who builds on formal models of competitive structure to develop his 'five forces' approach to analysing industry 'attractiveness'. These *five forces* are:

1 extent and intensity of competition
2 threat of entrants (new competitors)
3 threat of substitute products and services
4 power of customers
5 power of suppliers.

The approach is reproduced schematically in Figure 5.2 and is discussed now.

Extent and intensity of competition

The intensity of rivalry among existing firms depends on the number and respective sizes of firms operating in a given market. If there are large numbers of equal-sized firms, competition is likely to be more intense than if one or a few large firms dominate. Other relevant factors determining the extent of rivalry include the rate at which the industry is growing, the costs of established firms and the extent to which they have the capacity to respond to meet current demand. (We examine many of these factors in more detail in Chapter 6.)

Threat of entrants

The threats of entry often cause established firms to behave differently from firms operating in industries which are effectively sheltered from competition. The perceived threat of entry is likely to be much higher in cases where established firms are making excess profits. However, if established firms can raise entry barriers, then these entry threats are likely to diminish. Government regulation also plays an important role in determining the ease with which new firms can enter an industry. The extent to which entry poses a real threat to established firms depends on the importance of economies of scale, the extent to which products are differentiated and brand loyalty exists, the level and specificity of capital investments and the availability of access to distribution outlets. (We examine the importance of many of the legal and structural barriers to entry in Chapter 6.)

Threat of substitute products and services

The threat of substitute products and services will influence the intensity of rivalry. As we identified in Chapter 2, if substitute products exist, the price elasticity of demand for existing products is likely to increase, thus reducing the market power of established firms. Of course, established firms may choose to pursue strategies aimed at actively differentiating their products from rivals and gain market share and consumer loyalty in the process. The extent to which substitute products are successful in capturing market share from established firms depends in part on the extent to which they are of a superior quality to that of existing products and the level of costs incurred by consumers if they were to switch to alternative products (switching costs). Product innovation or low cost alternatives often mean that established products become obsolete. As we saw earlier in this chapter, the Schumpeterian and Austrian approaches view these issues as the primary drivers of competition and subsequent firm performance.

Power of customers

The power of customers depends on the degree to which they are dependent on the outputs of the established firms. If there are only a few large customers for an existing product or if substitutes exist (in the case of relatively undifferentiated products), then customers are likely to wield substantial power. In order to obtain favourable terms, large customers may threaten to internalise the buying function by integrating backwards (toward the source of their raw material inputs). In other words, customers may expand their production capabilities by adding a raw materials division, consequently reducing reliance on external suppliers. (We examine these issues further in Chapter 9.)

Power of suppliers

If large in size and small in number, suppliers of important inputs to a firm's production function can exercise power by raising the price, reducing the quality or even threatening to withhold certain key inputs.

It is these five forces which capture the extent of competition prevailing in a particular industry at a given moment in time. Porter argued that firms develop strategies in the light of the existence and strength of such forces. However, the approach is static and thus ignores the uncertainty associated with frequent changes in the competitive environment.

In contrast to economists, management strategists have emphasised the distinct internal features of firms to explain how competitive advantage can be gained and sustained. Porter argued that competitive advantage is the value a firm is able to create *in excess of costs*. He introduces the concept of the *value chain*, which disaggregates a firm into its strategically relevant activities, i.e. those that reduce costs or are potential sources of differentiation. The activities of the firm can be split into primary and support activities. Primary activities are those which are associated with the physical creation of the product or service. Support activities are those activities which support the primary activities and each other, for example by providing purchased inputs, technology and human resources. Once the firm's value activities have been disaggregated, the process of appraising these activities can take place. Each of the support activities is linked to each of the primary activities to a greater or lesser extent. The analysis attempts to examine how these links can be improved in order to increase the margin on each product in each of the markets the firm is operating in.

Porter argues that a firm must select and follow a generic strategy to add value and gain a competitive advantage over competitors. These generic strategies are: cost leadership, differentiation and focus.

Cost leadership

This is a strategy whereby the firm attempts to keep its costs lower than those of the competition. To do this the firm must identify cost savings at some point in its value chain and produce at lower levels of cost or, alternatively, change the structure of the value chain. For example, the firm may be able to gain this advantage by an exclusive deal with suppliers for raw materials.

Differentiation

This is a strategy whereby the firm gives its product some unique product characteristic which appeals to its customers. This leads to increasing margins and profits relative to competitors.

Focus

This is a strategy which can apply to cost leadership and differentiation. In both cases the strategy involves the firm focusing on a particular segment of the market. In the case of differentiation, this may involve identifying a particular group of customers and gearing the firm's product towards them. Under this approach, firms following generic strategies are most likely to add value and gain a competitive advantage over competitors.

Kay (1993) argues that firms are inherently different and thus dismisses the notion of generic strategies. He instead argues that firms can draw on what he terms '*distinctive capabilities*' in order to achieve competitive advantage over competitors.

What are distinctive capabilities?

There are three areas where a firm's distinctive capabilities may yield a competitive advantage. These are: innovation, architecture and reputation.

Innovation

If a firm is innovative it may obtain an advantage over competitors. However, this advantage only lasts for the length of time it takes for imitation to be effective. Innovation is particularly open to imitation. Even patents lapse or are vulnerable to new technology. Innovation advantages can only be maintained if the firm has other capabilities which make imitation of the technology on its own insufficient to erode the established firm's competitive advantage. We examine many of these issues in Chapter 8.

Architecture

Architecture refers to the firm's internal organisation. For example, the famous bootroom ensured long periods of success for Liverpool Football Club in the 1960s to the 1980s. However, if the market changes, these types of advantage can be eliminated by rivals (Kay, 1993).

Reputation

If a firm has a reputation for providing good quality and service, it will help add value and generate more sales. Reputation can be sustainable over long periods, making it difficult for entrants to compete on equal terms with a reputable incumbent.

Overall, the managerial approach argues that the strategic decisions made by firms affect their performance. Firms only obtain an advantage over competitors if they can protect their strategies against imitation. The ease with which firms can imitate one another is affected by institutional and economic factors. For example, institutional factors which may prevent imitation include the imposition of restrictive employment contracts which prevent individuals from using any firm-specific knowledge if they were to move to a rival firm. The 'corporate culture' of an organisation can yield advantages over competitors. For example, an organisation which gives long-term contracts to employees may be able to obtain a greater degree of commitment from its workforce, which enables it to work more effectively. Corporate culture is particularly difficult for other firms to imitate. Economic factors affecting the speed at which imitation takes place include the expected profits and the associated risks of pursuing a given strategy. Imitation is more likely to take place at a faster rate if the expected profits from imitating such a strategy are large. However, if there are high risks associated with adopting such a strategy, imitation takes place at a slower rate.

Although the managerial approach provides important insights into how firms can obtain and sustain competitive advantages over rivals, these insights have been neglected in much of the industrial organisation literature, especially in empirical studies. This is partly due to difficulties in measuring many of the variables used in the managerial literature to explain competitive advantages. However, a more fundamental disadvantage of the managerial approach is that it does not place enough emphasis on interactions between firms. In the managerial literature, the focus is mainly on the strategic options available to the individual firm. The literature does not consider the ways in which, having chosen their options, firms interact with one another at the level of the market in order to determine outcomes such as price and profitability. Since competitive market analysis is the primary concern of our text we tend to employ an approach which is implicitly based on the behavioural assumptions of the textbook models of competition outlined in Chapters 3 and 4.

Transaction cost analysis

In this text, the main focus is on how firms behave within a given competitive environment. We tend to view firms as units which use factors of production to produce goods and services.

Why do we have firms in the first place?

Any transaction, whether between two firms, two individuals or an individual and a firm, can either be conducted through exchange in the marketplace (external co-ordination) or co-ordinated within firms (internal co-ordination).

Which method should we use and why?

An approach which helps us address these issues is transaction cost economics. *Transaction cost analysis* examines the relative merits (or efficiency) of trade between two or more parties when resources are allocated through either the market or the firm.

In contrast to many of the approaches we have outlined so far, this type of approach assumes that information is not perfect. In other words, trade does not take place in a world where all trading parties have access to all the available facts pertaining to a trade transaction. This means that any parties involved in a trade transaction cannot behave in a fully rational manner because they do not have access to all available information. Not only do these parties not have access to all available information but they also find it difficult to process all pieces of information that they do have access to. This means that there are bounds on rational behaviour (bounded rationality). Given that information is often one sided, opportunities are available for individuals to act in an opportunistic manner. They can do this by failing to disclose facts that would make the transaction more efficient.

Why is information so important?

The provision of this information plays a crucial role in the competitive process. Under conditions of perfect competition information is perfect. In other words, buyers and sellers have perfect knowledge of market conditions. As a consequence one price prevails, leading to all firms making normal levels of profits. However, if information is imperfect, there may be asymmetric information between producers and consumers. In many situations, the seller of a product has more information about the characteristics of the product for sale than the buyer. Consumers, therefore, do not have enough information to make an informed choice about the products and services they are buying. This will sometimes have implications for the quality and prices of products sold by firms to consumers.

When information is not perfect, there are costs of using the market to conduct transactions and allocate resources. These are known as *transaction costs*. These costs include the time spent collecting information about the prices and qualities of products and services under offer, drawing up detailed proposals and contracts for transactions and, ultimately, enforcing the contract in a court of law if need be.

When should we use firms?

In many types of market transaction, transaction costs are high. This means that it is more efficient to bring the transaction/activity within the bounds of a firm. Firms are likely to be more efficient methods of conducting trade when the transaction is complex and carried out frequently and involves the utilisation of a specific asset. By bringing these types of transaction within the firm, savings can be made through specialisation in production, leading to technical and learning economies of scale and scope.

However, this is not to say that firms do not incur extra costs by bringing transactions within the firm. In fact, many of the savings achieved by conducting trade using the firm rather than markets are offset by monitoring costs specific to the firm. In other words, firms have to monitor the behaviour and performance of employees and ensure that the quality of goods and services produced is to a given specification. Overall, transaction cost analysis allows us to understand why firms exist and the types of organisational structures they adopt. We will assess many of these arguments again in Chapter 9.

Organisational ecology

Another approach to how firms and markets evolve over time has become known as *organisational ecology*. This approach draws on concepts developed in ecology and other natural sciences to examine how organisations and industries evolve. In this case, we are interested in the birth and death processes of organisations and the subsequent development and decline of organisations within industries over time. To some extent, such an approach can be regarded as more sociological than economic, but it certainly does yield important insights into how the populations and types of organisation within industries evolve over time.

Under this approach the evolution of organisations can be separated into four stages, namely organisational birth, organisational growth, organisatonal decline and, ultimately, organisational death. Of course, many organisations do not necessarily pass through all these stages of development. In fact, many organisations often move directly from the birth stage to the death stage without enjoying any period of sustained growth or even slow decline.

The success or otherwise of organisations, and the length of time they spend at any given stage of development, is ultimately dependent on factors specific to individual organisations (including the quality of their inputs such as entrepreneurial talent or managerial expertise) and external factors (such as general economic conditions and the availability of scarce resources). We now look briefly at each of the four stages identified in this evolution.

Organisational birth

The extent to which new organisations are created depends to some extent on whether there is an untapped demand for a product or service. Often the birth rate can be rapid if there is a large previously unsatisfied demand for products. To some extent, the birth rate will continue to increase in a given industry as long as each successive birth enjoys some degree of success. Eventually, of course, any demand is satisfied and the birth rate of organisations declines. Generally, organisations born first can be regarded as having first mover advantages over organisations who are born later. Older firms will have had time to build a reputation through establishing brand identity and thus enjoy the loyalty of a certain portion of consumers. Later entrants have less chance of survival, partly as they have to overcome the advantages appropriated to the 'first movers' and partly because more organisations are competing for scarce (physical and financial) resources.

It might also be the case that established organisations (in an attempt to protect their first mover advantages) are following particular strategies aimed at actively preventing the successful start-up and growth of new organisations. In this first stage of an organisation's life (whether it is the first into an industry or a late newcomer), it is crucial that it adopts the appropriate strategy to ensure survival. Many organisations decide the best route to survival is to operate as a specialist organisation, thereby concentrating their resources in a particular segment of the industry within which they are located. Alternatively, organisations may decide to operate as multi-product organisations by spreading their resources across several geographic or product areas. Each industry will require a different set of key attributes to ensure long-term success. Those organisations which have or can develop such attributes will survive, while those which do not will die. Marshall (1961 [1890]: 317) eloquently described such a process by likening young organisations to young trees in a forest 'as they struggle upwards through the benumbing age of their old rivals. Many succumb on the way, and only a few survive.'

Organisational growth

If an organisation survives the birth stage, then it can move into the growth phase of its development. Here again, an organisation must decide on the most appropriate organisational form and competitive strategy to fuel growth. Growth is crucial to ensuring the continued success of an organisation. This is because growing organisations find it easier to raise finance from capital markets to aid further expansion.

This expansion make it easier for the organisation to attract and retain talented personnel and allows access to scale economies, which leads to increased efficiency. Organisations can ensure growth by utilising expanded resource bases to invest in research and development. If such investments are successful, further growth takes place. Furthermore, the organisation may often use the skills and resources appropriated over time to change its organisational structure and diversify into new product areas. By doing this, an organisation can reduce the risks associated with any single product or service. If changes in the organisation's structure or competitive strategy are successful, then the organisation gains increased 'legitimacy'.

Organisational decline

This phase of an organisation's life can be detected when growth and profits level off. This slowing and ultimate decline in an organisation's growth and profits is, in part, related to the demand for the organisation's products and services. As markets reach saturation point, or new innovative products are introduced by rivals, the organisation finds it increasingly difficult to hold on to its accumulated resources. This problem is compounded if the organisation suffers from diseconomies of scale associated with problems of managerial co-ordination between different departments and divisions within its organisational structure. Overall, the declining phase of an organisation's development is often associated with a loss of confidence on the part of investors, which makes any new access to finance difficult.

Organisational death

If an organisation fails to organise its scarce resources more effectively (by introducing new products and services or by rationalising existing managerial and production processes) to halt the decline in its performance, it faces bankruptcy or takeover (death).

Overall, organisational ecology yields insights for economists as to how the evolution of populations of firms affects the competitive structure of any given industry. (For a more detailed treatment of this approach, see Carroll and Hannan, 1999.)

5.4   Why Do Firms Earn High Profits?

An important question which has faced researchers has been whether high profits enjoyed by established firms are a consequence of the type of market structure and anti-competitive practices adopted by established firms or of superior production and management techniques (distinctive capabilities) that allow larger firms to keep costs low and make higher returns.

The SCP approach views competition as imperfect, requiring government regulation to check the abuse of market power. However, the Chicago School argues that government interference leads to less competition. Their approach argues that the best thing government can do in a market context is to allow market forces to bring about the desirable performance. For example, there is no point in having a law which prohibits collusive activities, as these activities are inherently unstable. Therefore, the Chicago School holds that monopoly power (with the exception of government-created monopolies) is temporary.

In the context of structure and profitability, two things could cause a positive relationship between concentration and profits.

Collusive behaviour and anticompetitive practices

The SCP approach implies that, as an industry becomes more concentrated, firms find it easier to collude and erect barriers to entry to earn excess profits. Alternatively, firms can use individual market power to charge high prices, consequently earning high profits. The SCP approach tends to use industry-level data to capture differences in market power and competitive conditions across industries.

Efficiency differences

The Chicago approach suggests that it may be that bigger firms are more efficient (due to economies of scale) than their smaller counterparts and make higher profits as a result. In this case, market structure affects profitability not through concentration, but by the association between market share and profitability. Alternatively, x-inefficiencies are likely to exist in industries composed mainly of large firms, as established firms are more likely to be insulated from competition. The Chicago view uses firm-level data to capture differences in efficiency and profits across firms. The sources of firm profitability are neatly summed up by Demsetz (1973: 3) when he argued:

> Profit does not arise because the firm creates artificial scarcity through a reduction in its output. Nor does it arise because of collusion. Superior performance can be attributed to the combination of great uncertainty plus luck or atypical insight by the management of the firm.

These opposing views formed the basis of a substantial empirical debate. A discussion of this is outside the scope of this book. However, suffice to say that early research tended to find that concentration and industry-level variables were important in determining performance, while later work stressed the importance of efficiency differences between firms.[3]

Strategic groups: an intermediate concept

Although most analysis of markets has focused on industry- or firm-level data, some work has focused on the intermediate concept of the strategic group. Strategic groups can be defined as a group of firms which follow similar behaviour. These firms tend to compete directly with other firms in the group. Firms within these strategic groups tend to recognise their interdependence and act accordingly. Here we briefly discuss the concept of the strategic group and highlight some of the key contributions in this area.

Strategic groups can be defined on the basis of similarities in market-related strategies, firm-specific factors and industry supply characteristics:

- Market-related strategies include similarities in product quality, pricing practices, extent of product differentiation, branding and advertising.

- Firm-specific factors include the extent of vertical integration and diversification, ownership structure and firm size.

- Industry supply characteristics include economies of scale and scope, production processes and distribution methods and networks.

If strategic groups exist in an industry, then we would expect more variation in profitability *between* groups than within.

Due to the differing characteristics of strategic groups, the extent of competition can differ. For example, many industries are often composed of firms that can be classified into strategic groups which produce either branded or generic products. The extent and type of competition within each group is thus likely to differ considerably. This is why some groups of firms can earn higher profits than others within the same industry. The extent of the profitability differences between different strategic groups depends on the following factors:

- *The number and size of groups.* This refers to whether strategic groups are numerous and similar in size. If this is the case, competition is likely to be more intense than if smaller strategic groups are attempting to compete with large groups.

- *The extent to which groups follow different strategies.* This refers to the extent to which groups differ on discretionary decisions such as research and development and promotional expenditures.

- *The extent to which groups are interdependent.* This refers to the extent to which different strategic groups are competing for the same customers or whether

---

[3] Students may wish to consult Schmalensee (1985), Nelson (1991), Rumelt (1991) and McGahan and Porter (1997) for an extended discussion of the relative importance of industry- and firm-specific factors in determining the profitability of individual firms.

some segmentation of the market takes place. This segmentation may arise naturally over time as industry evolves or groups may actively attempt to divide the market.

It is likely that strategic groups of firms do exist within most industries. However, finding reliable methods to identify such groups had proved difficult. (For a more detailed treatment, see Lewis and Thomas, 1990.)

5.5   Conclusion

This chapter has examined the application of approaches prevalent in industrial organisation and strategic management to competitive market analysis. Industrial organisation and strategic management examines various factors that may cause profits to vary across firms, industries, and groups within industries. Various approaches were examined including the structure conduct performance approach, the Chicago School and the theory of contestable markets. All these approaches allow us a snapshot of competition at a given moment in time. The Austrian and Schumpeterian schools take a more dynamic view and regard competition as a process, not as a succession of equilibria. Those adopting a more managerial approach argue that an analysis of the forces determining competition is crucial in the formulation of the strategies which firms follow. This approach places emphasis on the role of the internal structure of the firm in generating and sustaining a competitive advantage over rivals. We have also examined whether industry- or firm-specific factors determine the profits of industries and firms. Overall, the approaches outlined in this chapter provide us with a broad theoretical understanding, which can be used for specific structural, strategy or policy issues related to specific competitive markets.

Discussion Questions

1 Using the evidence presented in Case Study 5.1, what forces determine rivalry between established firms?

2 Why is the structure conduct performance paradigm so widely used in the study of firms and industries?

3 Compare the SCP approach to competition analysis with that advocated by the Austrian School.

4 How can we identify strategic groups?

Further Reading

General background

Cook, M. and Farquharson, C. (1998) *Business Economics*. London: Pitman, Chapters 14 and 15.

Ferguson, P. and Ferguson, P. (1994) *Industrial Economics*. London: Macmillan, Chapters 1 and 2.

Advanced

Kay, J. A. (1993) *Foundations of Corporate Success*. Oxford: Oxford University Press.

Porter, M. E. (1980) *Competitive Strategy: Techniques for Analysing Industries and Competitors*. New York: Free Press.

Rumelt, P. (1991) How much does industry matter?, *Strategic Management Journal*, 12, 167–86.

6 Practical Analysis of Industry

Objectives

By the end of this chapter, the reader should be able to understand:
- and discuss the differences between markets and industries
- official approaches to market and industry classification
- measures of concentration
- determinants of concentration
- and describe a typology of entry barriers
- entry deterrence based on pricing and non-price strategies
- use of game theory to examine an entry decision.

Key Concepts

- absolute cost advantages
- concentration
- economies of scale barriers
- industrial classification
- industry lifecycle

- law of proportionate effect
- legal barriers
- limit pricing
- predatory pricing
- product differentiation barriers

6.1 Introduction

In Chapters 3 and 4, we examined four types of market structure (perfect competition, monopolistic competition, oligopoly and monopoly). In Chapter 5, we focused on defining various elements of market structure. These elements included the extent of product differentiation and vertical integration, availability of economies of scale, barriers to entry and exit and industry concentration. The traditional approach to the analysis of market structure assumes that the smaller the number of firms operating in a market, the more likely it is that competition is to be restricted. This implies that market structure contributes to profitability in such markets. In this chapter, we focus on two of the most common indicators or measures of market structure, namely concentration and barriers to entry and exit. In the study of competitive market structures, market concentration and barriers to entry and exit have been common measures of structure used. This chapter aims to quantify and assess the nature of concentration and barriers to entry and exit.

The rest of the chapter is structured as follows. Section 6.2 discusses how markets and industries can be classified. Section 6.3 outlines various measures of concentration and examines the determinants of concentration. Section 6.4 outlines a typology of entry barriers. Section 6.5 examines various strategies that can be adopted by established firms actively to deter the entry of new firms. Section 6.6 provides a summary.

6.2   Classification of Industries

In an analysis of competitive markets, we frequently use the concepts of industry and market. Markets can be defined in terms of geographic and product areas that firms cover. In these markets, firms produce similar goods and services from the buyer's perspective. In this case, close substitutes exist on the demand side of the industry. Product markets should therefore include all products that are close substitutes of the product in question. However, we are still faced with the problem of what to include in this definition. For example, Coca-Cola would be included in the same market as Pepsi Cola. However, would other types of soft drink (such as squash, cordial, fresh fruit and glucose) belong in the same product market? Do we include other types of beverage such as tea, coffee, and alcoholic drinks in the market definition? Defining markets by geographic areas presents us with similar problems. Is the relevant geographic market defined at a local, regional, national or international level?

An industry is defined as a group of products which are close substitutes from the firm's perspective. If we were to take the previous example, all soft drinks can be grouped together in the same industry. This is because firms use similar raw materials, technology, labour skills and production processes to produce these products. As a rule of thumb, we would expect industries to be of a wider grouping than a market.

Consequently, when we define markets or indeed industries, we are mindful of the type of products produced and the extent of close substitutes. We must also account for the ways in which these products were produced and the types of inputs used to produce these outputs.

So how do we define markets (or the wider concept of the industry)?

Type of product produced

Much of the analysis of firm behaviour within any given industry structure relates to the pricing policies of firms. Consequently, when defining industries, we are often concerned with a definition of industry whereby products and services are grouped together which are either close substitutes or complements.

Consequently, we can use the cross-elasticity of demand formula (E_{xy}) which we examined in Chapter 1. As we saw previously, E_{xy} can be calculated as the percentage change in the quantity demanded of one good when the price of another good changes. This can be expressed as follows:

$$E_{xy} = \frac{\% \text{ change in quantity demanded of good x}}{\% \text{ change in price of good y}}$$

If we find a positive relationship between changes in the price of good y and the quantity demanded of good x, then this would indicate that the two products or services are close substitutes, and consequently should be grouped in the same industry (e.g. tea and coffee).

Type of production process used

The type of production process used to produce goods and services may provide an appropriate method with which to classify firms into a given industry. However, this may cause industries to be defined too widely. For example, if 'engineering' were defined as 'a process using lathes', this would classify car and bicycle manufacturers within the same industry.

Type of raw material input

The type of raw material may provide a useful basis for grouping firms into a particular industry. However, again there are potential pitfalls with this type of measure. For example, the approach would suggest that woollen gloves and leather gloves belong to different industries, while soap and margarine belong to the same one.

In reality, even these approaches are an obvious oversimplification. As we will see in Chapter 9, firms often sell in many different markets. Although there are inherent problems in trying to define markets and industries, some decisions as to appropriate definition must be taken. Consequently, official statistics have defined markets or industries in different ways depending on the type of economic analysis being conducted. The official classification of industries in the UK is referred to as the *Standard Industrial Classification* (SIC). This system was introduced in 1948 and updated in 1980 and 1992. In 1992 the European Union (EU) introduced a new industrial classification system that was to be used across the whole of the European Union. The aim was to standardise industry definitions across EU member states. This made inter-country comparisons easier. The 17 sections replaced the ten divisions that had been used under the 1980 classification method. These sections were identified by letters from A to Q. These are reproduced schematically in Table 6.1.

Table 6.1 The EU Standard Industrial Classification, 1992 (by division)

Section (SIC 1992)	Description
A	Agriculture, hunting and forestry
B	Fishing
C	Mining and quarrying
D	Manufacturing
E	Electricity, gas and water supply
F	Construction
G	Wholesale and retail trade; repair of motor vehicles and household goods
H	Hotels and restaurants
I	Transport, storage and communication
J	Financial intermediation
K	Real estate, renting and business activity
L	Public administration and defence, compulsory social security
M	Education
N	Health and social work
O	Other community, social and personal service activities
P	Private households with employed persons
Q	Extraterritorial organisations and bodies

One major difference between the 1980 and the 1992 classifications is a more detailed breakdown of the services industries in the 1992 version. The sections can be subdivided into subsections by the addition of another letter. Subsections are then broken down into two-digit 'divisions', three-digit 'groups', four-digit 'classes' and five-digit 'subclasses'. The more digits there are, the finer the definition of the industry. The classifications outlined provide useful definitions when carrying out competition analyses of particular industries.

6.3   Concentration

Most modern industries are composed of a large number of small firms, numerous medium-sized firms and a small number of large firms. If we were to plot the

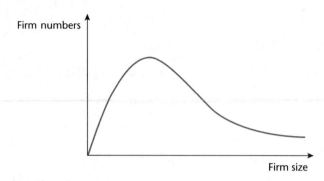

Figure 6.1 Distribution of firm sizes

number of firms against firm sizes in any given industry, we would be likely to observe a distribution which is positively skewed (as shown in Figure 6.1).

The curve shows that it is the small number of large firms which dominate the industries within which they are located. Table 6.2 shows the extent of this skew with reference to the numbers of firms by relative size in various UK industries in 2002. These are also the firms which have many articles written about them in the financial and business pages of academic and professional journals. The extent to which a few firms appear to dominate industries (whether defined along product lines or by geographic areas) poses an interesting puzzle to academics, managers and government policymakers. How much power or control do such firms have over the markets in which they are located? And, just as interestingly, why do markets tend to evolve in this manner in the first place? In this section of the chapter we are interested in quantifying the relative importance of firms within given markets and explaining how such markets have evolved over time.

How can we measure concentration?

Market structure can be characterised not only by the number of firms in the industry at a given moment in time, but also by how the sizes of these firms are distributed. For example, an industry consisting of 100 equal-sized firms will be very different from an industry with one large dominant firm and 99 smaller firms.

Concentration measures attempt to summarise the large amount of information on firm sizes and numbers by focusing on the distribution of firm sizes. Researchers and policymakers use various concentration measures to define industry structure. The extent to which industries are concentrated provides useful information about not only the structure of industry, but also on the interrelationships between the structure of an industry and the behaviour and performance of firms with that industry (see Chapter 5). We will now examine three commonly used measures of concentration: the concentration ratio, the Lorenz curve and the Herfindahl–Hirschman index.

The concentration ratio (CR)

The concentration ratio measures the size of the top firms in an industry as a proportion of the total industry size. The number of firms used in this calculation is

Table 6.2 Size distribution of UK enterprises, 2002

Sector	Turnover size (£ thousands)										
	1–49	50–99	100–249	250–499	500–999	1 000–1 999	2 000–4 999	5 000–9 999	10 000–49 999	50 000+	Total
Agriculture	67 340	29 465	29 145	10 215	4 230	1 545	600	175	110	10	142 840
Production: of which:	22 855	25 060	31 685	20 760	16 605	11 730	9 315	4 020	4 025	1 320	147 555
Mining and utilities	185	180	240	150	140	165	140	75	125	125	1 520
Manufacturing	22 665	24 875	31 625	20 610	16 465	11 565	9 180	3 950	3 900	1 195	146 035
Construction	31 845	20 815	45 550	20 560	12 905	6 890	4 180	1 295	990	210	175 235
Motor trades	7 685	14 000	17 410	9 500	6 925	4 415	3 560	1 360	1 180	225	66 265
Wholesale	16 595	15 320	21 775	14 390	13 085	10 110	8 480	3 590	3 080	740	107 165
Retail	18 965	44 550	67 095	33 490	16 915	6 815	2 910	770	620	265	192 390
Hotels and catering	4 490	31 260	47 080	16 005	5 725	2 305	1 085	310	245	75	108 580
Transport	11 580	16 355	12 395	6 290	4 770	3 290	2 555	890	820	285	59 235
Post and telecommunications	5 310	3 555	2 655	1 195	840	540	390	155	190	75	14 905
Finance	1 865	1 875	1 915	1 135	890	715	750	370	700	780	10 995
Property and business services	110 675	133 680	94 740	38 715	25 520	14 605	9 470	3 380	2 815	640	434 250
Education	2 280	2 525	1 870	790	625	390	385	200	340	90	9 495
Health	1 315	1 550	2 185	1 695	1 275	590	290	1 120	105	20	9 130
Public administration	38 920	41 090	33 940	13 105	7 055	3 385	2 065	770	640	185	141 160
Total	341 725	411 100	409 615	187 845	117 370	67 330	46 035	17 395	15 855	4 925	1 619 195

Source: Adapted from Office for National Statistics (2002), Table 2.

normally taken as three, four, five or eight. In practical terms it makes little difference as to the number of firms used. The formula used in this calculation is as follows:

$$CR_N = \sum_{i=1}^{N} s_i$$

In this formula, N denotes the number of firms used in the calculation, while s_i denotes the market share of an individual firm (i.e. firm i). For example, a three-firm concentration ratio (CR_3) measures the sum of the shares of the top three firms. When calculating the concentration ratio, firm size is measured by the number of employees, by firm turnover or by total assets. Table 6.3 calculates the measure for the top three, four and five firms using hypothetical industry data that comprises nine firms. In this example, firm size has been measured by sales. The concentration ratio is then calculated with reference to the total size of the industry and the market shares of firms located within the industry. Table 6.3 shows the concentration ratios based on the market shares of the top three, four and five firms. The values of these concentration ratios are 60%, 70% and 79% respectively. Obviously, the more firms we include, the higher the concentration ratio. Table 6.4 shows the concentration ratios for a number of UK industries.

Table 6.3 Calculation of the concentration ratio

Firm	Sales	Market share (s_i)
1	9000	22.5
2	9000	22.5
3	6000	15
4	4000	10
5	3600	9
6	2800	7
7	2800	7
8	2000	5
9	800	2
Total	40,000	100
$CR_3 = 60\%$	$CR_4 = 70\%$	$CR_5 = 79\%$

Table 6.4 Concentration ratios for selected industries in the UK

Industry	CR_5 (%)
Tobacco	99
Iron and steel	95
Motor vehicles and engines	83
Pharmaceuticals	51
Grain milling	63
Footwear	48
Brewing	38
Clothing	21
Printing and publishing	16

Source: Adapted from Office for National Statistics (1995).

Although the concentration ratio provides useful information on the structural characteristics of an industry, it only focuses on the top firms in the industry. Consequently, there is the potential for ignoring some important information by not taking account of the distribution of remaining firms. As a result of some of the difficulties associated with the concentration ratio, many researchers have adopted summary measures of concentration which take into account all firms.

Herfindahl–Hirschman index (H–H)

The Herfindahl–Hirschman index uses every point in the firm size distribution. It employs a weighting system to account for the relative importance (measured by size) of individual firms. This is done by squaring the market shares of each individual firm. As a result of summing the market shares of each individual firm, the larger firms receive higher weighting to reflect their relative importance in the industry. The higher the value of the index, the less likely a given industry is to exhibit competitive behaviour. In other words, market shares are concentrated in the hands of fewer firms. The formula used to calculate the index is:

$$H–H = \sum_{i=1}^{N} (s_i)^2$$

In this formula, N denotes the number of firms used in the calculation, while s_i denotes the market share of an individual firm. To help interpret the value of the H–H index, a variation known as the numbers equivalent can be used. This number equivalent measure is simply the inverse of the value of the H–H index. This variation provides the researcher with a rough approximation of the number of equal-sized firms which would generate a given value of the index. The formula for this is given as $\dfrac{1}{H–H}$. Table 6.5 calculates the Herfindahl–Hirschman index and its numbers equivalent. For example, in the table the H–H index is found to be 0.1545. Therefore, the numbers equivalent is equal to 6.47 (i.e. $\dfrac{1}{0.1545}$). This means that an industry with approximately six equal-sized firms would generate an index of 0.1558.

Table 6.5 Calculation of the Herfindahl–Hirschman index

Firm	Sales	Market share (s_i)	Market share^2 ($s_i)^2$
1	9000	0.225	0.0506
2	9000	0.225	0.0506
3	6000	0.15	0.0225
4	4000	0.10	0.01
5	3600	0.09	0.0081
6	2800	0.07	0.0049
7	2800	0.07	0.0049
8	2000	0.05	0.0025
9	800	0.02	0.0004
Total	40,000	100	0.1558

H–H index = 0.1545   Numbers equivalent = 6.47

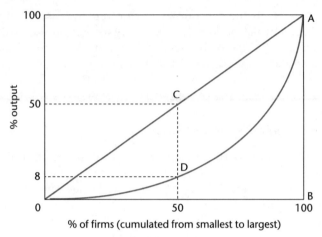

Figure 6.2 The Lorenz curve

The Lorenz curve

The Lorenz curve is used to show the share of the industry accounted for by various proportions of firms in the industry. An example of a Lorenz curve is shown in Figure 6.2. The vertical axis shows the percentage of industry output under consideration (i.e. cumulated from 0 to 100%), while the horizontal axis shows the percentage of firms cumulated from smallest to largest (cumulated from 0 to 100%). The line 0A is referred to as the *line of absolute equality*. If firm sizes are plotted along this line then all firms are of equal size. For example, at point C on the diagram we can see that 50% of firms account (cumulated from smallest to largest) for 50% of industry output. The implication is then that the other 50% of firms (cumulated from smallest to largest) account for the remaining 50% of industry output. It is assumed in this case that competition prevails, as all firms are equal sized and so firms are assumed to hold only a very small amount of market power each. However, if firm sizes are distributed along a curve which deviates from the line of absolute equality, then firm sizes are not equal. At point D, for example, the smallest 50% of firms only account for 8% of the total industry output, implying that the largest 50% of firms account for the other 92% of output.

This measure tends to focus on firm inequalities and, subsequently, ignores the number of firms in an industry. This means that a Lorenz curve for an industry with ten equal-sized firms would look the same as one for 1000 equal-sized firms. Consequently, although visually pleasing, the Lorenz curve can often give a biased picture of industry structure and thus should be used in conjunction with the concentration ratio or Herfindahl–Hirschman index.

What are the problems with quantifying industry structure using concentration measures?

Economists, management researchers and policymakers face several problems when using concentration measures to assess competitive conditions. These problems are related to how industry boundaries are delineated and how we treat large firms which often operate over large areas of geographic and product space.

Size of market

This will affect the importance of a firm within any given market or industry. The relevant market for a firm may only be on a local scale. National concentration ratios tend to be smaller than regional ones. For example, since the bus industry tends to consist of *local* monopolies, the national concentration ratios for the industry are relatively small.

International trade transactions

Many firms are involved in international trade transactions. For example, a firm might import its raw materials and sell some of its finished products abroad. This can cause problems when calculating and interpreting various measures of concentration. If imports are excluded from d~~ ~~ ~~ ~~ ~~ ~~ ~~ ~~~~ ~~~~~~~~oduction, sales, etc., the concentration measure used w~~ ~~ ~~ ~~~~ of importance of the top firms. Thus if we ~~ ~~ ~~ imported goods that accounted f ~~ ~~ ~~ ~~ ~~ ~~ $0.6 \times 60\%$). The opposite would

[

G   hat firms are diversified and
co   ufacturing plant or firm is
ass   belongs. For example, if we
hav   try X and 30% for industry
Y, tl   ity, output, labour) is allocated   from this type of data may
over-   the industries under con-
sidera

Chang

When   may be insensitive to
changes   istry. For example, we
might b   gest firms have a market share   ild be equal to 80%.
However,   with 50% of the market) and t.   :ture of this industry
has underg   ial to 80%.

So what   tion?

A number of   the structure and
thus the con   ies five of these,
namely, econ   ... factors and government regul.

Economies of scale

In Chapter 2, we examined the importance of economies of scale in determining a firm's optimal (most efficient) level of production. The costs of production also affect the structure of industries and the behaviour of firms. Economies of scale can often help explain why some industries are inherently more concentrated than others. These economies of scale depend on the state of technology prevailing in an industry. The minimum efficient scale in the industry to some extent determines the scale at which firms would wish to produce products. The relationship between the minimum efficient scale and industry size gives an indication of the number of efficient firms an industry would tolerate and so the likely level of concentration which yields efficient production. If the minimum efficient scale is large relative to industry size, then the industry will have a natural tendency to become concentrated. For example, suppose we have two industries, X and Y. For X the total market size is equal to 10,000 units, while the minimum efficient scale of production is equal to 1000 units. This means that the industry only supports ten efficient firms. In contrast, in industry Y, the total market size is again equal to 10,000 units, but the minimum efficient scale is at ten units of production. This means that the industry supports 1000 efficient firms. Therefore, as a consequence of the relationship between the minimum efficient scale and market size, industry X is naturally more concentrated (as it only comprises ten firms) than industry Y (which comprises 1000 firms). Table 6.6 shows this process.

Mergers

There are three main types of merger: horizontal, vertical and conglomerate. Horizontal mergers occur when firms combine their resources at the same stage of production and similar products and services are produced – in other words, where firms producing the same products merge (e.g. two manufacturing firms). Vertical mergers occur when firms combine their resources at different stages of production. These types of merger involve firms that are in both supplier and manufacturer stages of the productive process or that are involved in manufacturer and retailer/distribution stages respectively. Conglomerate mergers occur when firms combine their resources that are producing different goods and services. Benefits can arise from mergers through increased efficiency, through rationalising products and processes or by increasing the firm's market power. Overall, mergers lead to markets consisting of fewer, large firms and thus increase the level of concentration. Mergers are examined in more detail in Chapters 9, 10 and 11.

Table 6.6 Relationship between market size, MES and firm numbers

Industry	Market size	Minimum efficient scale	Maximum number of efficient firms
X	10,000	1000	10
Y	10,000	10	1000

Regulation

Government policy toward business and industry can also influence levels of concentration. By using regulations which influence the structure of an industry (e.g. by raising or lowering entry barriers) or firm behaviour (e.g. placing limits of advertising expenditure or prices charged), policy can influence not only the number of firms populating an industry at any given time, but also the size which these firms achieve. (Government policy is examined in more detail in Chapter 11.)

Industry lifecycles

Some economists have argued that concentration develops as industries and firms follow an ageing process or natural lifecycle (Dosi et al., 1997; Klepper, 1997). Under this approach the industry's lifecycle is composed of four stages of introduction, growth, maturity and decline. This is shown in Figure 6.3.

In the introduction or birth phase of an industry, firms invest in research and development to produce new products. The more firms invest in research and development, the more likely they are to achieve success. At this stage, the firms producing these products will have a first mover advantage and so charge high prices to achieve high revenues as a reward for being innovative. However, such revenues may not be sufficient to cover the levels of capital investment associated with research and development activities. There may also be some confusion and lack of awareness among consumers as to the usefulness of such products.

During the growth phase, established firms may become more profitable as the market grows. By producing at higher output levels to meet the demand for their product, successful firms gain economies of scale advantages over rivals, enabling them to expand further. However, this success attracts new entrants (increased competition) and a subsequent increase in industry supply, which ultimately leads to a decline in prices charged. These new rivals will attempt to imitate the successful products. At this stage established firms are likely to respond to such competitive threats by employing various pricing and non-price strategies. (For example, an

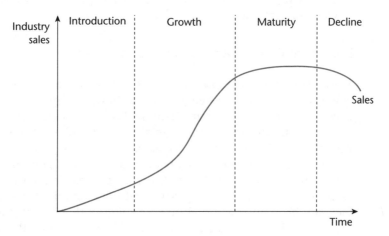

Figure 6.3 The industry lifecycle

established firm might increase spending on advertising to attract new and existing customers). During the maturity phase, growth and profits level off as demand for existing products reaches saturation point. At this stage, some firms may exit the industry in search of new opportunities. In the declining phase, the sales and profits of established firms decline, leading to a loss of confidence on the part of investors, falling share prices and eventually bankruptcy of many firms.

The industry lifecycle approach to assessing the evolution of industries has some drawbacks. McGahan (2000) provides an extended discussion of many of the issues raised here:

- Not all industries may go through the four stages identified. Changes in general economic conditions or technology may substantially effect the evolution of an industry.

- The importance of strategic decisions taken at the firm level may influence the path an industry takes. As industries reach maturity, firms are unlikely to remain passive spectators as the demand for their products and services declines. Instead, firms themselves may decide to invest in research and development activities or diversify into new product or geographic areas.

- As we have seen earlier in this chapter, it is often difficult to identify and define industries. An industry can be made up of several distinct strategic groups, which may all be at different stages in their lifecycle.

- The intensity of competition differs across different market structures, which in turn affects the evolution of an industry. For example, market concentration is likely to be inversely related to the industry growth rate. With rapid growth, established firms are unlikely to be able to expand capacity sufficiently to satisfy demand, so the opportunity exists for smaller firms to enter, leading to deconcentration. If sales are static or declining, established firms are likely to collude or exercise market power in order to protect current and future profitability, leading to increased concentration.

- The association between entry and exit rates affects the industry's lifecycle. In industries where new (small) firms enter, competition is likely to increase. However, if diversified entry takes place by large established firms, competition is likely to decrease.

Stochastic determinants of market structure

Most research that has examined the determinants of concentration has tended to emphasise the role of systematic factors in determining the structure of industry. However, chance factors can determine how the relative sizes of firms change over time. In fact, some evidence suggests that industries evolve into concentrated market structures through a sequence of random shocks to individual firm sizes (Gibrat, 1931). These arguments are embodied in the *law of proportionate effect*. According to the law of proportionate effect, the factors that influence a firm's growth, such as growth of demand, managerial talent, innovation, organisational structure and luck, are distributed across firms in a manner that is essentially random. If then firms' growth rates are determined in a random fashion, this results in a firm size distribution that becomes increasingly skewed towards a small number of large firms. In other words, those firms which have had a successive run of good luck over a sustained period of time grow to be large. This process can be illustrated using an analogy from gambling (Hannah and Kay, 1977: 103):

> If a group of rich men and a group of poor men visit Monte Carlo, it is likely that some of the rich will become poor and some of the poor become rich: but it is also probable that some of the rich will get richer and some of the poor will get poorer, so that the extent of inequality within each group and over the two groups taken together is likely to increase. The process works to increase industrial concentration in much the same way.

Overall, it is likely that systematic and chance factors play a crucial role in how the structural characteristics of an industry change over time.

6.4   Entry Barriers: Definition and Classification

In Chapters 3 and 4, the output and pricing decisions of firms under various types of market structure (perfect competition, monopoly, oligopolistic competition and monopolistic competition) were examined. Within this context, we discussed the importance of entry and exit in determining the profitability of firms in both the short and the long run. We argued that if there is sufficient freedom for new firms to enter and existing firms to exit, then a long-run equilibrium should exist where all firms earn normal levels of profits. However, when barriers to entry exist (e.g. under monopoly), established firms can make supernormal profits even in the long run. Overall, it is the relative flow of firms to and from industries which determines the nature and strength of competition. Box 6.1 outlines the expected effects of entry and exit under perfect competition, monopolistic competition, oligopoly and monopoly.

Box 6.1 Entry, exit and market structure

The importance of entry and exit varies across different market structures. The effects of entry and exit on the various market structures are now discussed briefly.

Perfect Competition

What is the nature of competition?
The model of perfect competition (introduced in Chapter 3) assumes that there is complete freedom of entry and exit. In other words, new firms find it easy to enter and compete with existing firms, while established firms are free to exit the industry. If an established firm charges a price above average cost for a given level of production, it will realise supernormal or abnormal profits.

Why are entry and exit important?
If established firms are earning abnormal profits, new firms will be attracted to the industry in search of a share of these profits. These new firms can enter the

industry and compete with their established counterparts without incurring any competitive disadvantage. The effect of this new entry is to increase the amount of goods and services available to consumers (shifting the industry supply curve to the right), which reduces the prices charged. As prices decline, any abnormal profits that established firms have enjoyed are competed away until the firms left in the industry are all earning a normal level of profitability. This is the long-run equilibrium. At this point entry has ceased, as there are no longer the potential profitable opportunities for new firms. This long-run equilibrium also coincides with the minimum point of firms' average costs and thus firms are using all their resources in the most efficient manner.

In perfect competition entry can be viewed as an 'equilibrating force', resulting in normal profits and an efficient allocation of resources. It is, of course, implicit in the notion of easy entry that firms have access to the necessary resources, which implies that a perfectly competitive market is characterised by the free flow of labour, capital, knowledge and all other inputs. The assumption of free exit is equally important. If exit is costly then firms might be reluctant to enter an industry in the first place, as capital investments may be lost on exit.

Monopolistic Competition

What is the nature of competition?

Under monopolistic competition (introduced in Chapter 3) firms produce goods and services that can be seen as broadly similar, or substitutable for one another. However, these goods and services are differentiated slightly. In other words, each firm produces a slightly different product, which means that consumers are likely to have some degree of loyalty to an individual firm. Consequently, established firms have some control over the prices they charge. This then implies that firms face a downward sloping (relatively elastic) demand curve for their outputs and the ability to earn abnormal profits in the short run.

Why are entry and exit important?

It is the entry of new firms in search of a share of the abnormal profits enjoyed by established firms that eventually brings about a long-run equilibrium where only normal profits are earned. Thus entry guards against the entrenchment of monopoly power. It might also be possible for entry to occur even after abnormal profits have been competed away. Some entrepreneurs may have a strong wish to be independent and to own their own firms. Even if profits are low, factors such as independence, status and leisure may be sufficiently attractive for owners of firms to consider entry into certain industries.

Monopoly

What is the nature of competition?

In the case of a pure monopoly, the dominant monopolist is effectively insulated from competition, by barriers to entry. Given that the monopolist faces a downward sloping demand curve and produces a unique product or service, it consequently has complete control over the prices it charges (assuming no government regulation). This means that the monopolist can earn abnormal profits not only in the short run, but also in the long run.

Is entry important?

At first glance one might assume that entry is not an issue as in theory monopoly represents long-run equilibrium. However, there are three ways in which the power of a monopolist may be threatened by entry considerations:

1 *Threats of entry*: A monopolist may be faced by potential entry. Therefore, while there is only one firm operating in a given market, there may be a pool of potential entrants, who are currently deterred from entry by the actions of the monopolist. In effect, this potential competition constrains the actions of the monopolist and may result in a more competitive equilibrium, where the monopolist may earn close to normal profits. Under these conditions, the monopolist faces uncertainty.

2 *Development of new products and processes*: A monopolist may be unable to prevent the development and entry of new products that could reduce its market power. In this case, the introduction of new products and new practices can lead to innovation, which leads to the downfall of established, less innovative and less efficient firms.

3 *Government policy*: Monopolies are often created and enforced by government policies which place strict limits on the number of firms allowed to operate in any given market. Government-created monopolies will fear no rivals as long as that government protection remains in place. If the government follows a policy of denationalisation and deregulation, then a monopolist faces greater competition.

Oligopoly

What is the nature of competition?

Competition in oligopolistic market structures (introduced in Chapter 4) is based on the recognition that a 'few' sellers account for a substantial proportion of total sales. As a result of the fewness of firms, the recognition of mutual interdependence determines how firms behave. The competition can be based on pricing and non-pricing strategies or firms may decide to adopt collusive strategies and essentially act as joint monopolists.

Why is entry important?

One can argue that it is under oligopoly that the conditions surrounding entry become important in determining the nature of market competition. While the market structures of perfect and monopolistic competition are affected by actual entry and the monopoly market is affected by potential entry, oligopolistic markets are affected by both types of entry. In oligopolistic markets, firms not only take into account the effects on entry conditions when making product differentiation, innovation and pricing decisions, but they may also erect obstacles to any potential threat of entry.

How do we classify entry?

There is no one simple agreed system of arranging the huge number of variables that may provide impediments to the entry of firms. However, most researchers agree that barriers to entry insulate established firms in an industry from competition and allow them to earn supernormal profits. This is because potential entrants normally have to incur costs above and beyond those incurred by established firms, which makes it difficult for them to compete on a level playing field. Such disadvantages faced by potential entrants can even be augmented if the government decides to give preferential treatment to established firms. Such entry barriers are not necessarily confined to the industry, but also exist between different groups of established firms within industries. Groups may arise from differences in products produced or ownership structure.

Barriers to entry can arise in a number of ways. For example, the structural conditions prevalent in an industry such as product differentiation, technology and vertical integration are to some extent given, but often give established firms inherent advantages over potential entrants. Firms can also pursue various pricing and non-price strategies (such as product differentiation, research and development etc.) that have the effect of increasing the barriers facing firms wishing to enter an industry. Barriers to entry can also differ between domestic and foreign markets, as a firm wishing to enter the latter may have to overcome additional regulatory and cultural barriers not necessarily present within a domestic market.

Potential pitfalls?

One of the potential pitfalls in any analysis of entry is that there is often some overlap in many of the barriers. In other words, it is not always clear whether the type of barrier observed is a natural consequence of the structure of the industry or is the result of firms putting deliberate obstacles before potential entrants. For example, (as we see later) product differentiation can be regarded as a natural outcome of the structure of the industry, where firms cater for consumer tastes by offering a wide range of goods and services. Alternatively, one might argue that firms deliberately differentiate products in order to reduce the price elasticity of demand for their products by ensuring customer loyalty, making it difficult for new firms to come in and compete on an equal footing. Thus it is possible to argue that product differentiation can be both a structural barrier and an entry-deterring strategy.

In the rest of this section and the next, we provide a classification of entry barriers and analyse how established firms adopt entry-deterring strategies to ensure long-term profitability. In our analysis, we do not necessarily argue that one entry barrier is any more formidable than the next. In fact, it is often the *type of potential entrant* which determines the degree of difficulty associated with any type of barrier. In other words, what might be a formidable barrier to a small newly formed firm may appear only a minor barrier to a large established firm wishing to diversify into new product or geographic markets.

Overall, the actual effect of entry depends on the speed at which entry is executed. Entry at a slow rate alerts existing firms to the danger of additional competition and allows them time to develop effective strategies to counter the threat. Faster entry may not allow firms to react as efficiently. Of course, the slower the rate of entry, or indeed if established firms can adopt successful entry-deterrence strategies, the longer any abnormal profits present in a market are likely to persist (see Case Study 3.4).

As mentioned earlier, structural barriers refer to all those barriers over which both existing firms and entrants have no direct control. They arise from the conditions of the industry structure. Under this heading we shall consider two broad categories of barrier: legal barriers and structural barriers.

What are legal barriers?

Legal barriers are defined and erected by government policies, through various Acts of Parliament and regulations. They arise because various forms of regulation affect either industry structure (the number of firms in an industry) or how firms behave. These barriers are very costly for potential entrants to overcome given that they have the backing of the law to enforce potential exclusion.

There are four main types of legal barrier to entry.

Registration, certification and licensing of businesses

In many markets, the number and sizes of firms are crucially affected by various certification and registration requirements. In these markets, firms must seek official permission to trade. Examples of such industries include public houses and off licences, minicab operators, defence equipment, casinos, airlines, financial and legal services. Established firms with some market power might be able to influence regulatory bodies to alter entry requirements over time to make it more difficult for potential entrants to enter the industry. Under this guise of 'maintaining standards' potential entrants who may be able to compete effectively with established firms could be prohibited from entering the market.

Monopoly rights

Monopoly rights may be granted by legislation. Governments may allow certain firms sole rights in the provision of goods and services for a limited or unlimited time. A common example of such sole rights is the awarding of franchised monopolies in a variety of industries, such as railways, mobile telephones and television stations. The argument put forward for these franchises is that these industries are either natural monopolies, where average costs can only be minimised if the firms operates at a sufficiently large scale, or industries that require a guaranteed share of the market to justify investment in technology and product development. (We discuss some of these industries further in Chapter 11.)

Patents

Patents are the deliberate creation of a property right so as to stimulate and encourage innovatory activity. Ownership of a patent confers monopoly rights and the potential of monopoly profit. It is this temporary monopoly status that is the sought-after return on investments in research and development. The downside is that a patent grants firms exclusive control over the output of new products and denies new firms access to the industry.

Government policies

Government policies can also indirectly bring about various legal barriers. These barriers can often be erected by governments to protect their domestic industries from the threat of entry by foreign companies. These types of barrier can come in several forms. For example, governments can impose tariffs and quotas, indirect and direct tax regimes, which may embody strategies such as subsidies and public procurement policies designed to help only the domestic firms. Such policies impede the free flow of goods, leaving foreign firms at a disadvantage. Governments also impose physical barriers such as frontier controls, which can lead to delays, customs formalities and expensive handling charges for foreign firms. Technical barriers might also be imposed by governments. These barriers refer to many constraints faced by foreign firms in a domestic market. These may include the need to meet specific technical standards, labour market regulations, transport regulations, exchange controls, language and cultural differences.

Overall, by effectively increasing the costs faced by entrants (whether domestic or foreign), governments can play an important role in determining the extent of entry impediments, and thus the extent of competition in industries.

What are structural barriers?

These barriers arise due to the inherent structural characteristics of an industry. In other words, the extent of product differentiation, the size distribution of firms, the availability of economies of scale and scope all determine the extent and nature of barriers to entry in any given industry. There are three main types of structural barrier to entry.

Economies of scale

As we discussed in Chapter 2, economies of scale exist when a firm's average costs of production decline as industry output increases. Economies of scale can act as a formidable barrier to entry in some industries and arise as a consequence of the types of production process and general economic conditions prevalent in an industry at a given moment in time. Barriers to entry of this nature can arise if fixed capital investments and the state of technology mean that the minimum efficient scale of production is large in relation to the overall size of the market. In a very extreme case, we can identify so-called *natural monopolies*, a condition where the market can tolerate only one firm, as the minimum efficient scale is almost equal to the total market size. Due to the very high fixed costs, entry is unattractive to any new firms.

This type of barrier can also exist when average cost at the less than minimum efficient size level of output is substantially greater than that at the minimum efficient size. This can be illustrated in Figure 6.4. The penalty to a firm for entering at, for example, half the minimum efficient size is the additional unit costs it will face, i.e. the distance AC_1 to AC_2. Given the nature of the technology, these costs are very much greater in industry B than industry A. In this example, it is the shape (slope) of the average cost curve that determines the size of the entry barrier facing potential entrants.

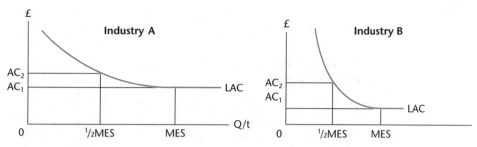

Figure 6.4 Economies of scale as a barrier to entry

Should potential entrants still enter the market?

Of course, a potential entrant faces a dilemma. It makes large capital investments and enters an industry at the minimum efficient scale, thus forgoing the extra costs of entering at below the minimum efficient scale. However, by making a large-scale capital investment, the entrant is taking a high level of risk. This is because entry on this scale substantially increases industry supply. This increase in supply is likely to lead to a fall in prices charged. Such an action may lead to retaliatory action on the part of established firms and even a price war, where all firms are likely to suffer losses (at least in the short run). The entrant's problems could be further exacerbated if there were significant economies of multi-plant operations and distribution networks. To compete with the existing firms in the first case, the entrant would be forced to enter as a horizontally integrated firm. In the second case, the firm would have to be vertically integrated. Both these conditions may make it difficult for an entrant to compete on an equal basis with the well-integrated, established firms. Alternatively, if the firm enters at a smaller scale (below the minimum efficient scale), it would mean it incurs the penalty of a higher average cost, making it difficult for it to price its products at the level charged by established firms. Case Study 6.1 examines how economies of scale act as a barrier to entry in various European industries.

Absolute cost advantages

This barrier exists where the long-run average costs of the entrant lie above those of the existing firm. Thus entrants face higher average costs at every level of output (see Figure 6.5). There are many reasons why entrants face higher absolute costs, as follows.

Established firms may be in control of superior production processes and own patents

As we noted earlier, patents are the deliberate creation of a property right for new knowledge, intended to protect an innovator from rivals. Although they may be regarded as an entry barrier they can also be viewed as increasing consumer welfare. This is because a patent system encourages firms to invest in research, with the promise of monopoly profits for successful innovations. Such innovations are likely to result in 'new' or better quality products and services, which ultimately leads to an increase in the variety of products and consumption possibilities facing consumers.

Case Study 6.1

Economies of scale as a barrier to entry in selected European industries

The extent to which economies of scale act as a barrier to entry varies across industries. For example the cost penalty that would be incurred by firms entering the electrical engineering industry at half the MES would be between 5% and 15%, while for footwear and clothing the penalty would only be 1% (see table).

Economies of scale are most prevalent in industries (such as chemicals and electricals) where the products produced incorporate complex technological features and involve established firms spending heavily on research and development. In industries where the methods of production involve less complex goods (such as food) economies of scale act as less of a barrier.

Industry	Cost of entering at half MES
Motor vehicles	6–9%
Chemicals	2.5–15%
Metals	>6%
Office machinery	3–6%
Mechanical engineering	3–10%
Electrical engineering	5–15%
Instrument engineering	5–15%
Paper, printing and publishing	8–36%
Rubber and plastics	3–6%
Drink and tobacco	1–6%
Food	3.5–21%
Footwear and clothing	1%

Overall, the table suggests that economies of scale act as a potent barrier to entry in most EU manufacturing industries.

Source: Adapted from Emerson et al. (1988), pp. 129–30, Table 6.1.1.

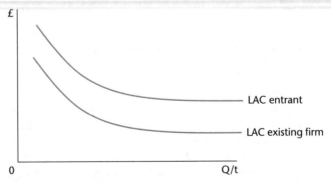

Figure 6.5 Absolute cost advantage as a barrier to entry

Established firms may have the exclusive ownership of superior inputs

Established firms have often populated industries for long periods of time and have (over time) gained control of various scarce factors of production. For example, they may have relationships with the best raw materials suppliers, or have recruited the best labour and management personnel. By gaining control of superior inputs, established firms force entrants to purchase lower quality inputs or get involved in a bidding war to attract scarce resources. An example of this is the control British Airways exercised over landing slots at Heathrow, forcing potential competitors to use less attractive airports.

Established firms may have access to cheaper sources for investment finance

Established firms tend to enjoy a better credit rating than potential entrants as they are seen to be of lower risk. New firms are viewed by financial institutions and capital markets as having an uncertain future. Consequently, any funds lent to such firms would carry a risk premium. This type of entry barrier is often referred to as the *capital requirements barrier*, which might be regarded as an all-embracing barrier that covers the problems of securing sufficient finance to enter the market at a realistic level of production.

Established firms often operate at one or more stages of the production process

The existence of vertically integrated operations such as the brewing, iron and steel and chemical industries can force an entrant to operate at more than one stage of production if it wishes to compete with the existing firms. Denying rivals access to customers or inputs through a variety of vertical exclusions can be classed as a restrictive practice. This is discussed more fully in the next section of this chapter.

Although entrants often have to incur costs additional to those incurred by established firms in order to persuade customers to adopt their products and services, they are often spared the costs of persuading the market to accept a new idea or a new product. Such costs have already been incurred by established firms at an earlier point in the industry's lifecycle. However, entrants may have a few advantages over established firms, as it is possible that existing firms may have overpaid for their assets. This means that entrants are at an advantage insofar as current asset prices are much lower. This might be true of an industry subject to rapid technical change, such as the computer software market, the media industry and mobile telecommunications.

Product differentiation

This type of barrier often arises because the existing brands and reputations of the established firms create 'loyal' customers. Therefore to enter the industry (successfully), the new firm needs to prise customers away from established firms by using promotional campaigns and strategies to stir them from their inertia. This can be achieved in one of two ways: first, by selling the same product or service at a lower price. However, this leads to a decline in revenue and may even send consumers the wrong signal. For example, the lower prices reflect a lower quality of products than that of the established firms. Second, the entrant could attempt to outspend existing firms in the promotion of new goods. However, by doing this, costs of production and distribution are increased. Either way, whether due to increased costs or reduced revenue, the entrant is faced with a squeeze on potential profits.

One of the most common types of product differentiation is through advertising. Although we examine this in much more detail in Chapter 7, we can introduce several important points.

High advertising implies additional costs to entrants

Due to either brand loyalty or customer inertia the new entrant must spend proportionately more on advertising per prospective customer than established firms. In other words, market penetration costs are high. This is an absolute cost advantage type of barrier.

Established firms enjoy economies of scale by advertising on a large scale

A new entrant, entering on a small scale, is not able to take advantage of various economies of scale in advertising. The large-scale advertisers benefit from an increasingly effective message as well as decreasing average costs of such advertising.

Advertising campaigns mean additional expenses

Finally, investment funds needed to create an advertising campaign incur high interest rates as this type of investment carries high risks. Not only is the risk of failure high, but these funds do not create any tangible assets that can be sold off in the event of failure. (We examine this again in Chapter 7.)

The types of entry barrier just described are important in determining structural conditions in any given industry. However, these barriers should not be regarded as permanent. Market structures can change over time and the height of entry barriers can rise or fall. For example, new deposits of a raw material can be discovered which reduces the absolute cost advantage to an established firm; a new technical process may result in changing the economies of scale facing both established firms and entrants; and the launch of a newly advertised product may also reduce the product differentiation advantages of the existing firms.

Overall, structural barriers to entry can come in various forms. However, when we analyse entry, what is important is not the existence of barriers, but how quickly these can be surmounted.

6.5   Entry-deterring Strategies

We have just considered 'structural' barriers, those that are present in the underlying conditions of the market. Fundamentally, these were causes that could not readily be altered. The barriers that we shall discuss here refer to those over which firms have some degree of control or discretion. As such, firms can erect or heighten such barriers through their own actions. These barriers often come in the form of implicit threats (to potential entrants) as to the likely retaliatory action taken by established firms should entry take place. The success or otherwise of any entry-deterrence strategy adopted by established firms depends crucially on how credible the threat of such action is. In general, large firms with substantial market power are likely to make more credible threats and be able to warn off potential entrants. This is often done by showing a commitment to an industry by embarking on large, irreversible capital expenditure programmes. By doing this, established firms illustrate that they would be unwilling (or unable due to barriers to exit) to leave the industry even in the face of intensified competition. Many authors have treated entry as some sort of game, where there is a high degree of interdependence in the entry decision (Dixit and Nalebuff, 1991).

Dixit (1982) examined the entry decision of a firm in the context of a game which encompasses the role of threats. This type of approach to analysing entry deterrence places emphasis on the role of threats, commitments and sunk costs in deterring entry. Firms do not hold a priori beliefs about one another, but instead try to predict other firms' moves using previous knowledge of past encounters. Firms also assume that their rivals' decisions are rational. In this game, there are two players comprising an established firm (labelled 'incumbent' in Figure 6.6) and a potential entrant.

Figure 6.6 illustrates a series of outcomes which depend on whether entry to an industry takes place. The outcome of this game depends on whether the established firm is *passive* (is not prepared to fight entry) or *committed* (in which case it

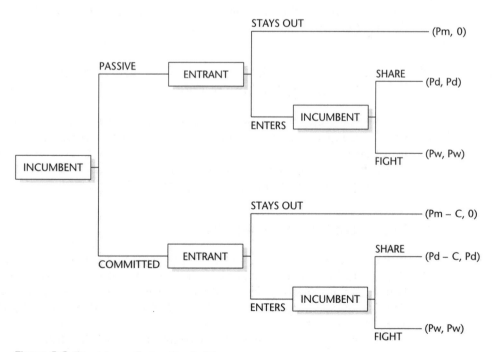

Figure 6.6 Game tree of an entry decision

Table 6.7 Possible outcomes of an entry game where the established firm is passive

Outcome	Decision	Consequence (shown in Figure 6.6)
1	If the established firm has not prepared to fight, and the entrant stays out of the market, then the established firm continues to make monopoly profits while the entrant earns zero	(Pm, 0)
2	If entry does occur, the established firm might decide to fight the entrant in a price war. If this happens, both firms are likely to make losses	(Pw, Pw < 0)
3	If entry does occur, the established firm might decide to share the market, in which case both firms earn positive profits	(Pd, Pd > 0)

has prepared itself to fight entry by prior spending that will help it to avert entry). In other words, we would expect a committed firm to be more credible if it has prepared itself to defend its market position.

The top and bottom halves of the tree show the situations where the established firm is passive and committed respectively. We can now examine the outcome of these two situations.

Passive established firm

There are three outcomes if the established firm has not prepared itself to fight in the event of entry. Table 6.7 shows these.

Is the established firm's threat to fight credible?
What is the equilibrium outcome?

No, the established firm's threat to fight in the event of entry is not credible, as it has no incentive to fight. In other words, it is much more profitable for the established firm to accommodate the entrant. Therefore, the solution would be that the established firm and entrant share the market, which is not as profitable as a monopoly, but more profitable than a price war (Pd, Pd > 0).

Committed established firm

If the established firm is committed to the market by making a prior commitment (C), i.e. the cost of erecting barriers, and the entrant knows this, what is likely to happen? In any measurement of the established firm's profits, we must, of course, deduct any expenditures it has made to establish its credentials through the threat. Table 6.8 shows the potential outcomes.

We can see from Figure 6.6 that the committed established firm is more profitable than the passive one. Overall, the prior spending by established firms to raise entry

Table 6.8 Possible outcomes of an entry game where the established firm is committed

Outcome	Decision	Consequence (shown in Figure 6.6)
1	The established firm will fight entry through a price war, if this is more profitable than sharing the market	(Pw, Pw)
2	The established firm will not fight entry through a price war, if this is less profitable than sharing the market	(Pd – C, Pd)
3	The rational entrant realises the threat of price war is credible and stays out of the market. Therefore, the solution occurs where the established firm earns monopoly profits minus the cost of the commitment, while the entrant earns zero. As long as the established firm's commitment is visible and irreversible, the threat is credible	(Pm – C, 0)

barriers sends a clear signal to potential entrants of the likely behaviour of established firms if entry takes place. In the previous example, the established firm has invested in specific assets to avert entry, and consequently has incurred costs that are likely to be unrecoverable (i.e. sunk costs). The existence of the prior irreversible commitment makes the threat of retaliation credible and indicates that the established firm is willing to fight a price war if entry takes place. Of course, the established firm could be bluffing!

We now turn specifically to several pricing and non-price strategies which established firms could adopt to erect entry barriers.

How can firms use pricing strategies to deter entry?

Firms can use several pricing strategies to deter entry. Two of the most common types are that of limit and predatory pricing.

Limit pricing

Fundamentally, established firms enjoy sufficient cost advantages to earn abnormal profits at prices that also deter entry. The theory of *limit pricing* is one such illustration of this strategy. There are many variants of this theory in varying degrees of sophistication and complexity. We develop the simplest, so as to capture the essence of the argument. The strategy is designed to ensure that entry is unprofitable. It is the highest price that an established firm believes it can charge without inviting entry. The level of the limit price depends on costs of the potential entrant, the potential entrant's estimate of industry demand and eventual likely share after entry. Regarding the last point the theory is built on the assumption (the Sylos postulate) that potential entrants behave as though they expect existing firms to maintain output at the pre-entry level in the face of realised entry (Sylos-Labini, 1962). This means that any entry is a net addition to industry output. Consider Figure 6.7.

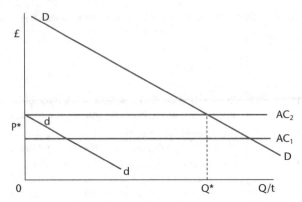

Figure 6.7 Limit pricing to deter entry

Figure 6.7 shows the limit price in the case of an absolute advantage, i.e. the established firm enjoys average costs at AC_1, whereas the entrant faces an average cost schedule of AC_2. The demand curve faced by entrants is dd, which is that part of the market demand curve DD that is not served by the established firm firm(s), which are producing output Q^* at price P^*. It could be thought of as the 'residual demand curve'. Since the entrant's average costs curve intersects the residual demand curve at P^* the entrant is unable to earn any profit. It is assumed that the established firm or firms are forgoing profits to keep output and hence price at the entry-deterring level. P^* is the so-called limit price.

How realistic is this theory of firm behaviour?

We can criticise the theory on several grounds. These are as follows:

- Is it more profitable to attempt to restrict all entry rather than retard the rate of entry?
- If an industry is growing it may be difficult to dissuade a potential entrant that there is no market available to it, if entry takes place.
- Could there not be a cheaper way of deterring entry, e.g. predatory pricing?
- The status of the entrant is all important. As we saw in Figure 6.6, there may be instances when existing firms may wish to seek an accommodation with potential large entrants.

Predatory pricing

Predatory pricing is a strategy adopted by established firms, designed to drive out new entrants. This involves setting prices at below average variable cost. Thus the established firm may forgo short-run profits in order to reduce the profitability of entrants or existing competitors. This may force new firms out of the industry and constrain the ability of existing rivals to expand. The consequence is that the established firms enjoy greater market power and increased profits in the long run. Case Study 6.2 gives a useful example of other types of predatory behaviour in the UK bus industry.

Case Study 6.2

Predation in the Scottish bus industry

Predation can come in many forms and is by no means merely confined to firms' pricing practices. For example, firms can adopt predatory strategies in relation to the quantity or quality of products and services supplied. In 1994, the Office of Fair Trading investigated two bus companies in Scotland which had adopted such strategies.

In 1990 Moffat & Williamson (M&W) won a contract to operate bus services that were subsidised by Fife Regional Council. On some of the routes M&W faced a competitor, Fife Scottish, who operated a commercial service. In 1992 Fife Scottish duplicated the subsidised service provided by M&W by additional bus journeys. This had the effect of reducing market demand for M&W. The OFT held that Fife Scottish was a dominant local operator and was able to absorb losses.

How can firms use non-price strategies to deter entry?

The following paragraphs introduce the ways in which firms can use various non-price strategies to deter entry.

Product differentiation

Product differentiation, especially advertising, can help to create or strengthen brand loyalties beyond what is natural to the market, thus reinforcing the structural barriers we examined in the previous section.

We can consider a few related strategies under this heading, which can lead to entry effects. Brand proliferation, common in, for example, the detergent market and the processed food market, can be an attempt by dominant firms to crowd the market with various brands and thus deny entrants sufficient market demand to recoup their sunk costs. Case Study 6.3 gives a useful discussion. In other markets, customers may face high switching costs, i.e. the cost of switching to another supplier. These customers are then 'locked in' with existing firms. Examples are bank accounts, computer software, hotels and stores (via loyalty cards). Consequently, these customers cannot be easily lured to other firms. Goodwill and reputation may also help to strengthen the market position of established firms, although this assumes that entrants from other industries do not have their own reputation which can be utilised to attract customers away from existing firms. Case Study 6.4 tackles many of these issues in the context of the UK banking industry.

Loyalty discounts, exclusive dealing, refusals to supply

All these types of strategy are intended to deny entrants access to supply of inputs or access to customers. An example was Capital Radio offering 'solus' advertising deals. This meant that, in return for exclusivity, the advertiser received a discount.

Case Study 6.3

Brand proliferation in detergents

Advertising is necessary to inform consumers of the factual attributes of products, promote brand image and stimulate demand. However, excessive expenditures on advertising and promotion and large numbers of brands offered by firms in many industries can often stifle or distort competition by making it difficult for new firms to offer something different. For example, in the UK household detergent industry and the US cereal industry, policymakers have criticised leading firms for spending excessive amounts on advertising and proliferating brands. In both cases, investigations by regulatory authorities (which are discussed in Monopolies and Mergers Commission, 1966, and Schmalensee, 1978) revealed that:

- Advertising appeared concerned with building up brand image and did not inform consumers about the factual attributes of the products.
- Excessive advertising was taking place for many similar products under different brand names. This was a waste of resources.
- New improved versions of existing products did not alter substantially the quality of the products.

But why did this make entry difficult?

- The large numbers of similar brands offered and expenditures on advertising by the established firms raised the capital requirements to enter the industry.
- This made it very difficult for new firms to raise finance to enter the industry and overcome the reputation advantages held by the established firms.

    The large number of similar products offered also made it difficult for new firms to find a market niche in which to sell their products.

The advertiser agreed not to advertise on any other radio station. The effect of these agreements was to limit the radio advertising market for Capital Radio's competitors. One of the most famous of 'solus tie' contracts was in petrol retailing in the 1960s in the UK. Independent retailers agreed to a long contract for the supply of petrol from one specific supplier. Some of these issues are discussed at greater length under the topic of vertical integration in Chapter 9.

Pre-emptive patenting

Patents can also be used as a strategy to deter entry and thus be seen as an endogenously caused barrier. In particular, this may be the case when a firm in possession of a new technology decides to apply for many patents to cover all possible spin-offs, so as to deny rivals the opportunity to 'invent around' the new technology to produce similar goods.

Case Study 6.4

Barriers to entry: banking for small business

In 2002 the Competition Commission published a report which was the outcome of an investigation into the supply of banking services to small and medium-sized businesses in the UK. The report found to some extent that competition in this market was somewhat limited as a consequence of the substantive market shares held by the largest clearing banks. In fact, in each geographic market examined (Scotland, England, Northern Ireland and Wales) the largest four banks accounted for almost 90% of certain financial services offered to small firms. This market power meant that there was a high degree of similarity across services offered, prices charged and barriers to entry faced by new providers which wanted to compete with the largest banks.

In general, several barriers to entry are likely to feature quite prominently in the banking industry. For example, previous evidence suggests that banks entering at below the minimum efficient scale are likely have average costs, which are around 5% higher than those of established counterparts operating at the minimum efficient scale. Minimum levels of capital and licensing requirements may also make it difficult for new banks to compete with established counterparts.

Specific problems

With reference to the specific market for banking services to small and medium-sized enterprises, product differentiation was found to be a substantive barrier to entry in three ways. First, a bank which had established and built up a reputation over time was more likely to enjoy the loyalty of customers. In fact, the investigation found some evidence of established banks offering preferential services to new customers or to those who threatened to switch to another bank. Second, barriers to entry were found because substantial switching costs from moving from one bank to another deterred customers from moving accounts and thus limited the extent of competition. Finally, the presence of established banks with branches across large geographical areas made it difficult for others to compete on a level footing.

Solutions

The overall effects of the barriers to entry outlined were excessively high prices and profits made by banks in England and Wales. Consequently, the Competition Commission proposed a number of *behavioural remedies* (such as abolition of certain charges, the introduction of interest on current accounts and improved information flows to customers) to increase competition. Collectively, these remedies would make it easier for customers to switch banks, and thus increase competition in the industry.

6.6   Conclusion

This chapter has outlined two of the main components of market structure, namely concentration and barriers to entry. We have outlined the importance of each in determining the extent and type of competition which is likely to take place in any given industry. The barriers discussed emphasise the role that the underlying structural characteristics of an industry can play in deterring entry, and highlight the ways in which established firms can actively deter entry. Often the threat of entry is enough to alter the behaviour of firms already in a given industry.

Discussion Questions

1 Are industries and markets different?

2 How can concentration be quantified?

3 Explain the significance of the numbers equivalent measures of the Herfindahl–Hirschman index.

4 Discuss how the relationship between the minimum efficient scale and industry size can determine the level of observed concentration in a given industry.

5 How useful are industry lifecycle theories to our understanding of industry evolution?

6 Utilising the evidence presented in Case Studies 6.1 to 6.4, outline a typology for the analysis of entry barriers.

7 Using Case Study 6.4 as a starting point, give examples of UK and European industries that are characterised by various legal barriers to entry.

8 Explain how the height of an entry barrier can be measured.

9 Outline the various pricing and non-price strategies a firm can follow to deter entry.

Further Reading

General background

Cook, M. and Farquharson, C. (1998) *Business Economics*. London: Pitman, Chapter 18.
Mochandreas, M. (2000) *Business Economics* (2nd edn). London: Thomson Business Press, Chapter 2.

Advanced

Dixit, A. and Nalebuff, B. (1991) *Thinking Strategically*. New York: Norton Books, Chapters 5 and 6.
Dosi, G., Malerba, F., Marsila, O. and Orsenigo, L. (1997) Industrial structures and dynamics: evidence interpretations and puzzles, *Industrial and Corporate Change*, 6, 3–24.
McGahan, A. (2000) How industries evolve, *Business Strategy Review*, 11, 1–16.

Part Three Analysis of Firm Strategy

7

Advertising and Product Differentiation

Objectives

By the end of this chapter, the reader should be able to understand:
- the various types of product differentiation
- the determinants of advertising expenditures
- how advertising can raise barriers to entry
- the relationships between advertising and prices.

Key Concepts

- advertising intensity
- credence goods
- experience goods
- search goods

7.1 Introduction

We saw in Chapter 4 that many modern industrial structures are characterised by oligopolistic relations between the large dominant firms. This suggests that firms are faced by the threat of continual and endless rivalry from other firms which produce close substitutes to their own range of products. Traditional economic theories suggest that close substitutability of demand would invite price competition as the main strategic variable. However, such competition leads to great risks and uncertainty for the major firms. Firms may prefer to engage in other forms of competition since the reactions to these strategies are likely to be less harmful than the reactions to price reductions. Price cuts can be met almost instantaneously, whereas it may take a considerable length of time for firms to react to non-price forms of competition such as advertising. By the time rivals have realised the success of a non-price strategy and begun to compete with similar advertising strategies, existing consumers may have to be prized away from the original advertiser. Advertising and product differentiation can be seen as reducing product substitutability and possibly creating a new market in which the firms have a more assured status and future. This chapter is structured as follows. Section 7.2 examines the various ways in which product differentiation can take place. In particular, it examines not only how product differentiation can evolve as a natural process over time, but also how it can be utilised by firms as a competitive strategy. Section 7.3 explains how advertising can determine the nature and extent of competition in different types of industries. Section 7.4 concludes.

7.2   Modes of Product Differentiation

Most modern markets are characterised by product differentiation. For example, there is no one identical type of car, perfume, radio station or hotel. Product differentiation can be viewed as the ability of producers to differentiate close substitutes, so that customers no longer regard them as similar products. This differentiation can occur by changing the physical attributes of a product or service. Alternatively, differentiation can take place in a psychological sense.

Products and services can be subject to vertical or horizontal differentiation. Vertical differentiation occurs when a product or service differs in quality from another. For example, one brand of lager may have a higher alcohol content than another and, as such, be deemed as a higher quality product. In contrast, horizontal differentiation occurs when products are of the same quality, but have slightly different attributes – for example, different colours of the same model of car.

Product differentiation can be due to many causes. We can divide these into natural and strategic causes. In the former case, differentiation occurs when products become different through a natural process not developed by producers. It is likely that producers exploit such differences, even if they occur naturally. Strategic product differentiation is directly controlled by producers through the pursuit of strategies such as advertising and promotion of primary product attributes or related additional services. It is often difficult to assess whether a product is differentiated to meet the many and varied characteristics of a producer's customers or is a deliberate attempt by the firm to appropriate brand loyalty advantages to reduce competition within the industry. Natural and strategic causes of product differentiation are now discussed briefly.

Natural causes of product differentiation

Brands and trademarks

Brands and trademarks can be exploited to differentiate similar products. Trademarks are normally words or symbols used by producers to denote particular brands. In many cases, firms which own trademarks have obtained exclusive property rights to exploit these. Examples are the Lacoste crocodile and the Armani eagle. This gives the firm some degree of monopoly power by reducing the number of substitutes and hence lowering consumers' price elasticity of demand for the product in question. Brands and trademarks can sometimes become synonymous with the products they are associated with (e.g. Hoover and vacuum cleaner). If this occurs the firm may lose its trademark protection. Case Study 7.1 discusses the importance of brands for a firm's revenues.

Community or national differences

In this case, the country or community of origin is the defining factor that differentiates goods and services. Products and services from different parts of the world are often deemed to be different and of higher quality – for example, Jersey cream made in Jersey, Devon custard, Russia vodka, Scottish whisky, Irish stout, Swiss watches and Italian clothes. Domestic producers can exploit such differences, for example by putting an Italian flag on a packet of pasta or giving clothes an Italian-sounding name.

Customer wants

Consumers have different characteristics, tastes and preferences. As a consequence, the type of product demanded varies from consumer to consumer. Differentiation by producers to meet these varied wants is often of a horizontal type – for example, colour of cars and size of clothes.

Geographical variations

The location of a producer can often differentiate a product or service – for example, the ease with which a shop or factory can be reached by consumers, as is the case when consumers make choices between the corner shop and the out-of-town superstore. It is also often the case that identical houses are differentiated by which part of the country they are located in. For example, London has traditionally been deemed a more desirable place in which to buy property than other parts of the United Kingdom.

Ignorance

Ignorance on the part of consumers can allow firms to exaggerate the degree of differentiation of their products and services. If consumer ignorance is present, producers may suggest that high prices reflect higher quality. This may even lead to these goods and services inheriting Veblenesque characteristics. Veblenesque goods are often luxury goods such as designer clothes or fine wines. Consumers tend to demand more of these goods as their price increases. Producers can often exploit consumer ignorance by advertising products which are harmful. In such cases, government regulations are required to protect consumers. Case Study 7.2 examines how advertising messages are regulated in the UK, while Case Study 7.3 examines a recent incident involving misleading advertising.

Case Study 7.1

Doughboy needs a decision

The Pillsbury Doughboy must be getting long arms from being pulled in different directions. Once again the 15-month regulatory review into General Mills' $10.5bn acquisition of rival food group Pillsbury from UK drinks group Diageo has led to question marks over the deal's status. The famous Doughboy brand remains at the centre of the negotiations between General Mills and the Federal Trade Commission. Tensions have mounted as General Mills has pushed back the target closing date on the Pillsbury deal, which will double its annual sales to about $13bn. Announcing the purchase in July 2000, it anticipated completing by the end of that year. General Mills has sought to ease competition fears by selling the Pillsbury brand baking mixes and other products to International Multifoods, another US food group, for $305m. General Mills already has Betty Crocker mixes, and the move would separate the top two baking mix brands. The sticking point is that General Mills would still control Pillsbury brand products – such as the dough business. It is thought the deal with IMC would allow IMC to use the brand name for 20 years and make royalty payments thereafter, as well as use of the Doughboy for a few years. The crux of the FTC worries appears to be the Doughboy and if, or how, he can be shared as a way of resolving anticompetitive questions in the deal. The protracted negotiations suggest the FTC does not like, or at least has doubts over, trademarks shared by two companies. However, two issues have surfaced.

One is that the Doughboy's value will decrease, if shared between two companies. Another, perhaps more serious, is that General Mills could feel less compelled to advertise its Doughboy products, thereby adding visibility to IMC's brand – a cake mix rival. Analysts downplayed the notion that General Mills would alter advertising for the coveted dough products business. 'I think at the end of the day General Mills is not going to get a free ride from IMC,' said Jeff Kanter, analyst at Prudential Securities. 'I don't see how this would create any disincentive to promote the brand.' Mr Kanter said the hurdles do not look like deal-breakers. He added that all parties involved want the General Mills–Pillsbury deal to pass; then the divestments to IMC can proceed. Indeed, IMC has used the Pillsbury cake mix buy as a catalyst to reorganise itself into a more consumer brand-focused company. Also, the recommendations by FTC staff do not always represent the final decision by the FTC commissioners, analysts said. As they meet to talk it over, perhaps as soon as this week, the impending finish-line could help resolution. 'Maybe it's going to be like Pepsi and Quaker, where it goes down to the wire,' Mr Kanter said. 'And Pepsi and Quaker ultimately went through.' General Mills and Diageo reiterated that expectations were for the FTC to complete its review in October and that they remain confident they will close the deal. Meanwhile, some analysts are worried about Pillsbury's business suffering under so long a period of limbo.

Source: *Financial Times*, 9 October 2001.

Case Study 7.2

Advertising and regulation

Introduction
As we have seen, much of the discussion in economics assesses the role of advertising in providing information to consumers to enable them to make informed choices. If consumers receive information via advertising that is misleading, it causes them to make decisions that are not appropriate, thus causing a misallocation of scarce resources. Evidence suggests that where goods and services are complex (requiring specialist knowledge on the part of consumers) it is more likely that misleading advertising may occur (OFT, 1997).

What is misleading advertising?
Misleading advertising can be classified as adverts that:

- contain false statements
- conceal or omit important information about the product in question
- create a false impression as to the properties, performance or outcomes of consuming particular goods and services.
- make false promises to provide services that will never be provided.

Who protects consumers against misleading advertising?
In the UK, a number of institutions, regulations and acts of parliament regulate advertising. Acts of parliament and regulation include the Trade Descriptions Act (1968), Consumer Protection Act (1987), Medicines Act (1968) and the Control of Misleading Advertisements Regulations (1988).

In 1962 the Advertising Standards Authority (ASA) was instituted as an independent body responsible for ensuring adverts (except those on television and radio) are accurate, truthful and follow guidelines laid down by competition authorities. The Independent Television Commission (ITC) and the Broadcasting Standards Commission regulate adverts on television and radio. The Financial Services Authority (FSA) deals with adverts for financial services. The Office of Fair Trading also has powers to act under the Control of Misleading Advertisement Regulations 1988. If advertising affects the health and safety of consumers or is aimed at inappropriate audiences (e.g. tobacco advertising to children), it is likely the Office of Fair Trading will become involved. Through its misleading advertisements team the Office of Fair Trading supports other bodies in stopping unfair advertising practices. Similar forms of protection are enforced in other countries (see Case Study 7.3, which highlights a recent case in the USA).

Case Study 7.3

FT

Unfair advertising: FTC brands Joe Camel unfair

The US Federal Trade Commission yesterday charged the tobacco company R.J. Reynolds with unfair advertising practices, alleging that its Joe Camel campaign targets children.

The accusation against the second largest US cigarette maker comes after investigators uncovered new information that was not available when the FTC initially exonerated Joe Camel three years ago.

It was unclear yesterday whether the FTC would issue an immediate cease-and-desist order or wait until RJR argues its case before an administrative judge. RJR has continually defended Joe Camel, the cartoon character in dark sunglasses who lounges on billboards and in magazine adverts. The new information came from the Food and Drug Administration, which passed on government statistics showing that the Camel brand's share of the youth market jumped substantially after the popular advert campaign began.

The documents also included an RJR survey showing that 86% of children aged 10 to 17 recognise Joe Camel and 95% of those children know the character is selling cigarettes.

Source: *Financial Times*, 29 May 1997.

New technology

New technology can also be used to differentiate a product – for example, the addition of Internet and e-mail features on a mobile telephone. Economist (1999) noted that Procter & Gamble had been successful in differentiating many of its products through new technological features. Examples of this included the Swiffer mop that captured dust and the Nutri-Delight orange drink which had a special formula to allow iodine to co-exist with certain vitamins and minerals and allowed children to gain weight.

Strategic product differentiation

Additional services

Additional services offered by firms can also be used to differentiate products. Even if products are identical, the conditions surrounding a sale may differ. By offering superior credit facilities, quicker delivery or a more comprehensive after-sales service, producers can effectively differentiate their products. By offering certain after-sales guarantees or warranties the firm is sending signals to consumers that it has confidence in the quality of the products it is selling. The overall bundle of products now being offered may now be vertically differentiated.

Variations in raw materials and other inputs

Inputs such as raw materials, labour and capital are rarely identical, even if the finished product or service is. However, the resulting goods and services are often marketed as being different from those of other firms. Firms may stress that their employees are better skilled, better trained and less likely to make errors or that their raw material inputs are superior to those of rival firms. This gives the firms some control over the prices or fees they charge.

Rate of change of product differentiation

Firms may be able to affect the size and importance of this variable. Products with a short time span and taking up a relatively low proportion of a consumer's budget can be subject to the planned obsolescence of desirability. Consumers will be urged to adopt new styles and models. In recent years, these characteristics have been found to be particularly prevalent in products such as electronic video games, home computers and mobile telephones.

Advertising

Advertising provides information and conveys persuasive messages. Producers can use advertising to create or exaggerate differences between products and services. If successful, advertising can convey a brand image and ensure consumer loyalty. The gains to the producer in the form of increased revenue from advertising can be large. Advertising is now a huge global business. In many industries it is the main strategic weapon used by firms to gain a competitive advantage in the market. In the UK advertising expenditures increased from £9.61 billion in 1987 to £14.23 billion in 2001 (figures in real terms).

Why do firms advertise?

Firms often spend vast amounts on advertising to enhance reputation or to provide consumers with valuable information on goods and services offered. For example, in 2001, Procter & Gamble was estimated to have spent £114 million on advertising. Other large firms such as BT, Ford, Vauxhall, Renault and DFS all had advertising expenditures exceeding £50 million. Firms advertise for many reasons.

To launch a product or service

Firms may use advertising to provide consumers with information regarding a new product or service. New products often require informative advertisements, aimed at educating a consumer as to the attributes of a new product or service. For example, the UK government and financial service firms had to spend heavily on advertising to provide consumers with detailed information before and after the launch of individual savings accounts (ISAs) in 1999.

To provide information on price, quality and availability

Firms may use advertising to provide consumers with information regarding the price and quality attributes of products and services. This is particularly important if prices and quality of products are changing over time. Such changes are often a consequence of increased competition or technological change. For example, mobile telephone operators in the UK have spent heavily on promoting quality and price attributes of various goods and services offered. Advertising can also be used to provide consumers with information on the location of the firm's sales outlets.

To increase or protect market share

Firms may use advertising as a strategy to gain a competitive advantage over competitors by capturing larger shares of the market. Here, advertising is used either to inform or persuade consumers that the firm's products and services are of a superior quality to that of their rivals. In a market that is growing, there is likely to be less need for advertising as there is a large pool of potential customers, whereas in a declining market, firms may advertise heavily to protect dwindling market share. In addition, firms may use advertising to protect their market shares from aggressive rivals.

To increase consumer awareness and increase profitability

Firms may use advertising to increase consumer awareness of the goods and services the firm has to sell. Over time this advertising is likely to lead to the firm building up goodwill and reputation advantages over its rivals. Over time this advertising can build up a brand image which can lead to the formation of entry barriers that prevent new firms from entering the market. These entry barriers effectively insulate the firm from competition, leading to increased profitability. The effect of advertising on a firm's profitability is shown in Figure 7.1.

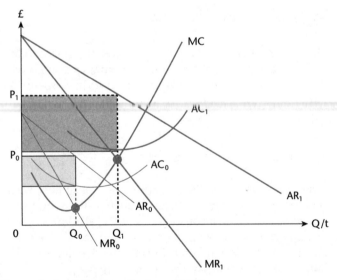

Figure 7.1 Effects of advertising on a firm's profitability

The firm operates in an industry where no advertising takes place. The firm faces a downward sloping demand curve (AR_0) and a corresponding marginal revenue curve (MR_0). Before advertising the firm maximises profits where MR_0 equals MC, producing at output level Q_0 and charging price P_0. The pale shaded area shows the firm's profit. If advertising now takes place, the firm's average costs increase from AC_0 to AC_1. However, the increased advertising has the effect of increasing demand, which increases from AR_0 to AR_1. Because advertising is a fixed cost, marginal costs are unaffected. The firm now maximises profits where the new marginal curve (MR_1) equals marginal cost (MC), producing at output level Q_1 and charging price P_1. The dark shaded area shows the firm's profit. The firm now makes higher profits after advertising than it did before. The extent to which firms make extra profits from advertising depends on the extent to which advertising promotes increased demand, the price elasticity of demand and the cost of that additional (or new) advertising. If demand is very inelastic, then increases in price lead to large increases in total revenue.

Oligopolistic industries are often characterised by non-price competition. One possible measure of the extent to which advertising dominates as a form of competition is to examine advertising expenditure in the industry as a proportion of total sales (otherwise known as *advertising intensity*). This can give us an indirect method of assessing the type of competition that takes place in particular industries. The Advertising Association (2002) found the advertising to sales ratios of selected product groups varied considerably (see Table 7.1). For example, in industries such as vitamins, shampoos, cereals and washing powders, advertising to sales ratios were found to be relatively high and were equal to approximately 24%, 20%, 8.5% and 8% respectively. In other industries, these ratios were found to be relatively low. For example, in cars, carbonated drinks, hairdressing and video recorders, the advertising to sales ratios were found to be 2.5%, 1.5%, 0.03% and 0.02% respectively.

In many industries such as toiletries and cosmetics (which includes deodorants, shampoos and soaps) advertising intensity is high, while in others such as soft drinks and cars the intensity is much lower. Remember that advertising intensity depends on two things: the actual amount spent on advertising and the actual sales of the products advertised. This means that using the advertising to sales ratio as an indicator of the intensity of non-price competition may be misleading.

Why is this?

- In many industries, the absolute expenditures on advertising are large (e.g. cars). However, so are sales. This means that when we calculate advertising intensity, the proportion of advertising to sales appears to be small.

- Advertising is only one form of product differentiation. Therefore, if firms are engaging in other modes of product differentiation, these are not captured by this measure.

The extent of advertising intensity in any given industry depends on many factors.

Why does advertising vary across markets?

Firm objectives

The level of advertising intensity in any given industry may depend on the overall business objectives of established firms in that industry. If firms are maximising

Table 7.1 Advertising to sales ratios of selected UK product groups, 2000

Product group	Advertising to sales ratio
Deodorants	21.08
Shampoos	18.84
Toilet soaps	17.70
Cinema	13.69
Air fresheners	10.12
Computer/video games software	9.60
Cereals	8.43
Washing liquids and powders	7.68
Vitamins	7.72
DVD players	6.43
Electric razors	4.90
Coffee	4.73
Hair dryers	3.53
Tea	3.33
Televisions	1.26
Trainers	1.45
Cars	1.09
Carbonated soft drinks	0.68
Cheese	0.82
Carpets, floor coverings and tiles	0.71
Beer	0.66
Rail travel	0.54
Domestic lighting	0.12
Cigarettes	0.05
Hairdressing	0.03

Source: Adapted from Advertising Association (2002), pp. 216–22, Table 22.1.

short-run profits, they may have little scope to spend heavily on promoting products and services. However, some firms might sacrifice short-run profits by additional expenditures on advertising, so that in the long run higher profits are secured. If firms are aiming to maximise sales or market share then expenditures on advertising are likely to be much higher, in order to stimulate consumer demand. Of course, firms in the same industry may follow different business objectives, so it may be difficult to assess the nature of competition in any given industry using only advertising intensity measures.

Market structure

Many authors have argued that advertising can aid in the growth of firms, consequently leading to industries dominated by a few large firms. Advertising can often lead to monopolistic and oligopolistic industry structures. The leading firms in these structures can then use advertising as a strategic tool to maintain or increase their market power. We examine the relationship between market structure and advertising expenditures later in the chapter.

Age of the industry

In new industries, firms must spend heavily on advertising their goods and services in order to increase consumer awareness and establish a market presence. Over time this may confer market share advantages to firms which do advertise, as consumers become aware of the products and services produced.

Extent of product differentiation

If the industry is characterised by a high degree of product differentiation, then consumers perceive that no close substitutes exist for the goods and services they consume. Consequently, firms have to spend heavily on advertising in order to capture market share from rivals.

Number of brands

If products are differentiated through branding by established firms, then consumers are likely to be loyal to particular products. If this is the case, firms must spend even more heavily on advertising in order to persuade consumers to switch from one firm's product to another. As we saw in Chapter 6, the proliferation of brands can lead to the creation of entry barriers to particular industries, thus insulating established firms from competition.

Type of product or service produced

The level of advertising intensity often varies by the type of product or service produced in a given industry (see Table 7.1). Evidence suggests that advertising intensity is generally lower in industries where durable goods are produced. Given the high price of durable products, consumers often undertake more detailed investigations as to the attributes of the products on offer. For example, when purchasing a hi-fi system consumers will tend to consult consumer information publications such as *What Hi-fi?*, *Hi-fi World* and *Hi-Fi Choice*, instead of relying solely on the informative and persuasive messages forwarded by advertisers.

Frequency of consumer purchase

Consumers who buy a good or service regularly are unlikely to need detailed information or to be persuaded by firms as to the desirable attributes of the goods and services that they are buying. Instead, consumers use their knowledge from previous purchases to guide them to appropriate consumption decisions. On the other hand, where goods are bought less frequently, consumers may need the help of advertisements to guide them in their consumption decisions. Imperfect information with regard to prices of goods and services may give producers some element of monopoly power. In other words, consumers may be unaware that different prices for similar products do not reflect quality differences. Therefore, if information is increased through advertising, consumers are more likely to shop around. As a consequence of increased competition, producers charge similar prices for products and services. Advertising and other forms of product differentiation may help improve information with regard to the prices and qualities of products produced. For example, other forms of differentiation that may imply information about product quality might include those firms with good reputations and those who are willing to provide warranties and guarantees with goods and services sold.

The government could also play a useful role in ensuring the provision of accurate information to consumers by public information announcements, the imposition of standards and licences when producing certain goods and services, and sponsoring and subsidising publications by consumer associations. Firms which advertise products frequently may send a signal to consumers about quality. Therefore, there would only be an incentive for a firm to advertise its products if it expected to capture and keep market share. Firms selling low-quality products would be unwilling to spend heavily on advertising as they would be unlikely to receive any repeat purchases from consumers. If consumers have access to good information, they would only be willing to pay high prices for high-quality goods and services.

Benefits of advertising

Advertising can be categorised as either informative or persuasive. If advertising is informative it is useful in providing consumers with enough information to make informed choices with regard to the goods and services they demand. If advertising is persuasive, it distorts the information that consumers receive, making it difficult for them to make informed choices. We will now examine each of these views briefly.

Advertising distorts consumer preferences

Information is a necessary prerequisite for effective competition and ensures that resources are used efficiently to produce the goods and services that consumers demand. Persuasive advertising simply changes the preference functions of consumers and can often lead to less competition, as firms which enjoy brand loyalty exploit market power by charging higher prices and earning higher profits. This view of advertising takes a negative view of its usefulness.

In a seminal work, Kaldor (1950) argued that because advertising is supplied jointly with goods and services, consumers are forced to pay for more advertising than they want and are thus 'unwilling accomplices in a waste of resources'. The amount of advertising supplied exceeds that demanded because it is generally provided as a 'free' service both to potential buyers and to those consumers who will never buy the good or service under consideration. Advertisers do not charge a positive price for advertising, since any charge would lead to an amount being demanded which is less than that required for firms successfully to achieve profit maximisation (see discussion relating to Figure 7.2). Consequently, there is an excess supply of advertising and a subsequent wastage of resources, which is financed by consumers who are forced to pay a higher price for the advertised goods.

The supply curve (S) relates the quantity of advertising to the price of advertising (P). The price can be regarded as the price paid to the advertising media by sellers or as the advertising component of the price paid by consumers of the advertised goods. D_c refers to consumer demand and D_f to seller demand for advertising respectively. Thus, Q_c is the amount consumers will be willing to pay for. This is at the intersection of D_c and S. However, the actual amount of advertising supplied is Q_f, where $D_f = S$. This is the amount advertisers regard as necessary to maximise their profits. The excess advertising and consequent waste of resources is the difference between Q_f and Q_c. The price charged at Q_f is P_f. At this price level consumers are only willing to pay an amount equal to the area OP_fAQ_b, given that they would only demand Q_b at that price level of advertising.

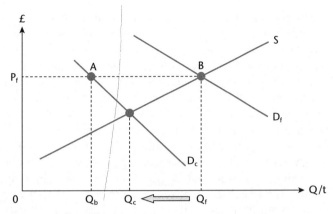

Figure 7.2 Advertising and welfare

Advertising helps consumers make informed choices

Informative advertising identifies the existence of sellers, provides information on the key characteristics and attributes of various products and services, and links the quality of a product to its brand (i.e. only high-quality brands are advertised heavily). This means that consumers are unlikely to pay higher prices for goods or services unless 'real' product differences exist. Furthermore, advertising brings buyers and sellers together by reducing the amount of time and costs that buyers incur searching for available goods and services.

Stigler (1961) and Telser (1964) contended that advertising reduces the costs of obtaining information. In other words, it is easier for a consumer to obtain information on the price and quality of products through advertisements than to engage in a lengthy search process to collect this information independently (see Figure 7.3).

In Figure 7.3, the cost of each additional hour of search is assumed to be constant and is summarised by the marginal cost function (MC). The benefit the

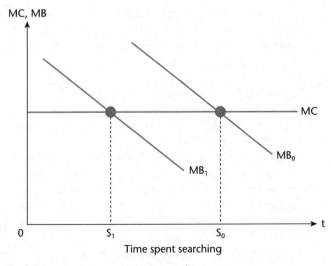

Figure 7.3 Optimal time spent on consumer search

consumers gain from each successive hour of search is characterised by a downward sloping marginal benefit function (MB). In other words, the benefits of gathering information on prices decline, as the consumer discovers more and more firms selling goods and services at low prices. The process of consumer search is likely to continue for as long as the marginal benefits of the search exceed the marginal costs. A consumer will continue to collect information as long as the increased knowledge obtained from the search is not outweighed by the costs (in terms of time or resources) used to collect this information. In Figure 7.3, the optimal amount of search is where $MC = MB_0$, at time S_0. The provision of information through advertising would have the effect of shifting the marginal benefit function to the left (MB_1) and reducing the optimal length of search time from S_0 to S_1. Given that advertising reduces the search costs of the consumer, the overall prices paid by consumers for products are likely to be lower in industries where advertising is prevalent. Overall, higher priced advertised goods may reflect a better quality product with a much smaller variability in that quality; or high prices reflect part of the search costs saved by the consumer; or producers who market 'own-brand' products at a lower price are simply exploiting the information spread by the advertised goods. The extent to which advertising effects prices is examined in Case Study 7.4.

Case Study 7.4

Does advertising reduce prices?

The extent of information available to consumers can affect the quality and prices of goods and services in a given market.

What does the theory say?
There are two views as to whether advertising increases or decreases price:

- Advertising increases consumer knowledge and increases the price elasticity of demand. In other words advertising reduces prices.

- Advertising will increase brand loyalty and/or consumer ignorance. The consequence is to increase the price elasticity of demand. In other words, advertising increases prices. Brand loyalty advantages can also lead to higher prices.

What does the real world say?
The majority of research compares the level and dispersion of prices between industries or market segments where advertising restrictions are imposed and those where there are no restrictions.

Benham (1972) examined the differences in the prices paid by consumers for eyeglasses in US states where advertising restrictions exist and those where they do not. Using data based on a national sample of 634 consumers, he compared the prices of glasses in various states. Benham found that eyeglasses were more expensive in states where advertising is restricted. MacKintosh and Frey (1978) examined the dispersion of prices for eyeglasses in New Orleans and Louisiana, where advertising restrictions were prevalent. The authors found significant differences in prices due to a lack of price transparency. They argued that if advertising restrictions were removed these price differences would decline.

Cox (1982) examined the relationship between advertising and the price of legal services in six US states in 1978. He grouped these states as to whether advertising regulations are restrictive (Alabama and Mississippi), moderate (Arizona and Indiana) or permissive (California and Wisconsin).

Cox found that higher advertising leads to lower prices. Uncontested bankruptcies were found to be on average $47 more expensive where advertising restrictions were in force, while divorces were on average $16 cheaper. Prices were found to be higher where: legal firms were large, reputation was deemed important and firms were less efficient.

Milyo and Waldfogel (1999) examine the impact of the lifting of advertising restrictions on alcoholic beverages in Rhode Island in 1996. The authors found that the prices of advertised goods declined (after restrictions were lifted), but those beverages that were not advertised remained at approximately the same price.

Kaul and Wittink (1995) surveyed 18 studies over a 20-year period that had examined the relationship between the extent of advertising and price in producer and consumer goods industries. From these studies the authors found:

- An increase in price advertising increased consumer sensitivity (i.e. price elasticity of demand) to price changes.

- An increase in price advertising led to intensified competition and resulted in firms charging lower prices.

- An increase in non-price advertising decreased consumer sensitivity to price changes.

Overall, the evidence suggests that advertising appears to reduce the variability and level of prices across several service industries.

Does information content of advertising vary by product type?

The extent to which advertising provides information crucially depends on type of product or service under consideration. Based on the research of Nelson (1974) and Darby and Karni (1973) we can provide a taxonomy of product types, comprising search, experience and credence goods.

Search goods are products and services which can be inspected by either touch or sight prior to purchase. Common examples include clothes, carpets, household and office furniture. In contrast, *experience goods* are products or services which must be consumed for an assessment as to quality to be made. Common examples include food, minidiscs, DVDs and university courses. Advertising is likely to be informative for search goods given that consumers can easily assess quality and product provider claims prior to purchase. Consequently, advertising expenditures are likely to be lower for search than experience goods. In fact, evidence suggests that advertising expenditures on experience goods are three times that of search goods (Nelson, 1974). However, consumers do have some control over their consumption of experience goods, as they can choose not to repeat purchase products if they are unhappy. The *credence good* is a product or service whose quality cannot be assessed either before or after consumption. Credence goods exist when a consumer is required to have special knowledge to judge the quality of the product or service. Common examples would be dental services, medical care, car repairs and financial services (Darby and Karni, 1973).

Some attempts have been made by researchers to assess the informative content of advertising. Resnick and Stern (1977) analysed 378 advertisements, and found that only 49.2% were regarded as informative. Abernethy and Franke (1996) analysed 91,438 advertisements relating to durable and non-durable goods. The authors found that advertising for durable goods provided on average 35% more information. In reality, it appears difficult to make a clear distinction between advertising that informs and advertising that persuades. To some extent, advertising can be thought to play a dual role of informing and persuading consumers as to the desirable aspects of goods and services. Regulatory intervention is often required to ensure consumers are not exploited.

7.3   Advertising and Competition

We have previously argued that there is little role for advertising and other forms of strategic behaviour under conditions of perfect competition. Under monopoly, this may also be the case given that the monopolist already faces an inelastic demand curve and so has substantial control over the prices it charges. However, under conditions of oligopoly and monopolistic competition firms may choose to engage in non-price competition through advertising. The effects of advertising are less clear. One view of advertising (outlined earlier) contends that advertising distorts consumer preferences, leading to a decrease in the price elasticity of demand, and allows established firms to increase their market power and profitability. The other view (also outlined earlier) contends that advertising increases competition by providing consumers with more information. The general hypotheses tested in the literature are either that high levels of advertising lead to increased concentration or that advertising increases entry barriers. We now examine these hypotheses briefly.

High levels of advertising lead to increased concentration

In this case, advertising leads to increased concentration through the operation of economies of scale. In other words, advertising increases the costs of production and the minimum efficient scale of production. This means that firms must be large to reach the minimum efficient scale to realise potential economies of scale in production and advertising. This has the effect of increasing industrial concentration in advertising intensive industries.

Advertising increases entry barriers

In the analysis of the effects of advertising on competition, entry barriers play a crucial role. It is a common argument that advertising simply increases the barriers to entry by increasing the minimum efficient scale of production for firms operating in an industry.

How does advertising act as a barrier to entry?

Advertising increases costs of production

Entrants have to spend heavily on advertising and other promotions to gain a foothold in the market. Consequently, entrants face additional costs when entering the industry. Furthermore, entrants may find it difficult to raise the necessary funds for entry, given that the returns to advertising outlays are likely to be uncertain.

High levels of advertising build reputation

Advertising leads to goodwill advantages and brand loyalty for established firms. This is often difficult for entrants to overcome. If the established firm is the first firm to pioneer a product in the market, brand loyalty will be high and any new entrants will find it difficult to capture market share.

Advertising increases demand

Advertising leads to increased demand for an individual firm's product. This in turn may lead to economies of scale for established firms. Economies of scale in advertising arise for two reasons. First, firms must advertise a large number of times before the signals from advertising reach consumers and are transformed into higher sales and profits for the firms. Second, as the firms' messages are passed throughout the economy, either by increased advertising or by word of mouth, consumers will respond to these messages by increasing demand. Consequently, economies of scale arise because increased numbers of advertising messages become more effective as they increase in frequency. In addition, large advertisers pay less per unit of sales than the small-scale advertiser. The effects of advertising as an entry barrier are shown in Figure 7.4.

Figure 7.4 shows the costs of production for established firms and entrants. In the figure, the average costs of production in the absence of advertising for established and entrant firms are shown by the curve APC. The minimum efficient scale of production is at Q_1. Average cost of production at this output level is equal to C_1. However, if advertising takes place (shown by ACA) the costs of production increase from APC to ATC. The average cost for established firms, ATC_{est} (equal to APC + ACA), is lower than that of entrants whose average costs are equal to ATC_{ent} (APC + ACA + AAIPC). The difference between the established firms' and entrants' costs is AAIPC, which represents the extra costs entrants incur in trying to penetrate the market. The minimum efficient scale in an industry where advertising is prevalent is Q_2. Consequently, the average costs are C_2 for established firms and C_3 for entrants. The entrant therefore suffers a cost disadvantage. This cost disadvantage is even higher if the entrant chooses to enter at a sub-optimal scale such as output

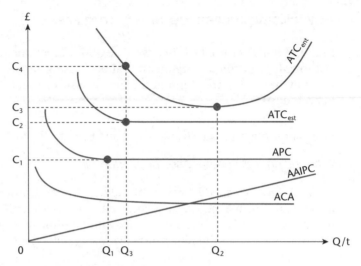

Figure 7.4 Advertising as an entry barrier

level Q_3, where average costs of production would increase to C_4. The cost advantages enjoyed by established firms may even allow them to set a limit price to make entry unprofitable to any potential entrants. Overall, this type of entry barrier allows established firms to exercise market power to increase profits and market share (Eckard, 1987; Paton and Vaughan Williams, 1999). Using the arguments developed in this section, we can now explicitly examine the relationships between advertising intensity and market structure.

Two alternative and conflicting hypotheses attempt to explain the relationships between advertising intensity and market structure. The first contends that increased concentration leads to a fall in advertising, while the other implies the opposite.

Increased concentration among sellers leads to a greater recognition of interdependence between them. As a consequence, they may decide to tacitly co-operate by eliminating competitive advertising. Thus increased concentration will lead to a reduction of advertising.

It is alternatively argued that increased concentration will force sellers to substitute non-price competition (i.e. advertising) for price competition. This hypothesis stems from the commonly used Dorfman–Steiner condition. This condition asserts that advertising intensity and concentration will be positively related. In industries where demand elasticity is high (such as perfect competition) advertising is low. By the same token, when elasticity of demand is low (as in oligopoly and monopoly), advertising intensity will be high.

Most analysis of advertising and concentration has examined the association between advertising intensity and some measure of concentration. If advertising leads to firms exercising market power, then advertising and concentration should be positively related. Early studies of advertising found a positive but insignificant relationship between advertising expenditures and concentration, implying that advertising will be at its highest under conditions of monopoly (see Comanor and Wilson, 1979, for a critical review). Later studies of advertising and concentration found an inverted U-shaped relationship between advertising and concentration, as

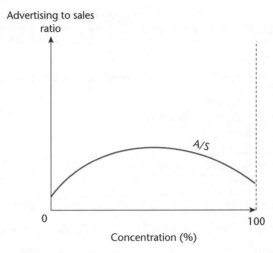

Figure 7.5 Advertising and concentration

is shown in Figure 7.5. Figure 7.5 shows that the advertising intensity (A/S ratio) increases under oligopoly, but declines again for monopoly. This relationship between advertising intensity and market structure implies that firms operating under oligopoly will compete on a non-price basis and so spend proportionately more on advertising than monopolists or firms operating under conditions of perfect competition.

There is some support for this relationship. For example, Sutton (1974) used data on 25 consumer goods industries and found an inverted U-shaped relationship between advertising and concentration. Buxton et al. (1984) and Uri (1987), who found a similar relationship between advertising and concentration, support this assertion. Taken together these findings lend some support to the view that advertising will be higher under oligopolies than any other type of market structure. Overall, the empirical evidence examined suggests that advertising intensity is much higher under oligopolies than under perfect competition and monopoly.

7.4   Conclusion

This chapter examined the role of advertising in determining company performance and considered the practical decisions firms must face when considering investment in product differentiation. We have seen that firms can use a variety of methods to differentiate products and services, in order to stimulate demand and increase market share and profitability. Our analysis suggested that oligopolistic market structures are the most conducive to large expenditures on advertising and other forms of product differentiation. At the level of the firm, the outcome of such strategies is variable and often uncertain. However, if successful, expenditures on product differentiation can lead to the appropriation of substantive competitive advantages over rivals.

Discussion Questions

1 Give examples of goods or services that have been successfully differentiated by:

a) advertising
b) geographical location
c) factor inputs
d) packaging
e) national differences
f) trademarks.

What is the effect of such product differentiation?

2 Why are firms motivated to advertise their products and services?

3 Outline the determinants of a firm's advertising expenditures.

4 Discuss the relationship between advertising and industry structure.

5 Discuss the differences between search, experience and credence goods.

6 How does advertising raise barriers to entry?

7 Using Case Study 7.1 discuss whether advertising increases or decreases prices.

Further Reading

General background

Cook, M. and Farquharson, C. (1998) *Business Economics*. London: Pitman, Chapter 18.
Davies, H. and Lam, P. (2001) *Managerial Economics*. London: Financial Times/Prentice Hall, Chapter 16.
Mochandreas, M. (2000) *Business Economics* (2nd edn). London: Thomson Business Press, Chapter 2.

Advanced

Bearne, A. (1996) The economics of advertising: a re-appraisal, *Economic Issues*, 1, 23–38.
Comanor, W. S. and Wilson, T. (1979) Advertising and competition: a survey, *Journal of Economic Literature*, 17, 453–76.
Kaul, A. and Wittink, D. R. (1995) Empirical generalisations about the impact of advertising on price sensitivity and price, *Marketing Science*, 14, 151–60.

8 Research, Development and Innovation

Objectives

By the end of this chapter, the reader should be able to understand:

- the meaning of innovation and the stages of research and development
- the reasons why diffusion of innovations can be slow
- why patents exist
- the market structures which are most likely to invest in research and development
- various research and development strategies
- the important issues facing firms which wish to invest in research and development.

Key Concepts

- Delphi technique
- diffusion
- innovation
- innovative milieux
- invention
- patents
- Schumpeterian hypothesis

8.1 Introduction

An alternative strategy to product differentiation, discussed in Chapter 7, is for firms to focus on research and development activity as a means of achieving a competitive advantage. This strategy is not too dissimilar to product differentiation in the sense that both create new products in the minds of consumers. If successful, both strategies have the effect of shifting the demand curve to the right and of reducing the price elasticity of demand. New products, as well as products which are successfully differentiated, have fewer substitutes and thus confer a degree of monopoly power on the firms which own and sell the products.

This chapter first discusses what is meant by innovation and then traces the various stages that constitute research and development. Special attention is paid to discussing the problem of diffusion and the importance of patent protection. After addressing the issue of the market structures most conducive to firms for investing in research and development and innovation, we examine the various general strategies open to firms when considering such an investment. This is then followed by a consideration of specific factors which affect an individual firm's decision to engage in research and development.

8.2   What Is Innovation?

Innovation is a part of the research and development process which seeks to introduce new products or technical processes that eventually render the existing range of products and processes obsolete. In studies of competitive market structures and business strategy, innovation is assigned a high level of importance, since not only does it confer market advantages on successful innovators but it can also be seen as a process that is fundamental to the development and evolution of an economy. In general, changes in technology affect the growth in economic welfare. Such changes can also have effects on output, product quality, levels of employment, trade, wages and profits. Thus the rate at which industries develop new ideas, launch new products and introduce new processes is of interest not only to firms, but also to governments, consumers and trade unions.

It is important to note that a distinction is made between *product* innovation and *process* innovation. *Product innovation* is seen as the development of a new product without altering the production process, whereas *process innovation* involves any technique that leads to a reduction in average costs, keeping input prices constant. Of course, there is an overlap in these definitions. From the point of view of a producer, a new machine would be classed as product innovation; whereas from the point of view of the buyer (the user), the machine would be seen as part of process innovation.

8.3   Stages of Research and Development

Let us now turn to an examination of what is meant by research and development and the process of innovation. Research and development can be thought of as passing through various stages. We now identify these stages and focus on the final stage, the *diffusion* or spread of an innovation. The quicker a new technology can be adopted or adapted to various uses, the greater the benefits to firms, industries, consumers and the wider economy. One possible cause for the slow rate of diffusion is the existence of patents. However, patents can also be viewed positively as an important stimulus for investments in innovation. The issue of patents is discussed at the end of this section.

Identification of R&D stages

Basic research

This refers to what may be termed as 'inventive activity'. An *invention* is the creation of an idea and its first reduction to practice. At its extreme, such activity is carried out regardless of any practical application in view. Hence basic research in molecular physics was carried out without any foreknowledge of the development of the valve to be used in broadcasting and communications. This type of research is unattractive to industrial firms due to the uncertainty of outcome. Consequently, it is normally carried out by government agencies and universities.

Applied research

As opposed to basic research, applied research has a stated objective. Following an investigation of potential economic returns, research is undertaken to determine the technological feasibility of the proposed application.

Development work

Generally, this can be considered as the bringing of an idea or invention to the stage of commercial production and, together with stage two, this can be referred to as *innovatory activity*. It is at this stage that resources are committed, as pilot plants or prototypes may have to be built. Although it is clear that at every stage of research and development the firm must review its progress, it is here that the selection process for the next stage is at its most important. A new product failure at the next stage would be very costly to the organisation.

Commercial production

This stage refers to the full-scale production of the new product or application of a new process. Notwithstanding the level of research and development carried out into the technical characteristics of the new ideas and the amount of market research undertaken, there still exists an element of uncertainty. We can thus define the difference between invention and innovation as the level of risk. Typically, the innovating firm must bear a degree of risk in the development and launch of a new product. The 'pure' inventor, however, is not interested in commercial applications, as his or her interest is in the generation of ideas and not the production of goods and services. Risks in this case are thus appreciably lower.

Diffusion

The final stage refers to the spread of the new idea through the firm as well as the copying and adoption of the techniques and products by other firms in the industry and other industries in the economy. One can also identify spatial diffusion, whereby ideas spread to other countries through transfers such as foreign direct investment, licensing agreement and joint ventures. This stage is discussed in more detail later.

These five stages discussed are not necessarily viewed as a linear process, whereby inventions, via innovation, lead to commercial production and eventual diffusion. Projects may be scrapped or revised at any time. Diffusion may be slow at first and then accelerate. There may also be extensive feedback from stages that can lead to the abandonment of existing projects, which then set into motion newer ideas and fresh projects. It is important to note that the stages of research and development outlined are not the only source of technological change for a firm. Technology can be acquired by copying techniques from other firms and industries, by entering into various collaborative and licensing agreements with other firms, or by acquiring the technology from suppliers of capital goods.

What factors affect the rate of diffusion?

The speed at which inventions are transformed into commercial goods varies from product to product and industry to industry. The greatest obstacle to the speed of technical change in an economy is the rate of diffusion. Some technologies seem to languish in oblivion and then suddenly take off, others may never get to challenge the existing technological process or products, while others still are rapidly adopted and spread quickly through the firm, the industry and the wider economy. It is important therefore to discuss the factors that help or hinder the spread of new ideas. We first identify the general factors that retard the rate of diffusion to other firms and industries (*inter-firm diffusion*) and, second, we focus on the specific factors that affect diffusion within a firm (*intra-firm diffusion*).

General factors (affecting inter-firm diffusion)

Labour fears

There is evidence that organised labour often resist the adoption of a new technology if they see it as a threat to their employment. In the UK print unions were reluctant to accept 'direct-inputting' technology in the 1970s. This technology allowed journalists electronically to transfer their copy direct to the photosetting department, thereby bypassing the compositing rooms. The three unions that represented workers in the compositing rooms refused to accept this and other innovations for a number of years. As a result, Fleet Street was slow to adapt to technical changes that were being adopted elsewhere in newspaper publishing.

Poor communications

Government reports (e.g. NEDC, 1983) have in the past highlighted the lack of communication and co-operation between inventors and innovators and the business community. The development of science parks and other initiatives has been an attempt to bring universities, the producers of new knowledge, and the immediate users closer together.

Management inertia

An important reason why some firms may adopt new products or new process quicker than other firms is that they are controlled by technically trained managers, attuned to the characteristics of the new technology. Managers with a poor technical background may fail to recognise the superiority of a new technology and only consider adopting it when existing capital needs replacing. It is also possible that firms could be run by a lethargic and over-bureaucratic cadre of managers who may move too slowly in seizing technical opportunities. Patel and Pavitt (1987) found that the rate of diffusion of four specific engineering innovations was much lower in Britain than in Germany. This was blamed on a lack of commitment to develop and commercialise new products and processes, as well as a lack of engineering expertise on the part of British management.

Protecting an older technology

There is some evidence to suggest that dominant firms may protect their existing market shares and status quo by either keeping new ideas secret or denying entry to firms with a newer technology. Maclaurin (1950) detailed how major communications firms in the United States (Western Union, Postal Telegraph and American Telephone and Telegraph) resisted the development of radio, preferring instead to buy up competitors and to enter into restrictive agreements. In addition, they attempted to prevent the Marconi Company from obtaining a franchise in Newfoundland. The UK Post Office also attempted to frustrate Marconi's new technology by refusing to connect their overseas service to Post Office telegraph lines.

Government or local regulations

Where an industry is faced with a cumbersome regulatory framework regarding standards for materials, design and safety, the adoption of a new technology may be sluggish, as amendments in regulations may be slow and bureaucratic. For example, Oster and Quigley (1977) found that local building codes significantly reduced the diffusion of technical progress in the building industry. Evidence of an opposite effect, whereby regulations stimulate the rapid diffusion of a technology, was provided by Hannan and McDowell (1984), who examined the adoption of ATMs (automated telling machines) by banks across the United States. Some states had restricted the number of branches allowed to a bank, and the adoption of ATMs was seen as a way of circumventing these restrictions.

Patents

In a free market new knowledge is a free resource, available to all firms. The consequence of this is that there would be too little or no research and development, as innovating firms would be reluctant to see their rivals enjoy a 'free ride' from their costly and risky investments. To shield innovators from too rapid a diffusion, governments offer patents as protection. In the UK, a successful patent grants a firm a 20-year monopoly on a product or process. The problem facing society is that an effective patent system may result in the slow diffusion of knowledge through the economy. There is little evidence that the patent system in the UK does result in slow diffusion, as many firms often enter into patent-sharing or licensing agreements.

Specific factors (affecting intra-firm diffusion)

Age of existing capital

The speed at which new technology replaces older technology is related to the age profile of a firm's capital stock. Faced with a new process, firms with older machines adopt the innovation at a faster rate than those firms which have only recently installed machines using the older process.

Degree of risk

A technology may be adopted only slowly if there is a substantial risk associated with its introduction. For example, the technology may require inputs that are either not readily available or may be unfamiliar to the firm. This may increase the costs of production and squeeze the estimated profit margins to such an extent that the firm is reluctant to apply the technology. Risks may also stem from uncertainties over the level of market demand. Oster and Quigley (1977) found that the effective demand for housing fluctuated widely, based on changes in the market for credit. These fluctuations inhibited the adoption of new technologies in the housebuilding industry. An application of capital-intensive methods of production could make firms more vulnerable to changes in demand.

Liquidity

It can be argued that the more profitable a firm, the better able it is to generate internal funds for the application of a new technology. It is implicit that investment in new technology is risky, and firms may have difficulty in raising external finance to fund such projects.

Degree of competition

There is some debate as to the effects of competition on the rate of diffusion. This mirrors the market structure and level of research and development debate, discussed later in the chapter. There are two arguments formulated here. Does more competition in the industry spur firms to adopt new ideas faster, as a means of gaining an advantage over rivals; or is diffusion faster where we have imperfectly competitive industries which enjoy the high profits and the protection of entry barriers to invest in new technology?

Size of firm

The introduction of an innovation may well require large inputs of capital and technical expertise which would tend to favour the larger firm. For example, Oster and Quigley (1977) found that in the house-building industry many of the innovations were in organisation, systems design and integration of housing components. These activities are usually found in large-scale production, a scale then not commonly found among the majority of house-building firms.

8.4   Patents

As discussed in the previous section, the problem facing governments eager to promote technical change is how best to encourage investment in new technology. A problem arises in that once a new idea has been created and developed under free market conditions, it is virtually costless to share this idea with other firms. Knowledge is a free good. However, such sharing of ideas would be a disincentive to undertake innovatory activity as the returns to such an investment would be greatly diminished. The granting of a patent to an innovator confers a *property right* over that new knowledge. The innovator owns an economic asset which can be sold, licensed or exploited by the firm itself. Its use is subject to the authorisation of the patent holder. However, granting such rights to an innovator also creates temporary monopoly power, which may compromise allocative efficiency. Governments must therefore attempt to find the right balance between the encouragement of research and development, on the one hand, and preventing the abuse of market power on the other.

In most countries for an invention or innovation to be 'patentable' it must meet three criteria:

- *It must be new*, in the sense that it has not been previously used, published or demonstrated in the public domain. There are certain ideas that cannot be patented, such as scientific discovery, mathematical formulae, mental processes, artistic creations, etc.

- *It should be non-obvious*, insofar as it would not have occurred to reasonably well-informed people in the field. In other words, it requires an 'inventive step' to have been taken.

- *It should also be capable of industrial application*, so that it can, at least in theory, be usable in some form as a piece of equipment or as a process.

Applying for patents can be costly to small and medium-sized firms. When filing a complicated patent application, consultants (patent agents) may be required to ensure that the patent is correctly drawn up so as to avoid possible imitations 'around the patent' and thus potential future litigation. Application fees, annual renewal fees (from the fourth year) and foreign patent applications add to the expense. Small firms must therefore weigh up the advantages of using a new technology with or without the protection of a patent. If a firm feels that it is too weak to defend and enforce its patent it may choose to open its ideas to the whole market, which at least prevents larger firms from 'stealing' the idea and patenting it themselves. Even larger firms may be in a position where the costs of policing and enforcing intellectual property rights are too high in their particular industry and thus the incentive to patent is non-existent.

Do patents encourage innovation?

A fundamental point in any discussion on patents is whether patents encourage industrial innovation. A number of issues arise:

- Does the patent system encourage investment in research and development or does it focus attention on patentable activity such as inventions? There may be no reason to assume that patented activity such as inventions is necessarily that which is of greatest economic benefit to industries and society.

- Patents may increase the risks of failure, by encouraging patent races. The cost of research and development increases as firms gain little return for their R&D investments. Thus firms face the potential risk of 'gambler's ruin', whereby an investment can lead to no tangible asset to sell off in the event of failure.

- By granting monopoly status, patents tend to protect innovating firms rather than inventing firms, and some firms may use a strategy of pre-emptive patenting to limit competition. It might be argued that greater competition is needed at the innovation stage to help the diffusion process.

- It is also important to determine the market structure that would be best served by the patent system – in other words, a market structure that lacks *other incentives* for investment in research and development. At a general level one could argue that monopolies would not view patents as an incentive to innovate as they already enjoy the security of not facing rivals. Instead, patents could be seen as buttressing their market dominance by adding barriers to entry. On the other hand, in theoretical models of perfect competition, patents would provide incentives to innovate. Without such protection their new knowledge would be immediately shared by rivals.

The last point is based on a simplistic view of market structure, where only the two extremes are considered. If we open up the analysis to include the wide variety of forms that characterise more realistic (oligopolistic) structures (which were discussed in Chapter 4), it is often argued that innovation is one of the main strategies for competitive activity in such markets. This could still be the case, even in the absence of patents, since competing firms may be slow through various market imperfections to imitate and adapt to new ideas, products and process. This delay could be caused by the lag effects of introducing a new technology, such as the need to acquire new skills, retrain labour, the risks of investing in new capital, buying unfamiliar inputs and accurately gauging the level of demand.

Schankerman (1998) noted that patent renewals in France in the four technology fields of pharmaceuticals, chemicals, mechanical engineering and electronics showed that there was a substantial incentive for R&D, but that it did not constitute the major source for such incentives. He also found that there were differences in the importance of patent protection in the various technology fields. The least important seemed to be in the pharmaceutical field, which he argued could be due to the strong level of price regulation in that industry.

8.5   Market Structure and Innovation

With reference to our discussions in Chapters 3 and 4, we can ask ourselves which of the four market structures are most likely to invest in innovation. It is clear that both *perfectly competitive* and *monopolistically competitive* markets, *in theory*, are not likely to devote resources to innovation as both models are built on assumptions of free entry. Any advantage gained through innovation would immediately be dissipated by the entry of rival firms which would copy the new products or process.

At first sight it would also seem that large *monopoly* or 'near monopoly' firms would also be uninterested in innovation. One of the traditional arguments against monopoly is that without the spur of competition the monopolist is content with its existing production techniques, since they are generating monopoly profits. Thus there is no incentive to invest in research and development to improve these production techniques. However, it has been shown, and claimed implicitly by Schumpeter (1950), that highly concentrated industries are often sources of great inventive and innovative activity. The reasons for this are not generally found in formal models of market structures.

The Schumperterian hypothesis

- Highly concentrated industries enjoy greater profits, which can be invested in 'risky' innovatory activity. Fragmented industries earn only 'normal' profits and have no 'uncommitted' resources. The higher profits earned by monopolies can also secure better inputs with which to exploit technological investments.

- The absence of competition allows the firm an environment of 'security' in which to carry out the risky projects. There are fewer potential imitators and the firm is free to consider speculative innovation, knowing that failure will not be exploited by rivals.

- Competition at high levels of concentration can still exist in the guise of near monopolies and highly concentrated oligopolies. Innovation may be an important source of non-price competition in these market structures.

- Monopolies are typically large and face a large market in which it may prove easier to exploit a variety of new ideas.

- There are potential economies of large-scale R&D production for the large firms operating under conditions of oligopoly and monopoly.

A contrary argument

An argument contrary to the Schumpeterian hypothesis can, however, also be made, which highlights possible *negative* effects a monopoly has on innovative activity:

- In the absence of competitive forces, management in a monopoly may become lazy. In addition, overbureaucratic structures can lead to possible control loss (discussed in Chapter 2) and x-inefficiencies (discussed in Chapter 3). All these may have the effect of reducing the amount of funds directed towards innovatory activity.

- Since there are so few potential rivals to a monopolist there are fewer firms doing innovatory work. Assuming that successful innovation is more likely the more firms there are, since the *intensity of research* as well as the *probability of success* is greater, it then follows that monopolistic structures have a lower level of successful innovative output.

- Monopolies which owe their market power to past successful innovations may view new innovations in the industry as displacing their current technology. The effect is that *net* returns are lower than those for new entrants which are unencumbered with an existing technology. In addition, the monopoly firm may be so 'tied' to an existing technology that to switch resources to a newer product or process might be considered too costly.

Finally, some economists have interpreted Schumpeter's arguments to suggest that at both extremes (perfect competition and monopoly) firms are adverse to large amounts of R&D. This would imply that the relationship between industrial concentration and R&D expenditures would exhibit an inverted U-shaped function. Scherer (1967) confirmed this sort of relationship when he found that R&D employment as a share of total employment increased with industry concentration up to around 50%, after which point it declined. These findings suggest the classic argument: that it is *oligopolies* that have the most incentive to innovate to free themselves from rivalry in markets. Similar arguments were discussed in relation to advertising intensity and market structure in Chapter 7.

However, given the lack of clear and consistent oligopoly theory much of the theorising is complex and speculative. In Chapter 4, we argued that oligopolists often seek co-operative solutions to reduce market uncertainty. Price competition reduces industry profits and the same could be said of non-price competition such as advertising and technical innovation. One would thus expect rational oligopolists to attempt to cover non-price aspects of competition as well.

Why do oligopolists find it difficult to collude over R&D?

For an oligopolistic structure of just a few firms it would be relatively easy to agree and decide on a common price. However, to determine what should be the optimal level of R&D expenditure for the group may prove impossible. Price-fixing agreements make it relatively easy to calculate the consequences for firms' returns over a period of time. Fixing an R&D effort does not lead to any easy prediction as to the likely output of research in the industry. If one firm were to be selected to do all the research for the industry, there is the risk that the other firms might be excluded from the ownership of that research output. If research were to be shared it would be difficult to co-ordinate the effort across the industry. Given the inherent uncertainty of research and the involvement of many firms involved, there may be a temptation to cheat by taking a free ride. This would further be compounded by the difficulty of enforcing and policing such agreements. An additional problem frustrating such agreements might be the concern over what would occur if the agreement were to break down. The breakdown of a price agreement implies only minor consequences in the short run. A breakdown of research agreements, however, would most probably have differential effects on the firms, since those that invested large amounts would suffer more than those with a smaller commitment.

This discussion has outlined the difficulties of entering into co-operative research agreements. This should not imply that these types of venture are never undertaken. Research agreements do exist and are usually of two types. The first is where the focus is on the 'pre-competitive stage' where firms share knowledge at the R&D stages but remain rivals in the product market. The second type of agreement is when firms extend their co-operation to include the product market. The aim is to enjoy greater security and higher returns and to recoup their R&D outlays with more certainty.

So far in this section we have considered the role of firms in oligopolistic and monopolistic market. These firms are typically large.

Does this imply that small firms are rarely involved in innovation?

It has been claimed (e.g. De Propris 2000) that although small firms invest proportionally little in research and development they can be more innovative than larger firms. The argument is based on a *systemic* approach to innovation as opposed to the linear, sequential approach outlined at the beginning of this chapter. This systemic approach argues that it is the *environment* in which a firm finds itself which affects the level of innovation which the firm undertakes. These environmental or external factors might then shape so-called *innovative milieux*, which are characterised by the following:

- Local firms sharing new knowledge. It may be argued that geographical proximity can help to develop a degree of social cohesion, which in turn helps firms to share new ideas.

- Regional and national organisations can also promote the spread of such knowledge.

- The existence of vertical and horizontal production networks often compels firms to share new technologies to avoid inefficiencies within the networks.

Thus although firms are small, existing in such innovatory environments does encourage firms to adopt and adapt to new ideas.

8.6   Industrial Research and Development Strategies

Economists have traditionally identified two fundamental reasons why firms undertake research and development. First, the activity is profitable and, second, successful research and development confers strategic advantages. The effect of successful research and development is to lower the average cost function, via process innovation, or to shift the demand curve to the right, via product innovation. Both these outcomes lead to increased profitability, assuming that competitors are unable to imitate the ideas either through institutional arrangements (such as patent laws) or through high market transaction costs.

However, in an economic environment where uncertainty characterises most decision making, it is unrealistic to assume that firms view policies such as innovation as a means of contributing to the maximisation of profits alone. We can achieve a closer appreciation of why firms invest in research and development by examining a wide variety of business strategies such activity can open up. Our discussion follows the arguments put forward by Freeman and Soete (1997).

Offensive strategy

An offensive strategy could be regarded as a strategy which is designed to give a firm a degree of dominance in the market, through the introduction of technological changes. The main focus of activity in the firm is to generate new ideas and to protect these ideas and associated spin-offs by patent application with a view to achieving monopoly status. The firm has to invest heavily in scientific resources of both labour and capital. Examples of such a heavy resource commitment to research were Du Pont's development of Nylon and Lycra, IG Farben's development of PVC and RCA's development of colour television. It is claimed that these types of firm may even invest in highly speculative basic research, although certainly not of the purest type. To be ahead of any other possible rival does imply that firms which wish to pursue an offensive strategy must concentrate on experimental development work, requiring the capacity to design, build and test prototypes and pilot plants. To be good at research and development also requires that the firm 'educates' the market as well as its own personnel to ensure that the technology is firmly rooted in the marketplace. This requires the production of training manuals, seminars, videos and other related support services. One can appreciate how Microsoft partly achieved its success by ensuring that its software was accompanied by an investment in the education of its consumers.

Defensive strategy

Changes in technology and continual product improvement force many firms to attempt to keep pace with such changes. In the absence of any other marketing strategy, to do nothing is to see market share collapse, as rivals introduce processes and products that marginalise the 'laggards'. The defensive strategy does not imply no research, but, rather, impacts the *timing* of the research. The defensive strategist simply follows the technology leads of offensive firms. The defensive firm may either lack the large technical resources needed to become an offensive firm or may wish to avoid the risks associated with a heavy commitment to such speculative investments, preferring instead to invest in proven processes and products. It may also be possible that the defensive firm may wish to improve on the technology by attempting to produce second-generation ideas, permissible within the constraints of the existing patent breadth. Empirical evidence confirms that, in most oligopolistic industries, defensive innovation is not only typical but also a rational reaction to new technology. This implies that these defensive firms must also invest in technical resources so as to react quickly to new ideas if they are to retain their market shares or even possibly 'leapfrog' over some of the weaker offensive firms.

Imitative strategy

Adopting an imitative strategy implies that the firm does not wish to produce a better product. Instead, it is happy to produce a product identical to that of other firms in the industry, either by a licence in the short run or by exploiting free knowledge in the long run. Investment in technical resources is low as the firm need not attempt any product adaptation or improvement and does not need to meet the costs of educating the market. It benefits from the information spread by the offensive and defensive firms. Nonetheless, for the strategy to be profitable, the imitator must posses certain advantages such as low costs or a captive market. One reason why Du Pont left the rayon market was its inability to compete with the low-cost producers. Imitating firms may also apply the new ideas where they benefit most from a captive market, for example demand from their own subsidiaries or markets protected by political patronage or tariff walls. These are markets from which the offensive firm is excluded. In some cases, government and capital market support can be used to exploit such strategies of imitation in order to diffuse technological change quickly and efficiently.

Dependent strategy

This strategy implies a subservient role with regard to the stronger offensive or defensive firms. These firms can be regarded as 'satellites' or 'subcontractors' of stronger firms and they initiate no investment in research and development. They accept the new technology handed down, often as a condition of maintaining supply relations with customers or suppliers. The new technology is often accompanied by technical assistance, the loaning of skilled labour and help with ancillary investments. The Japanese electronics and automotive industries is an example of this type of subcontracting and dependency strategy. This strategy may, under certain circumstances, propel firms towards vertical integration, should the dominant firm wish to protect its technology and investments.

Traditional strategies

The output of the traditional firm is not responsive to changes in technology. This is due to the nature of the market demand where consumers do not seek frequent technical changes in the products or where consumers may be ignorant of the new technology. Competition from rivals may be weak or, at the other extreme, so strong as to erode any abnormal profits that could be used in the development of new ideas. Differentiation, if important, would be focused on design changes which are non-technical. These industries may be likened to 'craft industries', such as hairdressing, restaurants and building contract work (see Case Study 8.1).

8.7   Investment in Research and Development

How should a firm best allocate its R&D expenditures?

In small firms the direction of investment may follow the aspirations and 'hunches' of the owner or technical director. In other firms, in industries where technology is changing rapidly in given areas, it is clear which direction such expenditures should take. There are firms, however, that may have large R&D budgets and a degree of discretion as to the allocation of such funds. Most of the issues discussed in the

Case Study 8.1 FT

Plenty of innovation alongside too much ambition

The short history of the Advanced Passenger Train, the tilting train developed in the 1980s, has become a case study in how not to introduce new technology. The trains were developed by British Rail engineers who went into overdrive in terms of introducing technical ideas, but with little thought as to how the new concepts would perform once the train was out on the track. Consequently, the four trains built never achieved full commercial service and were withdrawn unceremoniously in 1984, two years after the train made its debut.

'The engineers showed a lot of innovation but were too ambitious – they tried to do too much at the same time,' said Michel Moreau, president of the transport division of Alstom, one of the world's biggest three train builders, which is constructing the tilting trains for Virgin. Some of the ideas behind the 1980s' tilting trains were derived – with catastrophic consequences for the programme – from aircraft technology. They included a new type of brake, which attempted to slow the train's wheels with jets of high-pressure water. But, in operation, the water tended to overheat, causing a distortion of the brakes' metal components and forcing the trains out of service. Just as disastrous was the engineers' decision to attempt to tilt the train round corners by an angle of 12°. This turned out to be too much for the comfort of passengers, many of whom succumbed to travel sickness on some of the trains' first journeys.

Later generations of tilting trains have tilted by a more manageable 8°.

Source: *Financial Times*, 10 July 2001.

following fall into standard models of investment appraisal, which attempt to estimate the profitability of research and development by estimating the future level of customer demand and the level of development costs.

The major difference between the decision to invest in the replacement of capital goods and in research and development lies in the level of uncertainty attached to the latter type of investment. Risks attached to innovative effort differ from other risks in that they cannot be regarded as 'insurable risks' (i.e. risks which are repetitive and thus reasonably easy to measure). Risks naturally decrease as decisions focus more on the application and modification of established technology rather than on basic research and radical product or process development. With the risk constraint defined, let us now consider what factors may influence the discretionary use of research and development funds.

Market issues

The first issue firms may consider is whether the new idea meets an unsatisfied market demand. This may not be as difficult a problem as it first appears, since in many cases it is the customers who alert the firms to a gap in the market. Research has shown that a very large proportion of research and development comes about as a result of requests for product or process improvement from users.

Second, firms have to consider the growth potential of the new market. This may involve some form of long-term forecasting, which is, of course, highly speculative. Firms with a high commitment to innovation as an offensive strategy may attempt the *Delphi technique* to determine the future level of demand. The Delphi technique was developed by the RAND Corporation in the late 1960s as a forecasting methodology. The technique works by organising a group of experts, drawn from many different fields, who are encouraged to present subjective opinions as to the future of a market. These opinions are reached individually and then circulated to the other members of the group, who are then asked to revise their opinions in the light of what they have read. Through this process of *iteration*, a consensus is reached.

The problem with the Delphi technique is that it assumes that a collective consensus is always better that the views of one individual. An alternative approach to technological forecasting is *trend extrapolation*. Firms examine the developments of products using time series data and then attempt to forecast future developments. The problem with this approach is that one has to assume that all the relevant market variables remain constant into the future, which over a ten- or 20-year period is highly unlikely.

A third important issue to consider is the strength of rivals and the likelihood of their entry into a new product market. An example of a firm unable to withstand the entry of powerful firms was Lestoil, a small American company which developed and launched a range of liquid household cleaners. The success of the product attracted the attention of major manufacturers such as Lever Brothers, Procter & Gamble and Colgate Palmolive, whose entry Lestoil was unable to prevent.

Costs

If firms wish to determine the profitability of research and development investments, they must also attempt to estimate the level of development costs. Given that these costs are incurred well into the future and that they are costs that accompany an inherently uncertain and risky project, the chance of correctly estimating the level of costs is not high. Firms can reduce these costs by concentrating on less speculative innovations, but, even then, the estimating errors can be large.

The implication is that innovation which is anything other than a simple application of an existing technology incurs a much higher error in the estimated costs. Furthermore, there appears to be a tendency to underestimate the costs of such projects and much more so than for other forms of investment. The estimation of such costs is quite possibly dependent on in-fighting between the different interest groups within the organisation.

Marketing

There are many issues that need to be considered when firms are faced with the marketing of a new product. First, can the firm exploit its existing reputation to help the development of a new market? New firms with new products may be at a disadvantage from suspicious and conservative consumers. Second, the firm may have to consider whether the new product has clear and distinctive 'promotable' features. If, for example, the new product or idea is too complex for the average consumer to understand, or it appears unattractive, then the market may never fully develop. Distribution is another key element in the marketing strategy. If firms have well-developed distribution channels and dealer networks, then the new product can be promoted through these existing structures, accompanied by the necessary amount of promotion activity. The alternative is to rely on independent distributors who may have to be persuaded to adopt the new product or be prised away from existing suppliers. Finally, firms have to consider the price at which the new product is sold. It may be possible to overcome consumer inertia or resistance to a new product by a pricing strategy. For example, if a new product is subject to a taboo effect, whereby consumers will not pay a positive price for the product until they believe sufficient numbers of other consumers are already in the market, then the firm may be forced to charge a zero price to break the taboo and stimulate market demand. In the UK in the late 1980s there was much resistance to the new subscription satellite TV and the purchase of satellite dishes, which prompted Sky TV to give the dishes away free for a six-month period in order to establish a market for its service.

Production

Firms need to evaluate the demands placed on its production capabilities when considering an investment in innovation. Questions which have to be considered focus on whether the firm has sufficient capacity; the necessary capital; whether it has trained staff and the necessary technical expertise to see the project through. In addition, a new technology may require new inputs which involve the firm in new and unfamiliar supply relationships. As regards the issue of spare capacity, it may well be the case that the firm is prompted into developing new products simply to exploit its spare capacity.

Finance

Following this last discussion, it is clear that investment in innovation is speculative as the cash flows and losses are difficult to estimate. Firms hoping to attract external funds may be faced with a reluctance on the part of lenders and may well be forced to rely on internally generated funds. One problem which may frustrate the flow of funds is that the managers undertaking the research have much better information as to the likely success of the project than the financier, who is less able to monitor and control the use of such funds. Due to such possible information asymmetries, the projects may not be financed efficiently. The type of support that might be forthcoming would only be short term, since the risks of fluctuations in revenue and costs are much lower in projects with a short time span. Financiers may also be more able to monitor the performance of managers in the short run. It is therefore not surprising that many small and medium-sized firms turn to their own internal funds to finance innovation.

Timescale

A final consideration to be taken by a firm is to determine the speed at which the research and development should take place. The reason for considering the rate of development is the presence or absence of rivals. A tight oligopolistic market structure, characterised by powerful rivals, encourages rapid innovation, and as pressure from rivals declines the less pressing is the need to gain strategic advantages. Scherer (1967) developed a model which helps to explain the time choices faced by firms. This is illustrated by Figure 8.1.

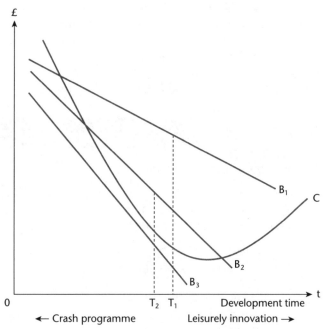

Figure 8.1 Optimum development time in oligopolistic markets

The model is based on the following assumptions:

- Research and development is carried out to maximise profits.
- Patent barriers do not exist.
- Rivalry is expressed through qualitative changes in the product.
- Each firm is responsible for its own research.

In Figure 8.1, C is the time–cost tradeoff function. A firm can innovate at a slow, leisurely pace or at a very fast pace (a crash programme) or at various speeds in between. To speed up the pace of innovation, costs rise due to:

- errors being made when the firm does not wait for a full analysis of various tests
- the necessity of maintaining parallel research as a hedge
- the potential of diminishing returns in the short run.

B_1 is a benefits function, which represents the benefits to an innovator of proceeding at various speeds. It is negatively sloped because:

- early completion of the project allows the firm to exploit the market over a longer period of time, and
- it improves the firm's market power over its rivals.

Being a profit-maximising firm, the firm selects the optimum time, where there is a maximum surplus over costs, i.e. where the slope of the benefits function equals the slope of the cost function. Development time $0T_1$ is thus chosen. The shape of the C function is largely determined by the level of technology. The slope of the B function is determined by market structure. If there are more or fewer firms, does the slope get steeper, e.g. B_2, and thus reduce the optimum development time? Is the slope affected by the relative size of the firms? These questions can only be answered by applying and analysing various oligopolistic markets. Scherer concluded that there is no clear, unambiguous answer. It is possible that entry of rival firms into the industry may shift the benefits function so far to the left (B_3) that the profit potential is so low and the potential number of imitators so high that *no* development is undertaken.

(See Case Studies 8.2 and 8.3 for more on innovation.)

Case Study 8.2

How a banker sees innovation

Warren Edwardes is a banker who has written on the topic of innovatory financial products. He notes that new products in the financial market enjoy a rapid diffusion for two reasons:

- The costs of producing such products are extremely low since no physical product is actually created or stocked in a warehouse. All that is required is that some documents are printed and relevant staff instructed in the promotion and sale of the product.

- They are difficult to patent. Many of the new financial products will use *basic ideas* and thus cannot be claimed to be 'non-obvious'.

Within this context, Edwardes identifies six types of innovation in financial markets:

- *Competitive innovation.* Due to the relative ease with which new products are adopted in the market all banks will be forced to be aware of and supply up-to-date financial products to clients to expand or protect their market shares.

- *Regulatory innovation.* These specific innovations are launched to circumvent regulatory or political restrictions, such as the creation of the eurobond market and credit and insurance derivatives.

- *Accounting innovation.* If corporate treasurers are faced with a requirement to pay for some services, a product could be devised to reduce such payments until some time into the future.

- *Taxation innovation.* These innovations can be used to exploit taxation regulations. Thus with the use of financial products, income streams can be converted into capital gains, which then attract a lower rate of tax.

- *Religious innovation.* These products were designed generally to meet the needs of Islamic banking, which prohibits interest payments. There are also examples of products which can help meet the needs of people wishing to invest in 'ethical' funds.

- *Ignorance innovation.* According to Edwardes such innovation is the 'ripping off' of customers, although not through any desire to mislead, but by 'creative financial engineering'. Thus customers may be happy with their returns, while remaining ignorant of the true potential returns.

Source: Edwardes, 2000.

Case Study 8.3

Creativity transforms user attitudes

Strategy and reality appeared to be at odds with each other. The chairman of JCB sought to expand from construction and agricultural vehicles into the industrial handling sector. Analysis showed this was dependent on manufacturing a forklift truck in order to build volume and establish a presence in the market sector. Such a move would not be easy. The market for forklift trucks was both mature and fiercely competitive. Forty different companies in Europe were already manufacturing forklift trucks and the market was oversupplied. There was no way a me-too product could be profitable. Product innovation was essential.

JCB quickly overcame the challenge. A dedicated 12-strong team produced a business plan within four weeks. Past experience has reinforced company chair Sir Anthony Bamford's positive attitude to innovation. He provides top-level support for creativity and sees sensible risk taking in a positive light. Although the initial projections suggested the initiative would not be into profit for several years, he took the view that, 'If the strategy is right we will find a way to get the numbers right.'

The company has a culture in which creative new ideas can flourish. This gave JCB the confidence to book the public launch of its forklift truck at a major exhibition when it was still no more than a concept. The forklift truck project team had to act quickly. They sought wherever possible to utilise components and mechanisms from existing JCB vehicles in order to minimise costs. But they adopted a completely fresh approach to forklift truck design involving use of a single telescopic arm from existing JCB digger machines. This has far stronger user appeal than conventional forklift trucks.

Confidentiality agreements signed by local companies, partners and suppliers allowed a great deal of expert input into the design of the new 'Teletruk'. Continuous attention to the life costs of the project allowed the team to 'get the numbers right' and improve the gross margins from those originally projected. JCB Industrial met its launch date target and its Teletruk went on to win various industry awards and be selected by the Design Council as a Millennium Product. Early sales are not only on track to meet targets; within the first month of production, JCB's chairman had already sent the team back to work on planning how volumes could be increased to allow expansion into new markets.

Source: DTI Innovation Unit Database, http://www.innovation.gov.uk/bcs/index.html

8.8 Conclusion

This chapter examined the role of innovation in determining firm strategy and also analysed the practical decisions firms face when considering investment in innovation. These decisions are extremely important since the outcome of such non-price competition is variable and often uncertain and thus carries great risks. However, successful investment in research and development can create a large competitive advantage for firms over their rivals and give them respite from the potential damage of price competition.

Discussion Questions

1 Give examples of firms that have gained monopoly status through successful innovation.

2 Discuss methods that can be employed to measure the extent of research and development present in a firm.

3 Read Case Study 8.2 and discuss to what extent innovations in financial products differ from innovations in non-financial products.

4 From the point of view of a production process, discuss the factors that may generate diminishing returns to innovation in the short and in the long run.

5 With reference to examples, identify those industries where there is a high propensity to patent and those industries where patents are less frequent. What factors determine such a distinction?

Further Reading

General background

Cook, M. and Farquharson, C. (1998) *Business Economics*. London: Pitman, Chapter 16.

Advanced

De Propris, L. (2000) Innovation and inter-firm cooperation: the case of the West Midlands, *Economics of Innovation and New Technology*, 9, 421–46.

Freeman, C. and Soete, L. (1997) *The Economics of Industrial Innovation* (3rd edn). London: Pinter.

Hannan, T. H. and McDowell, J. M. (1984) The determinants of technology adoption: the case of the banking firm, *Rand Journal of Economics*, 15, 328–35.

Maclaurin, W. R. (1950) The process of technological innovation: the launching of a new scientific industry, *American Economic Review*, 40, 90–112.

National Economic Development Council (NEDC) (1983) *Innovation in the UK*. London: National Economic Development Office.

Oster, S. M. and Quigley, J. M. (1977) Regulatory barriers to the diffusion of innovation: some evidence from building codes, *The Bell Journal of Economics*, 8, 361–77.

Patel, P. and Pavitt, K. (1987) The elements of British technological competitiveness, *National Institute Economic Review*, 122, 4, 72–83.

Schankerman, M. (1998) How valuable is patent protection? Estimates by technology field, *Rand Journal of Economics*, 29, 77–107.

Scherer, F. M. (1967) Research and development resource allocation under rivalry, *Quarterly Journal of Economics*, 81, 359–94.

Scherer, F. M. (1992) Schumpeter and plausible capitalism, *Journal of Economic Literature*, 30, 1416–33.

Schumpeter, J. (1950) *Capitalism, Socialism, and Democracy*. New York: Harper.

Taylor, C. and Silberston, Z. A. (1973) *The Economic Impact of the Patent System*. Cambridge: Cambridge University Press.

9

Horizontal and Vertical Integration

Objectives

By the end of this chapter, the reader should be able to understand:

* why firms seek to merge with other firms in the same market
* the extent of market power or efficiency gains such a strategy can bring about
* the benefits that vertical integration can confer on firms
* the range of vertical relationships that can exist in the marketplace
* and identify various vertical restraints imposed by firms and evaluate their contribution to allocative efficiency and competition.

Key Concepts

* backward vertical integration
* bundling
* contractual incompleteness
* foreclosure
* forward vertical integration

* horizontal integration
* resale price maintenance
* tying
* vertical integration

9.1   Introduction

There comes a time when most medium-sized firms consider further expansion so as to exploit potential economies of scale and scope and to make use of additional opportunities which a larger scale of operation can often deliver. In this chapter we shall examine two such strategies, horizontal and vertical integration.

Horizontal integration refers to the expansion of firms caused by mergers between firms who produce *substitute* goods. Such mergers occur so long as the owners or managers of firms believe it to be the most profitable means of expansion. Although much of the analysis of horizontal mergers is focused on the potential anticompetitive effects, there are other reasons why horizontal expansion may be attractive to firms. In addition to the potential increases in market power, we shall also consider possible efficiency gains as well as the opportunity of acquiring a firm at an attractive price. These issues are explored in section 9.2.

Vertical integration refers to the expansion of firms caused either by mergers between firms involved at successive stages of the production process or by firms developing their own vertical operations. A fuller explanation of vertical integration is given in section 9.3. In section 9.4 we examine the reasons why firms may be attracted to vertical integration. Our analysis starts with the transaction cost approach, which identifies the advantages of such a strategy in a general way. The section then considers specific issues such as technological conditions, uncertainty, supply conditions, etc. In section 9.5, we briefly identify some other types of vertical relationship which together with vertical integration can lead to anticompetitive behaviour. This behaviour is referred to as *vertical restraints* and is dealt with in section 9.6 of the chapter. Section 9.7 provides a brief conclusion.

9.2   Motives for Horizontal Integration

As we saw in Chapter 4 an oligopoly is characterised by interdependence. This interdependence means that a firm's success (or lack of success) in the market depends on how its rivals act and react to its strategies. This then creates uncertainty in strategic planning. One way of reducing such uncertainty is for firms to collude either explicitly or tacitly over prices, outputs, extent of differentiation, etc. Where such collusion is difficult to organise or control, mergers might be seen as an alternative strategy. There are a number of specific reasons why firms choose to merge.

Market power

A horizontal merger may grant a firm a larger market share or the removal of a close rival. One or both of these outcomes increases the ability of a firm to increase price without having to worry about the reactions of rivals. A merger can reduce the degree of oligopolistic uncertainty and reward firms with greater market power. This outcome may be of concern to the regulatory authorities. For a merger to be regarded as anticompetitive it must result not only in increasing the level of concentration but also in making *entry* for new firms more difficult. The second condition is important since price increases may be difficult to introduce in the market, if there are potential entrants waiting in the wings. (Government policy toward mergers is discussed in Chapter 11.)

As well as creating an increase in market power, horizontal mergers can also be used to protect the dominance of an existing firm. Should a dominant firm be threatened by the entry of a rival with a new product it might wish to take over the new firm as a way of protecting its status quo. The alternative would be to invest in the development of a rival new product. This latter strategy might not only take a long time, but might also carry a high financial risk, as we saw when examining product innovation in Chapter 8. Thus the cheaper alternative would be to acquire the firm. Since this alternative would benefit the firm in the long run, the firm may be prepared to pay a high price for the acquisition of the innovating firm.

Economies of scale

One of the most common arguments in favour of horizontal mergers is that the combined size of the two or more firms leads to economies of scale at a faster rate than could be achieved through internal expansion. These economies of scale can be classed as *plant economies* and *firm economies*. (The reader may wish to refer back to section 2.4 in Chapter 2, which dealt with economies of scale.)

- *Plant economies* refer to rationalisation of production processes, allowing greater specialisation and the realisation of technical economies. For example, two firms may own a number of small plants each, none of which operates at the minimum efficient size. A merger which results in the closure of some of the plants and a concentration of production in the remaining plants might see greater efficiency in those plants. To reduce average costs by *internal growth*, firms might be forced to reduce price to increase output and sales. As we have seen previously (in our analysis of the kinked demand curve), such price cutting may create unnecessary tension in the market, and if other firms react by matching such price cuts, then sales may not increase by much at all.

- *Firm economies* arise through the growth of the whole organisation. For example, marketing functions can be spread over a wider output without a proportionate increase in costs. Similarly, existing management expertise can also be applied to a larger organisation.

Farrell and Shapiro (2000) argued that, in most mergers, there are few genuine cases of efficiency gains due to general scale economies, since most of these efficiency gains could also be achieved through the firm's own internal expansion. What should really be considered are *merger-specific gains*, which cannot be achieved in any other way. These involve the integration of specific, *hard-to-trade assets* owned by the merging firms. These gains were referred to as 'synergies'. Thus, examples of simple plant economies just mentioned could be referred to as 'efficiencies without synergies'. Some examples of such synergies suggested by Farrell and Shapiro were as follows.

Co-ordination of joint operations

When two firms are linked by the joint management of a resource, such as an oilfield, there may be contractual and institutional problems which might create inefficiencies. If a merger were to lead to a reduction in such inefficiencies, then a synergy would exist.

Sharing of complementary skills

Consider a situation where one firm enjoys superior manufacturing skills compared to a rival, while the rival is better at distribution. In time it might be possible that both firms improve their areas of disadvantage. However, this might take too long to realise or might appear too risky a strategy. In this case a merger of the two firms might bring about a synergy. A similar example might be of a firm with a patent which can be fully and quickly exploited with the resources of another firm.

Improved interoperability

Two firms may develop what they consider to be separate products, e.g. two pieces of software which can be used interchangeably by end-users. However, because the two pieces of software were developed separately, they often conflict when used jointly. Moves to develop compatible software may be thwarted by the existence of a competitive culture which exists between the two firms. If a horizontal merger can bring about such compatibility or 'interoperability', then a synergy exists.

Network configuration

Assume two firms operate a rail service between two points A and B, with each firm owning a single track. Offering an 'out and back' service would imply that 'down' trains meet the 'up' trains. To solve this problem, sidings would have to be built and this would then lead to complex route planning and costly delays. A merger whereby the two lines could be used to serve traffic in one unique direction might be regarded as another potential synergy.

Motives of the 'acquired firm'

When discussing horizontal mergers one factor to consider is the motives of firms which *wish* to be acquired. These might be as follows:

- The acquired firm has suffered a loss of market share and is faced with decreasing revenues and potential financial ruin. A merger might then guarantee the continued existence of some part of the firm's resources, notably its workforce and some of its operations.
- The managers of the firm may be forced to sell to meet their legal and tax liabilities.
- Management may feel unable to maintain a rate of growth of the firm. These constraints may be caused by meeting difficulties in raising finance or possessing insufficient technical and organisational expertise to expand the scale of operations.

Since such weak firms may be desperate to seek a buyer, they may accept a price for the firm which is below the market price. Under competitive conditions, if there were many potential buyers all with access to perfect knowledge, the price would be bid up to the market price. In reality, however, there are few firms that have such knowledge or the ability to take over 'failing' firms. Thus the low price may attract some firms into a horizontal merger.

Studies of merger activities tend to suggest that a large proportion of mergers have not been successful. The practical problems of linking different product and distribution systems may lead to inefficient solutions. Merged information systems may also prove to be less efficient and senior managers may, for a significant time, face distorted information flows. Finally, a merger between two firms may create two separate and intransigent 'cultures'. Staff from one firm may find it difficult to adapt to and accept corporate practices of the other firm.

Let us now turn to a consideration of vertical integration.

9.3   Vertical Integration

Vertical integration can be defined as the ownership of an input used in the production of a firm's output or the ownership of a production unit that uses the firm's outputs. A production process can be thought of as a 'flow', starting from the extraction or acquisition of raw materials which are then processed into intermediate goods. These are eventually transformed into the finished product. Activities located at the initial stages of production are known as 'upstream', and those which are closer to the market for the final product are known as 'downstream' activities. Thus upstream or *backward vertical integration* refers to firms undertaking the production of inputs necessary for their production process, while downstream or *forward vertical integration* refers to firms moving into activities that utilise their outputs. Since capacity may differ at different stages of production, firms may also have to rely on external market transactions to make up their required capacity. Balanced vertical integration would occur if capacities at successive stages were equal.

Firms are attracted to vertical integration if it leads either to an increase in their revenue or to a reduction of their costs. Thus if profits of non-integrated firms can be improved through such a strategy, firms will consider vertical integration. When considering cost reductions, one may have to bear in mind that the strategy of vertical integration can generate additional costs to the organisation for the following reasons:

- The firm may find that using its own resources to produce inputs or to distribute its output may not be as efficient as using specialised firms in the market.

- As a firm integrates, management may face increasing costs of managing a larger organisation.

- Vertical mergers may attract the attention of anti-monopoly agencies, and consequently the firm may be faced with expensive legal fees.

The reasons for vertical integration are varied. The earliest explanations for vertical integration tended to focus on issues such as the technological advantages of linking successive stages of production, the risk and uncertainty attached to the supply of upstream products or the distribution of firms' finished products, the avoidance of government taxation and price controls and, finally, the desire to secure market power.

9.4   Reasons for Vertical Integration

Transactions costs approach

Williamson (1971) developed an alternative rationale to the classical paradigm. His *transactions costs* approach did not deny the earlier explanations, but managed to place most of these reasons into a more logically coherent methodology. Transactions costs differ from production costs in that they are associated with *market transactions* between buyers and sellers. In Chapter 5 we argued that these costs are the costs involved in negotiating contracts, monitoring performance, enforcing contractual promises and pursuing litigation in the event of breach of promises. Williamson argued that where the market fails to work well, i.e. proves costly, the firm 'internalises' that particular market transaction. It substitutes internal organisation for external market exchange. Whenever there is a large difference between external (market) co-ordination and internal organisation, there is a tendency towards vertical integration.

Why is it that the firm can be less costly at organising and coordinating production than the market?

According to Williamson, the firm benefits from internal organisation in three ways: incentives, controls and 'inherent structural advantages':

- *Incentives* cover the advantages of being able to avoid costly and time-consuming bargaining with other producers at different stages of production.

- *Controls* imply that the firm can benefit from stronger controls over intra-firm activity as opposed to inter-firm activity. Controls also imply that, through a process of organisational rewards and penalties, the firm has the ability to access more wide-ranging and more accurate information flows. In addition, should conflict arise within the firm, this can normally be resolved by the authority of senior managers rather than having to rely on expensive arbitration or litigation.

- *Structural advantages* may increase the economies of communication exchange. Thus staff within the organisation share common training, experiences and codes of practice, which ensures that the quality of the communications is improved.

Let us now move to the specific arguments for vertical integration. Most of these can be accommodated within the Williamson paradigm.

Specific arguments for vertical integration

Technological conditions

Vertical integration in certain cases may lead to the reduction of production costs. This may occur where there are complementary processes that need to be carried out quickly so as to save intermediate costs of delivery. A traditional example is the steel industry. Blast furnaces that make steel and the strip mills that shape and cut the steel are not only controlled by the same firm, they are also located within the same plant so as to conserve heat (thermal economies).

Uncertainty

The relationship between firms in successive stages of production is subject to many uncertainties. One of the major causes of such uncertainty is the lack of complete information. Vertical integration can help to correct such *information incompleteness*. Uncertainty creates a number of problems for firms in the organisation of production. The co-ordination of production involves many complex event variables, some that can be predicted, others that cannot. This is what Simon (1959) termed 'bounded rationality': the limited ability of economic agents to absorb and process information to make correct decisions. Success depends on how well firms can react and adapt to unanticipated events. There are two types of uncertainty:

- The first can be referred to as *primary uncertainty*. This is determined by factors external to the firm and the industry. These would include changes in technology, consumer demand and government policy. These factors would be regarded as outside the immediate control of the firm.

- *Secondary uncertainty* arises because of the lack of information facing decision makers. This information may be difficult to secure as vertically related firms may fail to disclose it or, worse, attempt to distort the information so as deliberately to increase the costs to their rivals.

Assured supply

Firms may be concerned about the risks of being let down by a supplier. To ensure a steady supply of inputs, firms consider backward vertical integration. Adelman (1955) reasoned that shortages in the supply of goods typically arise through lags in the growth of supply of those goods, while demand is growing strongly. Firms in the market for final goods are better able to judge the level of demand than firms producing the inputs. Under normal market conditions, price rations the availability of goods to buyers. However, in the short run, the prices of most standard goods do not adjust instantaneously to shortages and, instead, manufacturers ration the available supply. Therefore, there is a danger that buyers are not supplied with sufficient inputs to complete their planned output. This may even occur when firms have agreed specific contracts to ensure supply, but where enforcement of such contracts is difficult.

Externalities

An externality exists whenever property rights are poorly specified and a resource is not subject to effective ownership and control by its producer. Externalities arise when a vertical relationship leads to a situation where a firm is unable to prevent incurring additional costs brought about by the actions of its supplier or distributor. For example, some manufacturers might argue that forward integration into distribution is necessary to protect their 'brand'. Final demand may be too important to be left in the hands of inexperienced or inefficient retailers, who could damage the brand's reputation.

Complexity

Vertical relationships may be characterised by complex technical and legal relations that may prove too costly to arrange between two 'separate' firms.

An example of this is when a firm may wish to negotiate a long-term contract with its supplier or buyer. However, if the product is non-standard and surrounded with a great deal of uncertainty, such as frequent changes in product design or technology, the contract must be exhaustively specified to avoid all possible contractual ambiguities which could result in expensive litigation. An alternative might be to negotiate only a short-term contract. However, in some cases, vertical relations may require a commitment by a firm to long-term investments, and thus only a long-term contract is considered to ensure a guaranteed return on the investment. In these cases, neither long- nor short-term contracts are efficient solutions. Williamson (1971) referred to this as *contractual incompleteness*. The resolution of the problem is for the firm to integrate vertically.

A good example of complexity is the film industry, which comprises manufacturing and retailing stages. Each film is unique, and patterns of distribution of one film never quite coincide with those of another. Issues of pairing, regional exposure, repeat showings, television sales and degree of promotional effort determine a unique distribution strategy for each film. This implies complex contractual relations between the filmmaker, the distributor and the exhibitor. Contractual agreements would also have to be monitored with a sophisticated and costly inspectorate. It may be simpler and *cheaper* for filmmakers to integrate vertically forward with distributors and cinema chains or vice versa.

Moral hazard

Moral hazard occurs when an agent lacks the incentive to work in the best interests of the principal and the principal cannot observe the actions of the agent. In our context, moral hazard implies that a firm has no incentive to maximise revenue or minimise costs, when contracted by other firms at a different stage of production.

Assume a situation where a buying firm arranges a contract under conditions of uncertainty. It is possible for the supplier to bear the risks, but this means the addition of a 'premium' to the normal cost of production. Consequently, a much higher price is charged. The buying firm may regard this 'premium' as excessive and may decide to bear the risk itself by offering a 'cost plus contract'. The buyer remunerates the supplier for all costs and adds a mark-up for profit. This is sometimes typical of government contracts. However, there is now no incentive for the supplier to cut costs. The buyer might have to insist on monitoring the supplier's work. If this proves too difficult and costly, it may propel the firm to vertically integrate.

Specificity

Specificity arises when a firm invests in the production or distribution of custom-made products for specific clients. Thus firms are 'tied' or dependent on one another by investments in specific physical capital, human capital, sites or brands. This may leave the firm vulnerable to threats from clients in the event of disputes.

The consequence of the specialised asset is that a bilateral monopoly may arise. There is one firm buying and one firm supplying the input. For example, a shipper of antique furniture may have a limited demand for specialised padded wagons for long-distance rail transport. Given the level of demand, only one firm specialises in the production of such wagons. The two firms are now 'locked in' by the specific asset. Both can undertake 'opportunistic' behaviour to extract a higher price. The

Case Study 9.1

Vertical integration and transfer pricing

In 2002 GlaxoSmithKline were faced with the possibility of paying billions of dollars in unpaid taxes as it was alleged by US tax officials that they had deliberately concealed the revenues earned in the USA. The allegation surrounds sales of six major drugs sold in the USA, including the popular ulcer drug Zantac, between 1989 and 1999. The revenues totalled some $30 billion. The American Internal Revenue Service argued that Glaxo's US division *overpaid* its parent company for the drugs, to reduce the declared taxable profits in the USA. The main focus of the accusation is that 'transfer pricing' allowed the firm to overvalue the R&D costs incurred by the UK head office. In addition, the Internal Revenue Service claimed that the success of sales in the USA was due more to the marketing efforts of the firm in the USA than to the innovatory work done in the UK.

supplier may demand a higher price, threatening a refusal to supply, knowing that the buyer has no alternative source of supply. The buyer may demand a lower price with the threat of refusing to buy the supplier's output, knowing that the supplier is unable to find an alternative market. As a result, the market transaction is characterised by expensive haggling and high contractual costs, which may encourage the firms to integrate vertically.

Government policy

Through vertical integration firms are often able to avoid various government taxes, restrictions and regulations, when imposed on one stage of production and not on another. A market transaction which is subject to a sales tax or price controls can be replaced by an internal transaction and thus escape the restriction. Scherer (1980) noted that there was evidence to show that, in America and Europe, integrated petroleum firms showed low accounting profits in the refining and marketing stages of production, while enjoying much higher profits at the crude oil-extracting stage, a stage that attracted a much lower rate of profits tax. Case Study 9.1 is a further example of such a strategy.

9.5   Other Vertical Relationships

Vertical integration is only one of many possible vertical structures. Alternative relationships are often referred to as *principal–agent* relationships. Thus a manufacturing firm (acting as the principal) contracts a supplying firm (the agent) to produce its inputs. Contracts imply restrictions, and these restrictions are examined later in this chapter. It is clear that the fundamental reason why firms develop contractually specific vertical ties is to harmonise production, processing and distribution activities.

Why should firms choose this approach rather than rely on the advantages of vertical integration?

Generalising, we can argue that firms prefer to enter into such agreements for two reasons: first, to maintain some degree of independence and, second, to avoid the costs of entry into upstream or downstream operations. If we assume that firms wish to remain in their familiar stage of production and maintain their independence then vertical relationships can be used primarily to reduce uncertainty in the market. However, other factors may play also play a part. Harrigan (1983) suggested three alternatives to vertical integration:

- *Tapered integration* exists when vertically integrated firms rely on independent suppliers or distributors for part of their operations. Using such channels allows firms fully to exploit their capacity, ensuring that it is the 'outside' firms which bear the risk of market uncertainties. Furthermore, developing contacts with upstream and downstream firms may provide useful 'intelligence' regarding new product and market development. Harrigan believed that tapered integration was best applied in situations where technological interdependencies were absent and raw material inputs were plentiful.

- *Quasi integration* refers to a situation where a firm may not own the adjacent business unit, but is able to control all or part of the operation through franchises or other joint ventures. The strategy may appear attractive to those firms facing high risks of new technology and demand uncertainty.

- *Contracts* can specify the exact relationship between an agent and principal and can thus take a multitude of forms to reflect the minutiae of the different risks in the market as well as the market power of the firms involved. Harrigan claimed that the greater the level of monopoly power, the greater the possibility that firms would integrate. Where a market was characterised by 'competitive volatility' and principal firms possessed enough market power to monitor and enforce contracts, then contracting was seen as an appropriate solution. Such contracts mean that firms can gain advantages in vertical relationships without having to commit excessive financial resources to fund risky mergers.

9.6   Vertical Restraints

An alternative to vertical integration, which some firms may find too costly to monitor and organise, is to rely on an armoury of vertical restraints. Vertical restraints refer to the various restrictions imposed by firms linked by vertical relationships. Thus, if a manufacturer makes it a condition of supply that the retailer should charge a minimum price, a vertical restraint or restriction is said to exist. Unfortunately the word 'restraint' or 'restriction' has a negative connotation of wrongdoing. Such 'conditions' surrounding the sale of goods may have beneficial as well as harmful effects on economic welfare. If we consider the publishing of books in the UK we can identify at least three types of vertical restraint:

- No part of a published book may be copied and distributed without the permission of the owner of the copyright.

- Books may not be sold below a certain minimum price, determined by the publisher. In the UK this was known as the Net Book Agreement, a legal agreement that had satisfied the Restrictive Trade Practices Court. The agreement was formally abandoned in 1995.

- No paperback may be rebound by a buyer into a hardback edition.

Each of these restraints is anticompetitive. The first ensures that no other firm or individual is able to sell the same book. It thus serves as an entry barrier. The second ensured that there was no price competition between booksellers. The last is a form of price discrimination. Since the cost of hard binding a book is much less than the price differential, the publisher is, in effect, differentiating the product. Publishers believe that the demand for hardback books is less elastic than the demand for paperback books. Thus, by segmenting the market they can charge different prices.

However, the agreement also generates positive benefits. First, if books could be copied and sold by rival firms, publishers would see a drop in revenue and an inability to cover the full costs of publishing a book. The rival firms would be enjoying a free ride, having escaped the costs of contracting an author, typesetting and marketing. To protect firms from such 'piracy', the government defines strict property rights covering the written word and other media. The setting of a minimum price, or *resale price maintenance*, was argued to be in favour of protecting small booksellers who, it was claimed, provided useful services such as information and local availability of books. Being small, these booksellers were faced with high costs and, consequently, would be unable to cover these costs if prices of books were lower. It is also argued that price discrimination allows non-economic books (such as academic textbooks) to be published at a reasonable price, cross-subsidised by the popular books.

The Chicago School

As we saw earlier, vertical restraints may be viewed potentially as a force for economic efficiency, as anticompetitive or possibly as having a neutral effect. The debate in Europe and in America has tended to revolve around the views of the Chicago School (introduced in Chapter 5). The traditional thinking prior to the Chicago School arguments was that restrictions, by their very nature, reduced the independence of distributors, by controlling their ability to supply final consumers. Resale price maintenance was seen as little different from horizontal price fixing and was banned in most countries.

The Chicago School was a body of academic lawyers and economists who, in the late 1960s and 1970s, developed a line of research stressing a strict neo-classical approach to markets. Fundamentally, their approach was an attempt to separate vertical restraints from horizontal restraints, arguing that competition is defined within a market and therefore only horizontal and not vertical restraints can affect competition. Specifically, it was argued that manufacturers would not impose restrictions downstream as this would, in turn, reduce demand for their products. If restrictions are imposed it is because a potential efficiency can be realised. These efficiencies were the elimination of externalities and moral hazard problems discussed earlier in the chapter. Thus some perfume manufacturers may believe that selling their perfume at high prices, by attractive assistants and only in upmarket stores maximises their sales. To reduce price and allow downmarket chain stores to stock the perfume may, in fact, reduce total market demand.

The approach attracted a lot of criticism, and in more recent years the tide has turned away from the Chicago analysis and the focus is now based on a case-by-case approach. Restraints may be viewed as having possible entry barrier and collusive effects which lead to a distortion of the retail market, especially where there is little competition at the retail or manufacturing stage. Thus, resale price maintenance can be used as an alternative to horizontal price fixing, the latter being more obvious as well as illegal. Comanor (1985) also argued that the provision of expensive services and marketing may be inappropriate for established products where consumers are already familiar with the product and do not place a high value on additional services, the implication being that these additional services serve only as an additional barrier to entry.

Types of vertical restraint

Resale price maintenance

Mathewson and Winter (1998: 57) defined resale price maintenance (RPM) as:

> Any contract in which an upstream firm (e.g., a manufacturer) retains the right to control the price at which a product is sold downstream, usually in the retail market.

RPM is viewed with suspicion in most countries and has been consequently deemed to be illegal. This suspicion originates from two directions, one legal and the other economic. From a legal viewpoint, such price restrictions are seen to be contrary to the legal principle of *alienation*, which implies that as an individual relinquishes ownership of goods he or she should have no further rights over the use and disposal of such goods. The economic viewpoint is that such price restrictions result in a loss of competition. An example of the anticompetitive argument is the dealer cartel hypothesis.

Dealer cartel hypothesis

Retailers or dealers often group together for benign trade purposes and this can then develop into collusive agreements. Such cartels, as all cartels, are subject to potential instability brought about by independent action. Price discipline and thus greater stability can be injected into the collusive arrangements by RPM imposed by the suppliers. In addition, the RPM can protect the dealer cartel from the entry of 'discount' dealers.

Support for RPM also comes from a legal and an economic direction. A legal argument could be built on the notion that the owner of a good has the 'right' to offer any contract associated with the sale of that good that he or she wishes and that this 'right' supersedes the right of the buyer. The economic argument revolves around transactional hypotheses which identify distribution inefficiencies. Thus success in the production and marketing of a product depends on the actions of both manufacturers *and* dealers. It may be possible that individual dealer behaviour may lead to sub-optimal outcomes for both the manufacturer and other dealers. RPM may be used to correct these potential market failures. Let us consider one such example.

The service hypothesis

Demand for a good depends not only on price but also on the associated pre-sales services. These services include: convenient locations, availability of parking space, waiting time, displays and demonstrations and information provided by staff. The fact that we have retail outlets implies that retailers or dealers do supply such value added, otherwise consumers would buy direct from the manufacturers. To increase the final demand for their products, manufacturers have an incentive to ensure that retailers are providing such services. RPM increases the retail price and thus the retail margin, which allows retailers to invest in the provision of such services (see Case Study 9.2).

Foreclosure

Market *foreclosure* refers to the practice of firms refusing to supply downstream firms or to purchase from upstream firms. Complete or absolute foreclosure occurs when

Case Study 9.2

Volvo involved in car pricing cartels

Volvo Car UK has admitted supporting secret agreements to fix its car prices in the UK. The admission follows an investigation by the OFT, which uncovered evidence of an agreement by Volvo dealers not to offer discounts beyond set levels. Volvo Car UK Ltd – based in Marlow, Bucks – has now signed assurances to the Director General of Fair Trading, John Bridgeman, that it will not support price-fixing cartels operated by its dealers.

An investigation was launched by the OFT's cartels task force following a BBC *Panorama* programme in which former dealers alleged that a number of car manufacturers were fixing prices. Evidence emerged of agreements made by dealers to restrict the levels of discount available to private buyers and fleet customers. Further evidence indicated that Volvo ensured that dealers would comply with the set levels of discount by penalising them if they didn't. The situation arose following a decision by Volvo to reposition itself in the marketplace and to introduce a new dealer and commission structure. A series of meetings of dealers was addressed by Volvo managers, who then left the dealers to discuss future business strategy. Evidence obtained by the OFT suggests that the agreements Volvo has admitted supporting were made at these meetings.

Source: http://www.oft.gov.uk/News/Press+releases/1999/PN+24-99.htm

either a supplier obtains all the downstream outlets or a buyer obtains all the supplying outlets, to deny non-integrated rivals a share in the relevant market. Dobson (1997) argued the effectiveness of any potential foreclosures depends on three conditions being met:

- That a sufficient proportion of upstream or downstream firms are covered by the exclusive agreement.

- That there are substantial barriers to entry or an inability to expand output internally at the upstream or downstream stage.

- That the agreements are relatively long term.

Let us now consider whether such exclusionary practices can harm competition. Bork (1978) argued that the anticompetitive effects of foreclosure were exaggerated. He argued, for example, that benefits to an acquiring firm might well be offset by the losses of the acquired firm. If a firm acquires a downstream firm and then forces it to buy only from itself, this would increase the profitability of the acquiring firm. However, the downstream firm may see a loss of sales and profits if it can no longer sell other, possibly better quality, brands. In essence, Bork felt that foreclosure was an irrelevancy and what mattered was the degree of concentration in upstream and downstream markets. Vertical mergers and foreclosure were of little consequence in competitive horizontal markets. This view was challenged by Ordover et al. (1990), who suggested that vertical mergers reduce competition in the input markets. As a firm vertically integrates downstream it has less incentive to compete with other upstream firms in terms of price to attract downstream customers. Consequently, upstream firms can increase their prices and hence costs to the downstream firms. These higher costs result in higher prices charged to final consumers.

Krattenmaker and Salop (1986) suggested the following conditions could be applied to test whether market competition were harmed:

- *The ability of the excluded rivals to compete is reduced.* This is achieved if rivals' costs are increased as a consequence of foreclosure. Foreclosure need not, per se, increase the costs to the rivals, if there are abundant and comparable supplies from alternative sources.

- *Increased market power after exclusion.* It may be possible that the ability to foreclose does not increase a firm's market power due to the existence of powerful rivals or the entry of new firms. In the latter case, one could argue that exclusion harms competitors but not competition.

- *Do rivals have counterstrategies?* It may be possible that rivals are able to protect themselves from the foreclosure. The most obvious counterstrategy is to have access to alternative sources of supply. If rivals have no immediate access to such supplies, they may attempt to take over an input supplier or encourage the entry of a new firm into the supplying market by agreeing long-term contracts for the purchase of inputs. A further possibility is for the rival to consider 'self-entry', i.e. to set up the supply operation itself.

- *Exclusion must be profitable.* To exclude rivals from supplies implies lost revenue to the supplier. Thus the firm that implements a policy of foreclosure has to ensure that the increased profits of such a policy outweigh the profits forgone of lower sales.

Having identified and discussed the anticompetitive effects, we now turn to the consideration of other possible factors that may determine the extent to which firms pursue the strategy of exclusive dealing:

- *Free riding*. As discussed earlier, suppliers or manufacturers may attempt to capture and control the full benefits of services that are provided to final customers. Exclusive contracts prevent other firms from benefiting from specialised services associated with a particular brand. This encourages manufacturers to increase the level of such services.

- *Transactions costs*. The costs of monitoring and policing violations of exclusivity agreements may in some circumstances be too high. It may be very costly for a supplier to assess accurately whether a distributor is or is not stocking rivals' products. For example, firms would have to recruit an inspectorate to monitor compliance with contractual obligations. In such cases where costs are high, one would expect less reliance on exclusive dealing.

- *End-customer costs*. Exclusive dealing from the point of view of the final customer means that he or she cannot make a full comparison of different brands at one location. To save on such search costs, customers may prefer to shop at outlets that carry a larger selection of brands. The implication for distributors is that they may lose custom if they restrict their supply to a narrow range of brands. This may reduce the desire of such distributors to enter into such agreements.

- *Firm size*. Firm size may also influence the level of exclusive dealing, the suggestion being that larger firms can benefit from economies of scale and scope in distribution by developing exclusive dealerships. In addition, large firms are able to benefit from promotional economies that enhance the reputation of their brands. This increases final demand for their brands and places large firms in a strong position as regards exclusive dealing (see Case Study 9.3).

Exclusive territories

Manufacturers can also restrict their dealers territorially by allowing dealers to operate in specified locations. This can take two forms. The dealers are restricted to operating in a particular territory, but can serve any customer who approaches them. Alternatively, dealers may be forced to serve only customers from a specified location. Such territorial agreements affect the search costs to final consumers. If consumers wish to 'comparison shop' they may have to visit a range of outlets that are spatially differentiated. The effect is to increase search costs, and consumers may be unwilling to 'shop around'. This might then reduce inter-brand competition and increase industry profits. This is, of course, a different conclusion to the one discussed earlier under the heading of 'end-user costs' when we considered exclusive dealing. Implicit in this argument is that spatial distances between dealers significantly influence consumer search costs.

Quantity-dependent pricing

Quantity-dependent pricing as defined by Katz (1989) refers to the practice whereby the price a buyer pays for an intermediate good depends on the quantity bought. Broadly, there are three types of vertical restraint that fall under this heading:

Case Study 9.3 FT

Office of Fair Trading rejects complaint over personal computers market

John Lewis yesterday vowed to continue its fight against rival retailer Dixons after the Office of Fair Trading dismissed its complaint about the personal computer market. The OFT said Dixons had not infringed competition law by agreeing exclusive distribution agreements with two PC makers – a move John Lewis said restricted consumer choice.

Dixons welcomed the ruling, which it said proved how competitive the market for home computers was. However, John Lewis said it would study the full OFT ruling, due to be published next week, to see if there were any grounds for appeal under the 1998 Competition Act. If there were not, the department store group said it planned to ask Stephen Byers, trade and industry secretary, to look again at the act as it was obviously not providing enough protection for consumers. 'We could shrug our shoulders and walk away,' said Nigel Wreford-Brown, John Lewis's merchandise director. 'But we are unlikely to do that because there are important points of principle at stake.'

John Lewis brought the complaint against Dixons with rival retailers Tempo and Comet. The three complained that agreements struck between Dixons and two computer groups – Compaq and Packard Bell – stifled competition. Under the agreements Dixons is allowed exclusive distribution rights for certain products from both groups. However, the OFT said a wide range of computers was available through a variety of outlets – and that in general consumers did not appear to have a strong brand preference. The ruling said Dixons' market share in PCs was significantly less than 40% – the threshold normally regarded as an indicator of dominance.

The rival retailers had argued that Dixons' market share was in effect much higher, as it had 57% of sales made in stores. The OFT defined the market to include high street and specialist retailers, retails parks, mail order, the Internet and other direct methods of sale. It concluded that barriers to entry were not high. Dixons said the market for PCs was 'highly competitive and dynamic and indeed has grown even more so in recent months'. The group – which sells computers in its eponymous chain as well as through Comet and PC World – said its customers were the real winners.

Source: *Financial Times*, 7 April 2001.

- *Quantity forcing* occurs when a buyer is obliged to buy more than he or she would wish under normal circumstances. This practice can be accomplished by forcing the buyer to make a minimum payment for purchases up to a certain level. Forcing buyers to stock and sell more than they may wish has the effect of improving the service to ensure such sales are made as well as helping to reduce prices to final consumers.

- *Non-linear pricing*, or a 'two-part tariff', occurs when a buyer pays a fixed fee (a franchise fee) plus a price per unit. As more is bought so the average total cost declines. Kay (1990) suggested two reasons why suppliers may impose a non-linear pricing strategy. As remuneration increases more than proportionately with the total amount of business done with a particular supplier it may help to 'bias' retailers. Thus, an insurance company may wish independent brokers to recommend its policies over others or a breakfast cereal company may wish a supermarket to display its brand prominently on the shelves. Non-linear pricing can act as an incentive for dealers to promote the product. Second, if dealers stock only one product to capitalise on increasing their revenues, this then increases the 'switching' and 'search' costs to consumers. Consumers are less likely to search out and switch to alternatives if outlets carry a narrow range of products. This increases the market power of the suppliers.

- *Tie-in selling and bundling* again describe a situation where buyers are forced to buy more than they wish. *Ties* occur when a buyer wishes to acquire a product, but is forced, as a condition of supply, to accept additional products or services. The first good is referred to as the 'tying' good and the second is referred to as the 'tied' good. *Bundling* refers to the practice of selling two or more goods as a single 'package'. We briefy examine these two practices.

Why are suppliers interested in tying?

- *Price evasion.* If suppliers were facing government restrictions on the price of the products, they could then force their buyers to stock an unregulated product at a high price so as to regain some of their lost profits on the regulated item.

- *Protection of goodwill.* A supplier may wish, for example, to protect the quality of the product by insisting that repairs and spare parts to a machine be supplied only by the firm. The argument may focus on the technical complexity of the machine, and to have the machine serviced by non-approved engineers may harm the machine and damage the firm's reputation. Whether the argument is justified depends on whether efficient alternatives to the tying arrangement exist.

- *Economies of distribution.* Firms may tie two or more products if they are strong complements, to benefit from distributional economies. In theory, all assembled products such as cars are, in effect, a tying arrangement of many separate products such as engines, crankshaft, axles, wheels and other parts.

- *Price discrimination.* Price discrimination can also be achieved in the following way. Assume a monopolist supplier sells colour printers (the tying product) and ink cartridges (the tied product). The firm charges a competitive price for its printers but a 'high' price for the cartridges. Large customers (those with a low elasticity of demand) are forced to pay a higher overall price for printing services since they use proportionately more of the expensive cartridges than the low-intensity users. Resale is ruled out since the price of cartridges is the same for all customers. Thus price discrimination is achieved indirectly. Another example of this type of covert price discrimination covers the common practice of selling machines and expensive service contracts. The more machines that are bought the higher the overall 'price' paid.

- *Leverage.* Tying arrangements can extend the power of a monopolist into other related markets. The arrangement can create market power in the market for the tied products and prices can be increased. The amount of leverage a monopolist can exert depends on the extent to which tying arrangements can account for the whole tied market.

Why are suppliers interested in bundling?

Bundling, as just briefly described, refers to the practice of a seller offering several goods as one package. Thus, hotels offer rooms bundled with the use of other hotel facilities such as in-house movies, gyms and swimming pools. The prices of all these additional services are included in the price of the room, whether one uses them or not. Such bundling is profitable since customers can be sorted into different groups with different reserve prices and their consumer surplus appropriated accordingly. In other words, bundling can be used as a form of price discrimination. The example of 'block booking' in the film industry in Box 9.1 helps to explain the strategy.

In conclusion, we can draw a few strands together. The Chicago approach to vertical restraints, which argued that they are commercially legitimate, is plausible under a number of circumstances. However, one should not ignore the obvious strategic advantages that such a policy can present to firms. Vertical restraints can be used to change an industry structure or to preserve an uncompetitive status quo. In view of this dichotomy the most obvious conclusion is to treat each restraint on an ad hoc basis by examining the consequences of such actions. Thus if prices are considered

Box 9.1 Block booking in the film industry

Block booking refers to the practice of offering an exhibitor only a package of films, rather than the films individually. This policy increases revenue to the sellers. Assume a film distributor knows the reserve prices of two exhibitors. One exhibitor owns an 'art house', the other a cinema showing popular films. The reserve prices each exhibitor is willing to pay for two films, a foreign-language film and the latest 'blockbuster' are as follows:

Exhibitor	Blockbuster	Foreign-language film
Art house	7000	3000
Cinema	8000	2500

If each film were to be sold separately and the distributor could prevent resales we would achieve perfect price discrimination and the total rental would be £20,500 (7000 + 3000 + 8000 + 2500). However, under normal market conditions, perfect price discrimination is impossible and the best the distributor could earn would be to charge £7000 for the 'blockbuster' and £2500 for the foreign-language film. This would generate an income of only £19,000 (7000 × 2 + 2500 × 2). If the distributor practised block booking non-discriminatingly, he would sell the two-film package at £10,000 to both exhibitors. The total rental would rise to £20,000.

to be fair and entry is not retarded, the presence of vertical restrictions may be tolerated.

9.7   Conclusion

This chapter examined a range of horizontal and vertical relationships. The choice of which horizontal or vertical strategy to follow can only be resolved by an analysis of the potential costs and benefits present in any given market structure. What is clear is that there is no one particular unequivocal answer as to what constitutes an equilibrium condition for most firms. To understand why firms develop complex vertical and horizontal relationships one must appreciate the risks, the level of investment, and the extent of co-ordination and bargaining present in such relationships. One can then also understand why firms undertake integration if market contracts are a less efficient method of organising production and distribution. Clearly, all such relationships are beneficial to consumers if they result in lower costs, greater output and a control on the power of monopolies. However, both horizontal and vertical restraints can reinforce market power and frustrate greater competition and economic welfare. What is clear is that one cannot support or condemn such practices in any general sense. Only a careful analysis of the motives and effects of such actions can determine useful and practical solutions.

Discussion Questions

1 With reference to the Farrell and Shapiro arguments presented in this chapter, explain what they mean by 'synergies'. Give examples of such synergies in the real world.

2 Give examples of firms forced to vertically integrate backwards to guarantee their sources of supply and those that have had to integrate forwards to safeguard their distribution outlets.

3 It is claimed that one advantage of vertical integration is that communications within the organisation are better than between different organisations. Assess this claim.

4 It was reported in November 2002 that the Office of Fair Trading had been investigating Manchester United and the Football Association for their fixing of prices in the retail market for replica kit. It was reported that a replica shirt cost just £7 to produce, but retailed for £45. Present arguments as to why Manchester United might be justified in following this course of action and why the Office of Fair Trading could regard such a practice as anticompetitive.

5 The UK market for pubs is characterised by 'tied houses'. A 'tied house' is a pub owned by a brewery (or pub company) and is tied to selling what the brewery says. According to the CAMRA (Campaign For Real Ale) there are many pubs

which claim to be free but have done deals (such as accepting loans on generous terms) in return for guaranteeing to sell certain brands. Discuss the effects of this system on the market.

6 Explain how mergers between universities could be either horizontal or vertical. Assess the advantages of both such strategies.

Further Reading

General background

Dobson, P. W. and Waterson, M. (1996) *Vertical restraints and competition policy*, Office of Fair Trading Research Paper 12.

Farrell, J. and Shapiro, C. (2000) *Scale economies and synergies in horizontal merger analysis* (1 October 2000), Working Paper CPC00-015. Competition Policy Center. http://repositories. cdlib.org/iber/cpc/CPC00-015

Scherer, F. M. and Ross, D. (1990) *Industrial Market Structure and Economic Performance*. Boston, MA: Houghton-Mifflin, Chapters 14 and 15.

Williamson, O. E. (1971) The vertical integration of production: market failure considerations, *American Economic Review*, 61, 112–27.

Advanced

Katz, M. L. (1989) Vertical contractual relations, in Schmalensee, R. and Willig, R. D. (eds) *Handbook of Industrial Organisation*, Volume 1. Amsterdam: North Holland, Chapter 11.

Phlips, L. (ed.) (1998) *Applied Industrial Economics*. Cambridge: Cambridge University Press, Chapters 9, 15 and 21.

Williamson, O. E. (1989) Transaction cost economics, in Schmalensee, R. and Willig, R. D. (eds) *Handbook of Industrial Organisation*, Volume 1. Amsterdam: North Holland, Chapter 3.

10 Diversification

Objectives

By the end of this chapter, the reader should be able to understand:

- the difference between diversification as product and market extension and 'pure' diversification
- the reasons for diversification
- the concept of the 'coherent corporation' and its relationship with diversification
- the reasons why some firms may decide to reduce their commitment to diversification and concentrate on their core activities.

Key Concepts

- conglomerate
- corporate coherence
- cross-subsidisation
- deconglomeration
- economies of scope

- internal capital market
- predation
- reciprocity
- specific asset
- tie-in sales (tying)

10.1 Introduction

Diversification refers to a strategy where a firm is involved in the production of a number of different goods and services. Three different types can be identified.

Product extension

Firms can diversify by moving into familiar or related activities. A sweet manufacturer who sells a milk chocolate bar may decide to produce and sell a dark chocolate bar as a product extension. The firm may diversify further afield by marketing related products such as ice cream or snack foods. Product extension usually occurs when there are potentials for *economies of scope*. Such economies are realised when two related goods can be produced jointly at a cost lower than if they were produced independently.

Since almost all firms produce more than one type of product or offer more than one particular service, it may be true to say that all firms are, to some extent, diversified, multi-product firms. A steel manufacturer can produce different qualities of steel in various shapes and sizes; and even the sandwich shop can extend its product range by adding new ingredients to its fillings or offering a greater range of drinks.

Market extension

As a firm gains a specialisation in a given technology and product base, it may wish to exploit different markets, such as different industries, different social groups or different geographical areas. For example, a chemical company may decide to sell its chemicals not only to industrial users but also to the agricultural sector of the economy. The challenge of selling an existing product to a new market is the ability of a firm to ensure that it has the resources, the knowledge and the ability to exploit such new marketing opportunities.

'Pure' diversification

This type of diversification exists when firms move into unrelated fields of activity. Firms which are involved in different industries are often referred to as *conglomerates*. An example of such pure diversification is the British firm Virgin plc, which began as a record store, but is currently involved in aeroplanes, trains, financial products, soft drinks, mobile phones, holidays, cars, wines, publishing and bridal wear.

The first two types of diversification discussed refer to a strategy based on a core product specialisation. Conglomerates or purely diversified firms rely less and less on such a common base. Very few firms engage in 'pure' diversification. Most firms tend to enter adjacent markets rather than move into totally new areas of production and distribution. At times it may appear that a firm is involved in pure diversification, but on closer examination there may be a logical explanation why a firm has decided on a particular direction. For example, Mars UK, the confectionery firm, developed marine radar, aimed at the small boat market. At first glance this would seem to be an example of pure diversification. In fact, the company had developed a successful electronics business on the basis of technical expertise accumulated through its vending machine operations. Having spotted a gap in the market for a cheap and reliable radar, the company, Mars Electronic, invested in this new market.

Case Study 10.1

Diversification: internal expansion versus acquisition

A further issue that may be considered is the manner in which firms can diversify since diversification can be achieved either through internal expansion or by acquisition and merger. Internal expansion would require a consideration of the expansion of the existing plant, equipment, raw materials and application of skills and technical and managerial know-how. These factors are very much less important if a firm considers diversification through acquisition. The only requirement for the latter strategy is to select an appropriate firm and to manage the integration efficiently. Jacobson and Andréosso-O'Callaghan (1996) noted that diversification in Europe after the Second World War tended to be characterised by internal expansion, whereas American diversification was achieved through acquisitions. One explanation for this observed difference was suggested by de Jong (1993), who claimed that diversification strategy might depend on the industry lifecycle. New industries have opportunities to extend their product lines as the market grows and rivalry is less pronounced. This will encourage internal expansion. However, as an industry moves into a maturity stage, further market growth and new product development are constrained and firms will look towards the acquisition of new firms to maintain a diversification strategy. An alternative explanation was offered by Chandler (1990), who suggested that European firms' ability to raise finance for acquisitions and mergers was constrained by the smaller European capital market, unlike the American counterpart.

In this chapter we consider the reasons for diversification in sections 10.2 to 10.5 These reasons cover issues such as the desire by firms to secure more market power, to achieve greater growth, to lower costs and to exploit their *specific assets* in different industries (see Case Study 10.1). In section 10.6, we discuss the reasons for diversification as viewed from a newer perspective of the firm, developed by Teece et al. (1994) and referred to as the *coherent corporation*. It will become clear from the discussion in the various sections that diversification does not generate unlimited advantages and that, at some point, costs of diversification force firms to consider strategies of divestment or deconglomeration in order to refocus their attention on core activities. This is discussed in section 10.7, while section 10.8 provides a conclusion.

10.2   Reasons for Diversification

The basic reasons for diversification can be summed up under three headings, the market power view, the agency view and the resources view.

The market power view

This approach suggests that diversified firms might be able to exploit anticompetitive behaviour. Three examples of such behaviour are as follows:

- *Cross-subsidisation* or *'deep pocket' strategies*. This occurs when a firm relies on profits from its various operations to finance predatory practices in other markets.

- *Reciprocal buying*, which involves an agreement by which, for example, firm A purchases its inputs from firm B *on the condition* that firm B then purchases its inputs from firm A. Clearly, conglomerate firms are in a stronger reciprocal position than specialised firms, which may find that they have no need for the output of the buying firm. Thus specialised firms may be foreclosed from certain markets.

- *Mutual forbearance* is said to exist where large conglomerates recognise each other's power and decide to co-exist and accommodate one another in various shared markets.

The agency view

Due to a separation of ownership from control in the modern corporation, managers (the agents) may pursue growth through diversification strategies in excess of that necessary to benefit their shareholders (the principals). Managers may be tempted to do this for three reasons. First, their power, status and remuneration may be related to the growth of the organisation. Second, diversification in other activities may complement the talents and skills of the managers, thus making them indispensable to the organisation. Lastly, unlike shareholders, who are able to reduce business risks by diversifying their portfolios, managers are exposed to employment risks should the firm fail. Diversification of a firm might then be seen as a means of reducing the potential risks of failure faced by the firm and its managers.

A model consistent with the 'agency view' and which explains the issues facing firms which pursue growth through diversification was suggested by Baumol (1967). Baumol considered the effects of diversification on the firm's total costs. The first effect was the increase in fixed and variable costs due to increased production, which he termed the 'output' costs. The second group of costs which had to be considered were the costs of diversification concerned exclusively with the strategy of diversification. Assuming constant returns to scale, 'output' costs can be regarded as growing proportionately with the firm's output. However, diversification costs rise proportionately faster, as the rate of diversification increases. The explanation for these increasing costs is as follows:

- Diversification through mergers results in increasing business mistakes as the firm moves into new and unfamiliar areas of operations. These mistakes increase costs as 'poor' acquisitions are made.

- Acquisitions may have to be funded by a greater reliance on the capital market (as opposed to retained profits), which may result in higher interest rates as the firm accumulates more debt.

- As a firm develops new operations at a rapid pace it has to purchase more resources and apply these resources in an unfamiliar environment. Again, mistakes are made and costs rise.

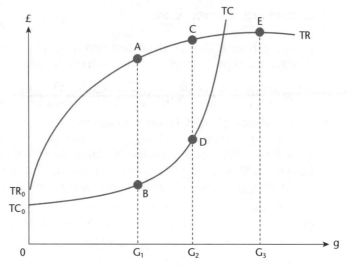

Figure 10.1 Growth equilibrium and diversification

Thus, as a firm diversifies it experiences an increasing cost schedule shown by TC in Figure 10.1, which shows the different growth rates of the firm (g) and the relevant total cost, total revenue and profits.

Total revenue rises as acquisitions and products are increased. There is, however, a limit to the increase in revenue. As the firm expands operations, so sales begin to increase at a diminishing rate and even possibly decline as returns to the marketing effort of ever-new products begin to diminish. The difference between total revenue and total cost is the profitability of the firm. At a zero rate of growth, the firm relies on its current products and earns a low profit ($TR_0 - TC_0$). As the rate of growth increases, so profitability increases and then eventually declines. The maximum profit is at the point of the greatest distance between total revenue and total cost (AB) and this corresponds to growth rate G_1. We can thus see that firms wish to grow through diversification to achieve higher profitability. However, managers may have other, equally important objectives, such as higher sales achieved through higher growth. This may be the case if their remuneration is tied to sales and the power of shareholders is weak. It can then be argued that managers pursue a strategy of growth maximisation, subject to a minimum profit constraint. Maximum growth of sales would occur at point E, but that level of growth results in a loss and managers would no longer be able to fund some of their future investments. If we assume the minimum required profit to satisfy the capital market and shareholders is CD, then managers aim to achieve a growth rate of G_2. The conclusion drawn from this model is that if we assume managers are growth maximisers, then the firm follows a more robust diversification strategy than if the firm attempted to maximise profits.

The resource view

Firms possess a range of resources and assets which can be exploited in other markets. If such resources can be sold in the market, to other firms, then the rationale for diversification would disappear. However, in cases where transaction costs are high, firms may be forced to exploit these assets themselves. Such assets have been given various names, such as *specific assets*, *core competencies* and *core capabilities*.

In the following section we consider and expand these general reasons. We consider these under four headings, market power, growth, cost reductions and specific assets.

10.3   Market Power

There is a belief that the diversified firm, relying on many different geographic and product markets, has a competitive advantage over the specialised firm, and that it can draw on resources from its many different operations to fight rivals in specific markets. It may also be the case that large near-monopolies and oligopolies seeking yet more market power may be reluctant to expand in one market as this would alert the anti-monopoly authorities. An alternative may be to cross over to related markets to escape the attention of the competition regulators. We consider four possible anticompetitive consequences of diversification.

Cross-subsidisation and predation

The diversified firm can outbid, outspend and outdo the specialised firm since it can rely on profits and cash flows from many sources. In essence it is a better fighter. A typical strategy for a diversified firm might be to undercut the prices of a specialised firm and force it out of the market. In order for this strategy to succeed the predator must have a 'deeper pocket' than its prey. Once the firm has left the market, prices are reset at the original or higher level. Such behaviour is referred to as *predatory pricing*.

Predation is, however, not as straightforward a strategy as one might think. First, predatory pricing is only profitable where entry barriers exist, otherwise the sacrifice of lower prices and lower revenues has been in vain, although it could be argued that the act of predation can also be used as a signal to potential entrants that the incumbent is a 'fighter' and is willing to sacrifice short-term profits to maintain or increase market share. This *reputation effect* may act as an entry barrier. Second, predatory practices imply that resources from one operation are being diverted to fight elsewhere. In a specialised firm, alternatives do not compete. Thus, while the diversified firm may have the capability of such a strategy, it may refrain from predatory practices since it would place its alternatives at risk. Finally, it may be argued that if firms wish to eliminate rivalry there may be alternative, less costly strategies than predation, such as collusive pricing or acquisitions.

Reciprocity

Reciprocity occurs when firms encounter each other in the dual capacities as buyers *and* sellers. Thus reciprocal buying is an arrangement whereby firm A buys inputs from firm B *on the condition* that B buys from A. Thus sellers realise that a buyer may shift purchases elsewhere if reciprocal transactions are not made. It can be argued that, in effect, all economic transactions involve an element of reciprocity, and in the extreme case of bartering transactions are based solely on reciprocal arrangements. The anticompetitive aspect of reciprocity might be inferred if some firms were *forced* into such transactions. Utton (1979) noted that the Federal Trade Commission in the United States argued that reciprocal trade would increase existing entry barriers and possibly create a new one, if potential entrants were excluded from a market by the existence of existing reciprocal trade agreements. To overcome such a barrier, the entrant would have to be diversified. A specialised firm has only a limited range of input demands, whereas a diversified firm has a much wider spread of purchasing requirements. Thus the diversified firm is in a *better reciprocal position*. Much of the evidence of anticompetitive effects of such strategies tends to be based on anecdotal evidence of cases that were brought before the courts. It may, however, be argued that reciprocity is just one method by which a firm can exploit its market power, *which already exists*, rather than a strategy of extending that power. Consequently, the practice itself can be viewed as not particularly harmful to competition.

Tie-in sales

In Chapter 9, we discussed the nature and effects of tie-in sales. We defined tie-in sales (or tying) as the sale of two distinct products where the sale of one good is conditional on the purchase of another. Thus a conglomerate supplies a buyer with good X on the condition that the buyer also purchases good Y from the conglomerate. In this way the diversified firm is able to increase revenues. The advantages of tying discussed in our previous chapter can equally be applied to the case of diversified firms.

Entry barriers

It may be argued that conglomerate mergers may increase the height of entry barriers through economies of scale, absolute cost and capital requirement type barriers. Tremblay and Tremblay (1996) noted that, in the United States brewing industry, large national firms attempted to fill all possible niches and market segments, through brand and product proliferation, to maintain their market power and deny market space to potential entrants, although it could also be argued that conglomerates may realise scale and scope economies which could lead to greater efficiency in various markets.

10.4   Growth of the Firm

A frequent justification for diversification is that it generates growth for the firm, with some commentators suggesting that diversification is the chief method of growth for medium-sized firms. Mueller (1969) argued that conglomerate mergers are a strategy which might be pursued by managers who are more concerned with the maximisation of the growth rate of the firm rather than the maximisation of shareholder wealth. To managers who are keen to maximise the growth rate of the firm, the opportunity cost of investments in the firm is equated with the returns on the additional projects in the organisation, rather than on returns on investment projects outside the organisation. The latter is the opportunity cost of shareholders' investments in the organisation. As a consequence the discount rate of managers for investment projects is *much lower* than that of their shareholders and this leads to higher investments by the managers. Such investments can be directed towards horizontal, vertical and diversification opportunities. However, any firm which wishes to maintain growth faces three possible constraints. First, the existing market may be declining or not expanding quickly enough. This implies that the firm is faced with *opportunities* for investments and acquisitions in new markets which can achieve better growth prospects than those in the existing product markets. These opportunities may reflect not just the changes in prices, tastes and other market conditions, but also the development of know-how and skills within the firm. Second, the firm may find that further expansion in its existing market may meet increasing rivalry from its competitors as it tries to encroach on their market share. Finally, the regulatory authorities may make it difficult for firms to expand into horizontal and vertical markets. As a consequence, managers may consider conglomerate mergers as an alternative strategy.

10.5   Cost Reductions

Let us now turn to the consideration of the argument that diversification can bring about cost reductions. This can be achieved in two ways: first, economies of scale and scope and, second, the reduction of risk and uncertainty. We shall also examine the argument that diversification can reduce a firm's tax exposure.

Economies of scale and scope

As we saw in Chapter 2 economies of scale can be realised if a firm can spread its indivisible inputs over a greater output. Such economies can also be achieved if a firm is able to spread its indivisible inputs over a greater *variety* of output. This is often referred to as *economies of scope*, whereby the costs associated with the production of two different goods are lower than if the two goods are produced separately. A frequently quoted example is that of fruit and sheep. A fruit grower has to leave enough space in between the trees to allow access for labour and farm equipment. The land between the trees can be exploited by grazing sheep. Thus the fruit grower can use one input, namely land, in the production of two products. In manufacturing, the cause of such cost savings would be the existence of technological interdependencies of the two goods.

The existence of such economies, however, does not necessarily imply that the fruit grower must diversify. The alternative for the grower is to rent the land to a sheep farmer. This market transaction produces the same outcome as the diversification strategy. If, however, the market transaction costs are too high, the grower may be forced to exploit the asset through diversification. We consider the problem of such market failure when we discuss specific assets.

We may be sceptical about the economies of scale argument for three reasons. First, economies due to the spreading of indivisible inputs over a greater output can also be realised by a specialised firm. Second, the argument assumes that the inputs are non-specific, i.e. that they *can* be spread over different activities. The sort of indivisible inputs that might work best would be managerial, marketing and financial functions. Finally, the inputs must be such that only diversification can lead to cost reductions, i.e. expansion by a specialised firm would somehow be insufficient to spread the cost of these inputs. Circumstances in which these conditions could be fulfilled are clearly limited.

Reduction of risk and uncertainty

All firms are vulnerable to adverse and unpredictable changes in demand and increased competition for their individual products. The more products a firm develops the lower is this vulnerability. One minimises the risk of such 'gambler's ruin' by investing in 'offsetting activities'. Stable cash flows can be achieved when firms develop products or services with different seasonal peaks. Examples of such offsetting activities are Wall's ice cream and meat products, Valor Gas's combination of heating and gardening equipment, and W H Smith's entry into the travel agency business. However, such activities are not always easy to identify, and in the absence of any obvious activity the best approach might be to select an activity at random. However, bearing in mind the potential advantages of exploiting familiar assets and technologies, firms rarely stray into random activities.

If the risks to various branches of a firm's activity are randomly distributed, or follow 'offsetting cycles', then their combined risks are lower. The conglomerate can thus enjoy more stable profits. Consequently, this ability to reduce risk via diversification can help firms to secure investment funds at a lower cost. From the point of view of the lender, however, it is not immediately obvious why a diversified firm should receive such advantageous treatment in comparison to the specialised firm. A lender in the capital market can reduce risk by diversifying his or her portfolio by making investments among a number of specialised firms. If the lender is a small investor, then the attraction of holding shares in one diversified firm may be clearer, although in practice the existence of financial securities such as unit trusts can channel such small-scale funds into managed diversified portfolios and reduce an investor's exposure to risk equally well.

One obvious advantage of risk reduction is the benefit to management, who are concerned with survival. Diversified operations are more likely to save a firm from 'gambler's ruin' should the firm invest in just one set of specialised operations. This reason for diversification is part of the 'agency view', discussed earlier in the chapter.

A further advantage of conglomerate mergers from the point of view of managers is their ability to manage internal operations efficiently. Traditional analysis would argue that the capital market rewards efficient management by increasing the market value of the firm and punishes inefficiency by decreasing the market value. In practice, investors in the capital market may be unable to secure correct information to judge the performance of management. This is even more the case if investors rely on managers for information flows. It would require a great deal of altruism for managers to pass on information that might reflect badly on their efficiency as managers. Bad performances might be explained with distorted facts or what these days is referred to as 'spin'. This *information impactedness* leads to a market transaction cost which frustrates efficient allocation of investment funds. Such transaction costs can be reduced by conglomerate merger and an organisational structure where senior managers have access to correct information. The headquarters of the conglomerate essentially performs the task of the capital market by allocating funds for investments. But unlike the capital market, headquarters has two advantages. First, the managers of the various divisions are subordinates to senior managers and can be ordered to provide good and accurate information. Accurate information flows since middle managers are under an implicit threat of discipline should they fail to provide such information and a promise of rewards if they do. The divisional managers also share confidential information with senior staff, which they would not do with external investors. Second, the headquarters of the conglomerate is able to carry out internal audits to guard against possible mismanagement by the divisional managers. As a consequence, the conglomerate acts as a miniature capital market, but enjoys better access to information and is more able to monitor the efficiency of the various divisions.

Tax reductions

Diversification can, under various tax regimes, reduce a firm's tax liability. Firms can offset losses in one activity with profits in another. A specialised firm that makes a loss obviously pays no tax, but the tax payable by other profitable specialised companies is not reduced.

Specific assets

Gorecki (1975) noted that some, if not all, firms possess *specific assets* that can be of value if exploited in other industries. These assets would include such things as a new technology, trade secrets, brand loyalty, managerial experience and expertise. If a firm wishes to capitalise on these assets, it faces a choice. It can either sell the assets in the market or diversify into the relevant industry to exploit the asset itself. The decision whether to sell or diversify depends on the extent of market imperfections surrounding such transactions. These imperfections increase the transaction costs. Gorecki identified the following imperfections:

- No market may exist due to the 'non-exclusion principle' and thus no price can be set. The existence of a price implies exclusion to those consumers who do not pay that price. If you do not pay the price of book, a cinema ticket or car, you are *excluded* from buying and enjoying those goods. If consumers cannot be excluded from a good or service, it follows that no price can be charged. An example of such a specific asset might be 'basic knowledge'. Since no one can be excluded from exploiting 'basic knowledge' such knowledge is non-patentable and cannot be sold at a price in the marketplace.

- It may be too difficult to transfer a specific asset independently of its owner. Gorecki suggests that a team of managers or skilled labour may be uniquely loyal to an owner and thus be unwilling to work for another organisation.

- The transaction cost of transferring the asset may be too high. An example might be if the nature of the technology is complex and no buyer has the necessary skills and facilities to exploit such an asset fully. In addition, the sale of technical know-how might include not only the blueprints and recipes for a new process or product but also 'learning by doing' skills. The latter would imply the training of technical staff in the buying company, which may be difficult if the staff have a different technical background.

- Market transactions are also subject to many potential externalities. For example, if B purchases A's brand or trademark, this may affect A's profits should B be unable to maintain a reasonable standard of quality. If B offers a poor-quality product and service, consumers might link the poor product and service with A's brand. As a consequence A's sales and profits could be affected. Another example of an externality might occur if negotiations between a seller and a buyer reveal production methods and strategies sufficient for the buyer to contemplate entry into the seller's industry. To guard against such externalities or 'spillovers', strict and complex contractual relations may have to be specified, which would imply expensive monitoring and policing costs.

In view of these market imperfections and high transaction costs, firms might feel it to be more advantageous to diversify. An example of the exploitation of specific assets would be Gillette's acquisition of Duracell, the battery manufacturer. At first glance there seemed no obvious economies of scope between the two products. Capital equipment and technical know-how are very different in both markets. However, what Gillette wished to exploit was its established marketing and sales operations in countries such as Brazil, China and India, by selling batteries to those countries as well as razors.

Sutton (1980) expanded these arguments to suggest that a firm in a dynamic context is facing continual changes in the economic environment. These changes affect the firm's specific assets which, over time, generate fresh opportunities and incentives. The value of any asset depends not only on its technical applicability in alternative industries, but also on the profits that can be earned from its use in the existing industry and in the alternative industries. Thus, market price changes as well as changes in costs affect the relative attractiveness of such assets in their alternative uses. Major and sustained changes in market conditions thus present diversification opportunities to firms.

10.6   Corporate Coherence

An interesting approach to the question of why firms diversify was provided by Teece et al. (1994). They argued, first, that firms are 'coherent' in that they do not diversify at random. That would imply an 'incoherent' strategy. Second, this coherence is stable over time. Companies such as Shell Oil, ICI and Boeing have tended to focus on a relatively narrow range of activities for close to a century. Teece et al.

ask: why hasn't Shell diversified into jewellery, Boeing into buses or ICI into super-markets? If coherence implies that a firm's different products are related, Teece et al. attempt to develop a theory that explains why firms diversify *coherently*.

As mentioned in the introduction to this chapter, few firms are truly specialised by producing just one product. In most cases, due to a natural variation in market demand, firms are forced to offer products in more than one size, colour, flavour or some other characteristic. In contrast, diversification refers to product extension, which is far more varied than the examples just given. Firms add new products over time which enjoy technical and market similarities with the existing product lines. Since a firm is considered coherent if its products are related, a measure of this coherence is then suggested.

A measure of coherence

To determine a measure of coherence, Teece et al. first constructed a measure of relatedness. This is computed on the basis that frequently observed combinations of activities within firms in the same industry are related. In other words, if firms in a given industry almost always involve themselves in two or more activities, then the activities are related. A measure of relatedness was computed on the basis of a sample of over 18,000 US manufacturing firms, active in 958 different four-digit SIC industries and with close to 67,000 activities. (SIC coding was discussed in Chapter 5.) The highest relatedness was between SIC 5181 and SIC 5182, which referred to beer wholesalers and spirits wholesalers. The measure of coherence is then presented as the weighted-average relatedness of one activity to all other activities in the firm. Their finding suggested that, as diversification increases, firms add activities that relate to part of their existing activities and that the strength of this relatedness does not change as the firms grow through further diversification. Teece et al. concluded that coherence is a *major characteristic* of diversified business operations.

A theory of corporate coherence

In an attempt to develop a theory that might explain corporate coherence, Teece et al. have attempted to redefine the firm in terms of enterprise learning, path dependencies and selection.

Enterprise learning

Learning is an important aspect of any economic and business activity. It is through learning that improvements to processes are made and new opportunities identified. Such learning takes place not only through the traditional trainer and trainee inter-action, but also through group interaction. The successful outcome of such learning is found in organisational 'routines'. There are two types of organisational routine, static and dynamic. *Static routines* cover activities which can be copied or replic-ated, although in time repetition may lead to refinement and modification and the development of new routines. *Dynamic routines* refer to activities by which the organisation learns and develops new processes, an obvious example being its research and development strategy. These routines are often difficult to classify formally and may thus also be difficult to apply to other firms and industrial organisation environments. Thus these routines can be thought of as a specific characteristic or asset of a particular firm, as well as ways in which firms can be differentiated from one another.

Path dependencies

The value of enterprise learning depends largely on what the firm has achieved in the past. Its past investments and routines shape its future because learning tends to be 'local'. 'Local' learning implies that firms develop opportunities that *lie close* to their existing knowledge and skills. The two most important aspects of the learning process for new products are the technology used and the market into which the new product is launched. To enter a new market with a new product may overextend a firm's learning range and the strategy may fail. Consequently, firms follow (or depend on) well-defined paths as regards investments in new products. Teece et al. identified three aspects of these path dependencies:

- *Complementary assets* help to construct paths for future growth. In many cases assets used by firms have alternative uses which can be exploited vertically and horizontally. Teece et al. illustrate this point with the example of Singer sewing machines diversifying into the furniture business as a result of their ability to build wooden cabinets to house their machines.
- *Technological opportunities* determine how far and how fast a firm moves down a certain path. Research and development undertaken by the firm identifies the technological opportunities present for the existing products as well as potential alternatives.
- *Convergence of paths* occurs when there are major shifts in basic knowledge. As the technological base of industries changes, paths may converge or diverge. For example, the development of digital electronics created a convergence between computer and telecommunications firms. Products once aimed at different markets and based on different technologies are now sharing the same core technology.

Selection

Selection implies that firms survive and prosper if they are efficient and decay if they are inefficient. The rate at which this selection takes place depends on the level of competition, government policy, technology and the amount of exposure to external debt. The more debt the firm accumulates, the greater the threat of discipline from the capital market. Teece et al. argued that the 'tighter' the selection process, the greater the reliance of the firm on its core competencies or specific assets.

In view of this theory, Teece et al. advanced the following hypotheses which could explain the existence of three different types of firm:

- The *specialist firm* is characterised by rapid learning, many technological opportunities and narrow path dependencies. These types of firm tend to be young, as the probability that technological opportunities remain promising falls over time.
- The *coherent diversifier* is characterised by quick learning, a broad path dependency based on generic technologies and 'tight' selection. As opposed to the specialist firms, these firms tend to be much older and to have weathered periods of recession.

- The *conglomerate* is defined by its slow learning, low path dependencies and a weak selection. Should selection become stronger then some of the more extreme cases might be 'weeded out' of the market.

What is clear in this analysis is that Teece et al. do not view conglomerates in any positive way, viewing them as largely temporary phenomena. In response to the question as to why some conglomerates seem to have prospered, they offer two arguments. The first is that conglomerates may serve as 'internalised capital markets', as suggested by Williamson (1975) and discussed earlier in the chapter. Teece et al. recognise that this may be a reason for their existence, but suggest that this existence could hamper the efficient allocation of capital if investors are denied information as to the efficiency on the individual business units. In their second argument, Teece et al. refer to such conglomerates as 'hopeful monsters' which have evolved through some form of organisational mutation. Some of these monsters have a number of characteristics which allow them to survive for a period of time, but in time, selection eliminates all but a few.

In view of the Teece et al. arguments for coherent diversification and 'incoherent' conglomerates, we turn next to an examination of whether there is any evidence for the failure of diversified firms and conglomerates, which would then lead to a process of *deconglomeration*. The term implies a firm wishing to divest itself of unrelated activities and to *focus* on its core activities (see Case Study 10.2).

Case Study 10.2

Flight of the navigator as Boeing spreads its wings: digital cinema is the next step for the aerospace group's diversification

The Boeing office has a perfect view of aircraft swooping into Los Angeles International Airport (LAX) with the distant Hollywood Hills and its famous sign as a backdrop. But this office is unlike any other in the world's largest aerospace group's empire. This is its Tinsel Town unit – home of Boeing Digital Cinema (BDC). Even the director of the cinema unit appears more Hollywood than many of Boeing's quirky rocket scientists. Frank Stirling, BDC chief, is telegenic, manicured and nattily dressed. He likes acting, and appeared in the movie *Apollo 13*.

Boeing wants to show off its diversity, hoping to turn investors' heads. It pulled up its roots from Seattle last September to move its headquarters to Chicago – in part to manage and develop a new image as more than just a manufacturer of jetliners. Digital cinema highlights just how far Boeing is willing to go in its search for ways of using and diversifying its technology to expand the company. It is starting to use technological discoveries and innovations made by its commercial and military operations outside its core aerospace unit. This push is turning Boeing more and more into a technology company. 'Boeing's value is in their engineering and technological capabilities; it is more than their machining and large-scale assembly,' says John Rogers, aerospace analyst at DA Davidson. 'Some people (still) think of them as an old-line manufacturing company.' Phil Condit, chief executive, describes his group as 'a company in transition; we are becoming a very different company'.

Nevertheless, some observers reckon the foray into digital cinema looks like a loss of focus, a turn away from Boeing's core. Indeed, entertainment is one industry where it is difficult to pick the next winner, and Boeing has no experience in movies. It also conjures up memories of some of Boeing's ill-fated attempts to diversify in the past. In 1974 its Vertol unit launched the first redesigned US-built trolley car since 1936 to help ease urban congestion in Boston. But the division failed because the cars contained many flaws, including poorly working air conditioning and doors opening in transit.

Mr Stirling's cinema division wants to replace the film that rolls through projectors. Its plan is to use Boeing satellite technology to beam a digital film directly to a movie theatre, where a Boeing-made receiver will store and feed it to the projector. Boeing's pitch to the movie studios is that digital transmission could slash 75% of the estimated $2bn it costs to print and distribute films. Moreover, movie directors increasingly shoot digitally. The project is a long shot, with theatres required to install equipment worth up to $300,000 to switch to the format. But analysts see a real possibility in selling the technology in general.

Cinema has a modest role in Boeing's diversification. The company's space, satellite and other businesses accounted for 19% of last year's $58.2bn in revenues, with military aircraft and missiles at 21% and commercial jetliners down to 60%. But cinema reveals a cross-section of technology, from building and using satellites to wiring complicated machines. Commercialising or selling such technological products could work for Boeing, as long as it skilfully tends to profit margins in bread-and-butter aircraft, analysts say.

Boeing's core mission is not likely to change. It will still build rockets, fighter planes, smart bombs, satellites and jetliners. However, its acquisitions of Hughes satellite, Rockwell's space and McDonnell Douglas's aircraft operations has left it brimming with cutting-edge technology and a lab called Phantom Works. The group is also developing an unmanned fighter aircraft; the X-37, an unmanned reusable space vehicle; and Connexion, a broadband service (television, Internet, aircraft data, remote flying possibilities) for aircraft.

Perhaps the most science fiction-like project, and most 'militarily secret', is Boeing's work with off-the-shelf technology to build a system that connects every system, person and vehicle in the US military. It calls its proposal to the government 'the integrated battle space'. Its goal is to make everything interact. Satellites, planes, tanks, missiles, and ground soldiers would all feed each other information. Flexible programming would allow aircraft to fly, tanks to roll and men to march locked into a battle sector's command and control. On leaving the sector, they would be logged off. 'You can only improve tanks so much if you treat them as an individual platform,' says Carl O'Berry, president of Boeing strategic architecture. 'If we pull this off, it's abundantly clear that it applies to virtually all aspects of life.'

Boeing wants to affect all aspects of life with its technology – from distributing movies through space to linking every platform, human and machine. This sounds like a company that wants to sell technology, not just aeroplanes.

Source: *Financial Times*, 16 April 2002.

Focus and Deconglomeration

In a study of 33 large, prestigious US firms over the period 1950–1986, Porter (1987) noted that most of them had divested more acquisitions than they had kept. A similar conclusion was reached by Scharfstein (1998), who analysed a 1979 sample of 165 conglomerates firms which had diversified into at least one other unrelated activity. By 1994 only 53 firms (32%) survived as conglomerates.

We now consider four reasons that have been suggested to explain why large conglomerates have become more 'focused' over the past two decades.

To increase profitability

One fundamental reason for deconglomeration is that as firms have become more diversified they have become less profitable, and as they became more focused, so their profitability has increased. Daley et al. (1997) noted that research had shown that stock market prices of parent firms which had sold off some of their activities had risen. They found that these price rises were higher in firms that sold off unrelated activities as opposed to related activities. This would then imply that the capital market viewed increased focus as a profitable strategy. If stock prices of diversified firms are consistently lower than those of specialised firms, it would suggest that shareholders have tended to penalise such firms. One could thus argue that unrelated diversification as a strategy is intended to benefit managers and not shareholders. Analysing the profitability of the parent firms which had divested themselves of their acquisitions as well as the units that had been divested, Daley et al. found that profitability did, in fact, increase for both organisations, which lent support to capital market optimism for firms who had become more focused.

Management inefficiencies

Managers in conglomerates may be viewed as 'jack of all trades and masters of none' and that a frequent exhortation to managers is to 'stick to what you know'. It may also become more and more difficult to provide sufficient incentives for managers as the number of activities increases.

Internal capital market inefficiencies

A previous argument for an advantage of diversification was that managers have better access to information and may thus be in a position to allocate capital more efficiently than the capital market. The opposing view is that managers in the large diversified firm are *less* efficient in the allocation of funds to their various divisions. Firms may prop up ailing divisions, at the expense of the profitable divisions. This behaviour was termed 'socialism in capital budgeting' by Scharfstein (1998). It is possible that divisions in a conglomerate bargain for funds and that the bargaining power of a division may be enhanced by investments that may not benefit the organisation as a whole. It may also be possible that head office 'buys' the co-operation of divisions by diverting investment funds in their direction.

Neglect of innovation

Porter (1990) argued that innovation stems from a focus on and a commitment to a specific activity. In time it is this innovatory activity which creates a competitive advantage for firms. In contrast, unrelated diversification makes little contribution to innovation. It tends to distract the firm from its focus and commitment to specific activities (see Case Study 10.3).

Case Study 10.3

Breaking up can be good to do

Spin-offs and carve-outs are a sign of today's difficult economic times. Diageo has announced the sale of Burger King, Canal Plus is to be broken up, and the split of AOL Time Warner has also been mooted. Many businesses and investors are questioning the rationale behind much of the frenzied acquisition activity of the boom years, as the perceived synergies seem less apparent in the current financial climate. Are demergers an admission of failure, a last resort, a portent of even more difficult times to come?

A study by Deloitte & Touche provides compelling evidence that proactive demergers create rather than destroy shareholder value. The study analysed the share price performance of the 118 largest demergers over the past ten years and concluded that most of those deals created significant increases in shareholder value for both the parent and separated business within a year of completion. This is in stark contrast to the market's initial reaction to a demerger announcement. The study reveals that corporate divorces are usually greeted with a 2–10% drop in share price, as investors expect a loss of scale and that assets will be sold cheaply. This reaction is usually misplaced. Although demerging creates diseconomies of scale for both separating entities, with the need to split and duplicate previously shared services, the additional costs are far outweighed by the clarity of purpose and renewed focus of each entity. Both management teams are able to concentrate on their core businesses, and decision making becomes easier, clearer and more commercial as the politics associated with taking sides are eliminated. In addition, the motivation of the smaller business rises with a greater sense of independence from its former parent and a newly found purpose and direction.

The study found that within one year of the demerger becoming effective, over half the parent companies had increased their share price in absolute terms by more than 12% relative to their share price the day before the demerger announcement. A quarter had increased by more than 50% over the same time. Similarly, for the young entities that went public, more than half increased in absolute value by 13% relative to the initial public offering price. Again, the best performing quartile achieved returns of more than 45%.

The benefits of a demerger – focus, transparency and accountability – do not come effortlessly. Demerging a fully integrated division is complex and it is not always obvious how the business should be divided, particularly for parts that are integral to both. Senior managers need to be reassured about the prospects of each entity before deciding where to pitch their flag, while the more junior ones will wait to see where the best managers go and then make up their minds. As jobs in both entities may shrink given the prospect of smaller teams, reduced budgets and responsibilities, creativity is required to manage egos, redefine roles and ensure value is retained from highly qualified staff.

Another challenge comes from the hard deadlines presented by an IPO or sale. The process requires a dedicated director to ensure deadlines are met. With mergers there can seem less urgency, with delayed decisions creating problems and destroying value.

Demergers also force separated companies to raise their game when it comes to dealing with their former other halves, as these often become their biggest new customers. For example, one technology company that was being spun off from its parent considered buying new computers from a competitor because it could get better service than under the old internal division procedures. As soon as the parent company realised what was happening, it set up a key account team to manage what was to become its largest new client.

Why don't more companies consider demergers? A 'grow and sell' strategy takes longer to execute than a 'buy and merge' one. Moreover, the 'buy and merge' approach means exciting M&A deals, performance awards on completion, bigger jobs, larger pay packages and higher industry rankings. However, as Deloitte's research shows, bigger is not always better; size may bring greater management burdens without necessarily any clear commercial advantages. Often, the best way to increase shareholder rewards is to keep executives firmly focused on their core competence.

So how can you tell if your company should demerge? Are you the best parent or natural owner for all your divisions? Can you add more strategic value and direction to each division than if they were standalone or part of another group? Can you redistribute internal resources (people and capital) more efficiently than on the open market? Can you deliver more synergy value through integration than a rival?

Do you actively reconcile your shareholders' expectations of your company and of your stock? Do your divisions have similar risk/return profiles or very similar (value or lifecycle) requirements for cash? Is the business as a whole more valuable than the sum of its parts? Are you readily classified against your peer group/industry by the financial community? Are you able to create an environment that encourages ambition and creative drive in all your management teams? Can you reconcile and fund equally deserving but competing projects? Are you satisfied that none of your divisions are being deliberately held back to grow others? Are you satisfied none of them have trouble attracting or retaining talented people? If you answer no to more than one of [these] questions, it is worth further investigation.

Source: *Financial Times*, 13 August 2002.

10.8   Conclusion

In this chapter we have considered what is generally meant by 'diversification'. Although it is popularly assumed that diversification is a strategy that moves a firm into unrelated businesses and activities, we saw that, in practice, diversification has a much wider definition, which includes product and market extension. The vast majority of diversification strategies fall into this large set. We examined the reasons why firms wish to diversify, and these fell into a number of categories such as market power, growth, cost reductions and specific assets. In addition to an economic analysis of diversification, we introduced the concept of corporate coherence, which attempts to explain the attractiveness of diversification as seen from a strategic management viewpoint. Finally, we noted some of the reasons why some firms may decide to divest themselves of a variety of businesses to focus, once again, on their core activities.

The direction that any diversification takes depends on the market opportunities, the nature of the technology facing the firms and the ability of management to exploit such opportunities. If diversification resulted only in advantages, then one could reasonably expect to see just a few large conglomerates in our economies. That this has not happened goes some way to show that there are limits to the ability of firms to manage ever-increasing commitments.

Discussion Questions

1 Why might some large firms be attracted to conglomerate mergers rather than horizontal or vertical mergers?

2 The argument that diversification benefits a firm through the realisation of economies of scale by the spreading of indivisible inputs over a greater output is of limited appeal according to some economists. Explain why.

3 Williamson argued that one reason for conglomerate mergers is the opportunity to take over inefficiently managed and undervalued firms. He argued that due to information impactedness, capital markets and shareholders were unable efficiently to 'discipline' poor management. Can you suggest why an efficient cadre of corporate managers are better able to exact better control within the organisation?

4 Give examples of firms that fall into the definition of Teece et al. of the specialist firm, the coherent diversifier and the conglomerate.

Further Reading

General background

Gorecki, P. (1975) An inter-industry analysis of diversification in the UK manufacturing sector, *The Journal of Industrial Economics*, 24, 131–46.

Penrose, E. (1995) *The Theory of the Growth of the Firm* (3rd edn). Oxford: Oxford University Press.

Teece, D., Rumelt, R., Dosi, G. and Winter, S. (1994) Understanding corporate coherence, theory and evidence, *Journal of Economic Behaviour and Organisation*, 23, 1–30.

Advanced

Montgomery, C. (1994) Corporate diversification, *Journal of Economic Perspectives*, 8, 163–78.

Utton, M. A. (1979) *Diversification and Competition*. Cambridge: Cambridge University Press.

Part Four Analysis of Government Policy

Government and Business

By the end of this chapter, the reader should be able to understand:

- why governments intervene in industry
- the rationale for competition policy and be aware of the evolution of such policies in the UK and Europe
- and assess the pros and cons of privatisation and how privatised industries have been regulated in the UK
- the differences between rate of return and price cap regulation.

Key Concepts

- franchising
- merger policy
- monopoly policy
- privatisation

- productive efficiency
- public interest
- regulatory capture
- restrictive practices policy

11.1　Introduction

In a free market economy, firms utilise scarce resources (in the form of land, labour, capital and enterprise) to satisfy the demands of consumers. The price mechanism is used to allocate these scarce resources so that firms produce goods and services at the lowest cost possible to those willing to pay the highest price. This implies that firms strive to make the highest profit because of the difference between costs and revenues. If this system (which Smith (1937) [1776] termed the invisible hand) works properly, then there will be an optimal allocation of resources in the economy. In other words, it will not be possible to make someone better off without someone else becoming worse off. This implies that any intervention in the economy by government would distort this efficient allocation of resources. However, in reality markets do not always work properly. If this is the case, we have market failure. Market failure can be defined as a situation where the market fails to provide certain goods or services or does provide them but in insufficient or excess quantities. Markets fail when externalities exist; when monopolies exist; and when goods are public in nature. These are now discussed briefly.

Externalities

When the market system works efficiently, market prices reflect the full costs and benefits of producing goods and services. If prices do not reflect all benefits and costs, externalities exist. Externalities exist when benefits or costs are accrued by someone not directly involved in the transaction – in other words, parties other than the buyer or seller of a product. Consequently, the true costs of production are not realised. For example, the sale of petrol may impose an externality in the form of pollution on society. However, this would not be a cost which would be borne directly by the producer selling the petrol or incorporated in the price the consumer pays for petrol. This is an example of a negative externality. On the other hand, externalities can also be positive. For example, company investments in training might benefit not only employers and employees of a firm, but also society as a whole. Overall, if externalities are negative, this is likely to lead to firms producing and consumers buying more products than would be the case if the true costs were realised for the product. The opposite would be the case for products which yield positive externalities. This implies then that when externalities exist, there is a misallocation of resources in the economy. To correct for such market failure, governments can impose taxes and other penalties on producers of goods and services that result in negative externalities. Alternatively, governments can reward producers of goods and services by creating positive externalities, through subsidies, tax breaks and other forms of favourable regulatory treatment. Overall, the efficient allocation of resources only exists if externalities are accounted for.

Monopoly power

As we saw in Chapter 3, under perfect competition firms set prices equal to marginal costs and output is at a level where all resources are fully utilised. At this level of output no individual can be made better off by increasing output without making someone else worse of. If all industries operate under conditions of perfect competition then there is allocative efficiency. At the other end of the competitive spectrum, the monopolist restricts output and prices products above marginal costs, thus leading to a consequent waste of resources. This distortion in resource allocation may lead to welfare losses. Regulation is therefore required to stop or curb monopoly power. This can be done via various policies to promote competition. Alternatively, if an industry can be characterised as a natural monopoly, governments can regulate prices or bring the ownership of the industry into public hands.

Public goods

Some goods have characteristics that make it difficult for a direct price to be charged for them, since no consumer can be excluded from the benefit. Such goods are known as *public goods*. Many consumers (without excluding other consumers) can consume these types of good. Examples of public goods include police and fire protection and street lighting. To charge a direct price for these services may lead to a free rider effect, whereby some consumers can receive the benefits of public good provision without paying for them. As a consequence, private firms would generally be unwilling to provide these goods. Governments are often left to intervene in the markets for public goods.

In this chapter we focus on the ways in which regulation is carried out by government in response to various market failures. In particular, the chapter examines how monopolies are regulated. We also examine the relative merits of organising production in the private and public sector when industries are characterised by natural monopoly. The rest of this chapter examines government intervention in industry via competition policy and other forms of regulation. Competition policy and regulation are primarily aimed at correcting various forms of market failure in order to increase competition and give consumers a wider choice of products and services. Governments often intervene (using industrial policy) to promote business and industry performance. This is done by pursuing policies aimed at encouraging new business formation, innovation and other developments, which might improve the competitiveness of UK firms within the international competitive environment. Industrial policy falls within the remit of the Department of Trade and Industry (DTI), which has instituted various initiatives in recent years aimed at increasing the competitiveness of UK firms through policies that will lead to improved productivity and scientific advances, ultimately feeding through to growth and performance of UK firms. In particular, the DTI aims to promote enterprise and improve efficiency and productivity; encourage research and development and innovation; and develop a strong and efficient regulatory framework which will ensure strong competitive markets. A detailed discussion of industrial policy is outside the scope of this chapter. However, a detailed treatment can be found in Griffiths and Wall (2001). The rest of this chapter is organised as follows. Section 11.2 provides a rationale for policies to promote competition and examines the evolution of competition policy in the United Kingdom. Section 11.3 examines the process of privatisation in the UK and subsequent regulation of these industries. Section 11.4 examines the related policies of franchising and competitive tendering. Section 11.5 of the chapter draws some conclusions. Case Study 11.1 provides an overview of the changing role of government policy.

Case Study 11.1

FT

Government and regulation

The past 20 years have seen a marked shift in regulators' role – towards helping businesses and markets to function.

It was not long ago that government–business relations were associated with taxation, investment incentives, public enterprises and regional development. The government was viewed as a substitute for markets where markets failed to operate. The classic examples were utilities, whose natural monopoly characteristics demanded supply by public enterprises. Although this view of government prevails in certain areas, there has been a marked shift in the past 20 years. Now business–government relations conjure up views of regulation, competition policy and public–private partnerships.

These developments have been driven by a changing perception of the function of government. From the 1940s to the 1970s, industrial policy aimed to correct 'market failures'; more recently there has been a growing appreciation of government failures. Thus the focus of government involvement in business has moved from substituting for markets to assisting them to function.

Alongside this change in attitudes, governments have acquired new analytic techniques for designing and evaluating policy tools, which permit the implementation of more sophisticated public policies at the microeconomic level.

Privatisation has been a big spur to change. During the 1980s and 1990s, some 2500 deals worth approximately $1100bn were reported in 120 countries. Huge segments of corporate activity around the world were transferred from public to private sector control. But the retreat of public sector ownership has coincided with the expansion of a new form of public sector activity – regulation.

Utilities

Regulation has been primarily associated with the utilities. In the absence of competition, the charges that utilities levy on customers had to be regulated. Regulation was originally conceived as a temporary expedient that would wither as competition emerged. In some sectors, such as electricity and telecommunications, this has occurred, but for the most part regulation has actually intensified. There are several reasons for this.

First, it is difficult to introduce competition into certain areas, for example water services and the core part of utilities, such as electricity and gas transmission systems. Second, the tools available to regulators have become increasingly sophisticated, for example in benchmarking performance and comparing costs. The belief that regulators can replicate the incentive mechanisms of competitive markets remains widespread.

There is little doubt that privatisation has brought considerable gains in efficiency, particularly in reducing the costs of running utilities. However, providing the right incentives for utilities to invest has been a tougher nut for regulators to crack. It is formidably difficult to determine the rates of return that utilities need to earn and it is even more complex to ensure that they are able to earn these returns over the long life of their investments.

The USA has attempted to solve this by fixing the rate of return that utilities earn (the so-called 'rate of return regulation') while the UK and much of the rest of the world has opted for 'price regulation'. Price regulation has encouraged the pursuit of operating efficiencies but potentially at the expense of investment.

Competition policy

The deficiencies of regulation have prompted policymakers to promote competition instead where possible. For example, in energy, competitive markets in supply have been developed separately from the core activities of transmission.

The emergence of potentially competitive markets in utilities has been one factor encouraging a greater emphasis on competition policy. Another has been the recognition that a tough public policy stance is required to avoid anti-competitive practices. As governments' role as provider of goods and services has diminished so their function as protector of the consumer has increased.

As in regulation, the tools of competition policy have become increasingly sophisticated. The principles of competition policy have been one of the greatest successes of economics in the past 20 years. While anti-trust regulation has been a focus of public policy in the USA for the past 100 years, it has only recently risen to prominence in Europe, led by the European Commission. The focus of US policy is on consumer protection, promotion of competition and arbitration through the courts. In Europe, however, many argue that policy has had a wider remit of the protection of small and medium-sized enterprises, employment and market integration. Critics suggest this is a source of confusion in European decisions.

In summary, the past 20 years have witnessed a pronounced shift in the role of government in business away from substituting for markets towards promoting them. This is happening at various speeds in different countries. It has been the focus of policy in the USA for a long time. It is being rapidly adopted in the UK and there is a growing appreciation of its relevance in Brussels.

These developments reflect not only a realisation of the limits of government but also the emergence of new tools of analysis. While it has not been widely appreciated, advances in microeconomic analysis over the past 20 years have given rise to more sophisticated policies towards corporate sectors. The USA leads the world in the quality of its economic analysis, so it is not surprising that it has been the source of most policy innovations. But these innovations offer policymakers around the world the opportunity of modernising the government of business.

Source: *Financial Times*, 28 August 2002.

11.2   Competition Policy

One of the themes running through this book has been that the extent of competitive forces determine the strategies which firms follow and ultimately how they perform. Under monopoly, when competition is limited or absent, consumers are often forced to pay higher prices than would be the case under conditions of competition.

Why is competition important?

Competition encourages efficient production

If industries are competitive there is efficiency in the production of goods and services. This is often referred to as *productive efficiency*. Productive efficiency is defined as the sum of two components which we introduced in Chapter 2. These are a purely technical (physical) component and an economic (or monetary) component. The technical or physical component of productive efficiency means that firms minimise the amount of inputs of land, labour, capital and enterprise to produce a given level of output. This is equivalent to the concept of x-efficiency, discussed in Chapter 3. In other words, firms which are technically efficient are also x-efficient. The economic component of productive efficiency is where firms are concerned with optimal level of production, which minimise the prices of capital, labour etc. Overall, competition allows the most efficient firms to survive and grow at the expense of their inefficient counterparts. In other words, competition leads to productive efficiency.

Competition encourages efficient allocation of resources

Consumption is also efficient under competition. This is because the competitive process leads to consumers paying a price equal to the firm's marginal cost of production for a given good or service. This means that the economy's resources are allocated to the production of goods and services demanded by the consumer (often referred to as *allocative efficiency*). Allocative efficiency refers to the welfare gains that accrue to society if all production takes place under competitive market conditions. However, allocative inefficiency arises when firms exploit monopoly power in order to restrict output and to charge a price above marginal cost. As we have already seen in Chapter 3, this creates a welfare loss to society.

What is competition policy?

Competition policy is normally aimed at promoting efficiency, innovation, price reductions and consumer choice. In other words, this type of policy aims to control firm behaviour (such as pricing and non-price strategies and merger activity) which will lead to the pursuit and exercise of market power. Competition policy is necessary to ensure that efficiency is rewarded and consumer welfare is maximised. However, some economists have argued that monopoly can be conducive for economies of scale and innovation. Competition policy can be classified under three main headings: monopoly, restrictive practices and merger.

Monopoly policy

If a firm has a large market share, it may have a dominant position that allows it to pursue policies to the detriment of consumers. *Monopoly policy* will attempt to prevent the abuse of such market power. The approach taken in the UK is to weigh the advantages and disadvantages to the *public interest* (defined later) of allowing firms to follow certain strategies which may reduce competition in a given market.

Restrictive practices policy

This type of policy examines cases where a firm or groups of firms are engaging in practices that may prove detrimental to consumers. Such practices may include price-fixing agreements, predatory pricing and vertical restraints (which we examined in Chapters 4 and 9 respectively).

Merger policy

Government intervention may become important if two or more firms propose a merger which may lead to a dominant position in the market for the newly formed firm. Historically, *merger policy* considers whether any growth of market power arising from a merger is in the public interest. For example, the regulator has to judge the benefits of rationalisation against the growth of concentration that a merger may bring. However, merger policy should not be so restrictive as to protect inefficient management from takeover.

Do policymakers face a dilemma?

Competition policy has to weigh up the efficiency gains that may result as firms grow in size (either by internal growth or by acquisition and merger) against the potential for large firms to exercise market power. Competition authorities often have a more complex task in assessing the benefits and costs of monopoly. On the one hand, the growth of large firms may lead to economies of scale advantages and lower production costs. On the other hand, the increased size of a firm may effectively insulate it against competition, thereby reducing the necessity to reduce costs. If no gains in productive efficiency are made from the monopolisation of industries, competition authorities must then assess if abuses of market power are taking place.

How is market power assessed?

Define the relevant market

Before assessing whether market power abuses are taking place, regulators must first define the relevant market for the analysis of competition. If a very narrow definition of a market is used, the extent of market power held by any firm may be overstated. In contrast, if a wide definition of the market is used, abuses of market power may be overlooked. Markets can be defined in terms of product groups or geographical area. Product markets should include all products that are close (demand or supply) substitutes of the product in question. The market definition will vary depending on the problem in question. Defining markets by geographic areas presents economists with similar problems. Is the relevant geographic market defined at a local, regional, national or international level? Any market definition must capture the true competitive environment.

Quantifying market power

To assess whether market power abuses are taking place, regulators must construct measures which can quantify market power. There are a number of sophisticated measures of market power. We outline two very simple and intuitively appealing measures next.

Measure 1

The Lerner index can be defined via the following formula:

$$L = \frac{P - MC}{P}$$

where P = price charged by the firm
MC = marginal cost

As we saw in Chapter 3 (under perfect competition), firms set prices equal to marginal cost. In fact, over a range of prices the marginal cost curve proxies the firm's supply curve. However, as we move away from perfect competition through imperfect competition (oligopoly and monopolistic competition) toward monopoly, a firm's ability to raise prices above marginal cost increases and, consequently, the firm enjoys market power. The Lerner index helps us quantify this market power. For example, if prices are equal to marginal costs (P = MC), this would indicate a firm that operates under conditions of perfect competition and enjoys no market power. However, if prices exceed marginal costs, competitive conditions deviate from perfect competition, indicating the exercise of market power by firms. This measure does have two limitations, which are that:

- estimates of marginal costs are not included in firms' annual reports
- perfect competition does not exist in reality, so all firms can potentially raise prices above marginal costs and enjoy some element of market power.

Measure 2

Market share of an individual or group of firms also provides a useful indicator of firm behaviour and so the likely conduct of firms in any given industry. Abuses of market power are more likely to take place in industries where a few firms hold large market shares (see Chapter 5 for a thorough discussion of such issues).

In reality, policy examines how market shares of established firms have changed over time and how potential entrants could affect the level of competition in a given market, if they decided to enter. There is also the possibility that the (countervailing) power of buyers in the industry may offset the market power of sellers, thus keeping prices at competitive levels.

What is the legal framework for competition policy?

Competition policy in the UK is the remit of the Office of Fair Trading (OFT) and the Competition Commission (CC). The Office of Fair Trading investigates complaints of anticompetitive practices and, if these complaints are found to be justified, refers the findings to the Competition Commission. The President of the Department of Trade and Industry or the Restrictive Practices Court takes final decisions as to the validity of any findings. Competition policy in the UK has evolved through legislation. The main legislative measures are now discussed briefly.

Monopolies and Restrictive Practices Act 1948

This Act was the first piece of UK legislation on monopolies and restrictive practices. The Act defined monopoly in terms of a firm or a cartel controlling one-third or more of industry supply. The Act also set up the Monopolies and Restrictive Practices Commission. The Board of Trade (now the Department of Trade and Industry) could, if a monopoly position were found to exist, refer the case to the Monopolies and Restrictive Practices Commission for investigation.

The Act also defined the public interest and argued that if a monopoly were in the public interest then it should be allowed to continue to operate. A monopoly would be deemed to be in the public interest if the firms in question were:

- efficient
- making full use of scarce resources (in other words, no excess capacity existed)
- meeting the wishes of the public in terms of price, quantity and quality
- developing new technologies
- expanding the market.

The Monopolies and Mergers Act suggested that each instance of monopoly had different defining characteristics and suggested a case-by-case approach to determining outcomes. As a consequence, each case would be judged on its merits. The Monopolies and Restrictive Practices Act 1948 found it difficult to cope with the volume of work with respect to restrictive practices. Consequently, new legislation was enacted to deal with such practices.

Restrictive Trade Practices Act 1956

The Restrictive Trade Practices Act 1956 aimed to ban all restrictive practices in UK industry. The Act set up the Restrictive Trade Practices Court to deal with collusive agreements between firms. The Act required that trade association agreements with respect to prices charged, production processes employed and conditions surrounding the sales of goods be registered, in a Register of Restrictive Trading Agreements. The newly appointed registrar had to bring these registered agreements before the Restrictive Practices Court. This Court would then decide whether the agreement in question was against the public interest. If so, the Court could declare an agreement void and issue orders that the parties involved in the agreement should cease such practices. The Restrictive Practices Court assumed that registered agreements were against the public interest. Firms could decide to end any agreement voluntarily or defend the argument in the Restrictive Practices Court. However, the onus of proof was on the firms. A series of defences or gateways were introduced by which firms could justify their agreements. An agreement was admissible under the terms of the Act if its outcome were to:

- protect the public against injury
- provide specific benefit to the public

- help prevent other restrictive practices
- help secure fair terms from suppliers or purchasers
- help protect jobs
- promote exports
- support another agreement acceptable to the Court.

Even if firms could prove the agreement was valid through one or more of the gateways, it did not necessarily mean the Court would grant the agreement an exemption. The Act had a clause that stated that if the agreement did not, on balance, serve the public interest, although satisfying one of the gateways, it could be terminated. This was referred to as the tailpiece. This Act was later augmented by the Restrictive Trade Practices Act 1976 (discussed later), Restrictive Trade Practices Court Act 1976 and the Resale Prices Act 1976.

Resale Prices Act 1964

The Resale Prices Act 1964 stipulated that resale price maintenance (discussed in Chapter 9) was anticompetitive and therefore against the public interest. The Act extended the power of the Restrictive Practices Court to include cases where resale prices were thought to be a problem. Consequently, firms wishing to impose resale price maintenance had to obtain permission from the Restrictive Practices Court. Firms involved in resale price maintenance were assumed to be guilty unless proven otherwise. Gateways were also introduced under this act. Price maintenance would be allowed if the abolition of such practices would:

- reduce the quality and choice of goods produced
- lead to a decline in retail outlets
- lead to injury to the public
- lead to increased prices
- reduce the quality or level of service provision.

In almost all cases, resale price maintenance was abolished. Notable exceptions were medicines and books. In the case of books, there had been what had become known as the Net Book Agreement. Under this agreement between publishers and booksellers, the publisher set a resale price for the book (net price) at which booksellers had to sell the book. The agreement was designed to allow publishers a reasonable return on books which had a limited print run. The agreement was also designed to protect small retailers from price competition emanating from larger rivals. The Net Book Agreement was abolished in 1995. Case Study 11.2 examines the end of RPM in medicines.

Monopolies and Mergers Act 1965

The legislation before 1965 was relatively successful in combating collusive practices in UK industry. The success of the Restrictive Practices Court in breaking up anticompetitive agreements led to a merger boom or a switch toward more tacit forms of collusion. The 1960s saw a merger boom in the UK, as firms searched for new ways to reduce competitive pressures. The Monopolies and Mergers Act 1965 was passed to deal with the rising concentration which had arisen from the wave of acquisitions and mergers in the UK. This Act gave the Monopolies Commission

Case Study 11.2

FT

The end of RPM in medicines: medicine prices set to tumble after court ruling

The last bastion of restrictive practices on the high street fell yesterday when a court abolished price fixing on over-the-counter medicines. Britain's leading supermarkets immediately moved to slash prices on a range of branded pain killers, vitamins and cold and flu remedies – some by as much as 50%. One supermarket group estimated the change would save consumers £300m a year.

The decision by the Restrictive Practices Court sparked warnings that many independent pharmacists could be put out of business, restricting access to medicines, especially in rural areas and among the elderly and infirm.

Yesterday's decision overturned 30 years of restrictive practices under the resale price maintenance rules. Books, the other area that had been protected, lost their status two years ago.

Consumers will now save hundreds of millions of pounds in a market worth about £1.6bn a year. Tesco, the UK's biggest supermarket group, and its rivals J Sainsbury and Asda said they would cut prices by between 40% and 50%. For example, a packet of 16 Nurofen tablets from today will cost £1.14, instead of £2.29. Six sachets of Calpol, the popular children's medicine, will fall from £2.75 to £1.37.

The ruling came after the Community Pharmacy Action Group, an umbrella body campaigning for the retention of RPM, withdrew from the High Court case after the judge said there was insufficient proof to back its claims.

The CPAG had argued RPM protected the viability of the UK's network of community pharmacies. Yesterday it said it still felt it had a strong case, but with a clear indication a victory was unlikely it did not make sense to continue.

John D'Arcy, chief executive of the National Pharmaceutical Association, the community pharmacy trade body, said supermarkets would indulge in headline-grabbing price cuts across a small range of drugs.

'Supermarkets will be able to use this to cherry pick where they want to offer price cuts,' he said. 'That will push independents out of business and as they offer a wider range of drugs than supermarkets the medicine range will contract.'

Mr D'Arcy said viable independent stores in economically successful areas would always thrive. Under more pressure would be smaller stores in secondary and tertiary retail sites – particularly those in rural and socially deprived areas.

'Pharmacies often go into a lot of areas where other retailers fear to tread,' he said. The Office of Fair Trading, which brought the court case, said it was delighted with the result. The OFT said: 'We felt that like every other product, there ought to be competition. We thought it was bad news for consumers that they couldn't shop around.'

The OFT said it would now remain on the look-out for any underhand practices across the retail sector. 'This is the end for legal price fixing, but we would love to hear about anyone who is illegally trying to fix prices.'

Source: *Financial Times*, 16 May 2001.

power to regulate prices charged and to break up monopolies. The Monopolies Commission now became the Monopolies and Mergers Commission. The Board of Trade (the precursor to the DTI) could refer a merger to the Commission if the merger would create a monopoly position. A monopoly position would exist if the new firm controlled one-third of the market or had annual turnover exceeding £5 million. This threshold was increased to £30 million in 1984. The Commission would present findings to the Secretary of State of the Board of Trade, who made a final decision as to whether the merger was in the public interest.

Restrictive Trade Practices Act 1968

After the 1956 Act, many firms had entered into agreements to share information regarding prices, quality and costs of production. The Restrictive Trade Practices Act 1968 made the registration of these agreements compulsory and subject to supervision of the Restrictive Practices Court. An information agreement could be exempted from the legislation if the agreement was of substantial importance to the well-being of the UK economy or where its main aim was to improve production and promote efficiency.

Fair Trading Act 1973

The Fair Trading Act 1973 led to the creation of the Office of Fair Trading and the appointment of a Director General of Fair Trading to oversee competition policy relating to monopolies, mergers and restrictive practices. Section 84 of the Act defined the public interest. A merger was thought to operate in the public interest if:

- it promoted or maintained competition
- it was in the overall interest of consumers and other market participants
- it led to a reduction of costs through economies of scale
- it stimulated innovatory activity and led to technical progress.

A reference to the Monopolies and Mergers Commission could be made if a scale or complex monopoly position existed. A scale monopoly was where one firm had a market share of 25% of the relevant industry. A complex monopoly position referral could even be made if two or more firms had a combined market share of 25% of the relevant market and engaged in concerted practices to affect competition. A reference could also be made if a takeover involved worldwide assets exceeding £70 million.

The Office of Fair Trading advised the Secretary of State for Trade and Industry on whether a merger should be referred to the MMC. If investigated, the MMC's role was to assess whether the proposed merger operated against the public interest. The Commission then reported to the President of the Department of Trade and Industry, who decided whether the merger should proceed.

The Act was extended to cover restrictive practices in the service industries (such as banks, travel agents and estate agents), nationalised industries and local monopolies. Overall, the Fair Trading Act covered monopoly pricing, mergers, restrictive agreements, predation, price discrimination and vertical restraints and led to major changes in the way monopoly and restrictive practices were investigated.

Restrictive Trade Practices Act 1976

The Restrictive Trade Practices Act (1976) brought together previous legislation relating to restrictive practices. The Act required registration of all verbal and written agreements to the Director General of Fair Trading. The details of these agreements were entered in a public register. At the end of 1999, over 15,000 agreements were disclosed on the public register. However, only about 1% of these agreements go to Court.

Competition Act 1980

The Competition Act 1980 brought together previous legislation that had aimed to deal with anticompetitive practices. In particular, the Act extended the provision of the Fair Trading Act 1973. The Act defined clearly what constituted restrictive and anticompetitive practices. These were defined to include price fixing, price discrimination, predatory pricing, vertical squeezes, exclusive dealing and tie-in sales. It also outlined how complaints of anticompetitive practices should be handled and the process of investigation if the OFT received a complaint from the Secretary of State for Trade and Industry or a member of the public. The Act allowed firms to comply voluntarily with OFT recommendations prior to reference to the MMC and made it easier for nationalised industries to be investigated. The aim was to promote efficiency in nationalised industries. Overall, the Competition Act covered predatory pricing, price discrimination and vertical restraints.

Companies Act 1989

The Companies Act 1989 established several procedures aimed at improving the investigation and administration of mergers. The Act required firms to notify the Office of Fair Trading with details of the proposed merger before it took place. The Director General of Fair Trading then decided whether a reference to the Monopolies and Mergers Commission was required. If no reference was made within 21 days of the notification, the merger was allowed to proceed. If an investigation ensued, firms could not acquire shareholdings in the other firm during the investigation.

Competition Act 1998

Until recently the Restrictive Practices Act 1976 dealt with collusion and the Fair Trading Act dealt with mergers, while monopoly power was dealt with by the Fair Trading Act 1973 and the Competition Act 1980.

The (new) Competition Act was ratified by Parliament in 1998. On 1 March 2000 the Act came into force, when most of the prior legislation relating to monopolies, mergers and restrictive practices was repealed. The Act aimed to rationalise the UK's competition policy and bring it into line with the competition policy adopted by the European Union. In contrast to much of the previous legislation already discussed, this Act is concerned with the effects on competition of firm behaviour rather than the form of any practice or agreement. The Act also increased the powers of investigation and intervention of the Director General of Fair Trading. The Competition Act set up a new Competition Commission to replace the MMC. This Commission came into being on 1 March 1999. The new Commission carries out the roles formerly administered by the MMC, but also hears appeals arising from any decisions made under the Competition Act (1998).

The Act is composed of two main components known as chapter prohibitions, referred to as Chapter I and Chapter II respectively. The Chapter I Prohibition deals with anticompetitive (restrictive) practices, while Chapter II Prohibition deals with abuses of dominant (or monopoly) positions. The chapters are only concerned with promoting competition within the UK. Section 60 of the new Act makes provision that any investigations and enforcement of the Act should be consistent with existing European Union policy. The following gives a brief discussion of Chapter I and II Prohibitions.

The Chapter I Prohibition applies to agreements between firms which prevent, distort or otherwise affect trade within the UK. These agreements can range from oral agreements to formal written agreements. Types of agreement which fall under the remit of the Act include:

- agreements to fix buying or selling prices
- agreements to share markets
- agreements to limit production
- agreements relating to collusive tendering
- agreements involving the sharing of information.

Exemptions can be granted if the agreement leads to an improvement in the production and distribution of goods and services or promotes technical progress that leads to substantial benefits for consumers.

Section 36 of the Act discusses the penalties firms face if violating either of the chapter prohibitions. The maximum penalty (which can run into millions of pounds) a firm faces is up to a maximum of 10% of annual turnover for each year that the violation takes place, up to a maximum period of thtree years.

The Chapter I Prohibition is closely related to Article 81 of EU legislation. However, if there is an overlap between Chapter I Prohibition and Article 81 in any investigation, the Competition Directorate General IV of the European Commission will take charge of the investigation. If an exemption is granted under Article 81, then the firms concerned will automatically receive a (parallel) exemption from the Chapter I Prohibition. However, an exemption from the Chapter I Prohibition does not automatically lead to an exemption from Article 81.

The Chapter II Prohibition is based on Article 82 of the Treaty of Rome and deals with the abuse of a dominant position. This is covered in Section 18 of the Competition Act. The investigation of a dominant position involves conducting a two-stage test, which assesses (i) whether the firm is dominant in the relevant product or service market and (ii) whether the firm is abusing this position. Practices that constitute abuses of a dominant position include situations where there are excessive prices being charged, price discrimination, predatory behaviour, vertical restraints and refusals to supply.

Since the Competition Act came into force in March 2000, the competition policy toward monopoly and restrictive practices has become much stricter. Further, amendments to the UK's competition regime are currently under way with the introduction of the Enterprise Act, which received Royal Ascent in November 2002. The Enterprise Act aims to encourage competition, productivity and innovation within a strengthened regulatory framework. With respect to competition policy, the Act aims to ensure competition prevails by reducing incentives for firms to engage in anticompetitive behaviour by imposing harsh penalties (up to five years' imprisonment) for managers found guilty of price fixing and related offences. Furthermore, the Act aims to ensure that policy uses quantitative and qualitative analysis to arrive at expert and independent decisions. For example, new regulations relating to merger enquiries are now based on economic analysis to assess the likely effects on competition rather than the somewhat vaguer public interest concerns. The process of investigation and enforcement of competition policies is to be made much more transparent, in line with many of the changes taking place within the European Union (Box 11.1). Case Studies 11.3 and 11.4 discuss recent merger and restrictive practices cases.

Box 11.1 The European Union approach to competition policy

Competition Policy and the EU

What are the aims of competition policy in the European Union?
Competition policy in the European Union is aimed at achieving a single internal market through the promotion of competition. In general, competition policy is aimed at preventing the development of dominant positions of firms by preventing mergers or strategies that may result in a lessening of competition.

How is policy formulated, administered and enforced?
The cornerstones of EU competition policy are Articles 81 and 82 of the Treaty of Amsterdam. Previously, Articles 85 and 86 of the Treaty of Rome were concerned with competition policy in the European Union. However, since the ratification of the Treaty of Amsterdam these Articles were renumbered Articles 81 and 82 respectively in May 1999.

Article 81 of the Treaty of Amsterdam deals with the regulation of restrictive practices within the European Union. This Article prohibits restrictive practice agreements between firms from the European Union member states which have the effect of preventing and restricting competition. These agreements can be horizontal or vertical (see earlier). For example, agreements to fix prices, production quotas and market sharing are deemed illegal.

One of the underlying aims of the Article is to integrate EU markets by removing distortions to competition. It is therefore not concerned with monopolies or oligopolies within member states. Any restrictive practice agreements were deemed illegal if they had the effect of distorting competition. Exemptions of agreements from Article 81 may occur if the benefits of the agreement outweigh the costs to the consumer: for example, if an agreement led to increased production, economies of scale and more efficient distribution processes, or technical progress, and where consumers were likely to receive lower priced or higher quality products.

Overall, this Article covers restrictive agreements, collusion and vertical restraints within the European Union. Historically, the policy toward restrictive practices within the European Union has been much stricter than that of the UK. In a recent case the European Commission fined Volkswagen and Audi €102 million for various restrictive practices which distorted competition within the European car market.

Article 82 regulates against abuses of dominant position through monopoly. A dominant position exists if an individual firm can prevent competition and behave independently of the competitive pressures facing its rivals and exercise control over production and prices. An investigation takes place if a single firm has a dominant position in the relevant market, which currently is defined as 40% of market share. A firm is abusing its dominant position if it is fixing prices, refusing to deal with certain customers etc. Overall, Article 82 covers monopoly pricing, mergers, predatory pricing and price discrimination. In contrast to Article 81, Article 82 does not offer any exemptions from activities that could be regarded as abuses of market power.

Both Articles 81 and 82 are confined to EU firms trading with other EU countries. These articles do not apply to domestic competition. The articles are investigated and enforced by the Competition Directorate-General IV (DGComp). The Directorate-General IV has the power to fine companies up to 10% of their annual worldwide turnover.

How are mergers dealt with?

Article 82 and Regulation 4064/89 (the European Council Merger Regulation (ECMR), The Control of Concentrations) have traditionally regulated mergers. The ECMR was passed in 1990, and was subsequently amended by council regulation, 13/10/97, which has been in force since March 1998. The ECMR covers mergers, acquisitions and joint mergers. Mergers qualify for investigation if they have a European dimension – in other words, if a merger has a fundamental effect on competition within the European Union. The ECMR outlines a number of circumstances under which a merger investigation may take place. These are as follows:

- if the firms involved in the merger or acquisition have worldwide sales exceeding €5 billion or have sales in the EU exceeding €250 million
- if the European-wide sales of each of the firms concerned exceed €100 million
- if the combined sales of the firms concerned exceed €100 million in at least three EU member states
- if two or more firms involved in any deal have sales exceeding €25 million in each of the same three EU member states
- where one of these firms has two-thirds of its market share in a single EU state.

Notification of any such mergers should be made to the Competition Directorate-General IV not more than one week after a bid has been made or a deal has been announced. Failure to do this may result in fines for the parties concerned. The Directorate examines the effect of a merger based on the effects on competition within the European Union. Most investigations assess whether a merger will lead to a dominant position for the newly formed firm in any product or geographic markets. Any investigation would weigh the effects on competition against the potential benefits (which may include scale economies or technological advances). The Directorate-General IV takes the decision as to whether an investigation should take place or if a merger should proceed. Overall, it is unlikely that a merger would be allowed to take place if it leads to or augments a dominant position, as this is likely to have detrimental effects on competition.

Current Developments

The European Commission is currently reviewing the ECMR in the light of globalisation of business, technological change, the enlargement of the European Union and co-operation with other supranational bodies. One of the most significant changes involves changing the proposed grounds for disallowing a merger from that of creating or augmenting a dominant position for the firms in question to a substantial lessening of competition test. Consequently, following an extensive consultation process (with other regulators, consumers, governments, businesses and other interest groups), the Competition Directorate-General IV is currently in the process of drawing up amendments to the ECMR for approval by the European Commission. These amendments will be accompanied by a set of best practice guidelines on the conduct of regulators and applications of economic-based competition tests in the analysis of merger decisions. (Monti [2002] provides a detailed discussion of many of the issues raised here.)

Case Study 11.3

Mergers in UK banking: Lloyds TSB and Abbey National plc

Following an investigation by the Office of Fair Trading, the proposed merger (takeover) between Lloyds TSB and Abbey National was referred to the Competition Commission in February 2001.

Background

The UK banking market is dominated by four clearing banks (Barclays, HSBC, Lloyds TSB and Royal Bank of Scotland/National Westminster Bank). However, in recent years deregulation and demutualisation of former building societies has meant that competition has increased in certain segments of the market (e.g. mortgages and wholesale banking). Competition was still limited in several parts of the industry, most notably personal current accounts. In this area, the four big banks were still dominant, partly as consumers have found it very difficult to switch bank accounts to new competitors. This was defined as the relevant market for analysing the competitive effects of the proposed merger. The Competition Commission examined the likely effects of the proposed merger on Lloyds TSB, the big four banks in general and the pricing of financial products.

What effect would the merger have?

By effectively removing a major competitor in financial services, it was thought that this merger would lead to a lessening of competition in the market for financial products sold to small consumers. In particular, a merger would mean that the market share of Lloyds TSB would have increased from 22% to 27% (which also meant the combined market share of the four leading banks would have increased from 72% to 77%). Although efficiency gains (through staff reductions and branch closures) were expected, it was thought that these gains would not be passed on to consumers in the form of more competitively priced products.

Conclusions and remedies

After considering various alternatives (including Lloyds TSB divesting one of its major subsidiaries – Cheltenham and Gloucester), the Commission decided that the effective removal of a major player in financial services (i.e. Abbey National) and the subsequent reduction in bank branches would mean a lessening of competition and consumer choice. Consequently, the proposed merger was rejected.

Case Study 11.4

Predatory pricing in UK newspapers: Northcliffe Newspapers fined £1.3m over predatory prices

The Office of Fair Trading has fined Northcliffe Newspapers, the regional arm of the Daily Mail and General Trust, £1.3m for selling advertising in a newspaper at a loss to drive a rival title out of the market. It is the first fine imposed on news publishers for predatory pricing. The OFT said yesterday it was investigating another unnamed local newspaper group.

Northcliffe faces a potential civil claim for damages from the *Aberdeen & District Independent*, the free weekly that originally complained to the OFT about pricing of advertising on the *Aberdeen Herald & Post*, one of three local Northcliffe newspapers. Any claim would relate to revenues lost after March 2000 when predatory pricing laws came into force. Northcliffe, which successfully contested a previous OFT ruling on the case, was last night considering whether to appeal.

The dispute dates back to 1996 when the *Aberdeen & District Independent* launched as a free weekly. The OFT was asked to investigate claims that advertising rates on the *Herald & Post* – later renamed the *Aberdeen Citizen* – were slashed at the new title's launch to discourage companies buying advertising space in it. In July 2001, the OFT upheld claims that the *Herald & Post* had indulged in predatory pricing. Under competition law, the offence occurs when a dominant undertaking deliberately incurs losses in order to deter competitors or remove an existing rival. Northcliffe took the case to the Competition Commission appeals tribunal, which in March sent the case back to the OFT, arguing that it had not sufficiently defined the market in question.

The OFT said 'further analysis' confirmed its original finding that Aberdeen Journals, which owns two daily newspapers as well as the *Herald & Post*, was 'dominant in the market for the supply of advertising space in local newspapers. . . . within the Aberdeen area'. It said the company had deliberately incurred losses on advertising in the *Herald & Post* to 'expel the *Aberdeen & District Independent*', its only direct rival, from that market. John Vickers, director-general of Fair Trading, said the practice continued, despite 'an OFT investigation already being in train'.

Source: *Financial Times*, 17 September 2002.

11.3   Privatisation and Deregulation

In this section, we discuss privatisation and deregulation. *Privatisation* involves the transfer and sale of assets from the public to the private sector. Examples have been telecommunications, water, gas and electricity. This transfer of assets from the public to the private sector may or may not be accompanied by a process of *deregulation* (or liberalisation). Deregulation involves policies aimed at altering the competitive structure of an industry by encouraging the entry of new firms. Where this is not possible governments can institute policies such as *franchising*, whereby services carried out by the public sector are franchised to private contractors. This policy has been used in industries where direct competition has been deemed undesirable. Indirect competition takes place as firms compete (often in auction contests) to gain access to such franchises. In the UK, examples of this are local bus services and operators of commercial train passenger services. The overall aim of franchising is to increase competition indirectly by encouraging firms to bid for contracts and licences to offer certain goods and services. The rest of this section examines privatisation and regulation.

What is privatisation?

Privatisation involves the transfer of assets from public to private ownership (see Table 11.1). The rationale for privatisation generally centres around the positive effects which competition exerts on the behaviour and performance of firms. In other words, by introducing competition, firms are more likely to follow strategies aimed at minimising costs and maximising profits. Many authors have argued that privatisation leads to productive efficiency.

Table 11.1 Selected UK privatisations by industry and year of first sale

Enterprise	Industry	Year privatised
British Aerospace	Aerospace	1981
Cable & Wireless	Telecommunications	1981
Britoil	Oil	1982
National Freight Corporation	Transport	1982
Associated British Ports	Ports	1983
British Telecom	Telecommunications	1984
British Leyland (Austin-Rover) Jaguar	Cars	1984
British Gas	Gas	1986
National Bus Company	Buses	1986
British Airports Authority	Airports	1987
British Airways	Airlines	1987
British Steel	Steel	1988
Water authorities (10 companies)	Water	1989
Electricity distribution (12 companies)	Electricity	1990
Electricity generation	Electricity	1991
British Rail (Railtrack)	Railways	1995
British Energy	Nuclear energy	1996

What are the arguments in favour of privatisation?

Several arguments have been forwarded in favour of privatisation. These are now discussed in turn.

Increased competition in product and service markets

The privatisation of industries has often been accompanied by increased competition. The introduction of competition leads companies to strive to minimise costs. The reduction in costs is likely to lead to a reduction in prices and a wider choice of products and services available to consumers. Overall, market forces will lead to less bureaucracy, waste and inefficiency. The extent to which advertising improves firm performance is by no means clear cut. Case Study 11.5 examines the extent to which privatisation leads to increased competition and improved performance.

Increased discipline of capital markets

Under privatisation management is likely to become more efficient and search for more profitable opportunities. It also leads to an increase in capital market incentives for managers and firms to perform well, as their job security depends on satisfactory performance. Evidence also suggests that there is a strong correlation between managers' salaries and firm performance.

Reduction in government controls

Privatisation leads to a reduction in the control which governments exercise over the strategies of nationalised industries. Firms are freed from the constraints imposed by government controls and pursue policies aimed at maximising profits. These firms are more likely to have clearly defined profit objectives. However, as we saw in Chapter 3, firms may not necessarily follow strategies aimed at maximising profits.

Case Study 11.5

Privatisation and performance

The extent to which privatisation has improved efficiency and performance has caused some controversy. As we saw earlier, public ownership of industry can be advantageous if introducing competition is difficult and where the industry can be characterised as a natural monopoly. However, by introducing competition, privatisation can lead firms to strive for efficiency gains, which ultimately feed through to improved performance.

What does the real world say?

Several studies have assessed whether privatisation leads to improvements in performance. For example, in a UK study, Parker (1991) examined the performance of six privatised firms over the period 1987 to 1990. The sample consisted of British Gas, British Telecom, Rolls-Royce, Associated British Ports, Jaguar and Enterprise Oil. Parker utilised performance measures relating to profitability and productivity. Profitability increased for British Gas, British Telecom and Rolls-Royce, but declined for Associated British Ports, Jaguar and Enterprise Oil. Productivity was found to increase for British Gas, British Telecom, Associated British Ports and Jaguar, but declined for Rolls-Royce and Enterprise Oil.

An international perspective is provided by Borcherding et al. (1982), who examined the results of studies which compared the performance of public and privatised industries. The survey analysed the result of 52 studies carried out across the USA, Germany, France, Canada and Australia. The authors compared the findings of studies that have carried out various tests of efficiency on public and private enterprises. The sample of 52 studies was drawn from five countries and a selection of industries including airlines, banks, bus services, cleaning services, debt collection, electricity, fire protection, forestry, hospitals, housing, insurance sales and claims, railroads, refuse collection, water and weather forecasting. The authors found that private enterprises outperformed their public counterparts in 43 of the 52 studies sampled. Based on the evidence outlined earlier, one might argue that privatisation does lead to improved performance. However, it is by no means certain that these improvements would not have taken place in the absence of privatisation.

They may instead pursue other objectives aimed at maximising size, growth or managerial satisfaction.

What are the arguments against privatisation?

Natural monopolies versus private monopolies

The process of privatisation may lead to the transfer of monopoly from public to private ownership. This may leave the privatised firms free to exploit monopoly power. This creates the problem of how best to regulate such new private monopolies.

Economies of scale and scope may be lost

If privatisation is accompanied by the break-up of monopolies into smaller components, this may lead to a reduction in the extent to which firms can achieve the economies of scale and scope under monopoly. This means that costs may actually increase after privatisation.

Difficulties in introducing competition

By privatising industries, competition should increase. However, substantial entry barriers face new competitors in these industries. For example, the introduction of competition when there is monopoly control of a network, as was the case in the gas industry or railways, may be difficult.

Do we need regulation in privatised industries?

Privatisation is likely to lead to incentives for firms to pursue productive efficiency. However, this will not ensure allocative efficiency, unless regulation is introduced to ensure that competition takes place. Another policy would be to pursue a policy of deregulation. In this case, the government actively removes various regulations, for example by removing entry barriers to encourage increased competition. Once an industry is privatised, government no longer has direct control over the objectives and strategies of these firms. As a consequence, there is often a need for regulation.

For effective regulation, the regulator needs information on future changes in costs and market conditions. In a stable market this task is relatively straightforward. In a dynamic market, where market conditions are changing constantly, it may be difficult to build up a detailed picture. Regulators attempt to balance the interests of consumers by promoting competition, while at the same time regulating prices to ensure that the shareholders of privatised firms receive a reasonable return on capital invested. There are two main ways of regulating prices known as rate of return and price cap regulation respectively.

Rate of return regulation

This ensures firms receive a minimum rate of return on any capital employed. In this case, the regulator fixes a required rate of return on capital (R*), which can be expressed as:

$$R^* = \frac{\text{Total revenues} - \text{Total costs}}{\text{Capital employed}}$$

This means that firms are guaranteed R*. The regulator allows firms to set a price which covers costs and a mark-up to allow capital equipment to be updated. Under this type of regulation, price reviews can be frequent. Therefore, it is more likely that a relationship between regulator and firms can build over time. As a consequence, there is a danger of *regulatory capture*. Regulatory capture occurs when the regulator ends up representing the interests of the firm rather than those of the consumer.

Price cap regulation

In the UK, the main type of price regulation used is price cap regulation. This regulation places a maximum limit on the prices that firms can charge. This has been of the form RPI minus an 'X' factor. Here the RPI denotes the retail price index (a measure of inflation), while 'X' is the amount by which the regulators feel that productivity gains can be made and thus costs reduced. In this case, the regulator would fix the 'X' factor based on the expected productivity gains in an industry over a given period.

The formula would work in the following way. Suppose for example, inflation in a given period was expected to be 4% and that the industry was expected to make productivity gains of 3% over this period. This would mean that firms in the industry could only increase prices by 1%. This type of regulation is therefore designed to make sure that any cost savings are passed on to consumers in the form of lower prices.

The formula used for price cap regulation means that firms which make productivity gains that exceed the 'X' factor can keep these savings and boost profitability. For multi-product firms, prices can vary within their portfolio of products as long as the average price corresponds with the price cap. The formula is relatively simple to operate and is transparent to consumers.

There are some inherent disadvantages of using price caps to regulate firm behaviour:

- If the 'X' factor is set too low, firms make supernormal profits.
- There may be a danger of regulatory capture. However, this is less likely than under rate of return regulation, as the information requirements of regulators are less onerous.
- Regulation is often complicated in industries where market conditions are changing quickly. This could lead to uncertainties for firms planning future investment programmes and non-price strategies.

Price caps vary from industry to industry depending on the structure and behaviour of firms in that industry and are generally reviewed every four or five years. In industries such as telecommunications, firms can vary the price of individual services as long as their overall service provision meet the price cap.

In the UK, separate acts of parliament have created a number of regulatory agencies to regulate previously privatised industries: Oftel for telecommunications, Ofgas for gas, Offer for electricity, Ofwat for water, Orr for railways. In 1998 Ofgas and Offer were subsumed under a new office known as Ofgem. The Secretary of State for Trade and Industry and the Secretary of State for the Environment grant firms operating licences (for electricity, gas, telecommunications and water) which outline general guidelines to which firms must adhere. The regulators have varying degrees of power.

In general, the agencies are responsible for:

- collecting and publishing information on competitive conditions in a given industry
- advising the Office of Fair Trading and the Competition Commission where appropriate of any abuses of market power or the existence of anticompetitive practices and enforcing competition law

- setting price and quality levels and investigating complaints
- altering conditions of licences granted to certain companies.

The Competition Commission and various parliamentary select committees reporting to Parliament oversee the overall activities of each regulator. These bodies can make rulings in cases where disputes arise between the regulator and a privatised firm (see Box 11.2).

Box 11.2 Regulation of privatised industries in the UK

Over the past 20 years or so, since the UK government's programme of privatisation began, the extent and type of competition has varied across industries. This box examines the evolution of regulation in telecommunications, energy, water and rail.

Telecommunications

Telecommunications was the first industry in the UK to be privatised. The incumbent monopolist, BT, was privatised in 1984 as a fully integrated company. The industry was initially a duopoly comprising BT and Mercury Communications. By 1998 over 200 operators existed within the industry. Regulation has been most active in the areas of national and international calls and rental of fixed lines. Regulation was introduced after BT was privatised in 1984 under the Telecommunications Act. This act set up the Office of Telecommunications (OFTEL) to regulate the industry. The RPI – X formula was set at –3% of any increase in the retail price index over the period 1984 to 1989. This was subsequently increased in the periods 1989–91 ($-4^{1}/2\%$), 1991–1993 ($-6^{1}/4\%$) and in 1993–1998 ($-7^{1}/2\%$). The price cap was subsequently reduced again over the period 1997–2000 ($-4^{1}/2\%$). Since privatisation the telecommunications industry has become much more competitive. This is partly as a response to changes in technology and the entry of new firms, particularly in the area of mobile phones.

Energy

Regulation of energy markets in the United Kingdom is carried out by the Office of Gas and Electricity Markets (OFGEM). Under the terms of the Gas Act 1986, the Electricity Act 1998 and Utilities Act 2000, OFGEM aims to promote competition and protect vulnerable consumers. It works in conjunction with Energywatch (an independent organisation set up by parliament in November 2000) to ensure the interests of consumers are served.

In the case of gas, the Gas Act of 1986 privatised British Gas as an integrated firm, which explored, produced and supplied gas. The Office of Gas Supply (OFGAS, the forerunner of OFGEM) undertook regulation. In the supply of gas, an RPI – X + Y formula has been used. In this case Y represents the costs (i.e. gas supplies) which firms are allowed to pass on to consumers. As competition has increased and productivity gains have been achieved the RPI – X + Y formula has been altered. For the periods 1987–1992, 1992–1997 and

1997–2000 the formulas were RPI – 2% + Y, RPI – 5% + Y and RPI – 4% + Y respectively. In 1992 competition was introduced when new rivals were allowed to use British Gas's networks if supplying large customers (measured as greater than 2500 therms per year). As a consequence, British Gas market share has fallen to 35% in this market. The Gas Act 1995 encouraged competition in the market where customers used fewer than 2500 therms. Other firms were allowed to use pipeline systems for the shipping and supply of gas. The pipeline charges for use of British Gas's pipeline were set at RPI – 5% for the period 1995–1997 and increased to RPI – 6$^{1}/_{2}$% for the period 1997–2001. By 1998 there were 70 new suppliers who had captured over 70% of the industrial and commercial markets. In response to a Monopolies and Mergers investigation, in 1996, British Gas split its operations into a gas supply company (British Gas Trading) and an exploration and production company (Centrica). Since 1998 regulation of the industry has been undertaken by the Office of Gas and Electricity Markets (OFGEM). Competition has increased in the market for gas with prices declining 37% between 1986 and 2002 (in real terms).

In the case of electricity, the 1989 Electricity Act privatised the electricity industry (in England and Wales) into three main activities, namely generation, transmission and regional distribution. In Scotland, the two electricity providers were privatised as fully integrated firms. Until 1998 the industry was regulated by the Office of Electricity Regulation (OFFER). It is now regulated by the Office of Gas and Electricity Markets (OFGEM). After privatisation 12 suppliers were given local monopolies (in corresponding geographic locations). However, since 1998, competition has been permitted between regional suppliers. Given the complexity of the industry, there have been many changes in regulation. In electricity transmission, regulators have adopted the simple RPI – X formula. This X factor was increased over the period 1990 to 1997, but has since been reduced again. Over the periods 1990–1992, 1992–1996, 1996–1997 and 1997–2000 the X factors were –0%, –3%, –20% and –4% respectively. A similar process has occurred in the transmission and distribution parts of the industry. However, in these segments, a Y factor has also been introduced which allows firms to pass on any unforeseen cost increases involved in the generation and distribution of electricity. Prices have declined by 28% since 1990.

Overall, regulation has been used relatively effectively to increase competition, which has subsequently meant a reduction in prices paid by consumers. At present OFGEM is reviewing much of its regulation and removing aspects no longer required.

Water

The Water Industry Act 1991, Water Resources Act 1991 and Competition and Service Utilities Act 1992 were instrumental in privatising and determining future competition in the water industry. After privatisation the industry comprised ten regional companies, which were responsible for water supplies and sewage. The Water Industry Act 1991 set up the Office of Water Services (OFWAT) to oversee regulation in the industry. To formulate price regulation, OFWAT has compared the performance of regional water providers (known as yardstick competition). The Competition and Service Utilities Act 1992 allowed rival firms to supply 'new' domestic customers and competition was extended to large corporate customers. Regulation in the water industry has been carried out using the formula $RPI + Y + K$, where K represents an amount required to improve networks to meet environmental and efficiency standards. The Water Industry Act 1999 introduced new measures to protect vulnerable consumers. A water bill proposed by the Department of Environment is currently under consideration by legislators. If approved this bill would see the setting up of an Independent Consumer Council for Water to protect the interest of water consumers. This will replace the current consumer (Watervoice) bodies. Water privatisation had led to increased investment, but in some cases increased prices.

Rail

The Railways Act 1993 and the Transport Act 2000 and *Transport 2010* (Department of Environment Transport and the Regions, 2000) have laid the foundation for the past and future regulation of the industry. The Railways Act 1993 privatised the rail industry and involved dividing railways into separate components. The first component involved a single firm (Railtrack), which owned and operated the rail network (specifically responsible for the track, stations and compiling train timetables). The Office of the Rail Regulator (ORR), which aims to promote and protect the public interest, regulated Railtrack. Railtrack charged individual operators for use of its network. The charges are based on the $RPI - X$ formula. Since privatisation in 1995 these charges have been set at $RPI - 8\%$ and $RPI - 2\%$ for the periods 1995–1996 and 1996–2001 respectively. Railtrack was placed into administration early in 2002. On 3 October 2002 Railtrack's assets and responsibilities were transferred and reorganised by a new not-for-profit body known as Network Rail.

Three firms control the rolling stock provision of the previously nationalised British Rail. To increase competition in the industry, the government offered firms the opportunity to bid for exclusive franchises to operate certain train routes. To encourage bidding the government offered the successful franchisees protection from outside competition. The nature of bidding for a franchise depends on the route under consideration. In cases where the franchise involves operating services on parts of the train network that are profitable, potential franchisees are offered fixed payments to run the network. The firm bidding the highest fixed payment wins the franchise. In contrast, for loss-making services of the rail network, firms bid for a lump-sum subsidy to run the service. In this case, the firm bidding for the lowest subsidy wins the contract. Charges are set by individual rail companies with reference to the subsidy set at the beginning of the franchise agreement. Regulation of these operating franchises is the responsibility of the Strategic Rail Authority (SRA). SRA monitors the performance of franchise operators and has the power to fine them if they do not meet the terms of their franchise contracts. In November 2002 the Strategic Rail Authority announced a revised package of measures aimed at encouraging franchise operators to improve the quality of services offered to consumers.

11.4   Franchising and Competitive Tendering

Franchising can be thought of as the allocation of exclusive rights to provide certain types of goods and services. This right, or licence, protects businesses from competition over the period of time that the contract runs. The aim of governments when granting franchises is to have an efficient industry that provides services that are available at competitive prices to consumers. Franchising is useful when restrictions on entry are required to ensure that firms have access to all available economies of scale and scope to achieve productive efficiency. This has been used in the United Kingdom where companies have been granted licences to operate specific product and service areas, for example in the provision of train passenger services.

Under franchising, there is no competition within the industry, but competition takes place when firms are bidding for a contract for the right to control part or all of the industry. This means that franchisers are subject to competitive pressure such that if they do not operate the franchise agreement to the satisfaction of the government, they will not have their licence renewed. Under a system of franchising, the extent to which the franchise is profitable depends on the cost and revenue efficiency of the franchisee.

Franchises can be characterised as either 'ownership' or 'operating'. Ownership franchises encourage investment as the firm is insulated from competition. Operating franchises encourage competition, but discourage investment in that there is a danger of a loss of contract at the end of the franchise agreement.

The award of a franchise contract is normally determined by auction. This can be done in one of three ways:

- *Cost per unit.* Competition is based on which firm can perform the service at lowest average cost. If competition in the auction exists, it is likely that prices will be bid to a level where average costs equal average revenues. This means that the winner of the contract who is awarded a franchise will earn normal profits. This type of bidding process ensures that competition takes place prior to the awarding of the franchise contract and ensures that no excess profits are made. As a consequence, the most efficient firm is granted the franchise to carry out a particular service.

- *Bidding by lump sum payment.* In this case firms bid a fixed sum payment to provide a good or service over a period of time. This method of franchise allocation is often used in cases of natural monopoly, where breaking an industry into many parts is not feasible. In the short term, the lump sum payment provides funds for the government.

- *Bidding by the lowest fixed level of subsidy.* In markets where prices have been kept artificially low by the government (possibly for some social reasons) any operation in the market will lead to firms sustaining losses (e.g. the provision of bus or train services to rural areas). However, if the government is willing to pay a subsidy equal to any shortfall a firm may make running a market then there is an incentive for firms to bid for the franchise contract. The firm which can carry out the service while making the smallest loss (i.e. requiring the lowest subsidy) would win the contract.

In allocating franchises the government must ensure that enough competition takes place prior to the awarding of the contract. It is therefore important to ensure there are enough bidders, that no collusion takes place, and that established firms do not have an unfair advantage.

11.5   Conclusion

In this chapter, we have argued that it is often necessary for government to intervene in industry when market failures take place. Such intervention can come in the form of policies to promote competition and regulate prices and output. Technological change and globalisation of product and financial markets have meant that competition policies towards assessing and regulating against abuses of market power have evolved in the UK since the Monopolies and Restrictive Practices Act (1948).

We have also seen that, as a consequence of natural monopoly, governments have felt the need to intervene in industry. Transferring ownership of assets from public to private ownership accompanied by liberalisation in order to encourage increased competition has been instituted in recent years. However, this has also been accompanied by regulations to ensure that competition prevails in these industries. In other industries, governments have offered franchise contracts as a means of encouraging competition and promoting efficiency.

Discussion Questions

1 Why do we need government regulation?

2 Outline the need for and scope of competition policies.

3 Using Box 11.1, outline the UK government's approach to the regulation of monopolies and restrictive practices. How does this differ from that of the European Commission?

4 Utilising Case Study 11.5, discuss the relative merits of privatisation.

5 Using Box 11.2, discuss the extent to which privatisation has led to increased regulation.

6 Define and discuss the differences between price cap and rate of return regulation.

Further Reading

General background

Mason, R. (2000) Microsoft: all good or all bad?, *The Economic Review*, 18, September, 18–21.

Scott, M. (2001) Economic policy for competition and consumers, *The Economic Review*, 19, September, 28–31.

Stewart, G. (1997) Why regulate?, *The Economic Review*, 15, September, 14–16.

Wilson, J. (1994) Competitive tendering and UK public services, *The Economic Review*, 12, September.

Advanced

Helm, D. and Jenkinson, T. (1997) The assessment: introducing competition into regulated industries, *Oxford Review of Economic Policy*, 13, 1–14.

Winston, C. (1993) Economic deregulation: days of reckoning for microeconomists, *Journal of Economic Literature*, 31, 1263–89.

Internet resources

Competition policy

- A huge resource of materials relating to UK competition policy can be found at the Office of Fair Trading (www.oft.gov.uk), and the Department of Trade and Industry (www.dti.gov.uk).

- A summary of findings of various investigations under the terms of the UK legislative measures we have outlined in this chapter can be found at www. competition-commission.gov.uk.

- Resources for competition policy in the United States can be found at the websites Federal Trade Commission and the Department of Justice. These can be found at www.ftc.gov and www.usdoj.gov/art/pubdocs.html respectively. The US Supreme Court website also holds a large resource of case summaries. This can be found at http://www.stolaf.edu/people/kecher/antitrust.

- Resources for the European Union can be found at the Competition Directorate General IV (DGComp) at http://europa.eu.int/comm/competition. This provides a vast amount of information on competition policy issues relating to monopoly, mergers and other restrictive practices. The website also provides various statistics on the extent of policy investigations across various industries.

- Resources from supranational bodies can be found at the World Trade Organisation (WTO) and the Competition Law and Policy Committee of the Organisation for Economic Cooperation and Development (OECD) at http://www.wto.org and www.oecd.org respectively.

Regulation

Resources on regulation can be found at various websites, including the following:

- Office of Gas and Electricity Markets (OFGEM) responsible for regulation in the gas and electricity industries (www.ofgem.gov.uk).

- Office of Telecommunications (OFTEL) responsible for regulation in telecommunications (www.oftel.gov.uk).

- The Office of the Rail Regulator (ORR) responsible for regulation in the rail industry (www.rail-reg.gov.uk). The Strategic Rail Authority instituted in 2001 also plays an important role in the management and regulation of the rail industry (www.sra.gov.uk).

- Office of Water Services (OFWAT) responsible for regulation of the water industry (www.ofwat.gov.uk).

Glossary

absolute cost advantages refers to an entry barrier where the long-run average costs of the potential entrant lie above those of the incumbent firm.

accounting profit a measure of profit that utilises data compiled in companies' annual reports. Calculated by deducting total costs from total revenues.

advertising intensity proportion of industry sales devoted to advertising.

Austrian School collective term to describe a school of thought emanating from researchers based at the University of Vienna in Austria. The school sees competition as a dynamic process driven by the introduction of new products and processes, along with the destruction of existing methods of production and goods and services. High profits are the result of successful innovation. The school tends to be against government intervention in the form of competition policies to industry.

average cost refers to the total costs of a given output divided by that output.

average revenue this is total revenue divided by quantity sold. In other words, average revenue is price and the average revenue curve is the demand curve.

backward vertical integration involves a firm moving ('upstream') into stages of production closer to sources of supply.

barriers to entry anything that raises the costs of firms outside an industry above those incurred by established firms.

bundling refers to the practice of sellers offering several goods as one package and thus being able to price discriminate and reduce consumer surplus.

cartel a formal organisation of independent firms that act collectively to improve their economic return by attempting to monopolise the market.

Chicago School collective term used to describe a group of economists emanating from the University of Chicago. The school argued that government intervention in industry leads to less competition rather than more. It argued that high profits are the reward for superior efficiency.

complements refers to pairs of goods where an increase in the price of one will lead to a decrease in the demand for the other.

concentration describes the distribution of market shares across a number of firms in a given industry. The size of firms is assessed with reference to data on sales, assets, employees, equity or output. Various measures of concentration can be utilised. The more common measures include the concentration ratio and the Herfindahl–Hirschman index.

conglomerate   a firm involved in many unrelated activities.

consumer surplus   exists when a consumer's reserve price (the highest price the consumer is willing to pay) is above the market price.

contestable market   this is a market where potential entrants and established firms face similar costs. Entry and exit conditions are free, which means that new entrants can withdraw and cover their costs on exit. This type of market structure implies that the behaviour of established firms is constrained not only by actual competition but also by potential competition.

contractual incompleteness   occurs when firms are unable to conclude efficient contractual agreements due to the presence of transaction costs.

corporate coherence   a term developed by Teece et al. (1994) to refer to companies that do not diversify at random.

credence good   a good whose quality cannot be assessed before or after consumption. Prevalent where the consumer must have specialist information or knowledge to assess the quality attributes of goods and services – for example, dental care.

cross-subsidisation   occurs when revenue from one activity can be used to support or subsidise other activities.

deconglomeration   the practice whereby conglomerates divest themselves of unrelated activities so as to focus more on their core activities.

Delphi technique   a method of making long-term demand and supply forecasts for product markets. The technique involves a process of iteration by which experts working independently eventually reach a common consensus.

determinants of demand   variables that help to explain the quantity of a good or service being demanded.

determinants of supply   variables that help to explain the quantity of a good or service being supplied.

diffusion   refers to the rate at which new products and processes are adopted within the firm (intra-firm diffusion), by other firms (inter-firm diffusion), by other industries and eventually by other countries.

diseconomies of scale   exist when the costs associated with an increase in the scale of production (long run) rise more than proportionately to the increase in output.

distinctive capabilities   internal resources specific to a firm that can be used to gain and sustain a competitive advantage over competitors. Innovation and managerial expertise are examples of distinctive capabilities.

economic efficiency   relationship between input prices or costs and output values.

economic profit   a measure of profit that includes all accounting costs and implicit opportunity costs. Accounting costs relate to fixed costs of production (such as rent, rates, interest on loans) and variable costs of production (such as wages and power). Opportunity costs reflect alternative or lost investment opportunities to which a firm could devote its scarce resources.

economies of scale   exist when the costs associated with an increase in the scale of production (long run) rise less than proportionately to the increase in output.

economies of scale barriers   entry barriers that arise when entrants are forced to enter and produce at a scale that places them at a cost disadvantage to established firms.

economies of scope   realised when the average cost of producing two or more goods is lower than if they were produced separately.

elasticity   degree of responsiveness of the quantity demanded of a good or service to changes in its price.

excess capacity   extra capacity that can be used at short notice to increase the output of firms. Often used as a signal to rivals that a firm is committed to an industry through substantial investments.

experience goods   goods and services that must be consumed for an assessment as to quality to be made. Examples would include music and food.

explicit collusion   covers collusive practices that require some formal communication to take place.

factors of production   refers to the inputs required to produce a good or service such as labour, machinery, buildings and land.

five forces model   introduced by Porter (1980) to examine the factors determining the level of competition facing established firms in any given industry. The five forces are entry threats, bargaining power of the firm's customers and suppliers, the threat of substitute products and services and the existing extent and intensity of competitive pressure.

foreclosure   refers to the practice of firms refusing to supply downstream firms or purchase from upstream firms.

forward vertical integration   involves a firm moving ('downstream') into stages of production closer to the final market.

franchising   a way of introducing competition into an industry where technical conditions mean that only a few large firms can efficiently compete. This involves utilising an auction to allocate exclusive rights to provide certain types of goods and services.

game theory   this approach plays an important role in a segment of industrial organisation theory ('the new industrial organisation'). The approach looks at particular competitive issues in the context of a game, which examines the strategic behaviour and outcomes of decisions made by firms with respect to price and non-price variables.

horizontal integration   expansion of firms caused by mergers between firms which produce substitute goods.

industrial classification   a method of defining an industry based on grouping firms producing and selling a similar goods and services, using the same technology. Standard Industrial Classification (SIC) can group firms by broad division, product class, group or activity depending on the economic problem at hand.

industry lifecycle   describes industry evolution as firms follow an ageing process or natural lifecycle. An industry's life can be decomposed into introductory, growth, maturity and decline phases.

inferior goods   goods for which quantity demanded decreases as income increases.

innovation   defines a stage of research and development between invention and commercial production. It covers the stages of applied research and development work.

innovative milieux　external environments which may encourage a firm to innovate such as local knowledge, regional organisations, horizontal and vertical links with other firms.

interdependence　the chief characteristic of oligopoly markets. Firms in an oligopoly are interdependent in so far as success for a firm will depend on actions taken by its rival and equally the actions of the firm will affect the success of the rival.

internal capital market　refers to the allocation of investment funds within the organisation. It is argued that managers allocate these funds more efficiently since they have access to better information flows than investors do in the external capital market.

invention　the first stage of research and development; refers to the creation of new ideas, regardless of any practical economic application.

law of demand　refers to the observed negative relationship between price and quantity demand. In other words, as price falls, more will be demanded and as price rises, less will be demanded.

law of diminishing marginal productivity　the hypothesis that as a variable input is increased at a constant rate while others are fixed, then, after a point, the increases in output become smaller and smaller.

law of proportionate effect　predicts that if firm sizes are subject to a growth process which is independent of size, their subsequent distribution eventually becomes skewed with a few large firms, several medium-sized firms and numerous small firms.

legal barriers　barriers to entry or exit that prevent or delay entry due to government legislation. Common examples are franchised monopolies, licences, registration, patents, taxes and tariffs.

limit pricing　a strategy often employed by established firms to deter the entry of new competitors. In this case, established firms set prices at a level which makes entry unprofitable. Established firms will often forgo profits in order to deter entry.

long run　a time period sufficiently long for the firm to vary all its factors of production (inputs).

marginal cost　addition to total cost as a result of producing one extra unit of output.

marginal revenue　addition to total revenue by selling one extra unit of output.

market equilibrium　at the equilibrium or market-clearing price, the amount demanded in the market is exactly equal to the amount supplied.

market structure　refers to the components that characterise the make-up of a particular industry. Individual components include the number of firms, the type of product produced and the extent of entry and exit barriers.

merger policy　assesses whether growth of market power arising from a merger is in the public interest. The benefit of rationalisation and subsequent increases efficiency against the growth of concentration that a merger may bring are analysed. The regulator has to judge the benefits of rationalisation against the growth of concentration that a merger may bring.

monopolistic competition   a market structure comprising large numbers of firms. Goods and services produced are slightly different. Competitive conditions lie somewhere in between monopoly and perfect competition.

monopoly   a market structure comprising one supplier and numerous buyers. A market that is normally characterised by high levels of fixed costs and substantial barriers to entry.

monopoly policy   applies in cases where a firm or group or firms have a large share of a market. This type of policy aims to prevent dominant firms abusing market power.

normal goods   goods for which quantity demanded increases as income increases.

organisational ecology   a methodology employed to examine the evolution of populations of firms over time. The main interest is tracking appearance of new firms, the death of existing firms and the changes in relative sizes of surviving firms.

patent   the deliberate creation of a property right over new knowledge. A patentee becomes the legal owner of a new product or process, and no other firm or individual will be allowed to copy the idea without the patentee's permission. Patents grant monopoly status and thus provide the incentive for individuals and firms to invest in innovation.

perfect competition   a market structure where there are many buyers and sellers. These buyers and sellers have perfect knowledge and there are no barriers to entry and exit. Firms are price takers.

predation   occurs when a dominant firm attempts to force a weaker firm out of the market. The usual strategy is to undercut the prices of the rival, even if this means selling at below marginal cost.

predatory pricing   a strategy whereby a dominant firm undercuts the prices of a rival, even if this means selling at below marginal cost. This can mean that the predator firm sacrifices short-run profits to gain higher returns in the longer term.

price discrimination   involves a firm with substantial market power charging customers different prices based on their relative elasticities of demand. By following this strategy, the firm can increase revenue and erode any welfare surplus which consumers might enjoy.

price leadership   refers to an informal or 'tacit' agreement that price changes set by a leader will be followed by most of the other firms in the industry. Also termed 'parallel pricing'.

price rigidity   refers to the observed phenomenon in oligopolistic markets that firms do not changes prices frequently, preferring instead to concentrate on non-price competition.

prisoners' dilemma game   an aspect of game theory. This will exist when there are gains to be made by players colluding. However, the collusive solution is unstable since greater gains can be made if one player moves independently.

privatisation   a process that involves the transfer and sale of assets from the public to the private sector. Industries that have been privatised in the UK include telecommunications, water, gas and electricity. Privatisation is often used to describe a number of policies including denationalisation, deregulation and franchising.

product differentiation   refers to (often small) differences between close substitutes. These differences can arise naturally or as a deliberate strategy employed by firms to gain a competitive advantage over rivals. Consequently product differentiation can be an important component of market structure or a firm's strategic armoury.

product differentiation barriers   impediments to new firm entry caused by brand loyalty or reputation advantages that have accrued to established firms.

production function   a technical specification of the relationship between inputs and outputs in a particular production process.

productive efficiency   the summation of technical efficiency (minimisation of input quantities) and economic efficiency (minimisation of input prices).

public interest   describes whether certain activities carried out by established firms have desirable or undesirable implications for competition, efficiency and consumer welfare. A strategy undertaken by a firm is likely to be in the public interest if it increases competition, firm efficiency or improves consumer welfare.

reciprocity   practice of firm A buying from firm B on the basis that firm B will have bought goods from firm A. Large conglomerates are thus in a better reciprocal position.

regulatory capture   when regulated firms and the regulator build up a relationship over time. Given that firms are normally more organised than the consumers the regulator represents, they have the power to lobby the regulator more effectively. This may lead to changes in policy toward the firms.

resale price maintenance   practice of upstream firms who fix a minimum (or possibly maximum) price to be charged in the downstream (usually retail) market.

restrictive practices policy   this type of policy is applied in cases where a firm or groups of firms are engaging in practices that may prove detrimental to consumers.

Schumpeterian hypothesis   argues that monopolies and near-monopolies are far from being lazy innovators, as traditional microeconomic theory would suggest. They enjoy conditions that allow them to invest in speculative research and development.

search goods   goods and services that can be inspected by either touch or visual inspection prior to purchase. Examples include furniture and clothing.

sequential games   an aspect of game theory. Rather than acting simultaneously, rivals will play their strategies sequentially.

short run   a period of time within which a firm is not able to vary all its factors of production (inputs).

specific asset   refers to assets that most firms posses which can be exploited in other activities and industries, e.g. an innovation, labour skills, brand, etc.

strategic groups   a group of firms which are similar in structure or which behave in similar ways. Members of a strategic group act interdependently. An industry can comprise one or more strategic groups. The differing competitive pressures and strategies employed across groups often lead to differences in performance.

structure conduct performance paradigm   a framework developed to examine the behaviour and performance of industries. Structural characteristics of industries influence or dictate the behaviour and performance of firms. Firm performance and behaviour can also affect the future structure of the industry.

substitutes   pairs of goods where an increase in the price of one will lead to an increase in the demand for the other.

tacit collusion   refers to collusive practices that arise out of industry 'understandings' and that have not been agreed via direct communication. One common form of tacit collusion is price leadership.

technical efficiency   relates to the actual physical ratios of material inputs to outputs in a firm's production process.

tie-in sales (tying)   occurs when purchases of one distinct product force buyers to buy another distinct product.

total cost   costs of production, which will include both variable costs and fixed costs.

total revenue   the product of price and quantity sold: thus refers to a firm's sales.

transaction costs   costs associated with carrying out market transactions. These include time spent collecting information about product attributes and prices. Transaction costs may also be involved in drawing up, monitoring and enforcing contracts.

tying   occurs when purchases of one distinct product force buyers to buy another distinct product. (Also known as **tie-in sales**.)

vertical integration   ownership of two or more stages of production.

welfare loss   describes the loss in society's welfare caused by monopoly.

References and Further Reading

Abernethy, A. and Franke, G. R. (1996) The information content of advertising: a meta analysis, *Journal of Advertising*, 25, 1–17.

Adelman, M. A. (1955) Concept and statistical measurement of vertical integration, in Stigler, G. J. (ed.) *Business Concentration and Price Policy*. Princeton, NJ: Princeton University Press, 281–3.

Advertising Association (2002) *Advertising Statistics Yearbook 2002*. Oxford: NTC Publications.

Alchian, A. (1963) Reliability and progress curves in airframe production, *Econometrica*, 31, 679–93.

Arrow, K. J. (1962) The economic implications of learning by doing, *Review of Economic Studies*, 29, 155–73.

Asch, P. and Seneca, J. (1975) Characteristics of collusive firms, *Journal of Industrial Economics*, 23, 223–37.

Asch, P. and Seneca, J. (1976) Is collusion profitable?, *The Review of Economics and Statistics*, 58, 1–10.

Bain, J. S. (1956) *Barriers to New Competition*. Cambridge, MA: Harvard University Press.

Baumol, W. J. (1959) *Business Behavior, Value and Growth*. New York: Macmillan.

Baumol, W. J. (1967) *Business Behaviour, Value and Growth*. New York: Harcourt Brace Jovanovich Inc.

Beardshaw, J., Brewster, D., Cormack, P. and Ross, A. (2001) *Economics: A Student's Guide* (5th edn). Harlow: Prentice Hall.

Bearne, A. (1996) The economics of advertising: a re-appraisal, *Economic Issues*, 1, 23–38.

Benham, L. (1972) The effect of advertising on the price of eyeglasses, *Journal of Law and Economics*, 15, 337–52.

Borcherding, T. E., Pommerehne, W. W. and Schneider, F. (1982) Comparing the efficiency of private and public production: evidence from five countries, *Zeitschrift für Nationalökonomie*, Supplement 2, 127–56.

Bork, R. (1978) *The Antitrust Paradox: A Policy at War with Itself*. New York: Basic Books.

Buxton, A. J., Davies, S. W. and Lyons, S. R. (1984) Concentration and advertising in consumer and producer markets, *Journal of Industrial Economics*, 32, 451–64.

Carlton, D. W. and Perloff, J. M. (1999) *Modern Industrial Organisation*. Harlow: Addison-Wesley.

Carroll, G. and Hannan, M. T. (1999) *The Demography of Corporations*. Princeton: Princeton University Press.

Chamberlin, E. H. (1962) *The Theory of Monopolistic Competition* (8th edn). Cambridge, MA: Harvard University Press [originally published 1933].

Chandler, A. (1977) *Managerial Revolution in American Business*. Cambridge, MA: MIT Press.

Comanor, W. (1985) Vertical price-fixing, vertical market restrictions, and the new antitrust policy, *Harvard Law Review*, 98, 983–1002.

Comanor, W. S. and Wilson, T. (1979) Advertising and competition: a survey, *Journal of Economic Literature*, 17, 453–76.

Cook, M. and Farquharson, C. (1998) *Business Economics*. London: Pitman.

Cookenboo, L. (1955) *Crude Oil Pipelines and Competition in the Oil Industry*. Cambridge, MA: Harvard University Press.

Cowling, K. and Mueller, D. C. (1978) The social costs of monopoly power, *Economic Journal*, 88, 727–48.

Cox, S. R. (1982) Some evidence on the early price effects of attorney advertising in the USA, *Journal of Advertising*, 1, 321–31.

Cubbin, J. S. and Geroski, P. A. (1990) The persistence of profits in the United Kingdom, in Mueller D. C. (ed.) *The Dynamics of Company Profits: An International Comparison*. Cambridge: Cambridge University Press.

Cyert, R. M. and March, J. G. (1963) *A Behavioral Theory of the Firm* (2nd edn). Englewood Cliffs, NJ: Prentice Hall.

Daley, L., Mahotra, V. and Sivakumar, R. (1997) Corporate focus and value creation: evidence from spin-offs, *Journal of Financial Economics*, 45, 257–81.

Darby, M. and Karni, E. (1973) Free competition and optimal amount of fraud, *Journal of Law and Economics*, 16, 67–88.

Davies, H. and Lam, P. (2001) *Managerial Economics* (2nd edn). London: Financial Times/Prentice Hall.

De Propris, L. (2000) Innovation and inter-firm cooperation: the case of the West Midlands, *Economics of Innovation and New Technology*, 9.

Demsetz, H. (1973) Industry structure, market rivalry and public policy, *Journal of Law and Economics*, 16, 1–9.

Department of Environment, Transport and the Regions (2000) *Transport 2010 – The 10-Year Plan*. London: Department of Environment, Transport and the Regions.

Dixit, A. (1982) Recent developments in oligopoly theory, *American Economic Review (Papers and Proceedings)*, 72, 12–17.

Dixit, A. and Nalebuff, B. (1991) *Thinking Strategically*. New York: Norton Books.

Dobson, P. W. (1997) The EC green paper on vertical restraints: an economic comment, *Competition and Regulation Bulletin*, London Economics, Edition 7.

Dobson, P. W. and Waterson, M. (1996) *Vertical restraints and competition policy*, Office of Fair Trading research paper 12.

Dosi, G., Malerba, F., Marsila, O. and Orsenigo, L. (1997) Industrial structures and dynamics: evidence interpretations and puzzles, *Industrial and Corporate Change*, 6, 3–24.

Eckard, E. W. (1987) Advertising, competition and market share instability, *Journal of Business*, 60, 539–52.

Economist (1999) Procter & Gamble: Jagers' Gamble, *The Economist*, 5 November, 88–99.

Edwardes, W. (2000) *Key Financial Instruments: Understanding and Innovating in the World of Derivatives*. London: Financial Times/Prentice Hall.

Emerson, M., Aujean, M., Catinat, M., Goybet, P. and Jacquemin, A. (1988) *The Economics of 1992: The EC Commission's Assessment of The Economic Effects of Completing the Single Market*. Oxford: Oxford University Press.

Fama, E. F. and Jensen, M. C. (1983) Separation of ownership from control, *Journal of Law and Economics*, 26, 301–26.

Farrell, J. and Shapiro, C. (2000) *Scale economies and synergies in horizontal merger analysis* (1 October 2000). Competition Policy Center Working Paper CPC00-015. (http://repositories.cdlib.org/iber/cpc/CPC00-015)

Ferguson, P. and Ferguson, P. (1994) *Industrial Economics*. London: Macmillan.

Freeman, C. and Soete, L. (1997) *The Economics of Industrial Innovation* (3rd edn). London: Pinter.

Gibrat, R. (1931) *Les Inégalités Economiques*. Paris: Sirey.

Goddard, J. A. and Wilson, J. O. S. (1996) Persistence of profits for UK manufacturing and service sector firms, *The Service Industries Journal*, 16, 105–17.

Gorecki, P. (1975) An inter-industry analysis of diversification in the UK manufacturing sector, *The Journal of Industrial Economics*, 24, 131–46.

Griffiths, A. and Wall, S. (2001) *Applied Economics* (9th edn). London: FT/Prentice Hall.

Haldi, J. and Whitcombe, D. (1967) Economies of scale in industrial plants, *Journal of Political Economy*, 75, 373–85.

Hall, R. L. and Hitch, C. J. (1939) Price theory and business behavior, *Oxford Economic Papers No. 2*, 12–45.

Hall, S., Walsh, M. and Yates, A. (1997) *How do UK companies set prices?*, Bank of England Working Paper.

Hannah, L. and Kay, J. A. (1977) *Concentration in Modern Industry*. London: Macmillan.

Hannan, T. H. and McDowell, J. M. (1984) The determinants of technology adoption: the case of the banking firm, *Rand Journal of Economics*, 15, 328–35.

Harberger, A. C. (1954) Monopoly and resource allocation, *American Economic Review (Papers and Proceedings)*, 44, 77–87.

Helm, D. and Jenkinson, T. (1997) The assessment: introducing competition into regulated industries, *Oxford Review of Economic Policy*, 13, 1–14.

Hornby, S. (1995) The theory of the firm re-visited: a Scottish perspective, *Management Decision*, 33, 33–41.

Ison, S. (2000) *Economics* (3rd edn). Harlow: FT/Prentice Hall.

Jacobson, D. and Andréosso-O'Callaghan, B. (1996) *Industrial Economics and Organisation*. Maidenhead: McGraw-Hill.

Kaldor, N. (1950) The economic aspects of advertising, *Review of Economic Studies*, 18, 1–27.

Katz, M. L. (1989) Vertical contractual relations, in Schmalensee, R. and Willig, R. D. (eds) *Handbook of Industrial Organisation*, Volume 1. Amsterdam: North Holland, 655–721.

Kaul, A. and Wittink, D.R. (1995) Empirical generalisations about the impact of advertising on price sensitivity and price, *Marketing Science*, 14, 151–60.

Kay, J. A. (1990) Vertical restraints in European competition policy, *European Economic Review*, 34, 551–61.

Kay, J. A. (1993) *Foundations of Corporate Success*. Oxford: Oxford University Press.

Klepper, S. (1997) Industry life cycles, *Industrial and Corporate Change*, 6, 145–81.

Krattenmaker, T. G. and Salop, S. C. (1986) Anticompetitive exclusion: raising rivals' cost to achieve power over price, *The Yale Law Journal*, 96, 209–93.

Leibenstein, H. (1950) Bandwagon, snob, and Veblen effects in the theory of consumer demand, *The Quarterly Journal of Economics*, 64, 183–207.

Leibenstein, H. (1966) Allocative efficiency versus X-efficiency, *American Economic Review*, 56, 392–415.

Lewis, P. and Thomas, H. (1990) The linkage between strategy, strategic groups and performance in the UK retail grocery industry, *Strategic Management Journal*, 11, 385–97.

Lipczynski, J. and Wilson, J. (2001) *Industrial Organisation*. Harlow: FT/Prentice Hall.

Machlup, F. (1952) *The Economics of Sellers' Competition*. Baltimore: Johns Hopkins University Press.

MacKintosh, D. R. and Frey, S. (1978) The prices of prescription eye glasses under advertising restraints, *Journal of Consumer Affairs*, 12, 323–32.

Maclaurin, W. R. (1950) The process of technological innovation: the launching of a new scientific industry, *American Economic Review*, 40, 90–112.

Marris, R. (1964) *The Economic Theory of Managerial Capitalism*. London: Macmillan.

Marshall, A. (1961) *The Principles of Economics* (9th edn), with annotations by C. W. Guillebaud. London: Macmillan [originally published 1890].

Mason, E. S. (1949) The current state of the monopoly problem in the United States, *Harvard Law Review*, 62, 1265–85.

Mason, R. (2000) Microsoft: all good or all bad?, *The Economic Review*, 18, September.

Mathewson, F. and Winter, R. A. (1998) The law and economics of resale price maintenance, *Review of Industrial Organisation*, 13, 57–84.

McGahan, A. (2000) How industries evolve, *Business Strategy Review*, 11, 1–16.

McGahan, A. and Porter, M. E. (1997) How much does industry matter really?, *Strategic Management Journal*, 18, 15–30.

Milyo, D. and Waldfogel, J. (1999) The effects of price advertising on prices, *American Economic Review*, 89(5), 1081–96.

Mochandreas, M. (2000) *Business Economics* (2nd edn). London: Thomson Business Press.

Monopolies and Mergers Commission (1966) *Household detergents: a report on the supply of household detergents*. London: HMSO.

Montgomery, C. (1994) Corporate diversification, *Journal of Economic Perspectives*, 8, 163–78.

Monti, M. (2002) Review of the EC merger regulation – roadmap for the reform project, speech made to Conference on Reform of European Merger Control, Brussels 2002. (http://europa.eu.int/comm/competition).

Mueller, D. C. (1969) A theory of conglomerate mergers, *Quarterly Journal of Economics*, 84, 643–59.

National Economic Development Council (NEDC) (1983) *Innovation in the UK*. London: National Economic Development Office.

Nellis, J. G. and Parker, D. (1992) *The Essence of Business Economics*. Harlow: Prentice Hall.

Nelson, P. (1974) Advertising as information, *Journal of Political Economy*, 82, 729–54.

Nelson, R. (1991) Why do firms differ and how does it matter?, *Strategic Management Journal*, 12, 61–74.

Office for National Statistics (2002) *Size analysis of UK business*, Business Monitor PA1003. London: HMSO.

Office of Fair Trading (1997) *Consumer detriment under conditions of imperfect information*. Research Paper Number 11. London: Office of Fair Trading.

Ordover, J., Saloner, G. and Salop, S. (1990) Equilibrium vertical foreclosure, *American Economic Review*, 80, 127–42.

Oster, S. M. and Quigley, J. M. (1977) Regulatory barriers to the diffusion of innovation: some evidence from building codes, *The Bell Journal of Economics*, 8, 361–77.

Parkin, M., Powell, M. and Matthews, K. (2003) *Economics* (5th edn). Harlow: Addison-Wesley.

Patel, P. and Pavitt, K. (1987) The elements of British technological competitiveness, *National Institute Economic Review*, 122(4), 72–83.

Paton, D. and Vaughan Williams, L. (1999) Advertising and firm performance: some evidence from UK firms, *Economic Issues*, 4, 89–105.

Penrose, E. (1995) *The Theory of the Growth of the Firm* (3rd edn). Oxford: Oxford University Press.

Phlips, L. (ed.) (1998) *Applied Industrial Economics*. Cambridge: Cambridge University Press.

Porter, M. E. (1980) *Competitive Strategy: Techniques for Analyzing Industries and Competitors*. New York: Free Press.

Porter, M. E. (1985) *Competitive Advantage: Creating and Sustaining Superior Performance*. New York: Free Press.

Porter, M. E. (1987) From competitive advantage to corporate strategy, *Harvard Business Review*, May–June, 43–59.

Resnick, A. and Stern, B. L. (1977) An analysis of information content in television advertising, *Journal of Marketing*, 41, 50–53.

Rumelt, P. (1991) How much does industry matter?, *Strategic Management Journal*, 12, 167–86.

Schankerman, M. (1998) How valuable is patent protection? Estimates by technology field, *Rand Journal of Economics*, 29, 77–107.

Scharfstein, D. S. (1998) *The dark side of internal capital markets II*, NBER Working Paper No 6352. Cambridge MA: National Economic Bureau of Research.

Scherer, F. M. (1967) Research and development resource allocation under rivalry, *Quarterly Journal of Economics*, 81, 359–94.

Scherer, F. M. (1992) Schumpeter and plausible capitalism, *Journal of Economic Literature*, 30, 1416–33.

Scherer, F. M. and Ross, D. (1990) *Industrial Market Structure and Economic Performance*. Boston, MA: Houghton-Mifflin.

Schmalensee, R. C. (1978) Entry deterrence in the ready-to-eat cereal industry, *The Bell Journal of Economics*, 9, 305–27.

Schmalensee, R. C. (1985) Do markets differ much?, *American Economic Review*, 74, 341–51.

Schumpeter, J. A. (1950) *Capitalism, Socialism and Democracy* (3rd edn). New York: Harper & Row [originally published 1942].

Scott, M. (2001) Economic policy for competition and consumers, *The Economic Review*, 19, September 28–31.

Shepherd, W. G. (1997) *The Economics of Industrial Organization* (4th edn). London: Prentice-Hall

Shipley, D. (1981) Pricing objectives in British manufacturing industry, *Journal of Industrial Economics*, 29, 429–43.

Sloman, S. (2000) *Economics* (4th edn). Harlow: Prentice Hall.

Smith, A. (1937) *An Inquiry into the Nature and Causes of the Wealth of Nations*, Cannan, E. (ed.). New York: The Modern Library [originally published 1776].

Smith, P. (1999) Demanding doughnuts: getting started, *Economic Review*, 17(2).

Stewart, G. (1997) Why regulate?, *The Economic Review*, 15(2).

Stewart, G. (1998) Do firms maximise profits?, *Economic Review*, 16(2).

Stewart, G. (2001) Entry and entry barriers, *Economic Review*, 19(2).

Stewart, G. (2001) Monopoly in UK banking, *Economic Review*, 19(2).

Stigler, G. J. (1958) The economies of scale, *The Journal of Law and Economics*, 1, 54–71.

Stigler, G. J. (1961) The economics of information, *Journal of Political Economy*, 69, 213–25. Reprinted in Stigler, G. J. (1968) *The Organization of Industry*. Homewood, IL: Irwin, 171–90.

Stigler, G. J. (1978) The literature of economics: the case of the kinked oligopoly demand curve, *Economic Inquiry*, 16, 185–204. Reprinted as reading 10 in Wagner, L. (ed.) (1981) *Readings in Applied Microeconomics*. Oxford: Oxford University Press.

Sutton, C. J. (1980) *Economics and Corporate Strategy*. Cambridge: Cambridge University Press.

Sutton, J. (1974) Advertising, concentration and competition, *Economic Journal*, 84, 56–69.

Sweezy, P. (1939) Demand under conditions of oligopoly, *Journal of Political Economy*, 47, 568–73.

Sylos-Labini, P. (1962) *Oligopoly and Technical Progress*. Cambridge, MA: Harvard University Press.

Taylor, C. and Silberston, Z. A. (1973) *The Economic Impact of the Patent System*. Cambridge: Cambridge University Press.

Teece, D., Rumelt, R., Dosi, G. and Winter, S. (1994) Understanding corporate coherence, theory and evidence, *Journal of Economic Behaviour and Organisation*, 23, 1–30.

Telser, L. (1964) Advertising and competition, *Journal of Political Economy*, 72, 537–62.

Tremblay, C. H. and Tremblay, V. J. (1996) Firm success, national status, and product line diversification: and empirical examination, *Review of Industrial Organisation*, 11, 771–89.

Uri, N. D. (1987) A re-examination of the advertising and industrial concentration relationship, *Applied Economics*, 19, 427–35.

Utton, M. A. (1979) *Diversification and Competition*. Cambridge: Cambridge University Press.

Veblen, T. (1908) *The Theory of the Leisure Classes*. New York: Macmillan (book available on the Gutenberg site: http://promo.net/cgi-promo/pg/cat.cgi?&label= ID&ftpsite=ftp://ftp.mirror.ac.uk/sites/metalab.unc.edu/pub/docs/books/gutenberg/ &alpha=853)

Williamson, O. E. (1963) Managerial discretion and business behavior, *American Economic Review*, 53, 1032–57.

Williamson, O. E. (1967) Hierarchical control and optimum firm size, *Journal of Political Economy*, 75, 123–38.

Williamson, O. E. (1971) The vertical integration of production: market failure considerations, *American Economic Review*, 61, 112–27.

Williamson, O. E. (1975) *Market and Hierarchies: Analysis and Antitrust Implications*. New York: Free Press.

Williamson, O. E. (1989) Transaction cost economics, in Schmalensee, R. and Willig, R. D. (eds) *Handbook of Industrial Organisation*, Volume 1. Amsterdam: North Holland, 135–8.

Wilson, J. (1994) Competitive tendering and UK public services, *Economic Review*, 12, September 31–35.

Winston, C. (1993) Economic deregulation: days of reckoning for microeconomists, *Journal of Economic Literature*, 31, 1263–89.

Index